The Hollywood
Writers' Wars

The Hollywood Writers' Wars

Nancy Lynn Schwartz

Completed by Sheila Schwartz

Alfred A. Knopf   New York 1982

THIS IS A BORZOI BOOK
PUBLISHED BY ALFRED A. KNOPF, INC.

Grateful acknowledgment is made to the following for permission to reprint from previously published material:

BELWIN-MILLS PUBLISHING CORP.: Excerpt from lyrics of "That Mittel-Europa of Mine" from *Meet the People 1955* by Henry Myers, Edward Eliscu, and Jay Gorney. Copyright © 1955 by Mills Music, Inc. Used with permission. All rights reserved.

LITTLE, BROWN & COMPANY: Excerpt from *Heyday* by Dore Schary. Used by permission of Little, Brown & Company.

TODD MCCARTHY AND JOSEPH MCBRIDE: Excerpt from interview with John Lee Mahin by Todd McCarthy and Joseph McBride. Copyright © 1980 by Todd McCarthy and Joseph McBride. First appeared in *Film Comment*, March/April 1980.

SIMON & SCHUSTER: Excerpt from *Front and Center* by John Houseman. Copyright © 1979 by John Houseman. Reprinted by permission of Simon & Schuster, a Division of Gulf & Western Corporation.

LIBRARY OF CONGRESS CATALOGING IN PUBLICATION DATA
Schwartz, Nancy Lynn, 1952–1978.
The Hollywood writers' wars.
Includes index.
1. Screen Writers Guild.
2. Trade-unions—Screen writers—California—Hollywood.
I. Schwartz, Sheila, 1929–   .   II. Title.
PN1993.S295S3   1981   331.88′11812′54   80–2728
ISBN 0-394-41140-4   AACR2

Manufactured in the United States of America
First Edition

Contents

Abbreviations

American Authors Authority (AAA) Plan

American Federation of Labor (AFL)

American Newspaper Guild (ANG)

American Society of Composers, Authors, and Publishers (ASCAP)

Association of Motion Picture Producers (AMPP)

Authors League of America (ALA)

Communist Political Association (CPA)

Conference of Studio Unions (CSU)

Congress of Industrial Organizations (CIO)

End Poverty in California (EPIC)

Hollywood Democratic Committee (HDC)

Hollywood Independent Citizens Committee for the Arts, Sciences, and Professions (HICCASP)

Hollywood Writers Mobilization (HWM)

House Un-American Activities Committee (HUAC)

Independent Citizens Committee for the Arts, Sciences, and Professions (ICCASP)

International Alliance of Theatrical Stage Employees (IATSE)

Joint Anti-Fascist Refugee Committee (JAFRC)

League of American Writers (LAW)

Motion Picture Artists Committee (MPAC)

Motion Picture Association of America (MPAA)

Motion Picture Producers and Distributors Association (Hays Office) (MPPDA)

National Industrial Recovery Act (NIRA)

National Labor Board (NLB)

National Labor Relations Act (NLRA)

National Labor Relations Board (NLRB)

National Recovery Administration (NRA)

Office of Emergency Management (OEM)

Office of War Information (OWI)

People's Education Center (PEC)

Screen Actors Guild (SAG)

Screen Playwrights (SP)

Screen Writers Guild (SWG)

Works Progress Administration (WPA)

Young Communists League (YCL)

Acknowledgments

I wish to thank the many people who helped Nancy with her work: Laurence Beilinson, Michael Blankfort, Allen Boretz, John Bright, Jean Butler, James M. Cain, Joe Cohn, Lester Cole, Norman Corwin, Sydney Davidson, Philip Dunne, Elizabeth Faragoh, Pauline Lauber Finn, Charles Glenn, Frances Goodrich, Albert Hackett, Lou Harris, Dorothy Healy, John Houseman, Roy Huggins, Sylvia Jarrico, Paul Jarrico, Michael Kanin, Charles Katz, Alexander Knox, Howard Koch, Ring Lardner, Jr., Emmet Lavery, John Howard Lawson, Robert Lees, Milton Lubovitsky, William Ludwig, Mary C. McCall, Jr., Richard Maibaum, Brian Marlow, Sam Marx, Arthur Ornitz, Abe Polonsky, Maurice Rapf, Dorshka Raphaelson, Samson Raphaelson, the Research Division of the Academy of Motion Picture Arts and Sciences, Fred Rinaldo, Allen Rivkin, David Robison, Budd Schulberg, Elizabeth Spector, Milton Sperling, Lionel Stander, Cleo Trumbo, Catherine Turney, John Wexley, Nathan Witt, and the staff of the Writers Guild West.

I would also like to thank Jeannette Mall and Elizabeth Leslie Schwartz for picture research, Victoria Wilson for editing, and Liz Dahransoff, Nancy Lynn Schwartz's agent.

Sheila Schwartz

Preface

My daughter, Nancy Lynn Schwartz, had a dream. Her dream was to tell the truth about what had happened to the joyous, creative founding members of the Screen Writers Guild whose careers had been truncated by the Hollywood blacklist. She was only twenty-five when she had finished her first draft of this present work.

Nancy loved people and hated injustice. She wept for hours about injustice after she saw *King Lear* at Stratford, Connecticut, and she was inconsolable after seeing *Spartacus* when she was only eight, in 1960. During the years that she was growing up, she breathed my political opinions: my unending sorrow about the Rosenbergs, about the plight of my teacher friends who had lost their jobs with the New York City board of education during the witchhunts, my unending belief also in the innocence of Alger Hiss, and my close relationship with one of the displaced Hollywood families. One of Nancy's unpublished stories deals with the horrors of this political situation as seen through the eyes of a young girl who must leave Hollywood because her father has been blacklisted.

During the sixties, our family marched in Washington against the Vietnam War and then, when Nancy went to the University of Wisconsin at Madison in 1969, she faced real danger for the first time.

The following year, temporarily worn out by the violence against the students, Nancy transferred to Sarah Lawrence, where she fell under the admirable influence of E. L. Doctorow, and it was there that her two dreams first coalesced. The first was to someday write for the movies and to be able to survive economically on this writing. And the second dream was to tell the story of the mistreatment of those Hollywood writers whose work she so much admired. Her dreams were strengthened at Columbia University, where she received an MFA in Film Studies, and finally, in 1974, at the age of twenty-two, she obtained a grant from the National Endowment for the

Humanities that enabled her to begin the research for this book. She traveled to many places to interview survivors: to England to see John Howard Lawson, to Washington, D.C., to see James M. Cain, to New City, New York, to see John Houseman, to Manhattan to see Samson Raphaelson, and to Woodstock, New York, to see Howard Koch and David Robison.

At the age of twenty-four, she felt it imperative to move west, to live in Los Angeles. She carried her files for this present book with her on the plane. "The most precious thing I own," she said.

In Hollywood she met Roy Huggins, showed him some screenplays she had done in college, and he offered her screen-writing work. Overnight, she was successful and able to sustain herself financially. During the next two years, each time I visited her, she was in a nicer apartment, and each time we worked on her files for this book. Gradually the book took second place to the exciting television writing work she was being offered.

In April 1978, she moved into a house with her fiancé, William Schwartz, and made an important decision. With an act of extraordinary will, she temporarily turned her back on screen writing and came to the McDowell Colony in Peterborough, New Hampshire, to finish this book. I met her at the airport and drove her to Peterborough. It was a joyous five hours, filled with our usual talk, silences, and love.

One month later, at the beginning of June, I again picked her up. She looked tired but was ecstatic that she had done what she wanted to do. She had finished a first draft of this book. It had been an extraordinary month for her. Daily, she had run four miles with Bernard Weissberger, a gentle man and outstanding historian. While at McDowell, the four episodes Nancy had written for the NBC miniseries "Wheels" was shown, and she knew the joy of seeing her first television writing on the little black-and-white TV at McDowell.

She left the first draft of *The Hollywood Writers' Wars* with me before returning to L.A. "Everybody writes for one person's mind and intelligence," she told me. "I write for yours. Read it, make comments, suggestions. Hold on to it until I can come back and work on it again."

In August she developed a terrible headache and slurred speech. The next day her doctor put her in the hospital for observation. She called me from Los Angeles. "Mom, come quick, it's a brain tumor." I took the next plane to Los Angeles, and they operated the afternoon I got there. Two hours after the operation the doctor told us, "'Malignant, the size of a golf ball."

During the next three days, Nancy was in intensive care. I sat there beside her, dazed, dozing, dreaming, waiting, not believing.

"Are there any old movies on television?" she asked me as soon as she was conscious.

I consulted the paper. "Yes," I told her, "but you won't be able to see the TV from the angle of your bed."

"I don't have to see," she said, "I just want to hear the dialogue. I know most of the movies by heart." And so until she was out of intensive care, she lay there, semidrugged, and listened to old movies.

She was moved from intensive care. We had eleven more days together. It was impossible not to believe that she would get well. She walked, talked, and did exercises every day with the physical therapist for at least an hour. She dictated some of her work to me, asked me to read aloud to her, spoke on the telephone, and saw her friends—so many friends that I worried they would tire her out.

On the day before she died, her physical therapist suggested that she be transferred to the new rehabilitation wing that was soon to be opened at Cedars-Sinai. "Instead of having your mother bring you every day for therapy, for weeks," the therapist said, "you could get large doses of exercise here and get it over with in a shorter time. You're still not steady enough on your feet, still lurch a bit. You wouldn't be here long."

"What do you think, Mom?" Nancy asked.

"It's up to you," I said. She was lucid, intelligent, humorous, perceptive, completely functioning at all times in the hospital, and able to make her own decisions. "Would I be able to work on my book?" she asked the therapist.

The therapist assured her that the rehabilitation center did not have a hospital atmosphere and that she could have a desk and typewriter in her room and could wear street clothes. "Then I think I'd like that," Nancy said.

The only bad night was the next one, the night she died. Suddenly, her vital signs started to fail and they reduced her painkillers. For the next five hours, from 11:00 p.m. to 4:00 a.m., while I begged for drugs for her and wept beside her bed, she tossed in agony. At one point a young intern came in and asked, "Nancy, are you awake or asleep?"

"I must be awake," she joked, "or why would I be feeling all this pain?"

Then the agony was too great for her to talk. She moaned, "The pain, the pain, I'm dying," and she was gone.

The major task that lay ahead of me was to finish Nancy's book, her memorial to those writers she so much admired.

Nothing can ever ease the horror, the sadness, the loss. But Nancy did accomplish her dream, and this book is here to bear witness.

Sheila Schwartz
New Paltz, New York

The Hollywood
Writers' Wars

1

It was 1933 in the United States, and the Depression was in its fourth year. In Los Angeles, oranges were a dime for three dozen, lamb chops were twelve and a half cents a pound, and lines of people waited at city garbage dumps to swarm over each newly delivered load. Il Duce commanded Italy. The Japanese were in Manchuria and Stalin led Russia. On January 30, 1933, Hitler became the chancellor of Germany.

The problem before the United States' new president-elect, Franklin Delano Roosevelt, was how to heal his ailing nation without assaulting the existing economic system or the personal freedoms inherent in democracy. On the eve of Roosevelt's inauguration, the gravest national crisis was in banking. Each day the public became more panicky, and the banking situation careened further out of control.

Two days before the presidential inauguration, the Federal Reserve issued figures that proved exactly how shaky the bank system was: they indicated that domestic hoarding alone accounted for a decline of more than $100 million in treasury reserves. It appeared to the public that the misers were the smart ones, and the next day, Friday, March 3, was marked by incredible runs on banks. To counteract this drain, the new president placed restrictions on banking in every state, and the following Thursday, March 9, he signed the Emergency Banking Relief Act.

On Sunday, March 12, Roosevelt delivered a fireside chat to the American people, of whom 17 million familes owned radio sets.

"I want to talk for a few minutes with the people of the United States about banking," he said. "I want to tell you what has been done in the last few days, why it was done, and what the next steps are going to be." He ended his gentle explanation to his constituents with these words: "It is your problem no less than it is mine. Together we cannot fail."

It was an invocation of collective destiny that left the American people touched, surprised, and reverent. In their minds it endowed Roosevelt with the wisdom and concern of a savior, and, as he introduced the sweeping recovery legislation that marked his first hundred days in office (against the nounced these measures as communistic), this image of salvation remained, opposition of Congress where a few representatives and senators even de- prompting one Texas congressman to call FDR "Moses leading us out of the wilderness."

In FDR's first hundred days, many pieces of legislation were enacted to help the people. Congress passed the Agricultural Adjustment Act, the Tennessee Valley Authority Act, and the Federal Securities Act. But most important was the National Industrial Recovery Act (NIRA), which many poli- ticians and journalists considered the most far-reaching legislation ever enacted by the American Congress.

The National Industrial Recovery Act sought essentially to regulate pro- duction, to prevent unwise overproduction and unfair wages, and to eliminate improper working conditions. The most important section of this act for labor was Section 7A, which gave employees the right to organize and bargain collectively through representatives of their own choosing. In addition, the NIRA sought to allot a total of $3.3 billion for public works, which the administration felt was crucial to generate new buying power so that increases in the price of goods would not exceed the wages of consumers. The provi- sions of the NIRA were administered by the National Recovery Administra- tion (NRA).

Critics claimed that the recovery bill was unconstitutional and that it would give Roosevelt dictatorial powers. Labor, however, was elated, and William Green, president of the American Federation of Labor (AFL), is- sued a warning that he would urge friends of labor in Congress to vote against the bill if Section 7A were in any way diluted. The NIRA was passed in the House and, by a margin of only ten votes, in the Senate. Roosevelt signed the act into law in June 1933.

The motto of the NRA was "We Do Our Part." Its symbol was the blue eagle. The agency immediately began to create codes for each industry, with the number of codes burgeoning until they reached 750. Admittedly, the NIRA seemed a bit unwieldly; but the spirit of joined hands and a better world prevailed, and for the first time in the United States there was govern- mental intervention in the economy on behalf of general welfare—interven- tion reserved hitherto only for wartime.

The NRA, because of Section 7A, gave tremendous impetus to member- ship in the American Federation of Labor, and figures nearly reached the peak achieved during World War I. By 1936, membership in affiliated trade unions had swelled to over 4 million.

The AFL espoused the simple trade-union philosophy of Samuel Gompers and was conservative and carefully apolitical, avoiding any socialist, fascist, or communist affiliations and resisting anything that appeared to be an attempt by left-wing groups to make headway in the organization. The AFL pointed out with pride that in the election of 1932 (despite the sufferings of the Depression and the union's disappointment with the labor planks in the platforms of both parties) it had refused to support either the socialists or the communists in the election.

The socialists and communists, despite their strong efforts, had flopped completely in the campaign of 1932 and had not been able to convince the American people that the time had come to scrap the existing economic system. One almost ritualized American tradition had always been to cry "communism" whenever labor-oriented issues arose, and now, despite the fact that one effect of the seeming success of the NRA was to push the left wing even further down the ladder of defeat, anti-NRA forces began to link communism and the NRA.

The most dangerous enemy to labor was William Randolph Hearst, who had started out as pro-union and anti–finance capitalism but after World War I shifted his position to rabid anticommunism. Hearst helped to create and continued to nourish heartily the "Red menace" scare in his chain of newspapers. On November 26, 1934, Hearst wrote to his editors: "Fascism will only come into existence in the United States when such a movement becomes really necessary for the prevention of Communism." Paradoxically, although he frequently accused members of FDR's administration of left-wing leanings, Hearst nevertheless maintained a pro-Roosevelt attitude in the early years of the New Deal.

During this period, the motion picture industry seemed like a magical kingdom, impervious to the economic catastrophes that were plaguing the nation. In 1933, at a time when the highest wage in the rest of the country went to newspaper printers, who received $33.88 a week, in Hollywood Greta Garbo was earning $5,000 a week. During the first four years of the Depression, Hollywood churned out celluloid lethe to lull the miserable Americans into forgetfulness, apparently affected by the national disaster only as it could be used for content in films such as *I Am a Fugitive from a Chain Gang* and *The Public Enemy*. On the very day that Roosevelt announced the bank holiday, the film *42nd Street* opened at New York's Strand Theater.

Therefore, it had come as a shock in January 1933 when Paramount and RKO declared their theater chains bankrupt and went into receivership. Although the inevitability of a collapse had been carefully camouflaged for years, the economic instability of the motion picture industry had suddenly become apparent.

After 1928, when the talkies began really to take hold, there had been a massive expansion in the movie industry, a boom period in which theaters were bought, built, or rented and huge sums of money sunk into equipment for the new process of sound. This overexpansion took place in the context of a monopoly: most studios controlled all three phases of motion pictures—production, distribution, and exhibition. (In time, these monopolistic practices aroused the attention of the Justice Department and led ultimately to lengthy antitrust litigation against the studios.)

With the end of silent pictures, the foreign market for American movies dropped. It took several years for the studios to devise a process of simultaneously shooting an English- and a foreign-language version of the same film. But the movie moguls were not worried, because they saw the movie houses as temporary temples providing a panacea for the Depression depressed. What they had not counted on was the possibility that Americans would reach a point at which they could no longer afford the diversion of movies. As the Depression wore on, there was a sharp decline in ticket sales in urban areas; and as revenues shrank, production was scaled down, with the result that there was a shortage of films for theaters.

To keep going, heavy loans were taken out from Eastern banks, and motion picture companies fell under the control and influence of bankers. During the boom period these bankers had encouraged expansion—even though it might have been unwise for the studios—by competing for the privilege of floating loans. So at the beginning of 1933, Fox, Warner Bros., and Loew's (MGM) were facing conditions similar to those at Paramount and RKO, although Loew's and Columbia, which had been more judicious in the boom period, had the healthiest stock and were in the most favorable positions.

Critics within Hollywood had reasons for, but not solutions to, the disastrous state of affairs. Samuel Goldwyn, whose independent studio was a relatively small operation, unable to compete with the big factories like MGM and Warner Bros., saw overproduction and high overhead as problems. He urged that a limit of fifty good films be produced a year rather than four hundred mediocre ones. With no trace of the malapropisms for which he was famous, Goldwyn told the *New York Times* on February 22, 1933, "The Industry is filled with incompetents who are coasting along on their reputations and receiving fat salaries. This is particularly true of the technical side of production. . . . A writer who turns in a good story or a director who does a fine job is worth all the money he gets. I believe the contract system should be eliminated entirely . . . director and writer should be free-lance."

Some of his sentiments were echoed far less gently by a young screen writer who was to develop a reputation as a radical troublemaker and to continue to plague the ruling powers throughout his career in Hollywood. In the *North American Review* of August 1933, in an article entitled "The Fall of Hollywood," Dalton Trumbo wrote: "Bankers, nepotists, contracts, and talkies. . . . On four fingers one may count the leeches which have sucked a young and vigorous industry into a state of almost total paresis."

Trumbo's criticism of the contract system extended to a radical suggestion that it be replaced by a royalty system of moderate salaries and profit participation in which writers, directors, and actors would "be free to work only in those pictures which, in their judgment, will be successful. They will not be penalized for having accepted a contract at a low figure during their early days; nor will the studio be penalized for having signed them at an extravagant salary during their decline. The quality of entertainment will rise, the profits will be corresponding, and producer costs will be reduced by more than half." Trumbo's helpful suggestions for collectivizing movie making did not endear him to the producers.

Almost every studio was experiencing internecine friction between the younger movie executives, who were allied with the bankers, and the older executives, the immigrant pioneers who had built their empires out of empty orange groves and were reluctant to relinquish any control. It was hard for these immigrants, whose successes were evidence that the United States was the land of opportunity, to let outside money men into businesses they envisioned as dynastic family enterprises.

The studio heads had made good in classic Horatio Alger fashion. Carl Laemmle of Universal, Sam Goldwyn, and Paramount's Adolph Zukor had come to the United States as teenagers. Louis B. Mayer and William Fox had immigrated as small children. Harry Warner was born in Poland, his brothers in America, after his peddler father had immigrated. Eddie Mannix, an amusement-park bouncer who had become a vice-president and Mayer's troubleshooter at MGM, and Winfield Sheehan, a former New York policeman who was a vice-president at Fox Film Corporation, were Irish-Americans. Spyros and Charles Skouras of 20th Century–Fox were Greek peasants who had waited on tables in St. Louis hotels. Sidney Kent, who preceded Spyros Skouras as president of 20th Century–Fox, and W. W. Hodkinson, the Utah correspondence-school salesman who founded and named Paramount, were both of British descent.

These clever immigrants created an industry that wed the principles of the assembly line to the European heritage of art under the patronage system. The studios were factories for art, run by ruthless overseers, who viewed their artists and employees with paternalistic, proprietary interest.

The studios were spread all over Los Angeles. MGM in Culver City, the Goldwyn studios on Melrose, near Paramount and Columbia; Warner Bros. in Burbank; RKO in the Valley; Universal on Lankershim; Fox Film Corp. on Pico (in an area later to become Century City); and, on or near Gower Gulch, what were referred to as the Poverty Row studios—organizations that included Tiffany, Liberty, Mascot, Majestic, and Monogram, which were all taken over in 1935 by Republic studios.

"They were bandits then," remembered producer Milton Sperling, who began as secretary to Darryl F. Zanuck, then production head at Warner Bros. "They were immigrants in a new business, repeating the pattern of capitalism in microcosm. They were religious men, many of them, but they were willing to violate nine out of the ten commandments to keep their studios running. They honored their fathers and mothers. Especially Mayer and Irving Thalberg. Mayer's mother's chicken soup was always served in the MGM commissary—35 cents a bowl."

Many industries are paternalistic, but the leaders of General Motors or U.S. Steel have never been referred to by their employees as "Uncle" (as in "Uncle" Carl Laemmle), and few industries resorted to the intimate, familial forms of economic and psychological manipulation used to retain absolute control in Hollywood.

In 1933 Los Angeles was an open-shop town. The only unions in the movie industry were the International Alliance of Theatrical Stage Employees (IATSE), which covered electricians, engineers, and grips, and the musicians' union. This arrangement suited the producers, who were anxious to avoid the loss of absolute power intrinsic to unionization. In response to the producers' desire to control all unions, on May 11, 1927, the Academy of Motion Picture Arts and Sciences was established, covering producers, directors, actors, writers, and technicians.

The Academy was organized at a small dinner party given by Louis B. Mayer in the private dining room of the Biltmore Hotel. At that meeting, Fred Niblo (director of the silent film *Ben-Hur*) was chairman. Niblo explained to the assembled guests the genesis of the idea for the association, how one night at Mayer's house, with actor Conrad Nagel and Fred Beetson (later president of the Motion Picture Producers and Distributors Association [MPPDA]), Mayer was playing solitaire while two of his guests were discussing the advisability of all branches of the industry getting together on some basis for the benefit and welfare of the entire production end of motion pictures.

According to Niblo, L.B. looked up from his game of solitaire and said to the two who had been discussing the idea, "Why don't you get together, then, and try it out?" So L.B. issued invitations to thirty-six people and invited them to dinner at the Biltmore. Mayer harangued his guests, convincing them that an organization such as the Academy would be far preferable to any craft organization that was antagonistic toward the producers. So the Academy was born and anyone who "had contributed in a distinguished way to the arts and sciences of Motion Picture production" was eligible for membership. The wording was vague enough to assure Mayer that he could keep out whomever he wanted. Functioning actually as a company union, the Academy managed to delay any serious labor organizing in Hollywood for over five years.

The motion picture producers felt reassured by the Academy. They were aware of the struggles against producers and managers in New York by Actors' Equity and the Dramatists Guild, and they congratulated themselves on the creation of an organization that would keep the industry free from strong talent organizations. Everything seemed safe and secure in the little kingdom until March 1933, when a series of events began that suddenly slapped Hollywood into an awareness of its connection to the outside world.

On March 8, 1933, the day before Roosevelt's bank moratorium, the studios were unable to meet their payrolls, except for MGM, which paid its employees in cash. Universal suspended all contracts; Fox notified its employees that salaries would not be paid; and Paramount, Warner Bros., Columbia, and RKO, due to meet their payrolls the next day, faced bleak prospects. The producers assembled in conference, awaiting word from New York. For the first time since the studios had formed, a general shutdown in the film industry seemed possible.*

Then executives of the MPPDA, which came to be known as the Hays Office, met secretly and formed a committee consisting of Sidney Kent of Fox Film Corporation, Nicholas Schenck of MGM, and Sam Goldwyn, which mapped out an emergency strategy. On March 9 a blanket wage cut was imposed. Those receiving $50 or more weekly would get a 50 percent wage cut. Those getting less would receive a 25 percent wage cut. The cuts were to last for eight weeks.

Louis B. Mayer called an enormous meeting of his stars, writers, directors, and department heads in the big Thalberg projection room on the MGM lot. Thalberg was on a cruise with his wife, Norma Shearer, but L.B. entered, theatrically (having kept his audience waiting for twenty minutes), followed by his ubiquitous strong arm, Eddie Mannix. L.B. played the role of a man in torment, looking sleepless and unshaven. He asked his employees to help him save the studio. The avuncular Lionel Barrymore spoke up and offered to take a salary cut for the good of MGM. Mayer looked at him dramatically, attempt-

---

* Wage cuts had been tried in Hollywood before. In 1931, at the Academy Awards banquet, a spokesman for the producers rose after dessert and, citing low stock prices, announced a 10 to 25 percent cut in wages. This occurred after Warner Bros. had already let nine hundred employees go. Universal had also cut salaries over $150 by 25 percent and Paramount had cut those over $500 by 25 percent. Warner Bros. had set a sliding scale for a wage cut, and the members of the International Alliance of Theatrical Stage Employees, who had a union contract and therefore did not have to accept any wage cut, were advised to do so by their union.

However, the Academy board of directors was opposed to this wage cut because of the embarrassing, well-known fact that Irving Thalberg was paid $4,000 a week. On June 27, 1927, in the *New York Times*, the board stated that the "Academy is not in sympathy with a move to decrease all salaries in excess of $50 per week without more specific consideration as to the merit of the decreases." By July 6, the pay-cut proposal had been withdrawn.

ing to convey gratitude so monumental he had no words to express it.

"Then," said Frances Goodrich (who, with her husband, Albert Hackett, wrote several films in the Thin Man series), "Ernest Vajda, a Hungarian who had written some pictures for Ernst Lubitsch, said he did not see why we should take a cut when Metro pictures were doing so well at the box office. He suggested that we wait and see.

"And then Lionel Barrymore—I'll never forget it—said in that famous voice of his, 'You are acting like a man on his way to the guillotine wanting to stop for a manicure.'

"Everyone got very pious and scared about the possibility that the studio might shut down, so we took the pay cut. Most of us had never had so much money anyway, and we preferred a few tough weeks instead of the end of the pastures of plenty."

Mayer swore that he would personally see that every penny of the cut would be reimbursed when the emergency was over. The group approved the pay cut with tears and solidarity. Samuel Marx, at that time story editor at MGM, swore that as they walked out of that exhausting, draining meeting, Mayer turned to his assistant Benny Thau and cheerfully asked him, "So! How did I do?"

"Oh that L. B. Mayer," said Albert Hackett. "He created more communists than Karl Marx."

Pay cuts were also accepted at Paramount, Columbia, and Warner Bros.

Lester Cole, a radical young working-class actor turned screen writer, had been at Paramount for about six months when the studio manager announced the wage cut. Brian Marlow, another writer at Paramount, said to Lester, "The grips and electricians don't have to take it. Just watch."

And on March 12, IATSE refused to accept the cut. With their union contract they could also take the projectionists out on strike. Leaders of the dozen locals of IATSE studio workers sent a signed statement to Pat Casey, the labor liaison of the MPPDA, declaring that they would not accept a 50 percent wage cut. On March 13, all studios were shut for the day, for the first time in movie history. Then the producers met with the members of the Academy to reach an accord acceptable to union and nonunion employees.

On March 14, the studio doors reopened. The union musicians in theater chains agreed to a 20 percent cut, and IATSE unions said they were willing to resume work, though they still refused to accept the pay cut. It was decided that the high-salaried contract employees would bear the brunt of the 50 percent reduction, middle-salaried employees (those making between $50 and $100 a week) would take only a 25 percent cut, and there would be no wage cut for those with very small salaries. But certain highly paid actors and actresses chose to go for several weeks without pay rather than risk a cut, which they feared might become permanent.

Charles Brackett, a silver-haired aristocratic lawyer from a Saratoga banking family who became a screen writer, waived his salary for four weeks, as did Maurice Chevalier and Constance Bennett. Brian Marlow was told privately by Merritt Hulburd, his story editor, of the studio troubles and was asked to take a 50 percent cut.

"I told him," said Marlow, "that since I had a few weeks to go on my contract, I did not feel justified in accepting a cut. I said I would be glad to take the company's note for what was due me and wait a number of years, if necessary. I didn't feel that I should receive a pay cut simply because collections were delayed. That was the end of it, as far as I was concerned."

Marlow belonged to the Academy at that time, and the Academy undertook to represent the writers in their relations with the producers regarding the cut. "They promised that they would check the books of the corporations and that as soon as conditions warranted it, full pay would be restored. That didn't mean it would be retroactive," Marlow said. "From then on we would receive only our contracted salaries. The Academy expected and promised us that we would be receiving them long before the eight-week period expired."

On March 15, production resumed at MGM, RKO, Warner Bros., and Fox. People were edgy, unhappy. They wondered in whispers how big a wage cut people like Jack Warner and L. B. Mayer were taking. Throughout March, locals of craft unions kept threatening to strike, but after that one-day hiatus the studios kept up their schedules. Nobody had any product to put in the overabundant theaters. Although the cost of admission had been lowered so that even the poorest would be able to find refuge in an occasional movie, audiences were down by 25 percent. Warner Bros. was the only studio working on a product-reserve basis, with twenty-six completed films in their vaults. The other studios were rushing films from completion to screening.

After the second week of April, most studios started to pay full salaries again. Goldwyn, to everyone's amazement, announced retroactive pay for the duration of the cut. Nobody expected that kind of beneficence from L. B. Mayer. Zanuck had promised that the eight-week pay cut would be restored to his employees, and when Warner Bros. extended the cut for another week, Zanuck resigned.

Milton Sperling was among the loyal opposition who left Warner Bros. with Zanuck.

"Personally," said Sperling, "I think the resignation was a fraud. It was Zanuck's way of breaking his long-term contract with Warner's. Zanuck hadn't cleared his assurance of retroactive pay to anybody upstairs." Two years later, when 20th Century–Fox was formed, Zanuck was at its head.

The wage cut had made several things obvious to the employees of the motion picture studios. It taught them that producers didn't think contracts were sacred. And they saw the protection that had rendered IATSE unions immune to any tampering with salaries. It was time to unionize.

The first tentative gropings toward unionization had begun before the industry faced the possibility of a shutdown, though even then there was a sense that "the nickel was about to drop." And now, with rumors of a wage cut circulating, writers began attempting to organize the "talent" (as the creative members of the movie industry were called), despite a vision of the bitter sanctions producers could and would use against unruly, ungrateful union forces.

The struggle started at MGM as a wage fight between the producers and the sound men and spread to the other studios. Columbia shut down for two weeks, putting eight hundred people out of work. It was tough on the studio, but Harry Cohn and the other producers were quoted as saying that they were damned if those union bums were going to push them around. The heads of other studios agreed to apply all possible pressure.

The next morning a "Help Wanted" sign calling for strikebreaking sound technicians was posted at the gates of MGM. The writers and actors felt queasy about going through the studio gates. There weren't pickets yet— just worried-looking technicians standing in clusters by the gate.

Employees shivered at the thought of how ruthlessly the studios could act. The workers—especially the talent—had no protection. Studio contracts had clauses reserving the right to cancel the employment of stars and featured players in the event of strikes that tied up production. And the writers knew that if the studios would do that to stars, they would do worse to the writers, who, according to Lester Cole, were regarded by industry executives as "the niggers of the studio system."

By mid-July 1933 the studios were bringing in nonunion sound men, and the rumors in the commissaries were that the executives figured they had broken the strike. After a tense, uncertain Saturday, production started up again Monday morning as if nothing had happened. The IATSE called out six thousand workers on a sympathy strike to retaliate against the studios' use of nonunion labor. The studios brought in more strikebreaking labor. Hungry, unemployed Depression victims were lined up at the studio gates like beggars at a soup kitchen, and secretaries sat at tables writing down their names, addresses, and qualifications. Louis B. Mayer, president of the MPPDA, explained the association's position to the *New York Times*: "We expect to keep on the job every man and woman who wants to be," he said. "Our wage scales are the highest in any industry on the Pacific coast, and will continue to be."

By the end of July, there was a slight drop in production, but it was considered minor. The producers had won, and their triumph was emphasized by the confusion in the union rank and file. The cameramen walked out, then walked back, claiming that they had never voted about supporting the strike.*

When the trade papers announced that union leaders had asked producers' representative Pat Casey for immediate arbitration, everyone in Hollywood knew the sound men were drowning. Pat Casey treated unions, except for the very powerful, with undisguised contempt. He favored apologies and a quick resolution, but he had little patience for discussion.

The next morning, legions of police and guards surrounded MGM's gates. One writer who asked what was happening was told, "Violence, fella. Them unions been threatening violence. Couple of fellas beat up a man they said was a scab. We gotta protect folks."

The IATSE sent out a statement that called the reports of violence ridiculous: "None of our men has been involved in an act of violence, in spite of intimations to that effect by the studios, who are trying to incite public sympathy for their side of the controversy."

Everyone in Hollywood knew that the police could easily have been extras and that the claims of violence held little truth. But there was no way to prove it to the rest of the nation. The workers in the motion picture industry were being treated to the spectacle of the studios breaking a strike.

What distinguished this display from former studio strikebreaking tactics was the existence of the National Labor Board, newly formed under the NRA, which intervened in the situation in late August. The strikers were to return to work at the studios. It was a victory of sorts, but the studios still held the power.

It was in this atmosphere that the screen writers were moved to unionize. The national pro-labor attitude was encouraging. The wage cut had angered writers, and the immunity of the IATSE to that slash had enlightened them. The leaking out of stock-dividend figures, which showed that MGM stockholders were receiving the highest dividend in years, infuriated them.

The Academy, of course, couldn't understand why the writers would want to organize when there was writer representation in the Academy. But as it was so precisely put in a statement attributed by some to Dorothy Parker: "Looking to the Academy for representation was like trying to get laid in your mother's house. Somebody was always in the parlor, watching."

Further, the Academy's idea of protective organization was to form a central artists' bureau through which studios would exchange talent, sets,

---

* James Wong Howe, cinematographer extraordinaire, wanted the cameramen to strike just to prove how dependent Hollywood was on the man behind the camera. Howe's favorite subject was the underestimation of the cameraman. Not that he was a union sympathizer. The idea of cameramen, who were artists, joining with stagehands and sound men offended his sensibility. It was a problem that would plague every talent organization in the industry.

properties, and stories, resulting in substantial savings to producers at the expense of medium-salaried actors, writers, and technicians, who would be hired through the bureau. The studios would also be able to sell and exchange stories they couldn't use. The formation of a union truly seemed the only course possible.

Prior to 1933, there had been a group called the Writers Club, which became an official branch of the Authors League of America (ALA) in 1920. The Writers Club was not a union but a confederation, and a social adjunct to the Club was housed in a cozy club in a ramshackle old house on Sunset Boulevard. There was a big fireplace and a dining room and billiard room, and of its round of social activities, none was more important or popular than the play committee, chaired by screen writer Jane Murfin, which around 1927 presented evenings of one-act plays with dinner. The writers in Hollywood saw the place as a kind of lost Lambs Club for those New Yorkers who had been wooed west. It substituted for all the cafés and nightclubs Hollywood didn't have.

Playwright, novelist, and magazine writer Rupert Hughes (whose nephew, Howard, had his own impact on Hollywood) was its president. Hughes

Rupert Hughes (novelist, playwright, screenwriter, whose credits include *Ladies' Man* and *No One Man*, and uncle of Howard) was president in 1933 of the Writers Club (an unofficial branch of the Authors League of America).

was a formal, pompous man who had helped to organize the Authors League. He also wrote biographies of George Washington and the AFL's Samuel Gompers, and such undistinguished motion pictures as *Ladies' Man* and *No One Man*. Hughes, who was described by author James M. Cain as "one of the goddamndest boring writers in history—I could fall asleep after one paragraph of his prose," nevertheless impressed visitors at his home with an array of six massive desks located throughout the house, each covered with a work in progress. He spent his days writing from desk to desk.

As rumors of the wage cut buzzed around Hollywood, writers realized that the Writers Club was not going to be an organization of sufficient vitality or commitment to really aid the writers in the industry. The Club was a remnant of the "lost generation," and what was necessary for survival was a dose of the found generation. The denizens of the Club were among Hollywood's most highly paid scribes, and it was the little writer, the hundred-dollar-a-weeker, who was really going to get hurt by a salary cut.

On February 3, 1933, over a month before the wage cut, ten writers met at the Hollywood Knickerbocker Hotel to discuss the betterment of conditions under which writers worked in Hollywood. The notes from that meeting explained that there had probably never been a more propitious time in the history of the motion picture industry for writers, acting in concert and presenting a determined and vigorous face, to take the place to which they were properly entitled.

The writers who attended this meeting included Lester Cole; John Howard Lawson, also politically very radical, who had come from New York's New Playwrights Theater; and Samson Raphaelson, an elegant Chicago advertising executive turned playwright, whose Broadway play *The Jazz Singer* had been turned into the first talkie by Warner Bros.

Also attending was John Bright, a Chicago newspaperman, who was only twenty-five. Bright was a flamboyant character, with a penchant for booze, big shiny cars, and hanging out in the black section of town near Central Avenue, who had written a novel called *Blood and Beer*, which had been turned by him and his partner, Kubec Glasmon, into a picture called *The Public Enemy*.

Edwin Justus Mayer was also there. He was an established writer and friend of F. Scott Fitzgerald. Another was Louis Weitzenkorn, who had written the original stage play *Five Star Final* and who had, in his youth, been editor of the *Socialist Call*. Though he had subsequently become a reporter and editor for the McFadden newspaper syndicate and then Hearst, he retained a sense of his left-wing origins. The other writers there were Brian Marlow, Bertram Block, and Courtenay Terrett, a former reporter for the *New York World*, who wrote the original story for a film called *Quick Millions*.

John Bright characterized the political orientation of many of those members at the first meeting: "There was no real Communist Party in Holly-

Among the writers who met in 1933 to discuss the formation of a writers' union:

Lester Cole (he had come to Hollywood after working as an assistant director in Gottfried Reinhardt's *The Miracle* and worked on such screenplays as *Charlie Chan's Greatest Case*, *Winter Carnival*, and thirty-six other pictures).

John Bright's films include: *The Public Enemy*, *She Done Him Wrong*, *Back Door to Heaven*, and *Glamour for Sale*.

Left to right: James M. Cain, Dorshka and Samson Raphaelson (his screenplays include *The Shop Around the Corner* and *Suspicion*). Raphaelson, after working for the *New York Times* and as an advertising man, wrote his play *The Jazz Singer*, which became the first talking picture.

Edwin Justus Mayer.

wood at that time, but several of us had working-class backgrounds or left-wing origins that we hadn't forgotten. Hell, we'd all come out of the Depression. We were all New Deal progressives."

Both Lawson and Raphaelson, though playwrights of different styles and philosophies, were familiar with the struggle of the Dramatists Guild in New York. At the meeting they pointed out that the task to be accomplished by writers in Hollywood was far less difficult than that successfully carried through by the Dramatists Guild, which had taken command of the theater at the height of its prosperity and at a time when there was a strong association of managers and producers.

The ten men agreed that the only possible hope for obtaining what they wanted from the producers lay in building a powerful organization among the writers, one of sufficient strength to be able to back up its demands by shutting off the source of supply of screenplays. They decided this could best be done by working slowly, holding a series of meetings to which each of the ten would bring one guest, selected as best fitted for membership by his or her reputation as a craftsman, sympathy for this movement, and by possessing sufficient courage to fight through to a successful conclusion.

After several suggestions had been made and discarded, the writers decided that through negotiation with the Dramatists Guild (to be carried out in New York), the moribund screen writer's subsidiary of the Dramatists Guild, which now existed only as the Writers Club, could be revived and turned over to the authority of the new group. It was believed by these ten that the Dramatists Guild would lend its utmost support to the new organization, even to the extent of prohibiting its members from selling any plays to recalcitrant movie producers.

The idea of royalties for screen writers was also enthusiastically endorsed, and it included not only a percentage of the gross but the right to audit studio books to circumvent cheating. The meeting ended with a few other exciting, enthusiastic proposals, including the determination of writer credits by writers instead of by producers.

Today, these sound like small, reasonable demands, but they were revolutionary at the time. In fact the movement of writers to unionize was met with opposition so violent that it contained the seeds of a struggle lasting more than fifteen years, one that became part of a larger battle ending in destroyed careers and ruined lives.

Hollywood in the thirties was a haven for orphan talent. With the advent of talkies, anybody who could write dialogue might have the keys to the kingdom. The studios sent raiding parties to Broadway to find actors, playwrights, and voice coaches for people like John Gilbert, whose voice had Hollywood deliciously abuzz with premonitions of doom.

Writers flocked to Hollywood following the lead of Ben Hecht, who cabled fellow newspaperman Herman Mankiewicz to come and make his fortune easily, with the caveat, "P.S. Don't tell anybody. The Competition is idiots."

Newspapermen saw Hollywood as a way to get out of the grimy, underpaid chaos of the city desk. The literary market was in bad shape as a result of the Depression. Authors found advances sliced in half or denied altogether. Pulps, which had been a regular outlet for writers, went bankrupt and folded. The slicks, responding to shrinking advertising, cut the size of magazines and concentrated on well-known names.

For aspiring playwrights, Hollywood was an easy place to make a few bucks so they could eventually get back to New York to work on their plays. Everybody boarded the Super Chief.

There were writers who had made the voyage to Hollywood before talkies came in. Many of them were women, such as the veteran Frances Marion, darling of L. B. Mayer and Hearst, who wrote screenplays for Marion Davies. Frances Marion was at one time the highest-paid writer in the industry. Her staff would each write a separate part of the script, for which only she would get credit.

Bess Meredyth, another hangover from the silent days, had written such masterpieces as *Ben-Hur*. She was snobbish, reactionary, and very rich and was called an iron butterfly, a politician, a brown-nose. Passionately devoted to L. B. Mayer, she was known as a big name-dropper who would constantly say such things as "I just talked to Darryl, I just talked to L.B." *Ben-Hur* was her big credit; she talked about it all the time. It was impressive that a woman could rise as high in the hierarchy as she had, but her reputation was not good.

Anita Loos was another producer's darling. She had started writing titles for D. W. Griffith at the age of fourteen, was sweet and docile, and worked hard. Professional and reliable, she associated only with stars and executives (and, now and then, a celebrity writer such as Aldous Huxley), apart from an occasional drink at the Trap (the bar in the alley behind MGM) with the boys. She was known to go to bed at ten o'clock, rarely went to parties, belonged to no organizations, and had little frame of reference outside of her professional world. She was considered by studio executives to be the perfect screen writer.

A deluge of writers came from the literary world. At the Garden of Allah, a Beverly Hills hotel on Sunset Boulevard that had once been the estate of silent-film star Nazimova, the stucco bungalows sheltered such literati as F. Scott Fitzgerald, Robert Benchley, Marc Connelly and Donald Ogden Stewart. Dorothy Parker and her husband, Alan Campbell, arrived in 1933.

From the radical New Playwrights, who had stunned New York with their audacious productions at the Cherry Lane Theater, came Francis Faragoh (*Pinwheel*), John Howard Lawson (*Processional*), and John Dos Passos. Allen Boretz, who with John Murray had written the play *Room Service*, came out to write for the Marx Brothers. In addition, there was John Wexley, author of the haunting Depression play *The Last Mile*, and Samuel Ornitz (a plump, bespectacled, guru-like man who was known as one of the few Angelenos to read the *New York Times* dutifully from cover to cover), author of the Jewish classic *Haunch, Paunch, and Jowl*. Even Sigmund Freud had been contacted by Goldwyn about coming to Hollywood to write a script about psychoanalysis.

And there were the Depression kids who couldn't quite believe their luck, kids who hadn't become successful on Broadway or in the literary world but who came out to Hollywood, got jobs, worked their way up to being screen writers, and marveled at the golden reversal of their lives. Julius Epstein and his brother Philip, the twin wits at Warner Bros., had come from the *Brooklyn Eagle*. Dore Schary, a young, solemn-faced man, had come from New Jersey.

Edward Chodorov, an aspiring writer who had hung out with his starving pal, Moss Hart, in New York, criticizing commercial theater, also came, as did a scrawny kid named Milton Sperling, who became friendly with Donald Ogden Stewart as he moved from his position as Zanuck's secretary to that of screen writer.

Fortune magazine noted as early as 1930 that MGM employed "more members of the literati than it took to produce the King James Bible." The numbers kept growing.

Some, like Stewart, who were enjoying the sunshine and the social life, worried about whether studio employment nullified a writer's self-expression. "A writer could work for a studio," Stewart remembered, "and he could express himself profoundly and honestly. But he had not the slightest control over whether what he wrote ever reached the screen. That, I learned, was in the hands of the producer, or the director, or any star actor or actress."

Stewart also learned that writers were not necessarily accorded the status in Hollywood that they received on Broadway. He remarked that at formal dinners one was seated "according to importance at the box office. Writers, if invited at all, sat at the bottom of the table, below the heads of publicity but above the hairdressers."

There was always an element of triumph about the largely uneducated studio heads who could own and manipulate the literati. Sometimes it took unpleasant forms. Milton Sperling said that many producers kept in their offices a goosing stick, which looked and functioned something like a cattle prod, and they found it amusing to use it on writers. "The cruelty," he remembered, "was intensified by the way people played along." The stakes were so big that many people submitted to this humiliation.

"Oh, they tried to own you," remarked Mary C. McCall, Jr., a glamorous, wisecracking magazine writer who became a "corpse ranger" at Warner Bros., spicing up dialogue. "I'm sure that Warner Brothers tapped my phone. They wanted to make sure you weren't dawdling or doing other work on company time."

"It was dull and lonely in Hollywood when we first came out," remembers Elizabeth Faragoh, "a barren life. There was nothing to do but to get ahead in the studio, save some money, and go back to New York. There was no life at all for most wives. We were completely excluded."

With the wage cut in effect, scores of writers joined the original ten to demonstrate their concern. During a meeting held at the Writers Club they rushed emotionally to the platform and, according to Brian Marlow in *Screen Guilds' Magazine*, "flung checks about them with the abandon of playboys and pledged their undying loyalty to the Guild in writing. This was an impressive demonstration and doubtless, in some Hollywood front offices, had a decided sans-culottes flavor."

The Screen Writers Guild (SWG) of the Authors League of America was then reorganized from the Writers Club, with a new constitution and by-laws. One hundred and seventy-three charter members each contributed a hundred-dollar membership fee, with some giving more for their less solvent brethren. A contract was drawn up by Guild attorneys and signed by 102 of the Guild's members. A committee formed to draft a code of working rules included Samuel Ornitz, Jane Murfin, Rupert Hughes, Oliver H. P. Garrett, Robert Riskin, S. N. Behrman, and John Bright.

At a meeting on April 6, 1933, John Howard Lawson was elected the first president of the new Screen Writers Guild. Frances Marion was elected vice-president, Joseph Mankiewicz (a rising young screen writer and brother of Herman Mankiewicz) secretary, and Ralph Block treasurer.

It seemed a very normal and logical process to Albert and Frances Hackett.

"We were used to organization," they remembered. "We were accustomed to Actors' Equity and the Dramatists Guild. We didn't feel dependent upon the industry, so we weren't intimidated by the nature of studio antagonism. We had successful Broadway careers."

But there was consternation among executive officers of the studios at this turn of events, particularly when the new Guild passed resolutions calling for no general booking agency (which the Academy had suggested), no collaboration with non-Guild members, no more pay cuts, and for withdrawal from the Academy. Also, unlike the Academy's procedure, writers didn't have to be invited to join the Screen Writers Guild. Anybody who had written or was writing for motion pictures was eligible, without distinction of sex. There were only two classes of members, active and associate, the latter being given limited voting rights.

The Screen Writers Guild incorporated as a nonprofit organization be-

John Howard Lawson (his films include *Blockade* and *Action in the North Atlantic*) was a volunteer ambulance driver overseas during World War I, working with Hemingway and Dos Passos. Lawson was a central figure in the Screen Writers Guild and in 1933 its first president. Fourteen years later he was cited for contempt of Congress, sentenced to a year in prison, and blacklisted.

At the time of the formation of the Screen Writers Guild, Joseph Mankiewicz, who had worked at MGM for one year (his films there included *Finn and Hattie* and *Million Dollar Legs*) lent the fledgling Guild $300.

cause this would protect members from personal liability for the acts of their union (members of the SWG were highly propertied—unlike those of other unions—and a corporation was desirable).

"The founding of the Guild in 1933," said Lawson, "made it inevitable that there be a struggle with big business to control the new forms of communication. I placed the emphasis on the creative responsibility of writers to have control of their material. As far back as 1933, I knew that this would be a fundamental struggle, so we opened up that first big meeting with a speech I made in which I said that the writers were the owners of their material."

"Most of the writers were young people," Milton Sperling remembered, "under twenty-five, under thirty. The Guild was an attempt to bring reality to Hollywood. It was an assault on the kingdom, a quixotic struggle. And the producers knew that even though the walls were high, once you let ideas in, content was next. It was an assault on a paternalistic kingdom, and they were going to fight back."

The immediate concern of wages was inseparable from a challenge to the sovereignty of the studios over the issue of film content. The wage scale for writers was based on credits, and credits implied a creative voice, if not a responsibility, for what was seen. The SWG movement was emphasizing that individuals were involved in this process that was dominated by one super-creator—the producer, as representative of the studio. But the producers felt they had the right to assign credits to anyone, even if this took the form of literary nepotism. As Ogden Nash once quipped, "Uncle Carl Laemmle / has a very large faemmle."

Irving Thalberg produced some of the finest films made at MGM in the twenties and thirties. But he was one of the worst offenders against the writing profession, seeing writers as interchangeable runners in a relay that he always won. He would secretly set multiple sets of writers to work on the same project and seemed oblivious to the idea that, even though they were working on a film that would be interpreted and orchestrated by others, those writers still maintained some creative rapport with their product.

The intensity of this rapport had developed with the talkies. Silent films truly were the province of the director, though writers always supplied plot outlines and title cards. But to novelists and playwrights, a relationship with their material was an inalienable right. Even those playwrights who cared little for their movie writing and viewed it as a way to earn survival money for the next assault on Broadway brought to Hollywood the dissatisfaction of Dramatist Guild enlightenment and union tradition.

Joe Cohn was head of several MGM units that produced the Andy Hardy and also the Doctor Kildare series. "When so many pictures were being produced," he reminisced, "you needed a reservoir of writers. If Sidney Franklin had to start shooting and a script still needed a scene that the writers hadn't been able to get, he'd call up Paul Osborn, the playwright, and say,

'Would you write me a scene?' Producers had to be able to pull writers in when they needed them, and they thought unionization would end all that. Thalberg was against a writers' union, but he wasn't antiwriter. Look at the writers he had. He hired the best."

A look at the roster in MGM's writers' building in 1932 proves that to be true: Herman Mankiewicz, Robert Benchley, P. G. Wodehouse (who preferred to work at home), Donald Ogden Stewart, Anita Loos, Dorothy Parker, Charles Lederer, and Ben Hecht. And many writers had great respect for Thalberg's talent and judgment. "I made good with a boss I respected," said Stewart. "Irving Thalberg became a sort of father, as he did for everyone who worked closely with him. And in trying to satisfy this father figure, I became absorbed in the techniques of screen writing."

It was difficult to explain to studio executives that the intent of the union, though led by many of these prestigious literary figures, was really to protect the young, beginning writers. A 1934 NRA digest reported that 50 percent of the screen writers in Hollywood earned less than $4,000 a year, 40 percent earned less than $3,000, 30 percent less than $2,000, and only 10 percent earned more than $10,000 a year.

Shortly after the Screen Writers Guild was established, full salaries were restored, and emotions cooled correspondingly. There was no longer a crisis, the bank moratorium was over, and box office grosses were picking up. "In short," said Brian Marlow, "the devil was well again. The bulk of Guild membership settled down to serious polo, yachting, and golf, and the business of maintaining and building the SWG devolved upon the inevitable five percent."

For the first time, the disparate writers at the studios had a sense of community action and were delighted to be working together. ("I'll tell you one thing, however," said Allen Boretz, "writers as a group are singularly unattractive. I used to take a gander at the pusses around the writers' table at Warners and wince.")

Said Donald Ogden Stewart: "My first year working in Hollywood eclipsed my memories of freshman year at college. Such fun, really!"

Apart from the socializing, the move toward unionization gave many writers a sense of commitment and common destiny that they had never before shared. With all of the purpose that the "lost generation" had lacked, the writers had entered the New Deal.

2

John Howard Lawson presided over a fascinating set of personalities at the early meetings of the Screen Writers Guild board. Legal counsel was a spare, elegant southerner named Laurence Beilinson, who had the eloquence of a courthouse orator. He was assisted by Elsie Wilkins, the Guild's executive secretary.

"Elsie came as close to running the Guild as anybody I ever knew," said Beilinson. "She was a delightful, practical Australian girl who was our general factotum. She wasn't very pretty, neither was she ill-favored, but she had a gift of holding writers' hands and getting them together, reconciling them, so to speak, since there were endless little quarrels that went on among them. As a matter of fact, almost everybody on the board was impossible."

Beilinson, who described himself as a barefoot Shakespearean Jew from Arkansas, had met Oliver H. P. Garrett (descended from Oliver Hazard Perry) through a roommate at Harvard, became his lawyer, and at his behest came to represent the Guild.

"Oliver was a fine reporter and a cynical idealist," said Beilinson. "He'd seen the worst of people in his career as a reporter covering the New York gang wars, and he had a just appreciation of the weakness of human nature, which he really needed, to be on that board."

Board members Ralph Block, Dudley Nichols, and Louis Weitzenkorn had been journalists, as had Laurence Stallings, who, with Maxwell Anderson, had written *What Price Glory?*

Stallings had written war commentary for the *New York Telegram* and had lost a leg in World War I. He had a habit of calling during the board meetings, which were (and still are) held on Monday nights, to say that he was on his way in from Santa Monica. When he'd arrive at 10:30 or 11:00 p.m., he would demand that everything that had transpired be reviewed and re-decided.

Grover Jones, another board member, was a witty, extremely conservative screen writer who had been satirized with his partner William Slavens McNutt in the Hollywood farce *Boy Meets Girl*. His first job in Hollywood had been at Universal, living on the lot, taking care of Carl Laemmle's hens on the studio chicken ranch. Calling himself the "lost soul from Chillicothe, Ohio," he glorified his humble origins as a coal miner's son and began every speech with, "Of course, I don't know much. I'm just an old coal miner."

Another board member, Howard Green, had been in line for the presidency of the Guild and was a bit disgruntled by John Howard Lawson's ascendance. Lawson was a very commanding presence. He had a slight limp that most people didn't notice, a booming voice, and the habit of smashing his fist into his open palm as he made a point. He often got into lengthy arguments with Ernest Pascal, who became the Guild's third president. The only woman on the board was vice-president Frances Marion.

"Everything was a source of argument on this first board," Beilinson said. "The arguments usually started with an article in the *Hollywood Reporter*, which would come out just before the meeting and antagonize the board members. They would decide to issue a statement. Most of them were ex-newspapermen, so they would immediately begin to argue about the statement. Once it was finally written, one of them would lean over to me and say, 'That sonofabitch calls himself a newspaperman? He doesn't even know how to write a lead.' "

The first big struggle that the new Screen Writers Guild faced concerned Roosevelt's National Industrial Recovery Act. After June 16, 1933, when the NIRA was signed into law, labor experienced an unprecedented explosion. Over six thousand people joined the Los Angeles unions in the first weeks of July. Organizers were at such premium that they were being sought through newspaper ads. Lawyers, doctors, newspapermen, and writers all wanted to unionize.

Despite the noble aims of FDR's blue eagle, the codes of fair practice, which each business or industry was supposed to formulate and which were intended to have the force of law, were riddled with illegal, antitrust practices. Because employers were allowed to regulate their own industries, the part that unions were supposed to play in the formation of the codes was precluded, and codes that were almost fascist were encouraged.

Lawson, as the Guild's president, spent most of 1933 and 1934 in Washington and New York, trying, without much success, to get the Dramatists Guild and the Authors League of America included in the NRA.

"Roosevelt wrote a letter to the Authors League," remembered Lawson, "in which he said that writers were artistic creators. The Dramatists Guild thought this was quite a victory, but the screen writers weren't happy. We of the SWG wanted to be regarded as both writers and workers. So I was caught between the SWG and the Authors League. The SWG wanted to send a message to Roosevelt telling him that he was wrong, that writers in the movie industry were indeed workers, but the Authors League and the Dramatists Guild got very angry about this, because they didn't want to hurt Roosevelt's feelings."

The situation was resolved, however, by the inclusion of the Screen Writers Guild in the NRA Motion Picture Industry Code. The NRA Code administrator assigned by Roosevelt to the movie industry was Sol Rosenblatt, who had been the attorney for the Democratic National Committee. The glamorous Hollywood deputy administrator slot was Rosenblatt's campaign reward. "Rosenblatt," said Lawson, "was undeniably on the side of the producers. A miserable individual, really."

Rosenblatt's brother-in-law, Lester Cowan, who later became the producer of *The Story of G.I. Joe* and other films, was at that time the assistant to, and then replaced, a man named Reed, who headed the Motion Picture Academy committee designated to represent talent in formulating the NRA Code for the industry. This was despite the fact that the writers had, in April 1933, withdrawn from the Academy. Eddie Loeb, of the law firm Loeb and Loeb, represented the producers' association, MGM, and Universal, and was extremely active in drawing up the Code.

"It was," said Beilinson, "one of the most blatant attempts to put the producers in permanent control of the business."

One can understand the furious fear of L. B. Mayer and his colleagues when the writers wanted to unionize. In 1934, the Authors League of America and the Screen Writers Guild issued a statement objecting to current efforts at censorship.

The statement read: "We wish to state herewith, resentment at and objection to the intemperance, hysteria, injustice, and in some cases outright falsehood which characterize certain expressions of the protest." They declared themselves against what seemed like, "an open attempt to regiment and standardize creative expression to the measure of limited groups."

One of the provisions of the NRA Motion Picture Code stated that nobody—no writer, actor, or director—could earn more than $100,000 a year. Another decreed that actors' and writers' agents could not function without being licensed by the producers, which essentially made them the producers' creatures. A third provision, said to be the inspiration of Irving Thalberg, was called the antiraiding clause. This stipulated that once a star's or a writer's contract expired, no other studio would woo him until the parent studio decided if it still wanted him or not. It was basically a tactic to keep salaries down.

Author Budd Schulberg remembered what had happened when the clause was first brought up at a meeting of the producers' association. His father, B. P. Schulberg, had recently left Paramount as head of production to become an independent producer. "I know," Budd Schulberg said, "that at one of the meetings of the producers' association, someone, either Mayer or Thalberg, suggested the nonraiding agreement, to force stars to stay where they were. . . . And my father said, 'You know we had a war to solve that. It was called the Civil War and it freed the slaves.' And everybody got furious."

Before the Code could be put into effect, copies of it were obtained, and Beilinson and other shocked representatives of Hollywood talent had them circulated. The announcement, in October 1933, of the salary-fixing board (that no salary was to exceed $100,000) caused the actors to join the writers in resigning from the Academy, and a massive meeting was held at the home of actor Frank Morgan. This was an extremely significant event in an industry built on the star system, and every important actor in town was there, among them, Ann Harding, Lee Tracy, Robert Montgomery, Eddie Cantor, Jeanette MacDonald, Fredric March, Paul Muni, George Raft, and Adolphe Menjou. Everyone there resigned in writing from the Academy (including Academy vice-presidents March, Montgomery, and Menjou), and the infant Screen Actors Guild (SAG) was consolidated, with Eddie Cantor as the new president.

The formation of the Screen Actors Guild coincided with a massive membership drive on the part of the Screen Writers Guild, whose membership had grown from 275 to 750 in a little over a year. "The proportion of Guild members to total writers," exhorted board member Brian Marlow in *Screen Guilds' Magazine*, "must be so overwhelming, so 99.44%, that producers will no longer be able to say with a straight face, as one did recently, that the Academy represents the screenwriter."

The Screen Actors Guild and the Screen Writers Guild sent a joint wire to President Roosevelt on October 8 that denounced the proposed "sinister provisions" of the NRA Motion Picture Code and stated that talent was not what had bankrupted the motion picture companies. What had caused the problem was "the purchase and leasing of theatres at exorbitant rates, caused by the race for power of a few individuals desiring to get a stranglehold on the outlet of the industry, the box office."

This telegram laid the foundation for a subsequent visit to Roosevelt in Warm Springs, Georgia, by SAG president Eddie Cantor, accompanied by writers Fannie Hurst and FDR intimate Robert Sherwood. On the subject of the ceiling salary of $100,000, Roosevelt said: "But that's more than I make. Why should an actor make more than I make?"

Cantor countered with the explanation that what Roosevelt didn't make stayed in the pockets of the American people, but if actors and writers made less, it just stayed in the pockets of the producers. Roosevelt conceded the point, and as a result of Cantor's visit, FDR issued an executive order that eliminated the two most offending sections of the proposed Code. In addition, Roosevelt ordered the formation of "five and five committees" (to consist of five writers, five actors, and five producers), which were supposed to work out amendments to the Motion Picture Code before it was finally promulgated.

The talent guilds soon discovered that a bargaining committee on paper was not a bargaining committee in fact. The writers and actors fought vainly to have the committees appointed, but as delay piled on delay, it became obvious that the producers were placing whatever obstacles they could find in the path of such appointments. Crisp, angry telegrams and bitter phone calls to Washington resulted in enough White House pressure to have Rosenblatt appoint the committees, and finally, by mid-July 1934, the producers announced that they were ready to negotiate.

And negotiate they did—bitterly, fruitlessly—until there was a complete breakdown in the talks, with the producers claiming that the demands were excessive and irrational. Both the actors and the writers wanted a guild shop in the industry, which meant contracts providing that the studios would employ only members of the Screen Actors Guild and Screen Writers Guild.

Among other working conditions the writers requested be included in the Code were the following:

1. that writers not be lent from studio to studio without their consent
2. that writers not be asked to write on speculation
3. that all notice of writer suspension or layoff be in writing
4. that producers transport writers to and from locations where their presence was required and that producers pay for the writers' room and board while on location
5. that writers receive screen credit according to their contribution to a picture and that no contract violate this
6. that all writers working simultaneously on the same material be notified of this by the producer
7. that agreements or understandings by producers, formal or informal, to blacklist writers be prohibited

The committees reached a total impasse and a brief to this effect was sent to Washington.

Shortly thereafter, Laurence Beilinson, as counsel now for both the Screen Actors Guild and the Screen Writers Guild, was summoned to Washington by Rosenblatt. He arrived there to find the deputy administrator contorted in anxious diplomacy, and Rosenblatt quickly disclosed his belief that the writers and actors could get nearly everything they wanted included in the NRA Code if they would "save the face of the producers." Rosenblatt assured Beilinson that the aim of a guild shop could indeed be obtained if the two guilds would agree to join in the formation of a central industry body similar to the Academy. In such a group, Rosenblatt promised, the producers would concede complete autonomy to each branch of talent, provided that the central body be allowed to function in an advisory capacity only. It seemed as if Rosenblatt's proposal meant an overwhelming victory for the guilds, but Beilinson didn't trust him.

"It's strange," Beilinson remembered telling Rosenblatt, "because both Mayer, who controls the industry, and Thalberg have said they would give guild shops 'over their dead bodies.' "

"It's only an illusion that Mayer controls the industry," said Rosenblatt. "Nick Schenck [chairman of the board of MGM] and Harry Warner [chairman of the board of Warner Bros.] really control the industry. I talked to them and they've agreed that you'll get guild shops if you withdraw that brief you're about to file with me."

"My brief," recalled Beilinson with pleasure, "would have been highly libelous, if it hadn't all been true. It exposed the unfair labor practices of the producers throughout the whole history of the studios, and it quite definitely made them look like the wrong people to be formulating an industry fair-practice code. The producers were afraid that the working conditions asked for by the guilds might be made a part of the NRA Code, and if that happened, it would mean that any violation on the part of the producers would become a criminal offense. As a group, the producers had violated every agreement previously entered into between themselves and the talent groups, so they had good reason to regard such a possibility with little relish. So what Rosenblatt wanted, in addition to having the brief kept quiet, was that working conditions not become part of the Code and only be contained in the contracts between the guilds and the producing companies."

Beilinson went back to Los Angeles to discuss the proposal with the guilds, and then laid down a set of demands, to which Rosenblatt acceded (ostensibly after conferring with and receiving the permission of Warner, Schenck, and Mayer). But Rosenblatt wanted the guilds to invite him to Hollywood to expedite the resolution of the matter.

"You're inviting yourself," Beilinson told Rosenblatt, "and you're doing so on the initiative of Messrs. Schenck and Warner. Suppose the thing blows up, after we've invited you and asked you to be the arbiter, and we don't get what we want? We'll be left with egg on our face."

After more haggling, Rosenblatt finally agreed to a clear correspondence that could be published in the event of a foul-up, and so the following telegram was sent to Rosenblatt:

> The complete deadlock in the producer actor five five committee and a like condition apparently soon to result in the writer committee creates a serious situation in actor producer relations. We feel that your presence in Hollywood is urgently required and request your good offices to help clear up the situation. [Signed] Robert Montgomery, SAG, and Ralph Block, SWG

Rosenblatt arrived in Hollywood on November 28, 1934, and attended the annual ball of the Screen Actors Guild with Beilinson. In the course of the evening, he asked Beilinson to have the guilds eliminate all of the extraneous demands that were put forth simply as bargaining points. Over Beilinson's protest, Rosenblatt explained that he intended to show the producers terms that, he said, were the "absolute minimum" and force them to accept without argument.

The next day, Beilinson met with producers' representative Eddie Loeb and Rosenblatt. Loeb suggested that they go to see Louis B. Mayer. The three of them went to MGM just as Mayer was leaving to visit his wife in the hospital. He insisted that the three men accompany him so they could talk en route.

"I found myself in Mayer's limousine," said Beilinson. "Loeb and Rosenblatt were following in a car behind us. The window was closed so the chauffeur couldn't hear. And Mayer kept talking about the Academy and how he was devoted to it. He would hate to see it go out of existence, and couldn't we change the name of the guilds to the Academy? I said I didn't care what he called it if we got our demands and a guild shop. He said that what the industry really needed was a czar, such as [Commissioner Kenesaw Mountain] Landis was for baseball, and then he said, 'Beilinson, you could be the czar, and that shows you how liberal I am. The position would pay $100,000 a year with a five-year contract.' And I said, 'Thank you, Mr. Mayer. I have a job.'"

The negotiations were futile. The producers flatly refused a guild shop, and the guilds, hoping to salvage the situation, said they were ready to accept an 80 percent guild shop. The producers came forth with another plan to create a new Academy. On Monday, December 3, Rosenblatt met at his Beverly Wilshire suite with guild representatives—for the writers, Ralph Block, Wells Root, Oliver Garrett, and Ernest Pascal, and for the actors, Robert Montgomery, Fredric March, Boris Karloff, James Cagney, and Kenneth Thompson. The committees were at a standoff. The producers wouldn't budge and the guilds were furious.

"You lied to us," Beilinson told Rosenblatt. "This isn't what you promised us at all."

Rosenblatt left in a huff, issuing a statement blaming the guilds for the breakdown of negotiations, whereupon Beilinson published the entire correspondence, exposing Rosenblatt as a liar and as the tool of the producers.

Nineteen thirty-four ended with the NRA five and five committees deadlocked. Briefs were sent to Washington, but there was little prospect of action on the guilds' recommendations until the administration and Congress decided the future of the NRA, due to expire in June 1935, and the disputed labor clauses. The guilds knew that even if the anticipated extension of the NRA favored collective bargaining, a long fight still lay ahead of them. But they were not discouraged.

"There are some defeats," stated the joint *Screen Guilds' Magazine,* "which are even more truly harbingers of future victory. If the two Guilds, in such a short period since their formation, have achieved a position and importance so great as to inspire the producers to such lengths to get rid of them, then the future of the organizations is bright indeed. It proves that Writers and Actors not alone are capable of craft solidarity, but also of presenting a solid front together. . . ."

On a lighter note, scribes around Hollywood were singing "The Screen Writers Marching Song" (words and music by Henry Myers):

I

Arise, ye movie writers, and cast away your chains.
Executives are human after all!
Shall they still rewrite our scripts, the children of our brains?
And shall we be a supervisor's thrall?
No! No! No! No! A million, million no's!
Not in vain our fountain pens are filled!
The writers all will join
And executives will loin
To monkey with the Screen Writers Guild.

II

They pay us weekly salaries, a measly grand or two,
And think we ought to work because we're paid!
Shall we yield and do our job? Will you? Will you?
Defend the rights the tyrant would invade!
Up! Up! Up! Up! Attack them from the rear!
Never shall the voice of art be stilled!
Through gory battle scenes
Drive your gleaming limousines!
Ye heroes of the Screen Writers Guild!

III

Ye Gentlemen and Ladies that push the fervent pen,
The time has come and Freedom is in sight.
The cudgeled brain grows weary. When a bottle is your yen,
Have at it! And remember, write is write!
Drink! Drink! Drink! Drink! Write a masterpiece!
Till twenty thousand pages have been filled.
They'll all be thrown away
But the producers have to pay
To members of the Screen Writers Guild!

Labor was not discouraged. Taking a cue from the movie industry, waiters at the Brown Derby restaurants walked out on strike after a wage cut. Picket lines were set up at the Beverly Hills and Hollywood restaurants, and stars and screen writers cheered the strikers, refusing to eat there until strike-breaking labor was dispensed with and the wage cut restored.

The second year of the Roosevelt administration had been both exhilarating and disappointing. Many of the New Deal plans that had been so progressive in theory turned out to be less satisfying in practice. After the summer of 1934, labor leaders realized that NRA officials lacked power to enforce the provisions of the act, so that by the end of the year, labor was relying on its own economic strength rather than on government officials. Before the year was over, Hollywood was also being affected by labor problems elsewhere in California.

In San Francisco, Australian-born longshoreman leader Harry Bridges took his dockworkers out on strike. The teamsters supported them, and police attacked the strikers with shocking violence on a day that came to be called Black Thursday. This violence resulted in the San Francisco general strike.

The general strike was an exhilarating show of the power of labor, but it antagonized the forces of reaction. As early as September 9, 1933, William Randolph Hearst had written to Walter Coblentz, one of his editors, "Business is also worried about turning the whole country over to the labor unions and will protest against that at the polls. . . . The labor unions, moreover, are never very grateful."

After the surprising strength of the 1934 general strike, agitating labor and communism were linked with increasing frequency by the antilabor forces. It was a trend that continued. The first of a series of attempts to have Harry Bridges deported was begun by the government, and in 1934 the Dickstein Bill was introduced in Congress, seeking to limit immigration of foreign professionals without the consent of the Secretary of Labor, unless the immigrant was a distinguished artist or the immigration involved a reciprocal trade of labor. Supporters of the bill claimed that it was designed to protect American actors and musicians, but the underlying motivation was fear of foreign agitators, presumably communists, contributing to the disruption of American labor.

Hearst's antagonism toward labor was exacerbated by the organizational attempts of the American Newspaper Guild (ANG). By the end of 1934, the ANG had more than eight thousand members, and it was carrying on an active campaign for protection under the NRA. California was the focus of the organizational struggle of newspaper writers, and the struggle centered on the case of Dean Jennings, a San Francisco journalist and member of the ANG who was discharged from the *San Francisco Call-Bulletin* for his labor activity.

The American Newspaper Guild vigorously supported his case and took it to the National Labor Board (NLB), which was empowered to act independently of the NRA. Over the protests of legions of publishers, NLB chairman Francis Biddle ruled that Jennings be given back his job or he would cite the *Call-Bulletin* to the NRA for loss of its blue eagle. The publishers' outcry was so great that FDR ruled that the labor board should have no jurisdiction over cases handled by an NRA Code unless the NRA body was unable to arrive at a decision.

For screen writers, who saw the newspaper publishers' sanctions against labor activists as a grim portent of what could happen in Hollywood, the Dean Jennings case was a reassurance that there would be some sort of federal intervention to maintain a balance between the forces of labor and employer in the industry. Hearst disagreed with the NRA, feared licensing of the press under it, and his papers criticized the act until it was declared unconstitutional in May 1935.

One of Roosevelt's plans that was meeting with success was the Works Progress Administration (WPA), which sought to employ artists to create works of art for the federal buildings being constructed. The WPA had a theater branch, the Federal Theater Project, which subsidized actors, writers, and stage technicians and enabled them to put on low-cost performances to divert the Depression multitudes. Some of the greatest theater in this country, written and performed in the thirties, was created under the auspices of the Federal Theater Project and its able director, Hallie Flanagan.

But one of the problems that beset the WPA and the Federal Theater Project and came to roost in the Hollywood writers' struggle was the fact that the times were not favorable to the idea of artists as a work force. The process of certification that an individual had to go through to qualify for the WPA was so humiliating (much like being certified for welfare now) that it deterred many of the people it had been created to help. The hangover of the Protestant work ethic still condemned the artist as a shiftless nonworker, and the underlying belief during the Depression was that artists should find themselves any kind of job rather than starve for lack of creative work.

As the country slowly began to pull itself out of the Depression and outgrow the consuming task of simple survival, a new form of political consciousness took hold. Writers began to speak out against social abuses in this country. John Howard Lawson, Sam Ornitz, John Dos Passos, and Theodore Dreiser all went to Kentucky to observe the condition of the miners in Harlan County and to protest, only to be chased out of the state by the vengeful mine owners. The possibilities of socialism were being examined and the publication *The New Masses* was dedicated to advancing the ethic of social consciousness everywhere.

* * *

Early in 1934, Upton Sinclair had announced that he would be a candidate for the Democratic nomination for governor of California. He explained his candidacy by saying, "I saw hundreds of thousands of persons driven from their homes; the sweep of an economic process which had turned most of California over to money lenders and banks. . . . And for every official who was sent to jail I knew that a thousand were hiding with their loot."

Sinclair's campaign was launched with a pamphlet, *How to End Poverty in California*, and his campaign became known as EPIC (End Poverty in California). Sinclair provided a figure around whom all of the angry, disillusioned, frustrated forces in the state could rally, and he easily won the Democratic primary in August of that year.

With a campaign funded and supported by the "little people," the lower-middle-class white-collar workers adoring this crusading figure, it looked as if Sinclair might indeed win the election against the incumbent governor, Frank Merriam. Then the reactionary forces of the state, led by the motion picture producers, panicked. Sinclair's utopian socialist schemes, they claimed, were totally impractical and would ruin them.

So the emperors of Hollywood's little kingdom set out to destroy Sinclair. There were progressives, of course, like Larry Beilinson, who opposed Sinclair on purely practical grounds. "Sinclair would have made a very bad governor," Beilinson said. "He was an impractical man and he would have broken the state with his pension plan [a "production for use" plan to support the unemployed, endorsed by the State Federation of Labor]. A very decent man, but thoroughly impractical. As a matter of fact, I think that was the first time I voted Republican in my life."

The heads of the motion picture studios set about utilizing their resources to defeat Sinclair. Millions of dollars were spent in creating fake newsreels in which bums, en route to California, claimed to have been drawn there by Sinclair.

"Louis B. Mayer had Felix Feist, a director of screen tests, making the anti-Sinclair films, and I thought it was a lousy trick. I was pro Sinclair," recalled Sam Marx.

Joseph Mankiewicz was instructed to write anti-Sinclair radio spots, and he didn't object. "I was against Sinclair," he remembered. "He wanted to raise taxes and I was against raising taxes. I still am."

The tactic that was most successful in raising money for Merriam, and that antagonized most members of the creative Hollywood community (which was largely for Sinclair), was the studios' extortion of money from its employees to contribute to the Merriam campaign. Warner Bros. deducted $100 from the salary of each employee. "A memo from Mayer and Mannix came down that said, 'Stop Sinclair.' Everybody was expected to contribute one day's salary to Merriam," recalled Sam Marx. "We were all indignant, especially the lesser-paid writers, although it was part of a continuous stream of demands from the studio heads to their employees. They were always hustling you for contributions to premieres, parties, and other funds."

"Mr. Mayer issued everyone a check made out for the amount of one day's salary in the name of the Merriam campaign," remembered Frances Hackett. "You were expected to sign it and send it in, and you were warned that if you didn't send the check in, when option time came they might not pick up your option. But we were damned if we were going to give our money to the likes of Merriam, so we simply didn't send in our checks. I suppose we were coerced, but not that hard. After all, they didn't break our contracts."

On October 24, 1934, the *New York Times* reported that the Screen Writers Guild had charged the motion picture producers with attempting to collect funds for Merriam with deceit. The producers of course denied the charges, but it was one more factor that antagonized them toward the Guild.

"Sinclair was something like Eugene McCarthy, a dreamer, but nothing particularly dangerous about him," recalled John Wexley. "Nevertheless, this Governor Merriam, the incumbent, was a horror, a dinosaur, even more backward than Reagan is. I was working at the time for Harry Cohn, at Columbia, and he had everyone contribute one day's pay to the Stop Sinclair Fund.

"In the middle of the executive-dining-room patio at the studio was a huge thermometer the set department had built, and as the people contributed, the red line went up toward the hundred percent mark. This fund paid for all the huge billboards on the highways, ads in the papers, the phony newsreels, and the circulars and leaflets to discredit Sinclair. Well, the thermometer was just short of the hundred percent mark because there were two people in the studio, out of the many hundreds of writers and technicians, who wouldn't cough up. John Howard Lawson and myself. And so Harry Cohn would play these little games. I actually wrote a sketch about it once because it was so funny.

"Harry's attempt to get my Merriam contribution stretched out over a period of some weeks. I was getting about $800 a week at that time, so one day's salary was equal to about $140 or $150. And Harry would bargain with me. He'd say, 'John, just make it an even hundred.' And I'd say, 'No.' He'd say, 'Well, just give me $50.' He was a peddler by nature. And then he came down to $10, a token $10, and I wouldn't give him that. He'd say, 'You know, you'll be marked lousy,' which was the word for 'blacklist' at that time.

"[Writer] Sidney Buchman held out for quite a while but finally gave in. Cohn threatened everyone. Robert Riskin and Frank Capra didn't want to contribute, but they finally gave in. The last holdouts were Jack and myself, and finally he fired Jack. And he got me to settle my contract with him, so that after sitting around for four months with no work, which he thought was punishing me but which I used to write a play, I had four weeks to go and he gave me two weeks' salary and I left. He warned me I'd never work again in the industry. I went over to RKO the next day at a salary of twelve hundred a week."

The behavior of the producers in the Merriam-Sinclair campaign was not only symptomatic of their political orientation and of the way in which they viewed as serfs the people who worked for them, but it also helps to explain their attitudes toward their children. Harry Rapf, third in command at MGM after Mayer and Thalberg, was a thickset, long-nosed man, with a mournful look around his eyes. Rapf's son, Maurice, was Budd Schulberg's best friend. They were inseparable, like brothers.

"I had become sort of socially conscious as I grew up," remembered

Left, Harry Rapf with his son, Maurice. Rapf Senior was an executive producer at MGM. Budd Schulberg said of him: "He was a good, hard-working man . . . and he made a kind of meat-and-potatoes film." Rapf Junior, at twenty-two just starting out as a writer at MGM, was invited to join the Guild: "I went that very night. . . . I never gave a damn about movie stars, but I gave a great damn about writers."

Schulberg. "My mother had known Upton Sinclair and she'd talk about socialism, although she was basically a pretty hard-nosed capitalist, a moneymaker. But she flirted with a lot of these ideas and cultivated people like Lincoln Steffens and Sinclair.

"I'm not sure how my consciousness started, but there was the Depression and unemployment and the apple sellers, the breadlines, and the sit-in strikes. It all affected me as it was affecting so many people of my generation at the same time. My father was one of the few somewhat liberal types out there. He didn't really oppose the Guild, and had come to his job as head of Paramount starting as a writer. "I think that combination provided a very different upbringing from that of most of the producers' kids. My father was basically liberal-Democrat, not antilabor. . . .

"Maurice's father was much more conventional minded, more square than my father. He was a good, hardworking man, basically simpleminded. I don't mean an idiot, because he did know his show business and he made a kind of meat-and-potatoes film. He didn't have the sophistication of my father. My family was much more permissive than Maurice's and I think Maurice felt closer to mine."

In 1934, Maurice and Budd went to Russia on their summer vacation from Dartmouth. "That's where we really became radicalized toward the Soviets," Budd recalled. "Until then, I was radically oriented but not radically organized. But 1934 was the year of the Writers Congress and it was fantastic. Maxim Gorky was the chairman in that little Tartar skull cap, and Jesus, the people who were there were really incredible."

It was in Russia during that summer that Budd and Maurice met Ring Lardner, Jr. Lardner had been a member of the Socialist Club at Princeton. Schulberg and Rapf were there under the auspices of the left-wing National Students League, which had organized delegations to the Anglo-American Institute for summer study at the University of Moscow. The three men came away from the Soviet Union inspired.

As Ring Lardner wrote in *The Lardners: My Family Remembered:* "It was my impression that the best hope for mankind lay with the Soviets. Only in Russia were massive construction and planning for the future going on at a time when the West was either locked in stagnant depression or, like Germany, headed resolutely back to barbarism."

"When Maurice and Budd went to Russia," remembered Joe Cohn, "everyone thought it was terrible. Somebody said, 'Get Harry Warner to talk to them,' and somebody else said, 'Those kids will make mincemeat out of Harry Warner.' "

"When Maurice and I came back to Hollywood from Russia that summer," said Budd, "there was a great complaint about it at the studio and so we went to see Thalberg. 'Send them to Thalberg' was the cry. It was like 'Go see the Wizard.' Thalberg was sort of the high priest of Hollywood and the producers, especially Mayer, felt he could straighten us out. He talked to us as people who had been trained to one day take over the reins of these studios and would be in positions of responsibility and power. He told us that he thought our politics were extremely immature and he was concerned about us because he assumed we would eventually take over the industry. No one doubted we would. We were in the line of absolute succession."

In a perverse way, Budd's radicalism gave his father a twinge of pride, because it was a social conscience sprung from learning, from reading books about philosophy and economics.

"My oldest son is a regular *New Masses* radical," he told the *New York World-Telegram*. "When he was up at Dartmouth he was editor of the student paper and he turned it into a radical paper, and all the alumni got stirred up. I didn't mind. The way I figure it, every man has got a right to speak what he believes."

B. P. Schulberg was unlike the majority of Hollywood's monarchs, and perhaps that's why he didn't last. He had an amused sense of tolerance. But other producers were puzzled to discover that they had armed the heirs apparent for revolt. In academe, these crown princes had developed a reverence for the word above the dollar sign, and it was not surprising that when they returned to their fathers' kingdoms they were not so sure their places were at the heads of dynasties. Nor was it surprising, though it shocked their elders, to discover that these young men were drawn to the organized Left. As enlightened crown princes, Schulberg and Rapf felt guilt for the suffering in the world, and acquiescence to a succession they didn't necessarily deserve seemed decadent to them.

Hollywood had not really become politicized yet. "There wasn't much in the way of left-wing organization in Hollywood at that time," said John Wexley. "There was an auxiliary of the New York–based John Reed Club, and it was sort of an intellectual club. Writers had coffee, read each other's stuff, chatted. There was no Communist Party in Hollywood then. Prior to the Depression, I think the left wing became rather Menckenite—at least I did— and we thought political action was quite futile because of Sacco and Vanzetti. But as the Depression continued, the left wing burgeoned from the placid Socialist Party into sterner stuff. The Communist Party came a little later, and it was slow in growing."

3

Gone With the Wind was a national best seller in 1936, and the news from Europe warned the American people of dire, irreversible changes, as violent as those of the Civil War. Sinclair Lewis published *It Can't Happen Here*, a warning against fascism, the black barbarism sweeping across Europe.

To many Americans, fearing the events in Europe, shaken by the Depression at home, uncertain about the future, Roosevelt did not seem to offer the needed political solution. Ironically, at the very time that some Americans were finding that solution in communism, believing that Roosevelt was just another liberal politician, there were many rich and distinguished Democrats who claimed that Roosevelt's economic planning abrogated constitutional liberties and American ideals. They accused Roosevelt of transforming the government from a republic to a communist model.

Roosevelt was already embroiled in severe conflicts over his New Deal policies. The National Recovery Administration was failing to achieve its hoped-for level of success.

Senator Robert F. Wagner had wanted to submit a bill to Congress in 1934 to create a labor board with subpoena powers and the authority to enforce orders directly through federal district courts. He felt that what was needed was a permanent regulatory agency such as the Federal Trade Commission that would deal uniquely with labor.

Roosevelt was attempting to have Congress extend the NRA, but in May 1935 the Supreme Court declared the NRA's system of codes unconstitutional. By the time the NRA expired in 1936, parts of its codes had already been considered by Congress, and the sections concerning labor and unionization were incorporated into the Wagner-Connery Labor Relations Act. Under the Wagner Act, Congress declared in unequivocal terms that collective bargaining was the policy of the United States. The act was passed on July 5, 1935, but unfortunately the Supreme Court's decision on the NRA had led employers to believe that the Wagner Act didn't have to be obeyed until a Supreme Court review.

The Wagner Act outlawed company unions, freed employees from interference or coercion in the exercise of their right to bargain collectively, and prohibited employer discrimination (i.e., blacklists) as a tool to discourage membership in a labor organization. Section 13 of the act guaranteed the right to strike, and Section 10 gave the act the force of law.

Laurence Beilinson wrote at the time, in *Screen Guilds' Magazine*: "It might be that the Act is unconstitutional as applied to the poultry business, but constitutional as regards the motion picture industry. Of all businesses, the motion picture is most clearly interstate. . . . If the constitutionality of the Act is upheld, the Guilds will gain greatly. The Academy will be definitely outlawed and that false face of the producers will be removed. . . . The producers will have to bargain with the Guilds. . . ."

Despite the encouragement that many sections of labor drew from the passage of the Wagner Act, the climate surrounding the National Labor Relations Act was exceedingly hostile. Employers universally despised it. There were many Roosevelt supporters, such as the *New York Times*, Warner Bros., and Hearst, who, nevertheless, were fighting hard against the act.

Nathan Witt, a tough, incorruptible Harvard Law School graduate who described himself as a "Yiddishe boy from New York" and wound up as executive secretary of the National Labor Relations Board, recalled the tense atmosphere surrounding the board. "When the AFL and CIO split in 1935," he said, "the AFL joined the employers in attacking the NLRB and me for ruling that the unit or representation of San Francisco longshoremen fell under the jurisdiction of the Harry Bridges union. They screamed that this union, the ILWU [International Longshoremen's and Warehousemen's Union], was run by Reds, that Joe Ryan should run the dockworkers, and that by supporting Bridges we proved that we were left-wing."

The response to the National Labor Relations Board, according to Witt, was the beginning of a common cycle of opposition to progressive agencies. The first step is public outcry from those who fear they'll be injured; in the case of the NLRB, it was the employers who screamed that it was unnecessary. The next step is constitutional attack. The Liberty League Lawyers, about sixty members of the American Bar Association, whose interests were those of big business, got together and issued an opinion (before the Supreme Court ruled) that the Wagner Act was unconstitutional. But the combination of Roosevelt's overwhelming majority in the election in 1936 and his attempt to pack the Supreme Court seemed to push the court into a more liberal position.

The third step in the cycle of opposition is an attack on how the agency is run. To discredit the agency, its administrators are accused of every sin, from incompetence to drunkenness to communism, with personal habits fair game for political slander. This results in top-level house cleaning. And finally, the employers take it over. The NLRB, which began with the vital, pioneering progressive lawyers and administrators culled from the state and local levels, ended up controlled by the employers who so despised it.

While Congress was dealing with Roosevelt's New Deal policies on a national level, it was also concerned with the impact of the turmoil in Europe on the United States. The McCormack-Dickstein Committee, composed of Samuel Dickstein, a rabbi's son from New York's Lower East Side, and John W. McCormack, a conservative from Massachusetts, had begun an investigation in 1934 of Nazi and other propaganda in the United States. The committee's report, dated February 16, 1935, stated that, despite a few isolated cases of fascist activity (such as that of an Italian vice-consul in Detroit), the committee had no evidence of any connection between these efforts and the fascist activity of any European country.

This committee was also concerned with the Communist Party in the United States, and Earl Browder (who during World War II was the leader of the U.S. communist movement) was questioned about the activities of the Left. The report of the committee concluded that

> the Communist Party of the United States is not a political party in the true American sense. . . . This committee does not believe that the Communist movement in this country is sufficiently strong numerically nor in influence to constitute a danger to American institutions at the present time. Its increase in activity during the past year is plain evidence that unless checked, such activity will increase in scope and interference so that they will inevitably constitute a definite menace. It is the duty of government to check and control, through appropriate legislation, the illegal actions and methods of such movements, and to protect itself and its loyal citizens against such subversive attempts.

In closing, the committee stated, "Whatever may be the result elsewhere, the constitutional rights and liberties of American citizens must be preserved from Communism, Fascism, and Naziism. The only ism in this country should be Americanism."

By 1935, the burgeoning left-wing movement among American writers and artists included New York's Group Theater and New Playwrights Theater, which had already been swept up in a movement to unite art and politics. According to playwright Clifford Odets, who claimed he was in the Communist Party from 1934 to 1936, with several members of the Group Theater: "In a time of great social unrest, many found themselves reaching out for new ideas and fighting for one's right. One believed that perhaps all of our problems could be worked out by some sort of socialism." To members of the Left, Odets's plays, such as *Waiting for Lefty* and *Awake and Sing!*, were perfect examples of proletariat art in the American theater. ("The function of revolutionary drama," wrote John Howard Lawson at the time, "is to circumvent a Freudian escape from truths people wish to avoid.")

The progressives wanted progressive plays that underscored the class struggle and the working-class fight for revolution. The cultural head of the American Communist Party, V. J. Jerome, expressed the belief that "agitprop [agitational propaganda] drama was actually better drama because Marxists better understood the forces that shaped human beings, and could therefore write better characters."

To many artists, it seemed that the communist movement represented a progressive force in American life. "The feeling in those days," recalled Budd Schulberg, "was extremely broad, that any man of good will opposed to fascism could join the Party."

"We felt," said John Bright, "that the Communist Party was leading the way in trying to work up as much feeling as possible against Nazis and aggression in Europe."

These feelings were echoed daily in the two New York left-wing publications, *The New Masses* and the Communist Party's *Daily Worker*. With the exodus to Hollywood of New York progressives such as Lawson and Odets and the growth of the creative intellectual community out there, it was not surprising that in 1936 the *Daily Worker* declared Hollywood the "West Coast Center of Progressivism." Clifford Odets is said to have been told by Moss Hart that he had persuaded many young writers to turn left and go west, where Odets had gone in 1935. "You mean my plays convert them?" asked Odets. "No, your salary," replied Hart.

The rise of Hitler and the proliferation of European refugees in Hollywood initiated a steady growth in political activity in the movie kingdom. "Being progressive began to be fashionable," recalled John Wexley. "It was considered a sign of decadence or of stupidity to be anything but liberal and very left. Collective security was the big thing that people were aiming for, and Hitler was the great danger. People really cared about Roosevelt's 'one-third of the nation' who were poor, weak, hungry. And since a lot of us writers were from the East and were used to expressing ourselves in one way or another on social themes, it was hard not to be a friend of the Soviet Union."

The Sunday salons at the home of Salka and Berthold Viertel in Santa Monica were a ritual and the center of Hollywood's émigré salons during the thirties. "At Salka Viertel's," said John Wexley, "in the small living room would be the three greatest writers of Europe: Thomas Mann, Lion Feuchtwanger, and Franz Werfel, in the same room with Pat O'Brien and myself." Berthold Viertel (poet, director, and model for Christopher Isherwood's Dr. Bergman in *Prater Violet*) and his wife had come to Hollywood in the twenties. Though her husband never achieved great success in America, Salka abandoned her acting career, took up screen writing, and became a well-known scenarist. A magnetic, eccentric woman with a buxom figure, Salka became chief writer for and confidante of Greta Garbo. It was rumored that the two women were lovers.

On Sundays, the Viertels' home overflowed with figures like Max Reinhardt and his family, George Cukor, Ernst Lubitsch, composer Bronislau Kaper, and the more progressive and cultured of MGM's literati. The gatherings there and at other émigré homes gave the huddled refugees a newfound sense of community and a vague hope that their Europe was not forever lost. These sessions also enlightened Hollywood residents, making them more aware of the situation in Europe.

"After Hitler in the thirties, Hollywood became the place where any antifascist movement went for dollars," remembered actress Karen Morley, who starred with Paul Muni in *Scarface*. "The progressive political movement was turning everyone into alcoholics, drinking at one benefit Friday night, one Saturday, and two on Sunday. You were smashed all the time."

"I gave $150 so many times to so many organizations," recalled Samson Raphaelson, "that at one point my wife, Dorshka, totaled it up and we were shocked. But we had the money and individual contributions of $150 didn't seem like so much. Jews, because of their fear of anti-Semitism, contributed to all the antifascist causes. I felt that if the world was going to go communist or fascist, I'd rather see it go communist, though I never joined the Party."

In his memoirs, *By a Stroke of Luck*, Donald Ogden Stewart described his conversion from sophisticated playboy-wit to communist wit as being a rather romantic leap toward humanity and away from his pleasure-filled, solipsistic life in which serious subjects were rarely discussed. Stewart began to read *The New Masses* and tried to do whatever he could in Hollywood for the movement, which included writing checks for migrant workers striking in the Salinas Valley and contributing to strike funds for Kentucky miners. His heroes were Clifford Odets and John Howard Lawson, and he joyfully joined the Hollywood Anti-Nazi League.

Stewart found that the movie executives, particularly Thalberg, were distressed at his political conversion for several reasons. They felt that foreign policy was not something screen writers should get involved in, especially since Germany and Italy were important markets for American films; for that very reason, Sinclair Lewis's anti-Nazi *It Can't Happen Here* was not made into a film. Second, the Hollywood establishment didn't want to look back to the ghettos, to their ethnicity and attendant vulnerability.

In 1978, screen writer Michael Blankfort, an Orthodox Jew who began his writing career as a theater reviewer for *The New Masses*, recalled in the *Los Angeles Herald Examiner*: "The Warners, Cohn, Mayer, Goldwyn, Selznick . . . dreamed hopelessly of being more American than the Gentiles who came before them. . . . I remember an occasion when Myron Selznick [David's brother], then Hollywood's most powerful agent, attacked me and my friend Budd Schulberg for creating anti-Semitism because we were involved in the left-wing struggles. . . . His view of fighting anti-Semitism, one he shared with many other influential leaders, was to hide our identity, keep quiet, change our names . . . and disguise in our films anything that might suggest that Jews were involved in the uncertainties of the times."

In 1979, John Howard Lawson recounted the following story in an issue of the *Authors' Guild Bulletin*: "When I arrived at RKO, I was informed that the studio would insist on only one slight change in my play [*Processional*]; the leading characters must not be Jews. I had always known that the play would be cheapened in the film version, but the Jewish theme was clearly the heart of the play. . . . By this time my personal plans and my Guild activities were already under way. . . . I felt I had no choice but to accept the conditions imposed and to salvage what I could from the original work."

There were, of course, members of the Hollywood writing community who were not set on fire by the political sparks that were flying. Allen Rivkin, in his *Hello Hollywood*, recalled the West Side Writing and Asthma Club, an organization started by a bunch of writers who were nostalgic for the college-humor magazines they had read or written for in the twenties and whose members included Don Marquis (author of *archy and mehitabel*), agent H. N. Swanson, Lorenz Hart, Richard Rodgers, Harry Ruby, and Groucho Marx. The club met at Al Levy's, a restaurant across from the Brown Derby on Vine Street, where the Huntington Hartford Theater now stands.

"The Eastern writers," said Rivkin, "nostalgic for the Algonquin type lunches of the past, but reluctant to mingle with the heavies at Musso and Frank's, were invited to join. We were fun. They were having those heavy anti-Nazi luncheons at the Vendome."

These same writers who didn't want a "heavy anti-Nazi luncheon" found that when they tried to move their forty-member lunch club to one of L.A.'s beach clubs, they couldn't get in. All the beach clubs were restricted against Jews. As a matter of fact, the Beverly Hills Tennis Club had just been founded because the Westside Tennis Club, the only tennis club in Los Angeles at the time, was also restricted.

It was decided that the members of the West Side Writing and Asthma Club would each host a monthly luncheon at their homes for the whole club. Grover Jones had a barbecue at his hacienda on Sunset Boulevard that featured musical Mexicans and half a cow on a spit. Preston Sturges held a luncheon at a restaurant he owned, The Players, and had a photographer take pictures of everyone, mount the prints, and send them to the subjects. The club folded because no one could top Sturges.

On April 27, 1935, the first League of American Writers (LAW) Congress was held in New York City, and was attended by four thousand writers. Addressing the congress, Donald Ogden Stewart cried: "Let us have no more million-dollar revolving staircases, no more star-filled symposiums of billion-dollar entertainment—but let us have some simple truths, against nothing but a plain background."

These sentiments reflected the prevailing progressive attitude toward the arts, which was articulated at this congress. The League took the place of the left-wing intellectual John Reed Clubs, which had flourished until the beginning of the popular-front period in 1934 and which sought to reach out for a large coalition of liberals, progressives, left-wingers, and communists in the fight against fascism.

The need for the League of American Writers Congress had been articulated in a statement in the *Daily Worker* on January 18, 1935: "The program of the LAW will be evolved at the Congress, basing itself on the following: [to] fight against imperialist war and fascism [and to] defend the development and strengthening of the revolutionary labor movement. . . ." The call

At Preston Sturges's restaurant, The Players: Sturges, Frances Dee, unidentified woman, and Joel McCrea.

for the congress was signed by many writers, including Theodore Dreiser, Michael Gold, and John Howard Lawson. Albert Maltz, a screen writer who had won the O. Henry Prize for the year's best short story in 1938, was active in the League of American Writers almost from its inception.

A call for greater responsibility in regard to movie content was accompanied by a cry for recognition of the importance of writers of movies. In 1934 Ida Tarbell, one of the country's most respected journalists and muckrakers, told the *Screen Guilds' Magazine* "the American screenwriter . . . has little or nothing to say about the production of the thing he creates. . . ." She called for protection of the integrity of a writer's endeavor and said that the producer "should not have the freedom to destroy, he should not have the freedom to rewrite, without the cooperation of the creator."

"The League of American Writers was a political mobilization of writers against fascism," Maltz recalled. "Fascism was the world enemy, the burner of books. On behalf of the LAW, I wrote a pamphlet, *We Hold These Truths*, which presented statements on anti-Semitism. We also transmitted funds to exiled antifascist writers, and helped to get writers out of Europe. We would take public stances on certain issues, and various members would write speeches for public figures. I wrote speeches for [liberal politician Robert W.] Kenny, and one for Edward G. Robinson. Even Roosevelt had a membership in the LAW at one point, but he asked us to keep it silent."

The League of American Writers grew larger each year, holding a congress biannually, and its members ultimately included Dorothy Parker, Donald Ogden Stewart, Dashiell Hammett, Langston Hughes, Vincent Sheean, and Norman Corwin. The LAW embarked on a campaign to inform writers of their power and their responsibility.

As Donald Ogden Stewart later wrote, in an introduction to *Fighting Words*, a book of essays based on symposia at an LAW congress: "Words are your weapon, a dangerous weapon. The soldier and the gangster both carry revolvers. Theodore Dreiser and William Randolph Hearst can both use the word 'liberty' and it doesn't mean exactly the same thing. To decide which usage is correct . . . involves a consideration of the difference in purpose of Dreiser's words and those of Mr. Hearst." Stewart ended by exhorting writers to "contribute to the sum of our democratic culture."

Budd Schulberg, in an article in the *New York Times* in 1939, remarked that he and his peers were the first generation that had never known a world without motion pictures, much as Marshall McLuhan later was to analyze the generation that had grown up with television. Schulberg quoted a screen writer friend of his as saying: "For a long time now, Hollywood has been developing its voice, until it has become the most powerful in the world. But it's like an overgrown child who is still encouraged to talk baby-talk. What we need most of all now are the people who can teach him how to act his age."

John Howard Lawson, attacking the situation far less gently, blamed motion picture executives for "repetitions, jokes, and indecent allusions in films." Lawson, whose *Processional* had rocked New York audiences with its children in overalls and masks, chanting against the Monster of Capitalism, screaming "Dynamo, Dynamo," and "Kill Henry Ford," claimed that writers in Hollywood formed a "veritable army—an army of high-priced and eminent privates who are in general thoroughly discontented."

After the National Industrial Recovery Act had been declared unconstitutional in May 1935, the Screen Writers Guild continued its struggle to unionize with increased bitterness. Producers continued their efforts to revive the writers' branch of the Academy, and on September 25 the Academy announced that it had concluded months of conferences between committees of writers and producers and that a revised Academy basic agreement and writer-producer code of practice had been drawn up. The producers proudly claimed that this new pact gave writers many of the concessions they had asked for in the last NRA five and five brief, which they had filed at the end of 1934.

Members of the Screen Writers Guild were furious. The Academy had refused to make any provisions covering the writers' requests for transportation and room and board while on location and had ignored the request that writers give their consent to being lent out. The question of a blacklist had been totally ignored, as had the request that there be no agreements between producers inhibiting competitive bidding on writers' services.

The most bitter blow was the Academy's stand on screen credits. The Academy said that producers had a right to tentatively determine credits based on an assessment of substantial contributions, to be made by the producer. If a writer disagreed with a producer's allocation of credits, he could appeal to the Writers Adjustment Committee of the Academy, whose judgment would be final. However, even if the Academy found that the credits had been improperly allocated on the screen, the producer would not be obligated to change them.

For writers in Hollywood, then as now, a screen credit is the only form of identity he has. Faceless, and generally three pictures down the road by the time a film is finally made, the screen credit, whether it reads "Screenplay by," "Original Screenplay by," "Screenplay Based on the Novel by," "Story by," or "Additional Dialogue by," tells the world the writer was there. A writer can work for years and make an exceedingly respectable living without ever seeing his name on the screen. Pictures get shelved, sometimes because the competition makes a similar vehicle; a performer won't play a certain part; or the picture is finally made after being rewritten by somebody else—generally somebody higher up in the writing hierarchy.

The level of income rises in direct proportion to screen credits, which prove a writer to be a good risk, and the writer with the longest and best list of credits has the safest berth. So, with the power of determining credits in the hands of the producers or the Academy, fear of obscurity was a strong enough deterrent to keep even the most outraged writer from joining with others in a unionization movement.

The Screen Writers Guild was determined to fight this attempt to reduce it to nothing more than a powerless company union. With a new slate of officers (president, Ernest Pascal; vice-president, Nunnally Johnson; treasurer, John Grey; secretary, Robert N. Lee), a huge membership drive was begun, under the chairmanship of Joel Sayre. Members were urged to find out if their collaborators were members of the SWG, and, if not, to use their best efforts to recruit them.

Among the writers who responded to this call in the summer of 1936 were new members Morrie Ryskind, Dashiell Hammett, Robert Benchley, George S. Kaufman, Theodore Dreiser, Alice Duer Miller, John Collier, Guy Endore, Lillian Hellman, Mortimer Offner, Laura Perelman, and Gottfried Reinhardt. Even those who had been sympathetic before but did not consider themselves joiners stood up to be counted. The Guild felt a sense of great

Director Ernest Pascal, Jesse Lasky, Jr., and Irving Cummings. Pascal served as chairman of the men's committee of the Hollywood Independent Citizens' Committee of the Arts, Sciences, and Professions (HICCASP).

optimism in this community spirit. When H. G. Wells came to Hollywood, the Academy of Motion Picture Arts and Sciences gave a banquet in his honor that was marked by the absence of customary celebrities. A few nights later, the SWG held a dinner for him, and everybody who was anybody was there. The Guild proudly claimed that its membership had reached 990, while the Academy had only thirty-five writer members.

After the utter failure of negotiations with the Academy and the producers, the Screen Writers Guild began to seek other methods of procedure. To strengthen their organization, the Screen Actors Guild had affiliated with the Associated Actors and Artists of America, an organization chartered by the AFL, which effectively made them a part of the AFL and of the California State Federation of Labor. Conscious of the strength the actors would get from such an affiliation, the Screen Writers Guild began working toward a closer association with the Dramatists Guild and the Authors League of America. The problem that remained to be solved, however, was that actors could strike simply by not showing up. The writers had to find some method of achieving a showdown in situations where studios had stockpiles of scripts and the writer's work was done long in advance of production.

The controversy between the Guild and the Academy was to climax in February 1936 with the Academy Awards. The Academy was pushing *Mutiny on the Bounty*, an Irving Thalberg production. The guilds were pushing *The Informer*, based on Liam O'Flaherty's novel about the Irish rebellion. To the guilds' delight, Dudley Nichols won an Academy Award for his script for *The Informer*. To its even greater delight, and to the disbelief of Hollywood—Nichols was one of the highest-paid writers in Hollywood and could easily have lived without the Guild—he turned the award down. Nichols wrote to the Academy:

Gentlemen:

My awareness of the honor given the screenplay of *The Informer* and my gratitude to those individuals who voted for the award only make this letter more difficult. But as one of the founders of the SWG—which was conceived in revolt against the Academy and born out of disagreement with the way it functioned against employed talent in any emergency—I deeply regret that I am unable to accept the award.

To accept it would be to turn my back on nearly a thousand members of the Writers Guild, to desert those fellow-writers who ventured everything in the long-drawn-out fight for a genuine writers organization, to go back on convictions honestly arrived at, and to invalidate three years work in the Guild, which I should like to look back upon with self-respect. . . .

Three years ago I resigned from the Academy and, with others, devoted myself to organizing the Guild because I had become convinced that the Academy was at root political, that it could not be made to function for the purposes to which it had been dedicated, and that in any

Nunnally Johnson with Joel Sayre.

Dudley Nichols was president of the Screen Writers Guild in 1937–38. Before coming to Hollywood he had been a foreign correspondent for the *New York World*. His films include *Stagecoach*, *Bringing Up Baby*, *For Whom the Bell Tolls*, and *The Informer*, for which he refused an Academy Award in 1936, explaining in a letter to the Academy that "to accept it would be to turn my back on nearly a thousand members of the Writers Guild. . . . I resigned from the Academy and . . . devoted myself to . . . the Guild because I had become convinced that [it] was at root political. . . ."

major disagreement between employed talent and the studios it would operate against the best interests of talent.

. . . A writer who accepts an Academy Award tacitly supports the Academy, and I believe it to be the duty of every screenwriter to stand with his own, and to strengthen the Guild, because there is no other representative autonomous organization for writers which aims at justice for employer and employee alike, and which is concerned solely with the betterment of the writing craft.

Respectfully yours,
Dudley Nichols

"Dudley Nichols," said actor Alexander Knox, "was an extremely intelligent man, a good journalist, who had forgotten more about the social history of his civilization than most of his contemporaries ever knew. That was why he consistently stuck his neck out and never gave it a second thought."

In addition to Nichols's refusal, the Academy was embarrassed by the presence of only twenty members of the Screen Actors Guild and thirteen members of the Screen Writers Guild at the Academy Awards dinner. The two guilds had sent their members wires advising them to stay away, since their presence would undermine the guilds and show the public that talent was at the beck and call of the producers.

The producers, wary of such a possible response, had arranged their own "private" party, to which each executive invited all of the prominent writers, stars, and featured players under his authority. The executives assured their guests that this was purely a social event and was quite divorced from any political aspect, so naturally many members of the guilds accepted, not wishing to offend their employers. However, the two guilds then discovered that the invitations weren't personal or social but were the effort of this group of organized hosts to pack the Awards dinner with names, for the purpose of convincing the public and the industry that the Academy was as strong as, if not stronger than, it had ever been before the two talent guilds had resigned in 1933. The turnout—tiny, considering that every writer and actor of any prominence in both guilds had been invited—demonstrated an exhilarating show of solidarity.

The lines were drawn for battle in Hollywood. The producers, and the writers who sided with them, knew that an insurrection of this sort had to be stopped. According to Sam Marx, the climate of distrust, "sparked by fears of communism, was growing in the front office, and Mannix, MGM attorney M. E. Greenwood, and his assistant, Floyd Hendrickson, began to place a number of employees under surveillance. Whitey Hendry [the Culver City police chief] was named head of the studio constabulary, and it began a new facet of studio operations—spying and undercover investigations."

Spring 1936 was about to erupt in the most brutal confrontation of writers and management in the history of the industry. Summer 1936 brought an even greater disruption to Hollywood—one which simultaneously minimized the importance of the Guild's struggle and brought the political community of Hollywood together in a concerted effort that for some initiated the best period of their lives. In July army officers began a revolt in Spanish Morocco that, led by generals Francisco Franco and Emilio Mola, and assisted by Mussolini and Hitler, would eventually overthrow the elected government of Spain. The Spanish Civil War had begun.

4

It had become obvious to the leadership of the Screen Writers Guild that big guns were now necessary to force from producers some sort of recognition of their organization. Although the Guild could count nearly a thousand members, fewer than one-third of them were employed at any given time, and the pressure on writers was intensified daily by the arrival of every aspiring college graduate with a vision of the gold and glory that were a screen writer's reward. Most of these new writers didn't care how little they were paid at first, if only they were able to get their feet inside the movie industry's pearly gates. The Screen Writers Guild hoped to protect the little writer not just from producers but also from other writers.

Some of these newcomers were lucky enough to begin as junior writers, turning out reams of stories that would be synthesized by other, more important writers. The junior writers were a gamble for the studios, but they proved to be a smart investment. They were like chorus girls—occasionally, out of the lineup, a star would emerge. Some of Hollywood's most successful writers, such as George Seaton and Robert Pirosh, began as junior writers. At Republic, they were fired at the end of the day before Thanksgiving, told the picture they'd been working on had been canceled, and then were rehired that Friday morning, just so the studio could save the one day's salary when they took Thanksgiving off. Other similar experiences gave junior writers a particularly strong sense of the need for a union.

Robert Lees, who also began his career as a junior writer, recalled: "Originally, there were four of us junior writers at Metro. We called ourselves the brain trust—it was in the days of Roosevelt, you know. There was Alvin Josephy, MGM story editor Eddie Knopf's nephew; Nicky Justin—who couldn't write, but was so funny everyone figured she could—kept us entertained. Then there was Fred Rinaldo and me. The head of the junior writers was a guy named Maurice Revnes. He was an absolute tyrant to our little group. When he wasn't scaring the shit out of us, telling us how many guys were standing in line to get our junior-writing slots at thirty-five dollars a week, he was making assignations with all the young actresses. Revnes was thrown out when he made the mistake of pursuing a girl L. B. Mayer was interested in, and we weren't sorry to see him go."

In his novel about Hollywood, *What Makes Sammy Run?*, Budd Schulberg described junior writers as "writers who aren't given anything to write, and if they do write something of their own, they can't find anybody to read it." But regardless of the frustrations, the junior writers were ready to hang in there, dreaming of one day being in the $2,500-a-week class of someone like Frances Marion, and knowing that outside those studio gates lay a Depression and a gaggle of hungry writers waiting to take their places.

There was no point in writers seeking union strength through a horizontal alliance with other crafts in the motion picture business. Prop men, electricians, and actors were not potential strikebreakers who would take writers' jobs in case of a walkout. The battle between producers and writers was essentially one of control of manpower and material in the writing field. The aim was a guild shop. Without it, the Guild could be nothing but a defensive machine whose only recourse would be to strike; and with the ravening writers at the gates of Hollywood, it would fold up and disintegrate in defeat.

In the summer of 1935, Authors League of America president Marc Connelly, leaders of the League's Associate Dramatists Guild and leaders of the Screen Writers Guild had met quietly in Hollywood. They concluded that jointly the SWG, the ALA, and the Dramatists Guild represented almost 90 percent of the creative writers in the United States. There had existed a rather loose agreement between the Screen Writers Guild and the Authors League since the Guild's inception in 1933, and there had been halfhearted negotiations for some closer alliance between the SWG and the Dramatists Guild, which already had a guild shop, but it had never been realized. At this meeting, however, the common danger liquidated petty disagreements among the three groups, and the leaders determined to attempt a consolidation of all writers in all fields into one unified organization.

Over the next six months, the three guilds worked secretly to achieve a plan whereby they could amalgamate. A solution to the biggest problem, a workable dues plan, was finally devised, and it was decided that writers would automatically be assigned by the Authors League to the particular branch, or guild, in the field in which they were then writing, and their work would be assessed accordingly for dues. Then the constitution of the Authors League was amended to embrace the respective constitutions and bylaws of all three groups. It was proposed that each govern itself, with the collective power of the entire organization invested in a council composed of thirty-six members, twelve from each branch, with each guild empowered to deal with its own problems.

On March 9, 1936, the board of the Screen Writers Guild met. President Ernest Pascal, vice-president Nunnally Johnson, treasurer John Grey, and secretary Robert N. Lee were locked for hours with their board, which included William Conselman, Frances Goodrich, Doris Malloy, Seton I. Miller, E. E. Paramore, Jr., Allen Rivkin, Wells Root, Joel Savre, and attorney Laurence Beilinson. The executive board invoked Article 12 of the Guild Code, which made it mandatory that Guild members refrain from signing contracts for services or material until a date to be specified. The plan was to invoke Article 12 until the membership meeting of the Guild, which was set for May 2. At that May meeting, the members would be asked to ratify the invocation of the article and to extend it until May 1938. Members would also vote on amalgamation of the Screen Writers Guild with the Authors League. Once the amalgamation was approved, the Authors League and the Dramatists Guild would also subscribe to Article 12 and impose a blanket embargo on all contracts and the sale of all material to motion picture studios until May 1938.

This would assure the perfection of alliances, so that one organization controlled all available manpower and material for writing for the screen. It would also give the Screen Writers Guild the clout to force producers to recognize and bargain with them. The aims of a guild shop and a minimum basic agreement would finally be reached, and the affiliation would protect the professional interests of all literary creators, which included producing adequate copyright legislation to establish and enforce the standard main contract.

In March, as the board met, John Howard Lawson was in Washington addressing a congressional committee on the subject of the Duffy Copyright Bill. The Duffy Bill, having already been passed by the Senate, was pending before the House Patents Committee, and though it purported to give authors protection against the mutilation of their works, it specified that "in the absence of special contract or notice by the author in the time he consented to the use of his work," the material could be edited, adapted, or arranged "in accordance with customary standards and reasonable requirements."

What it really meant was that writers would have no protection at all. Articles could be rewritten at will, plays doctored, and scenarios garbled, if the editor or producer felt that it was "reasonable or necessary." It was obvious that the industries purchasing authors' material—radio, motion pictures, publishing, and the theater—were being favored at the expense of the authors. The rights that the bill purported to grant in one section were cynically vitiated in subsequent sections by clauses leaving authors helpless to enforce rights that were supposedly theirs.

Lawson, in his speech before the congressional committee, stated that writers needed a tighter national organization to protect themselves from the sort of injustices the Duffy Bill was helping to perpetuate. Denouncing governmental reinforcement of employer sovereignty, he made the mistake of saying that writers were treated as office boys in Hollywood, which added fuel to the already caustic reaction developing against the proposed amalgamation of the three writers' organizations and the invocation of Article 12. From the April 25 issue of the *Motion Picture Herald* blared the following headline: "WRITER DICTATORSHIP LOOMS ON THE COAST WITH STRIKE WEAPON."

The *New York American* came out two days later with the following editorial:

> The action of the Executive Board of the Screen Writers Guild, ordering all members to refrain from signing contracts for services or materials beyond May 2, 1938, is an unwarranted and intolerable move to establish a closed shop for the writing profession in the motion picture industry.
>
> It is a radical, destructive scheme for "power" and "control" . . . and the motion picture producers are justly marshaling their forces to defeat the proposal. . . . The screenwriters are amply paid. They receive five hundred or a thousand or fifteen hundred dollars a week. In other businesses it would be said that they are enormously paid. The object of the Guild is either to secure higher wages for the writers who are already tremendously well paid, or else to prevent other writers from sharing in the benefits of these handsome salaries.
>
> The result of this Guild movement, if successful in forming a closed shop, would be to limit the amount of writing and consequently the amount of production and the number of productions. . . . Certainly, the working people who depend directly or indirectly on motion picture production would suffer seriously by a limitation of production. So the SWG movement is selfish and unjust.
>
> The Screen Writers Guild move is a device of Communist radicals who apparently don't mind cutting their own throats if they can only manage at the same time to cut the throats of the producers and workers generally.

The charge that communist radicals were running the Guild was no doubt partially aimed at Lawson, who had announced in *New Theatre* magazine, in November 1934, that he had joined the Communist Party. Praising Sam Ornitz's play *In New Kentucky*, Lawson wrote that Ornitz "had done a magnificent job in presenting the specific role of the Communist Party in the Kentucky situation. Ornitz shows that the radicalization of the miners led them to a Communist position. . . . As for myself, I do not hesitate to say that it is my aim to present the Communist position and to do so in the most specific manner."

The *Hollywood Reporter*, bastion of conservatism—and the producers' house organ—issued a similar attack on April 25. "Do writers want to do to the picture business what they so successfully did to the stage? Do they want to kill the goose that has been hatching all those beautiful golden eggs right in the pockets of the men and women who would now like to risk a new control?"

In *Screen Guilds' Magazine* in May 1936, Dudley Nichols retorted: "Writers happen to be people who think. Like all human beings they are concerned with money, but not money alone, thank God. . . . This golden goose is a myth, a ghost, to haunt the timid. Let us lay to rest the ghost and the goose with a laugh, a little common sense, and courage!"

The week and a half prior to the May 2 Guild meeting became a nightmare as producers applied pressure. In *What Makes Sammy Run?*, the only work of fiction to deal with this period, Budd Schulberg labeled it "Ten Days That Shook Hollywood." On April 26, the producers sent a telegram to all screen writers, setting forth their opposition to the affiliation, claiming that it meant control of the Guild by the East Coast.

Testifying before the National Labor Relations Board in 1939, Darryl F. Zanuck explained his opposition to the 1936 amalgamation: "I was personally opposed to dealing with a group of writers who were under control of another group of writers who hated the moving picture business. I was very violent in my belief on it. . . . It was obvious that the Dramatists Guild, the ALA in New York, who hate moving pictures and hate Hollywood, and make fun of it and ridicule it, and write plays lambasting it [plays like Moss Hart and George S. Kaufman's *Once in a Lifetime*, which Hollywood promptly bought and filmed] and who look upon anybody associated with moving pictures as a disappointed stage playwright, who hate the salaries that were made by screen writers because screen writers received ten times as much money for a picture as they received for a hit play, were endeavoring to get a lot of writers under their control."

Milton Sperling explained Zanuck's attitude in another way: "Zanuck took the SWG organization as a personal affront, with a sense of personal betrayal, because he had so much contact with writers and had built his studio on writers. I remember how in a moment of fury Darryl screamed, 'If those guys set up a picket line and try to shut down my studio, I'll mount a machine gun on the roof and mow them down.' "

The producers continued to make it quite clear that they weren't going to be coerced. On the same day they sent their wire to the screen writers, they also issued a statement published in the *New York American*, charging that "a few agitators among screenwriters are determined to establish a closed shop for the writing profession in the motion picture industry. . . . If it becomes necessary to seriously fight such a movement, the producers will use every resource at their command to defeat it." The statement continued:

> For years we have ignored the many false, malicious, defamatory and inflammatory articles and stories circulated by a few malcontents and disturbers among the writers. We know that the general group of screen-writers are constructive in their attitude toward the industry. . . . We do

not propose, however, to permit a few radical-minded and power-seeking individuals to disrupt the industry. We earnestly hope that the writers in general will refuse to follow false leaders, whose motives may or may not be sincere, but whose actions and utterances are exceedingly unwise and hurtful to the industry . . . The producers have no quarrel with the general body of screenwriters. We seek no quarrel and hope to avoid it. It is for the writers themselves to repudiate dangerous leaders and reject foolish counsel. . . .

The producers went on in the statement to distinguish between labor unions and organizations of creative employees:

Not by the wildest stretch of imagination can a writer, whose ability and value cannot even be standardized, place his interests and problems on a plane with a man who joins a union not only to protect his job but to establish standard wages, working conditions, and hours of labor.

The statement ended with yet another critique of the Guild's ultimatum as the inspiration of unwise radical leadership and was signed by Louis B. Mayer, vice-president of MGM; Darryl F. Zanuck, vice-president of 20th Century–Fox; B. B. Kahane, president of RKO; Harry Cohn, president of Columbia; Henry Herzbrun, vice-president of Paramount; Jack Warner, vice-president of Warner Bros.; and Charles R. Roberts, executive vice-president of Universal.

In the two weeks prior to the Screen Writers Guild's May 2 meeting, an opposition group was formed, led by James Kevin McGuinness and Howard Emmett Rogers. Their position was essentially that of the producers—that the SWG would be submitting to Eastern domination if the amalgamation were approved. "The day after everyone got the proposed ALA constitution in the mail," McGuinness later testified before the NLRB, "Howard Emmett Rogers came into my office with the document and said, 'What do you think of this?' I told him it was full of gags and catches. We talked to other writers like John Lee Mahin, Bill and Pat McNutt, and Waldemar Young, and we decided we should consult a lawyer."

They went to see Neil S. McCarthy, a powerful lawyer (whose clients included Howard Hughes) with enough wealth and clout to have a salad named after him at the Beverly Hills Hotel, a man who bred horses and raced them with his close buddy, Louis B. Mayer, and whose interests were on the side of the producers. Using the mimeograph and telegram facilities at MGM (though paid for, claimed McGuinness, by himself), the opposition group made up copies of a list of the weaknesses in the new ALA constitution, as outlined by McCarthy, and sent this list to all writers.

In the week before the May 2 meeting, with the blessing of the producers, the opposition organized a "flying squadron" that visited all the studios and made speeches denouncing the Guild's plan. The meetings and speeches

WRITER DICTATORSHIP LOOMS ON

COAST WITH STRIKE WEAPON

Amalgamation with Writers in Other Fields and No Contracts After May 2, 1938, Are Proposals Offered

A screen writers' dictatorship with an industry-wide strike as a weapon looms for Hollywood.

A closed shop for all writing talent in the United States in their dealings with the motion picture industry, and "one big union" through indicated alliances with the Screen Actors' Guild and the various studio crafts, is the aim of the Screen Writers' Guild. On May 2 the Guild is to ratify vital changes in the constitution and bylaws, intended to further its intention of getting an iron grip on the production of motion pictures.

Members of the Screen Writers' Guild at the forthcoming meeting will be asked to approve two major channels through which the closed shop is to be achieved in two years or sooner: (1) Amalgamation with writers in other organized fields; (2) no contracts for writing services or sale of writing material beyond May 2, 1938.

Only a dream several years ago, the plan has received strong impetus through adoption by the Dramatists' Guild and the Authors' Guild of similar constitutions linking the three groups in the Authors' League of America, which claims to control 90 per cent of the professional writing talent in the United States. The screen writers' group, with between 800 and 900 members, says it controls about 75 per cent of the major studio writers on the west coast.

Preliminary to the final action next Saturday, the Guild membership late last week voted unanimously for a united front in the closed shop drive.

Would Unionize All Writers

The plan is to unionize all writers, in whatever capacity, to control every source of writing material through "a minimum basic agreement with the producers so that all persons employed are members of the Authors' League and all sellers of material are members of the League." Eventual inclusion of radio and newspaper writers and others is provided for.

That the motion picture producers will not accept these terms without a struggle is anticipated by the Guild which makes provision in the revised constitution for conditions governing strikes.

See Increased Costs

The immediate results of recognition of these terms by the studios would be not only to subject the film companies to virtual dictatorship, but to increase negative costs, with higher film rentals also probable.

Sidney Howard, president of the Dramatists' Guild and screen writer, said that a minimum basic agreement "will be classed as Communism in Hollywood" but "we simple folk call it good business."

A preview of what may be in store for Hollywood is now being staged in New York, where the Dramatists' Guild arbitrarily has adopted a minimum basic agreement in its dealings with the Broadway producing managers, drastically curtailing their income and authority. The dispute came about largely because of Hollywood's

NEW CONSTITUTION OF AUTHORS' LEAGUE

The new constitution of the Authors' League of America which members of the Screen Writers' Guild will be asked to adopt May 2 at a meeting in Hollywood, described by the Guild as the most important since its inception, provides for:

The uniting of all writers in the United States in a common organization.

The obtaining of a closed shop for writers in the motion picture industry.

No strikes except by two-thirds approval of active Screen Guild members.

Self-government for each guild—screen writers, dramatists and authors—in its own field.

Separate constitution, bylaws and officers for individual guilds.

Election of Screen Guild officers by the membership.

Election of Authors' League officers by the membership at large.

Election of officers and council members for two years, instead of one.

Recall of officers by a 60 per cent vote of the membership.

All constitutional amendments are to be passed by a 60 per cent vote.

Members' assessments are subject to approval by the membership.

No assessment on incomes up to $2,500.

Appeal to membership in discipline cases.

Adequate machinery for admitting future guilds, such as radio writers and the Newspaper Guild.

Equal voice for East and West.

bankrolling of stage production, as a result of which, the playwrights claim, their royalties from play sales to picture companies have been held down. A total of 72 managers, a large percentage financed by the film industry, are pledged not to accept the Guild's terms.

The plan for amalgamation with the Authors' League is embodied in a new constitution approved by the members March 31 in New York which calls for a council of 12 from each of the component units, or 36 in all, whose purpose it will be "to promote and protect the general professional interests of all creators of literary, dramatic or musical material" and "to procure adequate copyright legislation and establish and enforce standard minimum contracts." Full control of the guild thus is vested in the League council.

In addition, a writer's membership in the League will cover his activities in all other affiliated fields.

The Screen Writers' Guild already has invoked Article 12 of the Guild code prohibiting members or signatories to the contract of April 6, 1933, from signing contracts or giving options

Screen Guild Hopes to Gain Complete Control of Manpower and Material Under "One Big Union" Idea

binding their services or material as screen writers after May 2, 1938.

Guild leaders concede that if they called a strike to force recognition, it would fail. However, they have faith in a weapon provided by the Authors' League in that the other Guilds would ban the sale of plays or other material to studios.

Three attempts by producers under the NRA to effect a 50 per cent salary reduction for writers are behind the formation of the Screen Writers' Guild, and the present moves are partly actuated by a desire to prevent a similar occurrence, declared Ernest Pascal, president of the Guild, in the current issue of *The Screen Guilds' Magazine*.

Dues Plan

Of the dues plan he said: "In six months, or in a year, when we work out a more equable one, it can and will be substituted.

"In this one, the salient points are these:

"1—Membership in the League, which naturally includes all three guilds, is uniform—$10 a year.

"2—Writers are automatically assigned to the particular guild in which field of writing they happen to be working at that time and will be assessed accordingly.

"3—All writers in all fields are exempt from assessment up to $2,500 income.

"4—A dramatist, therefore, pays relatively high assessments—but receives considerable service. An author of books or magazine stories pays relatively low assessments—and receives very little service. The screen writers' assessments fall in between, being one-half of one per cent of earnings, with a maximum of $250. This assessment, however, applies also to the sale of all material to picture companies from all writing in all fields.

"The only difference between this labor organization and any other labor union is that we are, under present conditions, unable to cut off the supply of manpower and material. The fight in the final analysis comes down to that simple proposition."

The plan, he said, "will tend to abolish the 'option' contract, where the advantage is always on the side of the producer and never on the side of the writer.

"Contracts, except for a very few, will have expired by May, 1938. We will be in the invulnerable position of controlling both material and manpower. Writers, the Authors' League of America, will hold the winning hand. And the producer, who has always proved himself to be a very shrewd poker player, will know it. It won't be necessary to call his bluff. Then without a strike, without any of us suffering from being out of jobs, it is only reasonable to conclude that we will gain all that we are after—Guild shop and a fair minimum basic agreement."

Oliver H. P. Garrett, former president of the Guild, declared that the proposed reorganization "is the only possible means of ultimately cutting off from any producer, proved unfair to writers, all possible material from the stage, magazines and books, as well as from unscrupulous screen writers."

The new setup has been designed to protect the autonomy of the affiliated groups, accord

(Continued on following page)

were held on company time and property. The squadron, led by McGuinness, was named "McGuinness's Flying Circus." His companions were Rogers, Patterson McNutt, and John Lee Mahin. They were dubbed "The Four Horsemen."

James Kevin McGuinness had been one of the early writers of *The New Yorker*'s "Talk of the Town." He left New York for Hollywood in 1927 and became one of Thalberg's pet screen writers and script doctors. He was under contract to MGM at over $1,500 a week and had an impressive list of credits. His father had been mayor of Drogheda, Ireland, and Jim was a florid, whiskey-drinking reactionary.

"He was a hard drinker," said his friend James M. Cain. "Never a sloppy drunk, you understand, but I don't think I ever saw him stone sober either. He used to beat against his shoes with a riding crop. That's how I always see him, his feet up on his desk, beating the cadence of his phrases, slapping first one toe, then the other. He was a genuine snob, too. Never lunched at the studio. Always ate at the club."

Nat Perrin, who wrote *The Big Store* for the Marx Brothers, recalled "McGuinness once said to me, 'In this world, some people will ride and some will walk. I'm gonna be one who rides.' "

So elitist was McGuinness that he finally married a baroness—Lucie von Lederman Wartenberg, formerly of Silesia. He was a large, handsome, persuasive man with the thin-mustached look and sound of Gable. He was known as a great wit and was always beautifully dressed in a bow tie and a vest. "I suppose some people thought McGuinness was charming," said Budd Schulberg, "but some people thought Goebbels was charming."

Even his enemies, and they were numerous, agreed that he had a presence. He was a leader.

"It was hard to relate the charming, relaxed McGuinness to the fellow caught up in the extracurricular witch-hunt," said Nat Perrin, "but his was an extremely conservative, actually reactionary position. If it hadn't been for him and his crew when the writers' struggle began, writer unionism and the idea of communism wouldn't have merged in the producers' minds."

The son of a labor leader, and a sour, hard-drinking, Irish-Catholic reactionary, Howard Emmett Rogers was not vocal like McGuinness, but he was also a producer's darling. Known as a master of suspense writing, he had been employed at MGM since 1932 and was making over $1,000 a week by the beginning of 1937.

"We called him the Gray Eminence because he was so deathly pale," said John Bright. "He never saw the sun."

"He was always white as a ghost from sitting in his office, playing the horses and talking to bookies," said Allen Rivkin. "He looked like a little whippet."

The McNutt brothers, the sons of a Presbyterian minister, had both come from New York. William Slavens McNutt had been a World War I correspondent for *Collier's* in France. He worked on *Ladies of the Big House, The Adventures of Huckleberry Finn,* and *Ruggles of Red Gap* during his career at Paramount. His brother, Patterson, had also been a journalist, writing sports columns for the *New York World* and producing a few plays in New York in the twenties. In 1936 both McNutt brothers were at Paramount, each earning well over $500 a week and anxious to stop a radical takeover of writers by Eastern Reds.

"They were terrified of radicals," remembered Samson Raphaelson. "They used to stand outside screenings of foreign pictures taking down names of everyone who went inside, for future reference."

In 1936 McGuinness, Patterson McNutt, and Rogers were well into their middle years, and they welcomed John Lee Mahin into their group. Mahin, a protégé of Ben Hecht's, had been signed by MGM in 1933 to a long-term contract. In 1936, he was only twenty-five years old.

"We were about the same age," recalled John Bright. "We'd both come out here about the same time and we were both Hollywood wunderkinds. I

James Kevin McGuinness testifying before the NLRB, 1938. McGuinness was one of the first writers of *The New Yorker*'s "Talk of the Town" before becoming a screenwriter at MGM. For his support of the split in the Screen Writers Guild he was, according to Ring Lardner, "rewarded by being made a Metro producer."

was at Warner's, where I wrote *The Public Enemy* and Cagney's next four pictures, and I just went up with Cagney. John Lee Mahin was doing that same thing at Metro, writing things like *Red Dust* for Harlow and Gable. He was one of the top writers at MGM, and he was being paid nickels. I knew him socially through a mutual friend, Courtenay Terrett. We used to drink and play cards and shoot the breeze. He was an alcoholic and so was his wife, [actress] Patsy Ruth Miller. He was a pretty calculating guy, a fairly good screen writer with a good popular touch, but he was making $250 a week.

"One night we were all together, Courtenay, Mahin, Cyril Garner, and me, and Courtenay said to Mahin, who was sitting getting quietly drunk in a corner, 'You're a fool, now that your pictures are making so much money, not to demand a better salary. Tell 'em you want more money or you'll quit.'

"And Mahin's reply became historic to me and my crowd of activists in the Guild. He said, 'I won't do it. The producers will take care of me. I know they will.' Well, they did. He ultimately became one of the most highly paid writers in Hollywood at Metro, and he was the producers' darling starting in 1936. He was totally their creature and he got a fortune for it."

To counteract the pressure from producers and "McGuinness's Flying Circus," meetings were being held all over town at the homes of pro-affiliation writers like Samson Raphaelson, Dorothy Parker, Sam Ornitz, and the Hacketts. At these meetings the older, more established Guild members explored the pros and cons of the proposed amalgamation, explained the ALA constitution, and showed the writers that the younger and lower-paid they were, the more they had to gain from this amalgamation of all the writers' guilds.

"The pressure at MGM," remembered Frances Goodrich Hackett, "was relentless. They had the big boys, you know, McGuinness, Rogers, Mahin, and Patterson McNutt. . . . The 'Four Horsemen' went around all the time, day after day, talking to writers, particularly the young writers, the ones who were just starting, warning them about the upcoming vote. So we proselytized, too. We walked around that lot and so did Lilly Hellman, and we talked to the young kids who were not aware of the problem but only on our lunch hour, so that no one could ever say we had used studio time for union activities. And we couldn't do our proselytizing on the phone, of course, because Thalberg's boys were always listening in."

"During my first couple of days in the studio," said Maurice Rapf, "I met all these marvelous writers because of the tremendous battle that was going on. They were preparing for the meeting to vote on Authors League affiliation, and they were trying to get as many votes as they could. I had just become a junior writer, thanks to nepotism, at MGM. And then, the first thing that happened to me was that Lillian Hellman came into my converted broom-closet office and asked me to join the Guild. It was most extraordinary."

It's not hard to imagine why young Maurice Rapf was impressed: a twenty-two-year-old kid, fresh out of Dartmouth, and into his office sails the formidable playwright—unbeautiful, wearing one of her extraordinary hats, and chain-smoking. He was impressed by this famous lady writer, acclaimed for her Broadway success with *The Children's Hour*, coming in and asking him, personally, to join the SWG.

"Now I never gave a damn about movie stars," Rapf said, "but I gave a great damn about writers. And here I was, my first couple of days on the lot, becoming friendly with all of these established, very well known writers. There were private meetings, like caucuses, of those who were totally in support of the affiliation. And I went to all of those and met the so-called radicals, mostly Eastern writers—Samson Raphaelson, Sam Ornitz, Dorothy Parker and her husband, Alan."

In an attempt to close the schism between the opposing factions, two nights before the proposed meeting, the Screen Writers Guild's board of directors met. Present as well were "flying squadron" members Mahin, McGuinness, and Patterson McNutt; Authors League president Marc Connelly; and such respected writers as Edwin Justus Mayer, Dudley Nichols, and Robert Riskin, who opposed the amalgamation.

The dissident conservative faction indicated several points that they thought should be changed in the ALA constitution to guarantee the Guild's autonomy and requested that the amalgamation be postponed until the provisions could be incorporated. The assembled writers decided, for the sake of Guild unity, to vote on the "principle" of amalgamation but to postpone the legal amalgamation until certain changes could be accomplished. Since time was needed to send the changes to the Authors League and to have them amended, the assembled group agreed to wait until May 16 for the final revisions.

To further show good faith to the conservative faction, the SWG board agreed to put certain members of the opposition on the election slate of officers, to be voted on at the membership meeting. Patterson McNutt and McGuinness were two of the opposition candidates, and they insisted that Robert Riskin also be included. Riskin was the foremost screen writer in the business, having written several of Frank Capra's most successful pictures, and, claimed Rogers, "We knew he was sane." Samson Raphaelson and Bert Kalmar were added to the slate as middle-of-the-road candidates.

The membership at large of the Guild was not aware as yet of the new coalition, and the producers were still hoping that the proposed amalgamation would be defeated. They decided that the good work of "McGuinness's Flying Circus" needed some eleventh-hour augmentation.

On Friday, May 1, Irving Thalberg presided over a three-hour meeting of all the producers, and they decided to call last-minute meetings on the next day at all studios except Columbia. So on Saturday, Thalberg spoke to a group of sixty at MGM; Henry Herzbrun addressed writers at Paramount; B. B. Kahane, Sam Briskin, and Pandro Berman addressed the RKO writers; Jack

Warner talked at Warner Bros.; Darryl Zanuck at 20th Century–Fox; and William Koenig at Universal. It was expected that from these talks a substantial number of writers would be persuaded to attend the Guild meeting that night and vote against Article 12 and the amalgamation.

That Saturday morning, when they arrived at the studio and opened their copy of *Variety*, the writers found nearly the entire issue consumed by an article headed "How Many of You Know What You Are Agreeing To?" The article included the legal opinion of Major Walker K. Tuller, a venerable Hollywood attorney and personal counsel for Louis B. Mayer. Major Tuller stated that not only would the amalgamation subject the Guild to the authority of the Authors League, but his studies also proved that with amalgamation would come the danger of violating the U.S. antitrust law and the Cartwright Act of California. Entering a final plea before that night's meeting, Bess Meredyth begged the writers not to endanger the future prosperity and success of all of them by surrendering control of their destiny to New York–based radicals.

Thalberg then held a lunch-hour meeting for writers in his projection room at MGM, where, three years earlier, Louis B. Mayer had requested the wage cut. About sixty writers attended this meeting. Maurice Rapf described it:

"I liked Thalberg very much. He was always nice to me. But the idea that he was a sweet, sensitive character was dispelled in five seconds at this meeting. He came in with Mannix, who was the studio manager at the time. The scene was similar to one you might find in Tammany, or even in the gangster movies—the hard guy and the so-called Little Czar, whom everybody loves. But Thalberg's speech was by no means sweet. What he said, in effect, was, 'You've all gotten a great deal out of this industry. It's been good to you and what you're proposing to do is to give it away and turn it over to outside interests, and we are not going to tolerate it.' Thalberg finished by saying, 'I simply want you to know what *our* stand, the studio's stand, is, and how we are going to feel about anybody who goes along with us, and how we are going to feel about those who don't. We have a lot to protect here, and we are going to protect it with everything we've got.'

"It was a very tough speech," Rapf said. "People had thought there was going to be a little discussion, but there was no discussion. He just spoke and left. People who had known him and worked with him and thought he was a nice guy saw him so tough and so hard that we were absolutely shocked. And I'll tell you, I don't think it had the effect that he wanted. I think it was quite the contrary. Even some of those who had been going along with the so-called studio point of view didn't like being told what they ought to do. And apparently meetings such as this one were being held in every studio."

Writer Richard Maibaum remembered, "Thalberg said he'd never allow a merger of the Screen Writers Guild and the Authors League because he had to protect the stockholders, some of whom were widows and orphans. It sounded as if he was beginning to believe his own scripts."

But McGuinness, testifying before the National Labor Relations Board in 1939, remembered this meeting differently. "Thalberg's talk," he said, "was an explanation of the obligations of running a motion picture company. He said the company had commitments for two pictures a year to Garbo and those pictures involved an expenditure of between two and a half and three million dollars. He said he had no quarrel with any writers' organization but he didn't want to be in the power of an organization governed from New York."

"I think he warned us," testified Thalberg supporter John Lee Mahin. " 'Let's not get to fighting amongst ourselves. This is a good business and everybody wants to be fair and square about the whole thing.' I was very moved by the speech myself."

Dalton Trumbo had been writing for Warner Bros. since October 1935 in the low-budget "B" unit, under producer Bryan Foy (dubbed the "King of the B's"), for $50 a week. He had never met Jack Warner until that Saturday, when he got a note from story editor George Bricker that called all writers to a meeting at 3:00 p.m. that afternoon in the Green Room of the Warner Bros. commissary. There were between thirty and forty writers at that meeting, including Luci Ward, Mary McCall, Jr., and Milton Krims, and writer-producers Walter McEwan, Frank Craven, and Robert Lord. The tables were arranged in a U, and Bricker presided over the first part of the meeting. Howard Emmett Rogers, James McGuinness, and Patterson McNutt spoke about the Guild being dominated by the East and said their own aim was to save the Guild from a split. When they finished, the writers waited in uneasy silence until Jack Warner came in.

"Warner entered," Trumbo later told the NLRB, "dressed in sport clothes, and he said he was sorry he'd kept us waiting, he'd been playing golf. He said it was a wonderful sunshiny morning and was wonderful golf weather, and this was a wonderful state and we were in a wonderful business. He said he remembered when he was a butcher boy and how now, when he got up in the morning, he had to think which car to take to work. He said that was how well the business had treated *him*, and that it had also treated us all very well. Therefore, he wondered, why were we kicking it around? He said the producers absolutely would not tolerate the passage of Article 12. He said our leaders were communists, radical bastards, and soap-box sons of bitches. He apologized to the two ladies present and said that he hated to use that language, but it was the truth, so he used it.

"He added that as a matter of fact, many of the leaders of the SWG were even then under investigation by the Department of Justice and that a lot of them were cooked geese. He said that he, personally, didn't care because he had five million dollars in cold cash and that the studio could close up tomorrow, as far as he was concerned.

"He said repeatedly, 'There are a lot of writers in the business who are active in the SWG now who will find themselves out of the business for good,' and it wouldn't be a blacklist because it would all be done over the telephone."

"Before the meeting to vote on the affiliation," said John Howard Lawson, "there was a compromise between the Screen Writers Guild and the reactionary faction. I was in New York writing telegrams by the barrelful to the Guild. I warned them that the alliance was dangerous. I warned them that you couldn't trust those producers' pets, and sure enough, they betrayed the Guild."

"I imagine," recalled Maurice Rapf, "that the studio people felt they were going to lose, that the writers would approve the amalgamation, so they sent these finks, their company stooges, in there, McGuinness and Rogers and the like, to stall. That's what it was, a stalling process, and it seemed to become a big love-feast. After the meetings with the producers at all the studios that morning, it was an incredible evening. I'll never forget that evening. It seemed like a great triumph."

The night of the meeting, Bess Meredyth, Sonya Levien, and Gene Fowler spoke against the affiliation. Richard Schayer, a writer who had been in the business for twenty years, said, "Screenwriting is a soft racket," and added that he saw no reason to rock the boat. "Especially when the Mothership [MGM] objects," quipped Dorothy Parker. Shortly thereafter she published an acid rebuttal to Schayer in *Screen Guilds' Magazine* titled "To Richard with Love":

> I do not feel that I am participating in a soft racket (and what the hell, by the way, is a hard racket?) when I am writing for the screen. Nor do I want to be part of any racket, hard or soft. . . . I want to earn my living, and naturally I prefer it to be a good one. . . . I have never in my life been paid so much, either—well, why am I here, and why are you, and why is Mr. Schayer? But I can look my God and my producers—whom I do not, as do many, confuse with each other—in the face and say that I have earned every cent of it. . . .
>
> When I dwelt in the East . . . I had my opinion of writing for the screen. I regarded it—all right, sue me—with a sort of benevolent contempt, as one looks at the raggedy printing of a backward six-year-old. I thought it had just that much relationship to literature. (I still do—all right, take it to the Supreme Court.) I thought, "Why, I could do that with one hand tied behind me and the other on Irving Thalberg's pulse." (Fooled you that time, didn't I?) Well, I found out, and I found out hard, and I found out forever. Through the sweat and tears I shed over my first script, I saw a great truth—one of those eternal, universal truths that

serve to make you feel much worse than you did when you started. And that is that no writer, whether he writes from love or for money, can condescend to what he writes. . . . What makes it harder in screen writing . . . is the money you get.

You see, it brings out that uncomfortable little thing called conscience. You aren't writing for the love of it or the art of it or whatever; you are doing a chore assigned to you by your employer and whether or not he might fire you if you did it slackly makes no matter. You've got yourself to face, and you have to live with yourself. You don't—or at least, only in highly exceptional cases—have to live with your producer.

Then, to the surprise of everyone who hadn't been at those heated last-minute meetings of the SWG board and the two factions, McGuinness and Patterson McNutt spoke in favor of the amalgamation, "in principle." The principle was to be voted on, pending ratification (by the boards of the Dramatists Guild and the Authors League in the East) of the amendments to the ALA constitution giving the Screen Writers Guild complete autonomy.

"These people," said Maurice Rapf, "who had been fighting, tooth and nail, to such an extent that there was real hostility in the studio environment, were suddenly getting up and putting their arms around each other. I saw Dottie Parker put her arms around Jim McGuinness, and she actually cried at that meeting. It seemed as if the writers had finally really gotten together and agreed in principle. Of course, there were people who were suspicious about it. The rumor had gone around before the meeting that it wouldn't really be a showdown vote, which was a shame because the way the sentiment was running, affiliation probably would have been voted in by the members. But what happened here instead was that you had a unanimous vote for the principle of affiliation. There wasn't anybody against it. You see, the progressives were trying to be very reasonable. They were trying to point out very clearly that the charges against this affiliation were unfounded.

"The progressives were assuring everybody that there was going to be no loss of autonomy, because we all knew that the union issue was at the core of the whole thing. But it was really being argued on political terms of Hollywood versus New York. You know, the $5,000-a-week boys were saying, 'We aren't like other labor unions, we need an organization more like a club.' And the progressives would point out that our contracts had economic conditions in them that screwed some of us and that not everybody got $5,000 a week like Ben Hecht did. But this claim that the SWG was in danger of being run from New York and Moscow was trotted out, and it seemed that granting autonomy would mollify the reactionaries."

A new slate of board members was elected. Ernest Pascal remained president and John Grey treasurer, with Nunnally Johnson the new vice-president and Robert Lee secretary. New to the board were James McGuinness, Bert Kalmar, Morrie Ryskind, Samson Raphaelson, and Robert Riskin, and the so-called radicals—Dorothy Parker, Dudley Nichols, Sheridan Gibney, Paul Perez, and Francis Faragoh—resigned. The rest of the board included Ralph Block, Sidney Buchman, Lester Cole, Edwin Justus Mayer, Mary McCall, Jr., and Wells Root.

Everybody was astonished. The *Hollywood Reporter*'s ominous warnings of civil war among the screen writers had resulted in the presence at this meeting of several members of the Hollywood Police Department. The membership approved the continuation of Article 12 until negotiations began between producers and writers for a minimum basic agreement; the coalition slate was cheered unanimously as the end to factionalism among writers; and the joyous writers adjourned to celebrate at nearby watering holes.

"I was opposed," said lawyer Beilinson, "to the attempt to force Article 12 and the affiliation from the beginning, but once the board adopted them, I felt loyally compelled to support them. But I always felt the attempt would end in disaster, as it did."

Three days after this "love-feast," two members of the newly elected SWG board of directors—Bert Kalmar and Morrie Ryskind—resigned. They were followed by sixty members of the Guild who, led by Rupert Hughes, also seceded. By the end of the week, 125 writers had terminated their Guild connections, and they announced on May 9 that they were going to form a new, rival association.

It was the producers, with their continued pressure, who had brought about the defection. They began, even before the May 2 meeting, to offer writers long-term contracts that would violate the May 2 cutoff date. One particularly staunch Guild member, who had never been much of a success as a writer, was offered a five-year contract at 20th Century–Fox, which he took. Forty years later, he still remembered the shame he felt but believed there was nothing else he could have done at the time. He was offered twice the salary he had been making, and he had a sick wife. Every day producers called writers individually and warned them about options that wouldn't be picked up and about how free-lance employment might be terminated unless they signed for five or seven years. The smaller the writer, the bigger the intimidation.

The rival association named itself the Screen Playwrights (SP) and declared itself against the idea of a closed shop, condemned the Guild for radicalism, and announced itself ready to listen to "sane proposals" and to undertake "sane negotiations" with the studios. It was immediately recognized by the producers. The SP announced that its criteria for membership were going to be much more stringent than those of the SWG, in order to keep their organization from growing too large. Studio screen credit for three pictures during the preceding two years was the requisite, and this effectively restricted the Screen Playwrights to the older, more established, more highly paid scribes. In 1939, before the National Labor Relations Board, Howard Emmett

Rogers objected to the Guild's flexible, open membership qualifications: "I will get any imbecile twelve weeks of work in any studio in L.A. if it does not have to be consecutive . . . and according to the SWG that man can go out an accredited writer and in a vote of vital importance, his vote could nullify mine or the vote of any man who had a stake in this business and credits to his credit." Junior writers, of course, couldn't get into the SP.

John Lee Mahin was elected the group's first president, and board members included Bess Meredyth, Waldemar Young, William Slavens McNutt, Kubec Glasmon, Frank Butler, Sonya Levien, William Conselman, Rupert Hughes, Grover Jones, and Gerald Geraghty. Members included Howard Emmett Rogers, Herman Mankiewicz, Patterson McNutt, and Robert Yost.

To the surprise of the Screen Playwrights, Robert Riskin, one of the "sane" members of the opposition, whom they had insisted should serve on the SWG board, did not resign. He saw no reason to do so and was angry with the SP for using him and for using stalling tactics with the Guild in an attempt to break it. The withdrawal of the conservative faction from the Guild's board nudged it, unavoidably, leftward. Dorothy Parker and Donald Ogden Stewart were appointed to fill the terms vacated by Patterson McNutt and McGuinness, which left the board with the following members: Ernest Pascal, John Grey, Seton I. Miller, E. E. Paramore, Sidney Buchman, Edwin Justus Mayer, Wells Root, Ralph Block, Lester Cole, Mary McCall, Jr., Robert Riskin, and Samson Raphaelson.

The members of the Guild were outraged. The Screen Playwrights were producers' stooges. When, during the NLRB hearings, Howard Emmett Rogers was asked, "Ever hear of Benedict Arnold? You know what they called him, don't you?" Rogers replied, "I think they called him a traitor. . . . I might also add that he was also a very good soldier."

And so the members of the Screen Playwrights, with a little help from the producers, began a crusade to eliminate totally the Screen Writers Guild.

"When I first got to MGM in 1936," recalled writer Catherine Turney, "John Lee Mahin came into my office and told me I should join the SP, that they were the group to be with, since they were all the high-priced, most prestigious writers. So I joined. Sonya Levien was similarly led down the garden path by Mahin and those guys. But as soon as I realized that they didn't have the interests of the writers, except for themselves, at heart, I resigned. I sent Mahin a note and told him they could keep the ten dollars, and I think the same went for Sonya. I got wise when the Hacketts sent me a furious note— how could you hook up with that crew, they're in the producers' pockets— and Phil Dunne came into my office and said, 'You look like such a nice girl, why do you want to go with them?' And of course, they were right, but it was my first week at MGM and Mahin had warned me that his group was favored by the producers and got all the best assignments, and that sounded good."

William Ludwig said of Sonya Levien: "She was the least political person I had ever met. She joined both the SP and the SWG, but she wasn't active in either. She was completely work-dominated and not political on industry matters. She had dear and old friends in every echelon. When the SWG conflict came, it probably moved her toward the Guild. She had many good friends on the extreme left, and her daughter and *her* friends were radicals. When the SP set up shop, it was done by a bunch of old boys at Metro, her friends, the Thalberg-echelon group. It seemed like a good career-move to join, but she had no philosophical position. I'd say to her, 'You know what this means?' and then I'd tell her and she'd say, 'Does it? I didn't know.' But she was the hardest worker I've ever known. She had a writing obsession."

The Screen Playwrights used the tactic of individual appeals to specific writers. Morrie Ryskind was their delegate to 20th Century–Fox; he had known Milton Sperling in New York and had watched Sperling's rise from Zanuck's secretary to fledgling writer.

"How can you betray Darryl after all he's done for you?" Ryskind asked Sperling.

Sperling then had a private meeting with Zanuck, who said to him: "We've gone through too much together. You've got to resign from that union. Look at all I've done for you. You gave me stories and I turned them into pictures."

"It was like Zanuck saying, 'I'm the magician,' " Sperling recalled.

Sperling found himself in a difficult personal struggle. People were kind to him on both sides, he thought, because of his youth. He had Ryskind and Zanuck on one side, saying, "You're like a son to me," and on the other side his Guild buddies, John Howard Lawson and Boris Ingster. "You're my real friends," he told Lawson and Ingster. "I don't know what to do. . . . Jack Lawson then said to me, 'You're free of obligations to us. We don't want to enforce discipline on anyone. You're a free agent.' " Sperling resigned from the Guild, but he never joined the Screen Playwrights. Later he rejoined the Guild.

Sperling is a perfect example of the writer who was caught in the middle of the Hollywood civil war of 1936, a struggle that went beyond simple union issues into the whole question of paternalism in the motion picture industry. Sperling could side with his friends in the Guild through membership in the Screen Playwrights. Zanuck had been good to him, had treated him like a son, given him chances and molded his career. But Lawson and Ingster were his friends. They were also young and connected to the larger world. When they looked at a newspaper, they saw what was happening in the world, not just what Louella Parsons said about the little kingdom. The producers and their stooges represented a stifled world-view.

It wasn't just that the producers were so much older, because they weren't. Thalberg and Zanuck were only in their thirties, and Walter Wanger wasn't much older. But with their claims of "You're like a son to me," their salutations of "Hello, boys," and the devotion that benevolent father figures like Louis B. Mayer extracted from his darling daughters Anita Loos, Bess Meredyth, and Frances Marion, the producers made Hollywood the fatherland and the studio the mother ship.

The susceptibility to and need for paternalism by the young migrants in Hollywood cannot be underestimated. They were orphans—rootless, insecure, lonely, cut off from home. And the attraction of the Guild and, soon after, of the Communist Party included father figures such as John Howard Lawson, Samuel Ornitz, Dudley Nichols—strong leaders who could unite a group of disparate waifs, who despite the fact that they were making more money than any other kids in the country still needed the warmth and approval of Papa to feel that they deserved the money they were making.

As the struggle between the Screen Playwrights and the Screen Writers Guild continued, it truly did take on the proportions of a civil war, with enemy lines drawn and brother set against brother. When Jean and Hugo Butler were first married, Hugo and Waldo Salt were both junior writers under Joseph Mankiewicz at MGM. Mankiewicz had been one of the founders of the Guild, its first secretary, but his brother, Herman, had been one of the leaders of the Screen Playwrights.

"I think Herman did it less out of political commitment than out of plain orneriness and a sense of what he was entitled to," recalled Sam Marx. "He was one of the old-time writers, the $1,500-plus group, who didn't want to be tied up with the kids. He felt why shouldn't he be with his drinking buddies, if they were all making so much money every week?"

But Budd Schulberg said, "I was shocked with Mank's siding with the SP. Once at lunch with me at Romanoff's he put up a fairly good argument in favor of Adolf Hitler, and it got into a shouting match, and I finally got up and walked away. Some of it was on purpose. He liked to needle you. But I think he may also have believed that it was simply not an appropriate activity for writers to organize like workers in other industries. Mank took out an ad in the trade papers saying, 'Writers of the world unite. You have nothing to lose but your brains.' He and my father always had a great deal in common in their attitude toward Hollywood, sort of an acceptance of it and enjoyment of it but at the same time a kind of mockery of it. Even so, I was surprised by Herman, who was so bright and such an incredibly witty man, joining what I considered the enemy."

In *What Makes Sammy Run?*, Schulberg made his hero one of the young turks of the Screen Playwrights, along the lines of John Lee Mahin, who uses the organization as a way of establishing himself as a good guy with the producers. This leads to Sammy's ultimate ascendance to the position so many writers yearned for—that of producer. In the same year they broke with the Guild to form the SP, Grover Jones, McGuinness, Howard Green, and Howard Estabrook all received writer-producer contracts. But for some the payoff wasn't as fat as they had expected. Schulberg incorporated such an incident, concerning Maurice Rapf, into *What Makes Sammy Run?*.

"I was working," said Maurice Rapf, "with Dick Maibaum, in the office next to Jim McGuinness's, and one day we heard terrible screaming. We were obviously curious but couldn't make out what was being said. So we used a trick I had heard of—if you put a glass to a wall, for some reason or other it straightens out the sound and you can understand what is being said. McGuinness was screaming at someone, I think his agent, about how Thalberg had promised him that he would be the producer of a big Nelson Eddy–Jeanette MacDonald musical called *Maytime*. Apparently, Thalberg had reneged on this offer. McGuinness was screaming, 'That sonofabitch, that dirty sonofabitch. He's got to learn that loyalty is not a one-way street!' And his agent was placating him with, 'Well, after all, you still have a great job,' and McGuinness was raging, really raging, saying terrible things about Thalberg. It was evident, whether Thalberg delivered or not, that the people who had led the split had received contracts and promises as their part of the deal."

One of the most disturbing results of the split was that, in its aftermath, it was not unlike the blacklist period of the fifties. People didn't talk to each other. The Screen Playwrights was viewed as a treacherous organization. The air was thick with threats. Every writer had personal conditions to face, but the result was broken friendships and scars that lasted for many years.

"When people who had been so close to you suddenly dropped off the train," remembered Nat Perrin, "there were inevitable bad feelings. And this bitterness had terrible ramifications. Families were split apart; it created problems with collaborations, because in many instances writers wouldn't work with people they considered traitors. It was the blue and the gray."

Things continued to get worse. "In 1936," claimed John Howard Lawson, "a panic hit the studios, and a blacklist blossomed in Hollywood. It was dangerous to talk about the SWG in the studios, and it was worth your life to be seen on a studio lot wearing an SWG button."

"There was a blacklist," Sperling remembered. "More of a graylist, really, a hesitation about hiring. It was emotional rather than institutional. There weren't immediate reprisals, however, and some options were picked up. Ingster, for example, stayed on at Fox and Lawson remained there for six months or a year, but Zanuck wouldn't talk to them."

Elizabeth Faragoh said that after the split, her husband, Francis, couldn't find any work. Rather than weathering the difficulties and finding out if he was really on a blacklist, they went back to New York. When they returned to

Hollywood a year later, he got a job at Columbia through his friend and fellow SWG activist Sidney Buchman, but Faragoh's standing salary of $1,250 a week had been cut to $500.

Philip Dunne said that he and Ernest Pascal refused to resign from the Guild and "it was the first time I began to hear the word *blacklist*. There were several people whose options were dropped, but both Pascal's and mine were renewed. I think Zanuck dropped the options also of some of the SP guys, but that was the sort of man Zanuck was. Ultimately, his interest was in writing."

"There was a great deal of intimidation," recalled John Bright. "It was a kind of graylist. Those of us who were active in the SWG were second choices for jobs. If you were a member of the SP, you were first choice for a job. All of the SP members were on the second floor of the Thalberg Building at Metro, a new building at that time. And those of us who continued to belong to the SWG were on the third floor. There was no physical traffic between the two factions because there was bad blood, really bad blood. Donald Ogden Stewart, Dorothy Parker, and the Hacketts—all SWG loyalists—were all on the third floor. We had no luncheon traffic and met the SP members from the floor below only in the elevators. The commissaries all over town were like armed camps."

"At Metro," recalled Nat Perrin, "the SP had its own table, where conservatives like McGuinness and Mahin, story editor Sam Marx, and occasionally actors like Tracy and Gable ate. The SP faction was noted for spinning dice every day to see who got stuck with the lunch check. The SWG had its own little table, a staunch island in the middle of a hostile sea."

George Seaton recalled that during 1936, SWG members would get pressured each lunchtime in the commissary by Rogers, McGuinness, or Herman Mankiewicz. Seaton and Robert Pirosh would pass by the Screen Playwrights' table, and one of the SP-ers would say, "You still in the SWG? You better get out of that commie organization or you won't be here long."

Seaton said that one day they were called in by Thalberg and they figured, "Better stock up on paper clips, this is it."

"We went to see him," Seaton recalled, "and Thalberg said, 'I understand you two are staying with the SWG. Why?' And we said, 'Because we don't believe in company unions and we do believe in the aims of the Guild.' And Thalberg said, 'Well, I disagree with you about that. I understand you're being harassed in the commissary. If anybody tries to threaten you, to tell you your job is in danger, you come and tell me. You're entitled to your opinions.' And he stood up and shook our hands, saying, 'God bless you both.'"

F. Scott Fitzgerald in his unfinished novel, *The Last Tycoon*, describes Monroe Stahr, the character based on Thalberg: "In spite of the inevitable conservatism of the self-made man, [he] is a paternalistic employer. Success came to him young, at 23, and left certain idealisms of his youth unscarred."

"Everybody had made Thalberg out a villain," said Seaton, who later became SWG president. "I'm sure he did his best to see that the Screen Playwrights won, and whether or not he gave us that speech just to keep us, I don't know. [Seaton and Pirosh had written the enormously successful Marx Brothers picture *A Day at the Races*.] But we were firm about staying with the Guild. The pressure of the SP made us SWG members for sure."

In 1939 RKO executive B. B. Kahane testified before the NLRB that he "had been in Hollywood since 1932 and had never seen any blacklist or heard of any blacklist."

Dalton Trumbo's memories were different. He recalled that Walter McEwan, executive assistant to producer Hal Wallis at Warner Bros., called him and suggested that he get in touch with Howard Emmett Rogers. "I asked him," said Trumbo, "if he was asking me to resign from the Guild, and he said, 'Not exactly.' I said, 'Because if you are, my signature to an SWG contract is worth exactly as much as my signature to a Warners Brothers contract, and since it exists in both contracts, it would be impossible for me to violate both.' " McEwan apparently said that it was all right. He wanted Trumbo to understand that there was no coercion in the phone call.

The next day, William Friedberg, assistant to Bryan Foy, called Trumbo and said he understood that Trumbo was to receive a six-week layoff and that if he didn't want it, Trumbo could tear up his contract. So Trumbo went to Foy's office, surrendered his contract, and left the studio.

Shortly after his exit from Warner Bros., Trumbo went to work for Columbia. There he protested that his contract was for the same amount he had been making at Warner Bros. even though he had two respectable "B" credits, for an original prison picture called *Road Gang* (loosely based on *I Am a Fugitive from a Chain Gang*) and *Love Begins at 20*. Edward Chodorov advised Trumbo not to make waves. "Dalton," he said, "I am telling you this as a friend. I understand that you have turned down a contract here, and I feel you should sign it because I'm afraid it will be a great personal tragedy if you don't."

Reporting on the situation in 1936 at the NLRB hearings in 1939, Trumbo, a waspish, feisty man, went to Columbia's president, Harry Cohn, and protested. "Cohn told me, 'I don't give a goddamn what you say outside of here. You will hear a lot of talk about there being no blacklist in town. As a matter of fact, there had been no blacklist since the blacklist of [actor] Conway Tearle, but now there *is* a blacklist and you are definitely on it and you have your choice of signing or staying out of the business. I took Mary McCall back into the business after she was out, and I'm giving you the same opportunity.' " Trumbo took the contract.

Lester Cole claimed that he too was blacklisted, at MGM, until the forties, largely due to the efforts of McGuinness and Rogers. "During the 1936 period," Cole said, "the only studio that would hire me was Republic, where I worked with a struggling young writer named Nathanael West on two pictures, *Follow Your Heart* and *The President's Mystery*. The blacklist couldn't hold because of the historical influence at work. In 1937 and 1938, antifascism was becoming popular and the studios were turning out more socially conscious pictures. You couldn't go to the right wing to do antifascist pictures, could you?"

In June 1936, the leaders of the Screen Writers Guild went to New York to consult with Marc Connelly and the leaders of the Authors League. The layoffs that had suddenly been hitting loyal Guild members in the weeks following the formation of the Screen Playwrights were an obvious form of studio sniping, although executives claimed it was "the time of annual list-shearing."

The Authors League reluctantly told the Screen Writers Guild to fight it out by themselves. Any interference would only add fire to the continuous accusations by the producers of East Coast radical manipulation. The leaders of the Guild, disheartened, returned to Hollywood, and the board rescinded Article 12. It seemed a futile and romantic gesture to continue to bind Guild members to that article while disloyal members were resigning and taking jobs. The notion of the mass vote on ALA amalgamation was abandoned; the Guild's board voted to amalgamate, and members were instructed to apply individually for membership to the Screen Writers Guild of the Authors League of America.

Most of Hollywood's best-known or highest-paid writers, including Jules Furthman, Zoë Akins, George Bricker, Stephen Morehouse Avery, Gene Markey, Charles Kenyon, Carey Wilson, Sam Engel, and Gene Fowler, resigned from the Guild. Of the nearly one thousand members proudly claimed by the Screen Writers Guild before the May 2 meeting, ninety-two were left with the courage or concern to appear for the final membership meeting.

The status of an organization in Hollywood could always be determined by the size of its meeting hall, because Los Angeles was a town of rented halls, and the meeting rooms of the Guild became smaller and smaller. "Finally we got down to one little room in the Hollywood Athletic Club," recalled Maurice Rapf. "That was when they found Herman Mankiewicz in the air-conditioning duct listening to the proceedings. Mankiewicz's brother, Joe, couldn't believe Herman would be that active in his opposition to the Guild. He said, 'My brother was a large man who was always sitting or lying down. The image of him crawling into a duct is hilarious. If he was in there, he must have gotten drunk and somebody pushed him in.' "

The Guild's final meeting was held in its offices at 1655 North Cherokee, a grimy, dilapidated building on a side street off Hollywood Boulevard, a few blocks from Grauman's Chinese Theater, and an appropriate place to mourn a lost cause.

"Ernie Pascal, our dear, wonderful president, looked around the nearly empty room," remembered Dore Schary, "and said, 'There's no point in going on. We can't even pay the rent.' By the late summer of 1936, the SWG had withdrawn from the *Screen Guilds' Magazine* so as not to embarrass the actors and had filed legal notice of dissolution. We'd broken up, but we had a sense of pride. We felt, 'screw everybody, *we* stayed.' We didn't have a real contempt for the guys who had signed the contracts. Just sadness and bitterness."

"I remember when I was a publicist," said Lou Harris, "and I was arranging a luncheon at Paramount for André Malraux. Charlie Brackett was there and so was Bill Saroyan, and Charlie kept saying, 'The Guild is dead. They've killed it. I don't think we'll ever revive it.' "*

"During that period," said Maurice Rapf, "we liked to call the SP fascists, but they weren't fascists, just extreme-right forces, and the *Hollywood Reporter* was their house organ. There was a lot of name calling and Red-baiting in the *Hollywood Reporter* in the thirties, and in 1936 it began to link the SWG situation more directly with 'communists.' The charges in 1936 were primarily that there were Reds in the East, but by 1937 they began to say that Reds were now in the West. They began to name people, including a lot of younger people like Budd Schulberg, Ring Lardner, and me. On a number of occasions the *Hollywood Reporter* lit into me and Schulberg because we were sons of producers, and they thought we were actually traitors to be engaged in any kind of activity for the Guild."

According to Schulberg, "This dynastic feeling was so strong that if you bucked it, as I did by saying to David Selznick that I was more interested in writing than in producing, they felt you were not playing your role. Selznick had been my father's assistant, and I was working for him in 1936. Ring Lardner and I did a few ends of things, the end of *A Star Is Born* and the end of *Nothing Sacred*. We were a kind of utility writer, getting seventy-five dollars a week, doing bits and pieces, but we never got to do anything on our own. I told Selznick I felt very frustrated and disappointed, and he told me that he thought it would be part of my training to write for a while, and after that to become an assistant and finally a producer. It was a line of succession. He was thirty-five then, and he mentioned that his little sons would someday work for me and this is how the dynasty would go on.

"David really believed in being true to this Selznick-Schulberg feeling, and he'd say, 'After all, we all have producers' blood, you know.' Even then I thought it was funny. Our whole family laughed at it. If we nipped our finger, or did something similar, my sister Sonya would say, 'Quick, put a bandage on it because we can't waste any of our producers' blood.' "

The anxiety that the elders of the community felt about the renegade crown princes was intensified that autumn when Irving Thalberg died. It

---

* The Guild would be dramatically revived, however, after a short time underground. See Chapter 6.

was September 14, 1936. A whistle blew at noon, and there was a moment of silence across Hollywood. "The whole little kingdom stopped for a moment," said Schulberg.

In F. Scott Fitzgerald's introduction to *The Last Tycoon*, he said of Monroe Stahr, "I want to show that Stahr left certain harm behind him just as he left good behind him. That some of his reactionary creations, such as the Screen Playwrights, existed long after his death just as so much of his valuable creative work survived him."

The anger of the elders toward the reckless young radicals exploded a month later at a meeting of the producers' association where Eddie Loeb, the lawyer for MGM, publicly denounced Budd Schulberg, Ring Lardner, Jr., and Maurice Rapf, accusing them of being communists whose chief purpose was the destruction of the motion picture business. Loeb demanded that the three troublemakers be driven from the community and the industry whose reins they were expected to inherit. Neither Harry Rapf nor B. P. Schulberg was at that meeting to defend their young, but a friend told Schulberg senior, who told the boys what had happened, and on October 20 Maurice wrote an impassioned letter to Eddie Mannix at MGM, refuting the charges:

> Frankly, . . . I approach you in particular with this problem because I've always felt you were a pretty regular gent. I tell you that the charges are unfair and ridiculous. I am not an individual going back on his beliefs in response to the pressure of a situation. I think you know me well enough to believe my integrity in this matter. . . .
>
> Ever since I have been able to work, I have been spending my time around the studio, either as an employee or as an observer. I have worked in the front office, in the laboratory, in the sound department, and finally, as a writer. Even in college, I concentrated, at the expense of other subjects, on literature and theatre, fields from which the motion picture borrows most. All of this was to make myself more fit to work in your industry, to build it up, to make better pictures. Why I should seek the destruction of the business on which my family and I are dependent is damn strange. I hope Mr. Loeb realizes that in tossing this slander to a committee of the industry's top men, he is playing with the lives of human beings, that he may very well ruin their careers.
>
> It appears that through all my careful course of training, I made one mistake in the eyes of the Hollywood producers. Since I had learned in college drama courses that the Russian theatre was the finest in the world, it seemed only right that I should see it. . . . Had I come back from the land of the Soviets with a report of the horrors I saw there, everyone would have called me a fine boy. But I made the mistake of telling what I *actually* saw and, in my possibly mistaken opinion, all these things were pretty good, certainly constructive, and nothing like the accounts of bolshevism which we read in the Hearst papers. What was still worse, I told people that if what I had seen in Russia was an example

of Communism, this could not be so bad. I was all of nineteen then and didn't know any better, but this made me a Communist in Hollywood's eyes, I guess.

I only discovered this when I found Mr. Mayer ignoring my hellos and Mr. Thalberg calling me to his office to warn me against the evil I had fallen into. . . .

Mind you, I don't go back on what I said in 1934. I told merely what I saw and nothing can change that. But does that make me a Communist? What have I done, besides this, to be called a Communist or a potential destroyer of the motion picture industry? The answer is nothing.

I am glad, in many ways, that the matter has come to a head. This bugaboo has been following me for a long time and I am glad to get it into the open. Its influence has held me back in my work at the studio. . . . With the exception of a bonus which you kindly gave me at the completion of *We Went to College*, I have received no recognition in the form of a raise. . . .

These are things on which I would like your advice. I am concerned . . . about the future, which isn't worth a damn unless this red bugaboo is destroyed. This is important, too, to relieve my father who is justly over-wrought by these unjust accusations.

I think I have spoken, more or less, for Budd Schulberg, too, who strings with me on this. I do not know Ring Lardner very well. I have not seen him in Hollywood. I remember him from several years back as an amiable young guy who liked liquor better than women and women better than anything else. If he's plotting the destruction of the motion picture business, I can't imagine why, since this is the perfect spot for him.

The producers must have believed Maurice's protestations for the moment, because it was actually several years before the three young radicals were exiled from Hollywood. In the meantime, they all got raises, they all got married, and the characteristics that had made Ring Lardner, Jr., the perfect inhabitant of the motion picture world—his love of wine, women, and words —suited him admirably in another context that was growing increasingly important in his life, as well as in the lives of many other glamorous, beautiful happy young Hollywood workers. This new context was the Hollywood Communist Party, where the love of liquor, ladies, and letters ranked second only to the passion for Marxism.

5

In Hollywood in the thirties, the Communist Party was barely distinguishable in policy and activities from the noncommunist Left. Just about everyone at that time was an antifascist liberal.

"There were a lot of liberals like me in Hollywood then," said Samson Raphaelson, "who weren't communists. But most Jews, because of their fear of anti-Semitism, contributed to all of the antifascist causes. I felt that if the world were going to go communist or fascist, I'd rather see it go communist."

"Communism was part of this brand of half-assed internationalism that hit Hollywood before it reached other parts of the country," recalled Alexander Knox with amusement. Boris Ingster, a Russian refugee who knew Russian communism, though he was not an active communist in the United States, said that the Hollywood Communist Party didn't have the slightest conception of what real communism was.

The alliance between the liberals and communism began in 1935 with the initiation of the popular front and grew enormously during the period 1937–1939. It broke only during the Stalin-Hitler Pact, from August 1939 to June 1941.

The outbreak of the Spanish Civil War provided a focus around which most of the progressive elements of Hollywood, communist and noncommunist, united. The liberals were outraged at the overthrow by fascist General Franco of Spain's legitimate, elected government (elected by almost the same huge margin as Roosevelt's over Landon in 1936).

Whether the British-backed policy of nonintervention blocked efforts to convince Roosevelt to let the Spanish Republican forces buy arms in the United States, or whether it was because of his fear, just before the election, of losing the Catholic vote, Roosevelt would not commit the United States to back the Spanish government and curb fascism in Europe. So Hollywood found itself with a new purpose—generating support for the Loyalists and sending medical supplies to them, since it couldn't send arms. The spasmodic Hollywood anti-Nazi activity coalesced at this point and the Hollywood Anti-Nazi League—the first of a long line of antifascist organizations—was born.

The Anti-Nazi League, formed by Dorothy Parker and Oscar Hammerstein II, was a true attempt to develop an organized front against fascism. With a cultural commission, a woman's commission, a religious commission, a professional commission, a labor commission, and a youth commission, the League announced that its purpose was to generate active propaganda against nazism, with the individual commissions operating in their areas of expertise. The professional commission, for example, was in charge of planning adequate legal defense measures and exposing violations of law and justice in the United States and Germany.

The chairman of the League was Donald Ogden Stewart, the vice-chairman was Marian Spitzer, and the secretary, Alan Campbell. Besides Hammerstein and Parker, the League's sponsors included Eddie Cantor, actresses Florence Eldridge and Gloria Stuart, Rupert Hughes, Richard Left, Ernst Lubitsch, Fredric March, Edwin Justus Mayer, and Judge Isaac Pacht.

"Dottie Parker and I arrived at the politically conscious stage of our lives at about the same time," recalled Stewart.

The leftward leanings of both seemed predicated less on dogma than on a desire to help suffering humanity, a kind of sentimentality felt for the underdog. All of her friends found it amusing to imagine the willful Dottie subjecting herself to CP discipline. The news media was not only amused but irked by the politicization of the former Algonquin Round Table members, ridiculing "the startling conversion to the Loyalist cause of hitherto class-unconscious intellectuals. Most surprising of those hearing the call of the proletariat was the bittersweet wit of poetess Dorothy Parker," wrote *Newsweek* in 1937.

The boredom and loneliness experienced by many screen writers and their wives, and the insecurity and divisiveness resulting from the Guild's dissolution, were assuaged by the burgeoning political activity in Hollywood after the outbreak of the Spanish Civil War. In a town of isolated residences and little cultural activity outside movie making, political involvement provided a connection for the Hollywood castaways—not just with the rest of the world but between husbands and wives. Fund-raising get-togethers for Spain and similar fetes given by the socially conscious were really the first social activities in Hollywood intrinsically unrelated to the making of motion pictures. Therefore, for the first time politically aware Hollywood wives had a broad social framework into which they could meaningfully channel their activities. They had been interested onlookers in the Screen Writers Guild–Screen Playwrights struggle, but they had still been outsiders.

"I remember," said Elizabeth Faragoh, "that in 1936 we were playing poker for Spain. (William Faulkner was the most marvelous poker player.)

We made it clear that there would be no poker at all if the women couldn't play. We were all grateful for this political connection. In Hollywood, politics was an oasis in the intellectual desert."

"The possibility that things might go badly for the Spanish Loyalists was unthinkable, unbearable," remembered Karen Morley. "We really believed that things would get better, and we were terribly shocked and dismayed by Roosevelt's munitions embargo."

A glance at the 1936 datebook of Samson Raphaelson's wife, Dorshka, gives a good picture of the synthesis of politics and social life at that time. On successive Saturday nights in April and May were the following events: Anti-Fascist League banquet; a dinner for Prince Lowenstein, a Catholic who had fled to America to spread the word about Hitler; the wedding of screen writer Jesse Lasky, Jr.; Scottsboro party; dinner at Dorothy Parker and Alan Campbell's.

"We were blessed in that period," remarked lawyer Charles Katz, "not only by having great creative people on fire politically, but also in having a genuinely dedicated trade-union leader, Harry Bridges, moving in the streets. Sparks flew! Men like Robert Sherwood, Bridges, and brilliant European refugees crossed paths. The combination was terribly exciting."

Screen writer Paul Jarrico, the son of a socialist-Zionist lawyer from Boyle Heights, the old Jewish section of Los Angeles, was twenty-two in 1937. He had changed his name from Israel Shapiro to a more homogenized-sounding screen-credit name.

"In the summer of 1937," he said, "at a meeting at the Philharmonic Auditorium where André Malraux was raising money for ambulances in Spain, a very moving and exciting big meeting, I ran into a communist or-ganizer whom I'd known since my Young Communist days at Berkeley. She said, 'What are you doing?' I told her, 'I've just gotten a job in Hollywood as a screen writer.' She said, 'Would you like to be put in touch with some people in Hollywood?' and I said, 'Sure.'

"The next thing I knew I was invited by a few young communists to meet at the Hillcrest Country Club, one of the classiest, most expensive and snobbish joints in town. They were looking me over, and I was looking *them* over. At the university there had been a difference between being a member of the Young Communist League and being a member of the CP, but Holly-wood had a branch of the regular CP, and it was arranged for me to transfer to this group from the Berkeley group.

"The number of communists in Hollywood kept changing, but during the late summer of 1937 there were only about twenty or thirty in Hollywood working in the industry as writers, producers, or actors. Within a year there must have been forty or fifty members, and by 1939, until the Hitler-Stalin Pact, there must have been about one hundred."

The variety of movements that proliferated during those years, from the

Paul Jarrico (*Tom, Dick, and Harry, Song of Russia, Little Giant*) testifying in Washington before the House Un-American Activities Committee, 1951. His father was a lawyer in L.A. defending Wobblies and immigration cases; his uncle ran for lieutenant governor of California in 1930 on the Socialist ticket. Jarrico's first script was seen by Dore Schary, who recommended him to Nat Perrin, a producer at Columbia. "I worked primarily at Columbia, RKO, and MGM," Jarrico said. "Louis B. Mayer was quoted to me once as having said that he knew I was a communist and that he wouldn't have me on the lot for a minute except that I was such a good writer."

Spanish Refugee Committee to the Anti-Nazi League, undoubtedly would have existed without the CP, but what the Party did do was to lend a structure and a context to political efforts in Hollywood. It probably did more for its members than it did for society.

Later on, those who left the CP and made their views known during the Cold War purge would criticize the Party for its intractability, for its rigid adherence to the Party line, and for the often boring discussions that filled the meetings. Nevertheless, it served a variety of functions for the people who joined it—so much so that some of the victims who paid most dearly for that involvement later were to look back with nostalgia on what they considered the high point of their life.

The Communist Party suffused everything with meaning. If you got drunk, you did it for Spain, at a meeting to raise ambulance money. The Party removed the guilt surrounding Hollywood's enormous salaries by having members pledge a certain percentage to the different causes, as well as to the Party itself. (There were of course those who didn't like to part with so much cash, and it is said that writer-director Robert Rossen once argued with a CP treasurer that his pledge should be based on his net rather than his gross income.)

Another reason for CP nostalgia is that Hollywood was a transient world. People moved from assignment to assignment, switched studios, suffered the anxiety of ignored options. The struggle of the Screen Writers Guild had brought the old working-class dynamic of the employers versus the poor, powerless labor force right up to the front step of the Garden of Allah. Writers ricocheted from coast to coast, hoping to make it on Broadway and, when that failed, to stockpile their Hollywood cash for the next assault on New York. The Party, despite its shifts in line and in nomenclature (this year's fraction was last year's cell), was something of a constant. In Hollywood it was the progressives' Café Royale.

"The Hollywood CP was like Sunset Strip," recalled writer-director Abraham Polonsky. "Thousands of people used to go there, hang around a little while, and then pass on to someplace else. The group ultimately stabilized to some degree, but it shifted as people came from the East and Europe."

In the world without roots, peopled by orphans from urban centers and European refugees, the Party also provided a family of sorts that would not evaporate, as so many organizations did, when the specific motivation went away. John Howard Lawson was the great, exacting father figure, and Sam Ornitz was a gentler guru, fated to be cast more as an educator and never quite relinquishing his grudge that he wasn't a leader. Dalton Trumbo, who joined the Party later than did Ring Lardner, Jr., served as a mentor and friend to a younger group composed of Lardner and fellow writers Ian McLellan Hunter and Hugo Butler.

The Party's attitude toward women was more progressive than that of most other sectors of life in Hollywood and so fostered better male-female relationships. Party meetings included both writers and their wives, husbands, or lovers, not just because it was more usual to have gatherings of couples, but because the Party was both an ideology and a life style. The CP offered community services and channels for the energies of spouses who didn't work in studios. It lent a vibrancy to life and placed the Hollywood union struggle in the context of the union struggle throughout the United States and throughout history. (Lawson was particularly well known for always relating current events back to a historical pattern.) The Party channeled leisure time and work time. And for writers, disgusted by the anomie of the previous "lost generation," it was an affirmation that they were the found generation.

"There's no doubt," recalled Charles Glenn, a columnist for the *People's Daily World*, the West Coast CP organ, "that some Party members were responsible for nurturing the careers of others. Once I was urged to become a

Abraham Polonsky (*Body and Soul, Force of Evil*). Before coming to Hollywood he had studied law at Columbia and taught at City College in New York from 1932 until the war. He was called to testify before HUAC in 1952, pleaded the Fifth, and was fired from 20th Century–Fox. (He wrote about the friendly witnesses: "What these people were betraying was a way of life they had enjoyed tremendously. A social relationship of excitement and dedication and the fun of working together. . . .")

writer for Metro by someone at Stanley Rose's bookstore, or maybe Musso and Frank's."

Writer-producer Roy Huggins joined the Party and later left, becoming a friendly witness. Speaking about the CP's aid to writers, he said: "There were left-wing writers who wouldn't have worked without their politics—awful writers, but they were politically smart. Becoming a communist was just another way of being Sammy Glick."

In *Confessions of a Red Screenwriter*, the rationalist manifesto published by friendly witness Richard Collins, he explained, "When I joined the Party, I was handed ready-made friends, a cause, a faith, and a viewpoint on all phenomena." Some of the writers thought this ideology was wonderful. Others later viewed it as a surrender to authoritarianism, an escape from freedom.

Prior to the 1937 organizational surge in the Communist Party, there were isolated Marxist study groups attended by many of the young members of the Hollywood Left.

"I was seventeen," recalled Jean Rouverol Butler, "and it was 1935. I was in a Marxist study group with Budd Schulberg and a few others. My political concerns were always along very simple lines—would something be good for the little man? I thought in terms of the little man versus the fat cats. But I left the group because I was a young girl who wanted to be an actress and writer and all I was reading were these heavy theoretical tracts. I knew I wanted and needed to read literature, so I went off to do that."

By 1937, some of the Young Communists in Hollywood had graduated from their Marxist study groups and YCL meetings to being regular members of the Hollywood section of the CP. "The older members who were in when I joined in 1936," said Ring Lardner, Jr., "were people who felt a passionate commitment about it."

Among the earliest members were John Bright, John Howard Lawson, and writer Madeleine Ruthven. The Hollywood section was an island unto itself. Far more underground and secret than the Party in New York, the Hollywood branch did not, like its East Coast counterparts, bear the name of a black or a socialist hero. John Howard Lawson was in essence the leader of the CP in Hollywood from about 1937 to 1950, when he went to jail. He was on the county board of the Los Angeles CP, although according to former Party organizer Elizabeth Spector there wasn't much of a relationship between the Hollywood Party and the state and county CP. The basic tie was between the Hollywood Communist Party and the national office. The Hollywood section had regular dues and a structure based on the Party constitution.

According to most of the Party organizers and functionaries interviewed, the Hollywood CP was handled with special care, given the kid-glove treatment. "In return for continued support," said Sydney Davidson, a CP functionary, "in terms of names, activities, and money, the Hollywood Party members were given preferential treatment. There was little mixing between the downtown rank and file and the Hollywood people. Of course, there were exceptions. Harry Bridges was invited to Hollywood parties, and he cut a swath of broken hearts. Representatives from the county, from central and national committees, such as V. J. Jerome, would occasionally meet with the Hollywood people, particularly Jack Lawson. But there was this snob element. There was some resentment of the Hollywood Left among the rank and file."

"I remember," said a former organizer, "that whenever you were at a meeting at a home, you always had to have a drink so that in case anyone walked in, you'd look as if you were at a party. I remember one writer saying, 'What do you think of my great Marxist library?' and there wasn't a book around. Then he pushed a button and the bar swung out and there was indeed a great Marxist library. But I think he used the bar more than the books."

"The normal situation in the Communist Party," said Elizabeth Glenn, a former CP functionary, "was if they were active in politics or in the unions, they did not do active open Party work. In the Hollywood area, it was all sheltered. Discussions were held at homes, and there was a rigorous screening process before introducing someone at a recruiting meeting."

"When the issue of secrecy comes up today," she continued, "the Left is critical. It's hard to place oneself back in conditions of the time. Secrecy was carried to extremes. We weren't keeping secrets from the enemy. It meant you were keeping your political beliefs from people you wanted to influence, and in a way it was unproductive. But to break secrecy had to be a Party decision."

"The biggest mistake was in the Party's staying underground, the cult of secrecy," said Dorothy Healy, Los Angeles County CP chairperson. "If we had been public, would it have made a difference to noncommunists? Of course, there are legitimate reasons for the question of security. My life has been easier for being outspoken, telling my political nature. More people should have been. The right wing didn't hate me the way they hated those they couldn't peg."

The secrecy of the Communist Party in Hollywood added a little thrill for some of the members. All young people yearn for secret societies. The Party had dull duties, of course, such as collecting dues and selling copies of the *People's Daily World*. "I once asked Michael Gold," said John Wexley, "if I should join the Party, and he said, 'Don't. They'll have you out collecting dues. Write plays.'"

But the excitement came in secret names, aliases, and a sense of the forbidden that occasionally had the feeling of a game. Ring Lardner, Jr., said that he found himself in a situation at MGM where, on the phone, he would refer to Party meetings as "the poker game." Lardner also used to participate in a high-stakes poker game with the head of the MGM music department. He didn't like the idea of his poker playing becoming common knowledge, so on the phone he'd refer to the poker game as "the meeting." So Lardner spent his evenings going to poker games he called meetings and meetings he called poker games.

The secrecy of the Hollywood Communist Party was such that, according to many who joined, Party cards were not issued, though the House Un-American Activities Committee (HUAC) later "produced" some. Ring Lardner, Jr., speculated that the organizational secretary of the Hollywood section probably had a list of members in order to coordinate dues payments, but that the secretary most likely used partial names or pseudonyms for the members.

The county organizer was a man named Nemmy Sparks, and John Stapp was the liaison between the county and the Hollywood CP. The talent section was subdivided into various groups, called either fractions or cells.

"When I first joined the Party," said Paul Jarrico, "there was just one branch. Shortly after I joined, they formed a new branch, and then a third one was added in early 1937. At that time it was decided that this should be what was called in CP terminology a section, which consisted of two or more branches. It was getting large enough to be a section and to have a section committee and a section organizer. As we got bigger, there was a lot of work. I mean just literature and dues and all sorts of organizational things that all of us had done as volunteers. But basically there was too much for anybody who had another job at the same time, so when we got bigger, there was a paid organizer. He wasn't paid very much, and he generally was not a Hollywood person."

Writer Martin Berkeley claimed in his testimony before HUAC that the Hollywood section was organized in his home. "From the time I got out here, in January 1937," testified Berkeley, "all of us were working pretty hard to recruit members. And we felt that . . . there was no real organization . . . there were a few study groups, but that is about all. It was felt that numerically we were strong enough to have our own organization, which was called the Hollywood section. In June of 1937, the meeting was held in my house . . . because I had a large living room and ample parking facilities. It was out on Beverly Glen. . . . We were honored by the presence of many functionaries from downtown, and the spirit was swell." Berkeley named many people as having been at the meeting, including V. J. Jerome, Harry Carlisle, Donald Ogden Stewart, Dorothy Parker, Alan Campbell, Dashiell Hammett, and Lillian Hellman.

Fractions were basically separate bodies of communists from the same union, such as the writers' fraction, which was composed of the communist members of the Screen Writers Guild. There was an Actors Fraction and a Directors Fraction as well. The members of a fraction were not necessarily in the same branch, however, because the branches were often influenced by geographical factors.

"People who lived in the Valley," said Jarrico, "generally didn't like to make that long trip over the mountain in the days before freeways. But as time went on, there were too many writers for one branch. There were more writers than any other cultural worker in the Hollywood CP. Branches in general would run to no more than twenty people. So by the time we had fifty, sixty, seventy writers, we couldn't all have been in one branch. The writers' fraction got together to discuss writers' questions—content and Guild matters."

Dues were paid to the branch, and it was the branch that conducted general Party business in meetings usually held weekly. But the writers' fractions were separate meetings, called together whenever necessary. "It might just have been called together when there was some particular crisis in the Guild or during a period like the disintegration and subsequent reorganization of the Guild," said Ring Lardner, Jr. "Through 1937 we probably did meet regularly every week."

"People have some confusion about the word *fraction*," said Paul Jarrico, "because sometimes there were noncommunists involved in fraction meetings. In theory, it was just a communist meeting within the communist membership of a guild—writers, actors, or directors who met to discuss guild-related matters. But sometimes there would be fellow travelers at these meetings. If our fraction were having a particularly important meeting concerning the Guild, certain progressive writers would show up, and as time went on, that confused HUAC and the stool pigeons. People who were not communists attended what were supposed to be fraction meetings but which were actually 'fraction-plus meetings'—fraction plus some friends.

"At the fraction meetings we would discuss what should be done, to decide on priorities in the Guild and what position we should take in Guild meetings. If there were an important issue on which we were going to vote, every member of the fraction would more or less be bound to vote with the fraction of this particular issue."

"The goals of the Communist Party," said Maurice Rapf, "were to strengthen the unions, to help in political campaigns, and, during the war, to fight fascism. As a member of the CP, it was a very clear responsibility for me to work with the Screen Writers Guild. That was my area of operation."

During the growth period of 1937, the Party actively recruited members. How did the CP members keep from recruiting each other, considering the amount of secrecy in the branches?

"We knew who the other communists were," said Paul Jarrico, "even if we weren't in the same branch. We would meet, for instance, at Guild meetings or over luncheon tables at studios and begin to sense who was a member of the Party and who was not, just from the conversation. People met socially and knew about each other's politics, so that despite the general policy of secrecy, the communists could recognize each other."

Explaining the great appeal at that time of the CP to thinking people,

Budd Schulberg said, "The Marxist explanation for what was happening in society was most convincing. Once we were told that we could be communists and still support the New Deal and Roosevelt, and that the CP was simply a more advanced group going in the same general direction, it was pretty heady and convincing stuff to us."

Schulberg was recruited to the Communist Party by Stanley Lawrence, a CP organizer who also tried, unsuccessfully, to recruit Samson Raphaelson.

"Stanley Lawrence was my first true international communist, I guess," said Raphaelson. "All of the others were sort of Hollywood types. He was well built, tall, had extremely thick glasses, could be very congenial, and seemed absolutely brilliant to me. He was economic-minded. He could explain the theory of surplus value, which I have, to this date, still not mastered."

The paradox of the wealth and luxurious life style of these Party members was occasionally very funny. "All these people knew that an awful lot was happening in the world and Hitler was growing stronger," Budd Schulberg said. "And there they were, sort of fiddling while Rome burned, and I think the CP gave them a sense that they were doing something more serious and more socially useful, which would compensate for the waste of so much of their talent. Dialectical materialism by the pool . . . some of it was hilarious."

Ellenore Bogigian, a long-time worker in state Democratic politics and an observer of the Left in Hollywood, remarked, "Commitment is either total dedication and self-deprivation, like the resigned political life of Dorothy Healy, who had nothing and wanted nothing besides her politics, or commitment is for the upper middle class, who can afford it. Commitment is always a luxury with these people, and they rarely have to choose between their commitment and their luxury."

The young Hollywood communists never thought they would have to make a choice—certainly not in 1937. "The CP," remembered Milton Sperling, "represented the best interests of writers in Hollywood." He never joined, but there were gentle attempts to recruit him. There was a girl he was wildly infatuated with, a fresh-faced beauty who became a Party organizer, and he almost joined the Party just to be near her.

"Most of the people I came to know as communists," recalled Ring Lardner, Jr., "were brighter and more admirable and more likable than other people. I once proposed the slogan 'The Most Beautiful Girls in Hollywood Belong to the Communist Party,' but it wasn't taken seriously, even by me. The facts just seemed to sustain Bernard Shaw's thesis that revolutionary movements always attract the very best and the very worst elements in the existing society. Budd Schulberg and his bride, Virginia, known as Jigee, seemed to me just about the ideal representatives of our generation. Jigee made us feel pleased about being communists in the sense that someone as beautiful and sophisticated and charming as she was part of the Movement. She certainly contributed to making the Movement romantic to us."

Virginia Ray picked up the nickname Jigee from her sister Anne, a stuttering child who couldn't pronounce her whole name. Both Virginia and Anne were dancers. Virginia had appeared in a Sonja Henie movie and was a Busby Berkeley girl. She was about five feet two inches tall and thought her sister had better legs; she always thought her own were too short. Nevertheless, she was considered exquisite; many men called her the most beautiful woman they had ever known. She had extraordinary coloring that everyone talked about, a perpetual flush on flawless skin, huge dark eyes, a pert straight nose, a wide curling mouth, fine teeth, and thick, straight, glossy brown hair with red highlights.

Virginia (Jigee) Ray Schulberg with her daughter.

Bobby Lees had known her at Fairfax High School in Hollywood, which Virginia and her sister had attended. "We were a tight little group," he said, "the young Hollywood progressives. Our girls were dancing girls in some of the musicals. Amber Dana was one—she later married Waldo Salt. Marion Edwards was a dancing girl who wanted to be a serious actress. She married Irwin Shaw after she worked in his play *Bury the Dead*. I danced in *Dancing Lady* with Virginia Ray."

Through Bobby Lees, or the Fairfax High School grapevine, Jigee was introduced to Maurice Rapf, who immediately fell for her. He introduced her to Budd, who also became infatuated with her.

"Budd and Maurice and I had been taking out two Goldwyn girls and Jigee," recalled Milton Sperling. "She was like a solitaire set off by two lovely, though less beautiful, ladies."

It was all casual at the beginning, but then they really began to compete for her. What made Jigee different from the other girls was that she was very well read. Milton Sperling was impressed by her reading list. She had read all the right books—and after all, she was just a chorus girl. "With characteristic smartness, she went with Budd. He was the only true writer among us, and she knew he'd hit fast and big.

"When she and Budd were going together, and then when they first were married, we used to have Marxist study groups in B. P. Schulberg's house in Benedict Canyon. B.P. never suspected, of course. Jigee was the hostess, and I think we couldn't deny the appeal of meeting in a fine Beverly Hills house to talk of revolution with such a glamorous young hostess. These study groups usually numbered eight to twelve people and most of them were men—young writers—and everyone was a little in love with her."

Seventeen men interviewed have confessed to having been in love with Jigee. "She was always at the center of some drama," remembered Jean Butler. "It was as if she'd been created to be at the center of politics and romance."

"All the Jewish communists were attracted to her," remembered her brother-in-law writer-producer-director Melvin Frank, "because she was this gorgeous gentile princess who was accessible because she was a communist."

"I think that Jigee was always deeply grateful to Budd for legitimizing her, for opening up a world where she could operate as an equal, thinking, respected member of a community," recalled Sylvia Jarrico, Paul's wife.

Jigee married Budd on New Year's Eve 1936. She left the road-show life of hangers-on and writers' girls and found new status as the wife of a prominent writer, daughter-in-law of a former studio chief. Her married status didn't make her suitors any less ardent, however. As the young screen writers married and grew into a circle of couples, Jigee was always at the center. The men clustered around her, and she was not part of the circle of writers' wives. She didn't seek out the company of women, and they didn't like her much, unless she set out to charm them, and then none of them was immune to her captivating force. Even women whose husbands she was reputedly sleeping with found themselves liking her. Marriage left Jigee curiously unpossessed; new realms of conquest were constantly opening to her, and her circle of admirers grew.

Jigee made the Marxist study groups seem like glamorous evenings out. She didn't have the sharp wit of Dorothy Parker, but she was smart in a literary way and could on occasion be devastating, as when she referred to a sharp-tongued acquaintance as Malice in Wonderland. Jigee herself could be malicious, but it seemed charming in her because it gave her an aura of absolute candor, of someone who would speak her mind without caring about consequences. At that time, women were more guarded and wouldn't freely state their opinions; it seemed a more masculine trait. But Jigee didn't care. Her outspokenness came from the self-assurance of being attractive.

Ring Lardner, Jr., first got to know her when he and Budd were working together on *A Star Is Born*. Ring married Silvia Schulman, shortly after Jigee married Budd (both couples had been warned by a paternal David Selznick about the dangers of interfaith marriages). The two young couples saw a great deal of each other, and Ring fell in love with Jigee. It was a love that was to last throughout her lifetime, and Ring, never ending up with her romantically, remained one of her closest friends and confidants.

Her sister Anne said that Jigee was a woman with little capacity for self-examination, but Budd was proud of having such a fine creature for his wife. He had a certain sense of inferiority about his appearance and was insecure about his stuttering. In their little group there were three stutterers: Budd, Anne, and Sylvia Jarrico. A picture of the young Schulbergs in 1937 shows Virginia in shorts—small, ruddy, her hair haloing her head. Budd looks like a kid—tall, broad, with curly hair. He looks at once shy and self-conscious and like a proud conquering hero.

Another reason Jigee was so attractive to the young Hollywood Left was that she was always a little bored with the study of Marxist texts. "We were serious, but not too serious about the Party," recalled Lardner. "Anybody talking of devotion to the working class in a terribly serious way was looked on as something of a joke."

The young left wing in Hollywood—a yellowing photograph shows them at Malibu, dressed to kill in the days before jeans were the official casual uniform. The men are just past being boys, looking a little amused and diffident at being in such a wonderful, rich world of politics, beauty, and luxury. The women are radiant.

6

Though members of the Screen Playwrights and the studio heads thought that the Screen Writers Guild was dead after the summer of 1936, it was not. It was being kept alive through secret meetings at various people's homes.

"After the Guild fell apart," remembered John Howard Lawson, "it was sustained underground, which was something unusual and dangerous for writers, the fact that they stayed together without industry support."

The meetings were held at the homes of writers Dorothy Parker, Lillian Hellman, Samson Raphaelson, Dudley Nichols, Lester Cole, Mary McCall, Jr., Ernest Pascal, Wells Root, Donald Ogden Stewart, Dashiell Hammett, John Howard Lawson, Sheridan Gibney, Oliver Garrett, Sam Ornitz, Nathanael West, and others. The secrecy made the meetings seem extraordinarily similar to the meetings of the Party during that period. To some writers, looking back on that time, the memory of the two clandestine activities is indistinguishable.

"I remember," said Raphaelson, "going to dark cottages in the Hollywood Hills where there would be one lamp, and under the light people would be writing down the names of those joining the Screen Writers Guild."

"It was a dramatic reappearance," said Lawson, "in 1937, when the SWG emerged from a group that had a dissolved charter and came out a full-blown organization. Red-baiters said it was due to the communists that the Guild was reorganized, but the majority of the people who sustained the organization were not communists. They were just individuals who saw the need for an organization, who realized that the struggle for the Guild was both economic and creative."

Donald Ogden Stewart (*The Barretts of Wimpole Street*, *The Prisoner of Zenda*, *Holiday*, *Keeper of the Flame*, *The Philadelphia Story*) was born in Columbus, Ohio, was graduated from Exeter and Yale, and became a staff writer for *Vanity Fair*. In 1930 he went to Hollywood. "It suddenly came over me that I was on the wrong side . . . gradually I began to form the image of a worker whom I wanted to have the same sense of freedom that I had had at college. Over in the corner of my imagination there crouched the image of a little man who needed my help—the oppressed, the unemployed, the hungry. . . ."

Dorothy Parker; her husband, Alan Campbell; and Donald Ogden Stewart. Parker and Stewart were both on the executive board of the Screen Writers Guild. She was one of the founding members of both the Motion Pictures Arts Committee to Aid the Republic of Spain (she went to Spain in 1937) and the Joint Pacifists' Refugee Committee. Parker and her husband went to Hollywood as a writing team in 1932 (their joint screen credits include *Sweethearts*, *Here Is My Heart*, *A Star Is Born*, and *Trade Winds*).

What gave these individuals the hope they so desperately needed to continue their struggle was the possibility that the Supreme Court would soon rule on the Wagner Act. A favorable ruling would, however, also be an aid to the cause of the Screen Playwrights, who despite its status as a company union was finding it difficult to squeeze a contract out of the executives, whose purpose the organization had already fulfilled. The one bargaining point that the SP members wanted they found denied to them, and this was an injustice they objected to simply because they were writers, regardless of their politics. They wanted an end to "chiseling tactics" on the parts of directors, supervisors, and minor production executives, who would suggest slight changes in scripts and then assume partial screen credits for their endeavors. "It was then that they found out," recalled Lester Cole, "that whether they were house niggers or field niggers, writers were still the niggers of the studio system." Ironically, if it hadn't been for the SWG, the SP might never have obtained the benefits promised to them for their union-busting activities.

But early in February 1937, the Screen Playwrights, led by the Gray Eminence, Howard Emmett Rogers, met with the producers to announce that the Screen Writers Guild was re-forming. A provisional contract was signed on February 10, 1937, which was to go into effect if the Wagner Act was upheld. On April 12, 1937, the Supreme Court declared the act constitutional.

The Screen Writers Guild reappeared and began organizing to petition for a hearing before the National Labor Relations Board, and on April 19, 1937, one week after the Supreme Court ruling, the SP contract went into effect. As a result, the Academy relinquished control over credits, and Frank Butler, Grover Jones, Waldemar Young, and Gerald Geraghty were among the triumphant signers of the first SP charter. To make certain that whatever gains the SWG might achieve through the NLRB would be minimal, the SP contract was for five years; but triumphant as its members were, the SP still found itself at the mercy of a stronger group. Under the new SP contract, *directors* were given the right to story credit.

The Screen Writers Guild had its first open meeting on June 11, 1937. It was attended by more than four hundred writers, most of whom had been active in the old Guild; there were stories of blacklisting because of their activities about many of them. The meeting was held at the Hollywood Athletic Club, the site of that crucial, fatal "love-feast" in 1936. The old officers were present and took an active part in the rejuvenation ceremonies, but a new slate of officers and board members was elected. Dudley Nichols was the new president, Charles Brackett the vice-president, Frances Goodrich the secretary, and John Grey the treasurer. It seemed a conscious retort to the Red-baiting critics that the officers were writers who, though decidedly not communists, were all staunch Guild activists. There were a few left-wingers on the board, such as Donald Ogden Stewart, Dashiell Hammett, Lillian Hellman, and Dorothy Parker, but they were balanced by such conservatives as Mary McCall, Jr., Morrie Ryskind, Albert Hackett, and Brian Marlow. Young Philip Dunne and Ring Lardner, Jr., were alternates.

Although the meeting was open to all writers, unusual precautions were taken to prevent any attempt by the Screen Playwrights to control the militant body, which had turned out in force to hear Ralph Seward, counsel for the NLRB, outline the rights of employees under the Wagner Act and explain how, under the act, the Guild could petition for recognition by the producers. Howard Emmett Rogers, who had been discouraged from attending by Dudley Nichols, was asked to leave when he sought admission, and the situation threatened to turn extremely ugly. Some attempts were made in the audience to heckle the SWG revival, but the steering committee, bent on harmony, managed to avoid any open row.

The political climate in Hollywood at the moment, coupled with the Guild's new thrust toward organization to bolster its membership before filing with the NLRB, produced an interesting split within the Guild's ranks—one that was inherent in the nature of the Guild, in the nature of the writers, and in the nature of Hollywood in that era. It was a split chronicled amusingly in an exchange of articles in the *Screen Guilds' Magazine* between Mary McCall, Jr., and Donald Ogden Stewart.

The fight began when, on the night of a Screen Writers Guild executive board meeting, a quorum did not show up. Many board members, Donald Ogden Stewart included, had gone to a mass meeting to hear Ralph Bates, the British journalist and novelist, give a graphic account of the war in Spain. Bates had just returned from fighting in the trenches to spread the word about the slow murder of democracy in Spain. The drama of his presence was enhanced by the fact that Ralph Fox, another British writer, who took Bates's place so he could come on this lecture tour of America, had been killed by the fascists in his first battle.

The large turnout was also attributable to the identification of the Spanish Civil War as the "writers' war." The League of American Writers had polled hundreds of writers throughout the country, and the only one who proclaimed support for Franco and his fascist forces was Gertrude Atherton. Ernest Hemingway and John Dos Passos had both enlisted in the ambulance service in Spain; André Malraux was commanding the international air squadron defending Madrid; and Vincent Sheean, the progressive correspondent whose autobiography, *Personal History*, had been an enormous best seller in 1935, was in Spain as an observer.

McCall, objecting to the lack of a quorum at the meeting, suggested that those members who were at the mass meeting for Spain were engaging in an activity incompatible with the duty of writers, which, she believed, was to write and to concern themselves with matters that applied solely to their craft. She went on to quote Yeats's words to the Irish parliament:

> "Art knows no politics—art knows no morality."
>
> Nobody goes to anybody's house any more to sit and talk and have fun. There's a master of ceremonies and a collection basket, because there are no gatherings now except for a good cause. We have almost no time to be actors and writers these days. We're committee members and collectors and organizers and audiences for orators. . . . Our jobs are rapidly becoming a kind of hobby, like tambour work. . . . I don't think a writer or an actor ought to live in an ivory tower out of the world. He's got to be interested in what's going on. He must possess himself of the most accurate information he can get on the events, the tendencies, the spirit of his day. . . . I'm not suggesting that we make mental geldings of ourselves in order to keep perspective.

But, McCall continued, this perspective must not be allowed to take precedence over all other aspects of working life. She described how she overheard a question being asked in Beverly Hills: "What can a writer, employed by a major studio, do to further the coming of the proletarian revolution?"

The response was, "Aside from inserting one revolutionary sequence or perhaps only one revolutionary line of dialogue into a script, there is very little he can do." McCall added, "I was then engaged in constructing a starring vehicle for Miss Marion Davies. For the life of me I couldn't find a spot in that script for 'up the workers.' "

"Yes," she remarked in closing, "I do think there may be a showdown between the extreme right and the extreme left, and when and if it comes, I want a chance to watch it . . . I want to write about it, because I'm a writer."

McCall was answered by Stewart.

> One gets [from Miss McCall] a distinct impression that Hollywood is at the present time a veritable bee-hive of political activity, both radical and reactionary. Frankly, I beg to differ. During the past year I have attended practically all of the "radical meetings, symposia, and benefits" (as Howard Emmett Rogers and his followers in the MGM branch of the DAR will be glad to tell you at the drop of an American Legion button), and I can assure Miss McCall and her possibly alarmed readers that 99 and 44/100 percent of Hollywood is still sleeping peacefully in its options. I can also assure her that if she should ever wish "to do something" about any good cause, she will find herself surrounded by the most enthusiastic apathy it has ever been her privilege to sink into.

Stewart went on to cite Hemingway, Dos Passos, Malraux, Thomas More, Byron, William Blake, Shelley, Baudelaire, and Voltaire.

At all times in the past writers and poets have taken part in politics without sacrificing any of their integrity as artists. Victor Hugo was exiled from France for his attacks on the current would-be Hitler, Napoleon. . . . The example of these men would seemingly give some small excuse at least for a Hollywood writer to interest himself in what is going on in Spain or permit him to attend an anti-Nazi mass meeting without feeling that he is betraying the artistic demands of his contract with Harry Cohn.

Nor are all the "good causes" which Miss McCall resents as occupying the valuable time of Hollywood artists entirely devoted to affairs across the Atlantic. Collection baskets have been passed—speeches have been made—on behalf of the nine Negroes unjustly condemned to death in Scottsboro, Alabama. . . . Would Miss McCall have us believe that it is a betrayal of our duty as writers when we interest ourselves in the fate of some of the miserable and wretched of this earth in some more practical way than the sale to a magazine of a beautifully written account of an electrocution?

It has always been my feeling that a man is an artist primarily because he is gifted or cursed with a greater degree of sensitivity not only to the beauty of the world but also to its terror and pain. . . . It has long been one of the stock criticisms of Hollywood that in our sunny golden-goose existence we are all too disposed to hide our well-massaged bodies from . . . those cold cruel winds of pain and despair which, in our days of adversity, were the sources of our sensitivity to the miseries of our fellow-sufferers, and the very well-springs of our creative urge. Whether or not this criticism is just, . . . certainly Miss McCall's indignation at the efforts of the organizers of the good causes sounds not so much like the desire of the true artist for the high lonely peak as the reminiscent whine of the well-fed [screen playwright] to be "let alone" in his feather-bed. It is a painful surprise to find so courageous a fighter as Miss McCall . . . counselling . . . adherence to the banners of those defenders of the goose that lays the golden eggs.

Stewart's reply generated a certain amount of fireworks, but the entire exchange was symptomatic of an unfortunate divisive tendency that was to become more political and nearly destroyed the SWG. Writers like McCall, who fought against the Guild's involving itself with world politics, were in no way reactionary, as Stewart's characterization might suggest. They were merely liberals, like McCall, and later like William Ludwig and Emmet Lavery, conservatives who perceived their union purely as a labor organization—and one with a tenuous existence in a hostile industry. Because of this they fought attempts to politicize the Guild, fearing that politics would further weaken the union. What was unfortunate was that in the course of time, particularly after the end of the Second World War, the forces of reaction and the forces that wanted a politically neutral Guild were nudged into a seemingly unavoidable coalition against the forces of the Left in the Guild.

The hostilities resulting from the split with the Screen Playwrights had intensified in the months during which the Screen Writers Guild was reorganizing underground, and as the climate in Hollywood became increasingly more political, the debate over union involvement in politics exacerbated that hostility. It was not unique to the SWG, however. During this period the AFL and the Congress of Industrial Organizations (CIO) split, and the AFL became the bastion of Gompers's philosophy of trade unionism, while the CIO leaders were further to the Left politically and claimed that a labor union should be a political and social agency as well as a business bargaining agency. Pressure from AFL national president William Green brought the ouster of CIO locals from the State Federation of Labor in 1937.

Though it did not really become a controversy until several years later, during the Hollywood Ten hearings, when it was exploited for all it was worth, the issue of radical thinkers inserting left-wing propaganda into their art was beginning to be raised in Hollywood. It was not magnified as an issue, because the thirties was the era when Hollywood, especially Warner Bros., was turning out a batch of "socially conscious" pictures that dealt with issues like crime and unemployment. However, as Abe Polonsky was later to point out about social realism, the movie companies would have willingly followed Stalin in those days had that made for commercially successful entertainment. And radical politics, though it irritated the studio heads, were not yet a reason for wholesale blacklistings.

"Louis B. Mayer was quoted to me once," said Paul Jarrico, "as having said that he knew I was a communist and that he wouldn't have me on the lot for a minute except that I was such a good writer—a quote that I liked. It was obviously harder to get anything progressive made at MGM than it was at other studios because of the politics of Louis B. Mayer. He was a power in the Republican Party and was alert to political questions.

"Warner Brothers had made a reputation as good, patriotic Americans, and they made some of the best anti-Nazi films and more political films than were made anyplace else. But they also, when they decided to be anticommunist, were more anticommunist than anybody else and made more anticommunist films, most of which were failures commercially. The Warner brothers and L. B. Mayer thought politically: they had political motivation, intent, and drive. They cared. Harry Cohn at Columbia and Darryl Zanuck at Fox were more open to progressive content if it could be sold to them in terms of its commercial attractiveness. They didn't care what the picture said. They just wanted to know whether it would make money."

Disagreements between members of the Screen Writers Guild, such as the exchange between McCall and Stewart, were now pushed aside as internecine warfare that was doing a disservice to the Guild, whose main function was to recruit new members and to petition for a National Labor Relations Board hearing on the writers' case. During the summer of 1937, new members such as Paul Jarrico received letters from Philip Dunne, chairman of the SWG's membership committee, welcoming them and informing them that the Guild was "counting on your cooperation to help us win the struggle for recognition before the NLRB."

It was decided by the regional and national labor relations boards that the SWG's case would be the first to test the applicability of the Wagner Act to the motion picture industry. The Guild had petitioned the board for an election to determine what organization should be the sole collective bargaining agency for film writers. If it was determined in these hearings that the movie industry was indeed involved in interstate trade, then the industry would be eligible for unionization under the Wagner Act. Once the motion picture industry had been declared eligible, it would then be possible to legally define a screen writer, and determine which was the appropriate bargaining unit, the individual studio or the entire industry. The question was whether or not screen writers qualified as labor under the Wagner Act. The Screen Playwrights and the producers were already screaming that the writers were artists and therefore not eligible to unionize.

The NLRB hearings on the screen writers' case had been set for autumn 1937, and as lawyers for both sides were preparing their briefs, the Screen Playwrights initiated a series of attacks on the Guild that were calculated to weaken it, both structurally and spiritually, before the impending trial. The smoldering strife between the Authors League of America and the Screen Playwrights over the matter of recognition of the SP or of the ALA-affiliated SWG broke into the open at the beginning of August when the Authors League asked Rupert Hughes, president of the Screen Playwrights, either to give up his membership in the SP or to resign from the League, in which he had been an early activist.

Hughes refused to do either, charging the ALA with "regimentation." This was an obvious attempt to force the hand of the SWG in a court action. The SP said it would ask the court to enjoin any attempt by the ALA to prohibit joint membership in both the ALA and the SP. Hughes, for the Screen Playwrights, contended that such a prohibition violated the writer's constitutional rights and was subject to review by a federal judge. An open-letter battle in the trade papers between Hughes and ALA President Marc Connelly had all of Hollywood giggling with the polysyllabic lambasting being hurled from both sides. But Connelly won when he called Hughes a "syncretist." Nobody knew what it meant and everyone rushed to look it up in the dictionary; while Hughes was polishing his meanest retorts, it was discovered that *syncretist* merely meant "one who attempts the union of conflicting parties or principles." Hughes had obviously thought it was a far more pejorative term, and a *Variety* wag reported that "lexicons are being torn to pieces by maddened combatants looking for more words to sling."

The battle between the two groups of writers climaxed in a quarter-million-dollar libel suit filed on behalf of the Screen Playwrights against the Screen Writers Guild. The basis for the lawsuit was the publication of a letter from Philip Dunne to P. G. Wodehouse, the British creator of the character Jeeves and a member of the SP. In his letter Dunne charged the SP with being a company union, organized by the producers to destroy the Guild. In the complaint the defendants named were Dudley Nichols, Charles Brackett, Frances Goodrich, Dashiell Hammett, Lillian Hellman, Edwin Justus Mayer, Dorothy Parker, Samson Raphaelson, Morrie Ryskind, and Donald Ogden Stewart.

"The letter I wrote Wodehouse at the time was never intended to be used in public," said Dunne. "It was quite obviously a little jejeune, and I even called one of the Guild executives—perhaps it was Ernie Pascal, or Dudley Nichols—either boring or ponderous. I later apologized to the fellow for it,

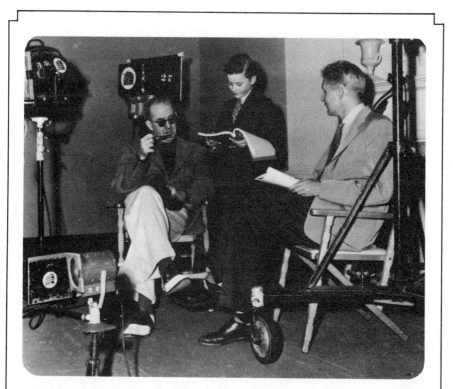

At right, Philip Dunne (his films include *The Count of Monte Cristo, The Last of the Mohicans, Suez, How Green Was My Valley, The Late George Apley,* and *Forever Amber*) with John Ford and Roddy McDowall. He came to Hollywood in 1933 after graduating from Harvard and working for a few years in banking. He was chairman of the Screen Writers Guild membership committee 1936–37 and was in 1940 the first witness brought before the Dies committee. He was later blacklisted.

but the SWG president, Nichols, was pleased because my criticism of a Guild member showed that my letter was an individual matter, not a political one. Of course, I was convinced that the hatred of the SP, and particularly of Wodehouse, for the members of the SWG was not just because of the union but was an anti-Semitic matter. Wodehouse, you know, was later accused of collaborating with the Nazis."

Philip Dunne, the son of humorist Finley Peter Dunne, who had created the Irish tavern philosopher Mr. Dooley, was extremely sensitive to anti-Semitism, remembering the surprise of his father in New York in the twenties and thirties when he found that several of the clubs he frequented would not accept the membership of some of his literary chums, who were Jewish. Dunne came from the private-boarding-school world, where he had known John Lee Mahin. Dunne's brother had roomed at school with Mahin, and the heritage—not unlike Ring Lardner, Jr.'s—of Long Island, polo playing, and Harvard had left him with perfect manners but an empty bank account. His father's fortunes had been wiped out in the Crash. Dunne worked for a few years in banking, and in 1933 the young aristocrat came to Hollywood, where his first job was to write the dialogue for *The Count of Monte Cristo*. He re-called that he had never finished the book and had made up every line, except for one from Dumas: "The world is mine." From the time Dunne arrived in Hollywood he was a firm liberal Democrat and Guild activist. He later became the Guild's vice-president.

Ironically the Wodehouse suit came before Robert W. Kenny, then a Los Angeles judge. The jovial, humorous politician claimed that this was clearly a political matter and so issues of libel didn't apply. Kenny threw the case out of court and was to prove himself a friend to writers again and again during the next ten years. He became a member of the legal team that nego-tiated the first SWG contract and later defended the Hollywood Ten.

Throughout the Screen Playwrights–Screen Writers Guild battles, the Hearst papers continued, as they had since 1936, to give very favorable publicity to the SP as an organization and to its leaders as individuals. "Hearst," recalled John Bright, "spent a fortune trying to make a star out of Marion Davies, but the American public said No. He had formed Cosmo-politan pictures for her, and her films were released through MGM. Hearst and Mayer were close friends, so it wasn't surprising that his Los Angeles and San Francisco papers were practically house organs for the Screen Play-wrights."

It was in this atmosphere that the National Labor Relations Board hear-ings finally began on Monday, October 4, 1937, in a simple judicial chamber in the Pacific Electric Building in downtown Los Angeles. The group gathered there knew that the eyes of the world were on the movie industry and that the outcome of this hearing would affect that industry as a whole, not just its writers.

The defendants in the case included the Motion Picture Producers and Distributors Association; the Association of Motion Picture Producers; Pat Casey, the labor-contract executive for the producers; and the production corporations of MGM, RKO, 20th Century–Fox, Selznick International, Walter Wanger, Universal, Republic, Goldwyn, Columbia, Armour, Warner Bros., First National, Paramount, B. P. Schulberg, Walt Disney, Grand National, Hal Roach, and Monogram. Counsel for the companies was led by the diminutive Milton H. Schwartz, who was representing at least eight of the producers, and Major Walter Tuller, representing Paramount. Representing the NLRB was William J. Walsh, the twenty-six-year-old chief counsel for the Los Angeles office of the board. Leonard Janofsky, a man with bushy eyebrows and a quick temper, represented the Screen Writers Guild, and Neil McCarthy represented the Screen Playwrights.

Presiding over the hearings was special examiner William R. Ringer of Indianapolis, a man with a bristly mustache, silver-rimmed glasses, and a profound ignorance of the motion picture industry, forcing labor representative Walsh to call various witnesses to the stand to explain the different aspects of the motion picture business. Responding to Ringer's lighthearted comment that his only previous contact with the movie industry was as a paying customer, Schwartz muttered, "Well, boys, we'll be out of the trenches by Christmas." McCarthy exclaimed, "And I took this case for a flat sum!" From the beginning of the hearings it was apparent that precedent-setting revelations would be made. The amounts expended by each movie company for raw film and other studio materials were introduced in an attempt to show that the use of raw materials coming from states other than California defined the movie industry as being engaged in interstate trade. Janofsky then quoted recent Supreme Court decisions on Wagner Act cases in which gross incomes of corporations had been taken into consideration. Despite violent objections on the part of the counsel for the producers, Ringer ruled that testimony concerning the income of movie companies and the grosses of motion pictures was pertinent, thus opening the way for minute examinations of motion picture finances.

The first witness called was RKO production chief B. B. Kahane, who explained the role of the producer. He admitted under questioning that the script was the framework for the entire motion picture. The next witness, John Arnold, head of MGM's cinematography department, made much of the independent function of the cameraman, claiming that the cinematographer was the "only man privileged to interpret the mood the director intends for any scene." Under cross-examination by Janofsky, Arnold reluctantly admitted that a cameraman must still look at a script. Then director Henry King was called, and he claimed that the director sometimes functions as a screen writer.

Movie executives were obviously going to be uncomfortable at having such an open examination of their studios' finances, and the claims of ignorance of witness Nicholas Nayfack, a minor MGM executive, concerning his company's gross income caused Walsh to indicate that from that point on he would call only top studio executives who did know what the company profits were. The producers were grim when the hearings ended on Friday afternoon, though a lighter note was introduced by examiner Ringer, who canceled the Saturday morning session so that young Janofsky, who had been married the night before, could have the weekend for his honeymoon.

As the hearing progressed, there were alternations of humor and violence. McCarthy and Janofsky clashed at one point over a document, meeting in the middle of the floor in such a bitter vocal fight that they were on the point of squaring off. McCarthy already had his jacket off when Ringer ordered them to take their seats. The two attorneys apologized, and Ringer remarked mildly, "I take it for granted this is not your customary conduct."

Comedy was provided when the court began to call writers as witnesses. Grover Jones traced his career from coal miner to film scenarist. He claimed to be the man who christened Poverty Row at the studio, having applied the title when he had to pay rent for studio space because his producer claimed he couldn't. And Jones never got the money back. He also proudly claimed to have been fired from "practically every studio in Hollywood, including some of those that weren't even painted."

Remarking that "most screen writers are lice when it comes down to honor," Jones minimized the care given and the role played by the writer in making a motion picture: "A writer takes an assignment, doesn't know what it's all about, but hopes for a miracle. He hands it to the director, who is in the same state of mind." He illustrated his claim by saying, "I wrote *The Trail of the Lonesome Pine* in three weeks and a half, and it turned out to be rather successful—I don't know why, but it did." He then ended his statement, saying that "it [screen writing] is my art, and I am going to stick to it."

A more dignified note was introduced when Charles Brackett, the Screen Writers Guild's vice-president, took the stand. (Brackett and his collaborator, Billy Wilder, were later responsible for some extremely successful films, including *Ball of Fire, Midnight,* and *Ninotchka.* "If I were casting a picture and I needed a perfect Supreme Court judge, it would be Charlie Brackett," Wilder said of his partner. "He was a right-wing Republican conservative, of the Truman Bracketts of New York, a formal man, always impeccably dressed, who made entries in his diary every evening.")

Brackett was a perfect witness for the Guild, not just because his presence was so dignified and magisterial but because he was a professional writer, whose primary concern was that of dignifying his profession. He rendered slightly ludicrous the taunt that the Guild was dominated by New York radicals.

Brackett testified that the writers feared to join the Screen Writers Guild

Charles Brackett was president of the Screen Writers Guild in 1938 and 1939. His collaboration with Billy Wilder resulted in such films as *Ninotchka, Hold Back the Dawn, The Major and the Minor, Five Graves to Cairo, The Lost Weekend, A Foreign Affair,* and *Sunset Boulevard.*

until after the Wagner Act was passed, thus ensuring them against trouble. In an eerie exchange that portended a later hearing with another McCarthy, Brackett was asked by Neil McCarthy to name the members of his union. Brackett replied: "I do not choose to name the names of members of my organization."

Janofsky added, "Mr. Examiner, my client doesn't wish to name these names because of the blacklist."

"There is no such thing as a blacklist," McCarthy snapped. "Instruct him to name the names."

The definition of a screen writer had been given the previous week by Brian Marlow, who cited as his authority the by-laws of the SWG, adopted in 1933. At that time, any scripter working for an established studio or as a freelancer was declared eligible for membership. A writer was also eligible if unemployed, provided that he had received a screen credit in the prior eighteen months. Marlow testified that the customary hours of a working writer were 10 a.m. to 5 p.m., with many writers doing much of their work at home. Marlow was questioned by McCarthy about "the poker game," which all writers were supposed to have going in their office. It was an obvious metaphor for freedom of writers from discipline and studio constraints.

"My last poker game was in 1931," said Marlow. "I lost."

Sheridan Gibney, who wrote *Anthony Adverse* for Warner Bros., testified that he had had some arguments with producers, but minor ones. He said producers had final say in the writing of a script.

After Brackett's testimony that he had earned $50,000 from Paramount the year before, though none of his stories had been filmed, McCarthy belittled the writers' attempt to unionize. But then Sherman Lowe was called to the stand, and he disproved the contention that all screen writers were overpaid and lived in luxury. Lowe had been a contract writer for ten years, first at Republic, writing serials, then at Warner Bros. In this time he had seen his salary rise from $35 a week to $85 a week at Republic. When he reached Warner Bros. he hit his all-time high of $150 a week. He said he had been required for all those years to keep fixed hours, from nine to five, with an hour for lunch, and that any failure to adhere to strict time limits drew criticism from producer Sol Siegel. After several years in a barren little office at Republic, he now had an office at Warner Bros. with a comfortable chair and a couch as well. Lowe lent a note of sadness to the proceedings. He represented the little man, who really needed the protection of the Screen Writers Guild. He was not the glamorous, political, highly paid screen writer who frequented Musso and Frank's and the Trocadero. He was part of Hollywood's firmly entrenched community of underpaid hacks and fringe people, the weary studio employees who became part of Nathanael West's grim vision in *Day of the Locust*.

The hearings ended in Los Angeles on October 23. Just before adjournment, the Screen Playwrights, led by James Kevin McGuinness, Patterson McNutt, John Lee Mahin, and Howard Emmett Rogers, testified that they already had individual contracts with producers, did their work wherever and whenever they pleased, from golf course to bathtub, were never required to keep hours, and were, in general, highly paid creative artists who needed no union. McGuinness was nearly jumped by members of the Screen Writers Guild when he claimed that Thalberg had supposedly encouraged the formation of the SP because at a party Ralph Block had said to him, "Irving, we need an organization of writers because writers get drunk, they work on other stories on your time, and if we had an organization which was strong enough, we could discipline them and stop them from doing that."

To counter accusations that, in the wake of the split, the Guild's board of directors had been discriminated against, McNutt testified that during the four months he was a member of the SP board of directors, he was without employment. This was, he claimed, because "for the previous year, my picture credits had been of such a character that employment was not easy to find for me. Not having good standing as a screenwriter is the only reason that most writers can't get employment."

"When writers come out to Hollywood," he said, "and get on the gravy train, they finally get the idea they belong there as a matter of course, no matter what they turn out."

McNutt said he never threatened SWG board members that they'd lose their jobs if they didn't resign. How could he, he asked, since he himself had been out of work until September 1937? Moving on to the question of work versus art, he said that he worked at home or on the golf course and had fluid hours. Secretaries were paid overtime for working late, but writers weren't, and they shouldn't be, even though screen writing was a "ditch-digger's job mentally. I mean, it was mentally exhausting."

But, he continued, it was a creative process. "Every time you do a story," he claimed, "you have a baby." McNutt, who had written *Curly Top*, the Shirley Temple picture (in which the darling of the orphanage hides a beloved pony in her bed), claimed that out of love of his craft he worked on vacation at home by his pool with writer Harlan Ware and that there was never any question of employee status.

And so, on a sustained note of conflict, the NLRB regional hearings in Hollywood closed after seventeen days and half a million words of testimony, and the proceedings were sent to the national board in Washington, where, it was believed, there would be no decision before the first of January 1938. In the meantime, the screen writers' proceedings had started a clamoring in the industry for hearings, and the directors, art directors, decorators, and set designers were all waiting for their turn. By mid-October, there were already thirty movie industry cases pending.

Two weeks after the end of the hearings, Dudley Nichols came to New York and reported to an Authors League of America meeting that the Screen Writers Guild had grown from almost no members to 540. He said he expected the SWG to be certified by the NLRB, since the Screen Playwrights was a company union and had only 100 members, a figure that was due to the new status and revitalization of the Guild.

The hearing of the screen writers' case in Washington began early in December, and the Screen Writers Guild was encouraged by the presence of a seeming friend at court, Donald Wakefield Smith. Smith was a member of the three-man National Labor Relations Board and in court was openly sympathetic to the screen writers, observing that he knew something about the habits of film producers because at one time he had been counsel for the American Society of Composers, Authors, and Publishers (ASCAP). Strong sympathy for the Guild was also shown by NLRB chairman Warren Madden during the hearing. When an executive at Fox named Wright spoke about the freedom given to writers, Smith remarked, "I don't believe there is any such elysium this side of heaven. I won't believe they live in this happy state where nobody has anything to bargain about. It sounds like nonsense."

The rulings on the screen writers would have certain important implications for the entire movie industry, but it was not only these rulings that were making the producers extremely nervous. Viewing the existing combination of the production, distribution, and exhibition branches of the motion picture industry as a violation of antimonopoly legislation, Congressman Boren of Oklahoma had already raised the possibility of introducing national legislation that would make each branch a separate unit. Congressman Pettingill had introduced anti–block booking legislation, which would forbid movie companies from forcing bad pictures on movie houses in order for them to get good ones. And now, should the NLRB rule that the movie industry was engaged in interstate commerce, the Interstate Commerce Commission would be empowered to license movie companies, which meant that studios would be required to submit to the commission detailed reports of their financial setups and trade practices. The commission had the authority to deny licenses to any corporation violating antitrust laws. It was the possibility of such legislation that struck terror in the hearts and pocketbooks of the major movie corporations, and it was to their great relief that Congressman Boren was told the House Committee on Interstate and Foreign Commerce would be too busy to consider his bill during the 1937–38 session.

This bit of relief was undermined by the information that the issue of screen writers as employees versus independent contractors might overturn the Social Security tax setup in the studios. The writers suddenly realized that if they were to be considered independent contractors instead of employees, neither the federal nor the state government had the right to collect from them old-age pension or workmen's compensation deductions, which would mean that if they were classified as independent contractors, the deductions that had already been made were illegal, and they could sue the studios for 100 percent refunds. Brian Marlow estimated that he had paid up to $3,000 a year in Social Security. Multiplying one Marlow by the number of writers—some making more, some making less—throughout the studios, the producers were faced with a sudden, nightmarish alteration of their cash flow.

On the other hand, it represented a savings to the studios in the future if writers were classified as independent contractors, because in California an employee had to pay 1 percent of his total earnings to Social Security, while the employer had to add 2.7 percent, which meant that for every $5,000-a-week employee the studio had to put up $7,020 per year. The classification of independent contractor was, for the same obvious reason, more attractive for the more highly paid studio workers.

While the case was being considered—first in Los Angeles, then in Washington—clashes between the Screen Writers Guild and the Screen Playwrights continued outside the courtrooms. One feud was over the issue of screen credit. On an MGM picture, *Lord Jeff*, James Kevin McGuinness was given credit for the screenplay, which infuriated the other four writers on the picture, who were members of the SWG. McGuinness claimed that "four members of the SWG worked a total of sixty-four paid-for weeks during which they produced one-fourth of 1 percent of the dialogue per week and one half of 1 percent of the story per week. One Screen Playwright worked seven weeks and produced 12 percent of the screenplay per week and 9 percent of the story per week."

The studio backed up the SP's allocation of credits, which only intensified the animosity.

While the screen writers' case was being presented in Washington, the Screen Writers Guild was preparing for the possibility of a favorable NLRB decision by formulating a potential collective bargaining agreement between writers and producers as well as voting on a new Authors League of America constitution that, though making the Guild part of the ALA, would grant it almost total autonomy. The measures were heartily approved by the Guild membership.

Two trends—only seemingly contradictory—were becoming evident in Hollywood unionization: while unions felt the absolute need for local autonomy, they also were seeking affiliation with a larger body (like the SWG with the ALA or the SAG with the Associated Actors and Artists of America and the AFL), which promised greater clout in the case of a strike.

Consistent rumors that William Green and other leaders of the AFL might make a secret deal with the International Alliance of Theatrical Stage Employees (IATSE), giving its officials jurisdiction over all workers in the industry, was greeted with strong opposition. The three talent guilds—Screen Writers Guild, Screen Actors Guild, and Screen Directors Guild—formed the Inter-Talent Council to encourage a commitment to mutual protection from domination by an organization such as the IATSE. The SAG, however, which already had a ten-year closed-shop contract with the producers, was not particularly eager to enter an autonomy fight with two guilds still unrecognized by the NLRB or the producers.

Yet despite the basic ineffectuality of the Inter-Talent Council, the motivation for its organization was a reflection of resistance throughout Hollywood against IATSE. IATSE craft locals, whose requests for autonomy in the movie industry had been consistently ignored or denied by union officials, were galvanized finally by the radical leadership of Jeff Kibre, who founded a branch known as the IATSE Progressives, which dedicated itself to freeing the locals from IATSE domination. Kibre's fight had a sound basis—the IATSE was controlled by gangsters and just before Christmas 1937, Willie Bioff, personal representative in Hollywood of IATSE president George E. Browne—the sole power in control of twelve thousand members of the studio locals—was exposed. That is to say, the record of a jowly character from Chicago named William Bioff, alias Morris Bioff, alias Henry Martin, alias Willie Bioff, was exposed. Chicago police records showed that at various times Bioff had been arrested for burglary and pimping. Police suspected him of complicity in the murder of Tommy Malloy, a former business agent of the Motion Picture Operators' local in Chicago. Malloy had opposed the leadership of Bioff and Browne and had been machine-gunned to death on his front lawn. Bioff had also been arrested several times on vagrancy charges, one of the methods used by Chicago cops to run known criminals out of the city. Bioff and Browne were surrounded by squads of bodyguards, with names like "Dago" Lawrence Mangano and menacing bulges under their vests. Bioff was called back to Chicago in the midst of the progressives' accusations. They wanted him kicked out of the union, but he wasn't.

This, then, was the sort of leadership from which Jeff Kibre was trying to free his progressive IATSE locals. His demands for autonomy were based not only on the accusations of IATSE racketeering but also on the union's capitulation to the devastating rise in studio unemployment at the close of 1937. By the end of February 1938, nearly 40 percent of studio employees were on the street. Paramount had laid off 1,400 workers; MGM was virtually shut down for six weeks. The Universal writing staff was pared to fourteen, half of them contract writers. The producers, who were supporting IATSE officials (in what the progressives claimed was an attempt to intensify dissension in the union at a time when united action was needed to meet the unemployment crisis), gave numerous reasons for the slowdown in production. Claiming that the previous winter's production costs had suffered because stars caught colds and had to lay off in the midst of shooting, the producers said they were slowing down production during this rainy winter season to avoid unnecessary additional production costs.

Studios were also in trouble, executives explained, because of the loss of certain Italian markets. Italy had canceled plans for an MGM first-run circuit, and, according to the *Hollywood Reporter*, it was "believed to be in retaliation for the treatment accorded Vittorio Mussolini by certain Hollywood elements." What the *Reporter* was referring to was an antifascist demonstration by the Anti-Nazi League and the Spanish Refugee Committee, organized by Ring Lardner, Jr., at Warner Bros., against Il Duce's son, whose visit to Hollywood, given the passionate support there of the Spanish Loyalist forces, had not been in the best diplomatic taste.

The studios were following the old employers' tactic of trotting out economic instability whenever labor was agitating. It was hard to reconcile the unemployment and studio pleas of poverty with the reports of five major companies that they had experienced a 25 percent average increase in net profits in 1936 and 1937. The aggregate net profit of Columbia, Loew's, Paramount, 20th Century–Fox, and Warner Bros. was over $34 million in 1937.

Under the auspices of the IATSE Progressives, a studio unemployment conference was organized in January 1938 by delegates from twelve unions and guilds, including the carpenters, cartoonists, directors, electricians, plasterers, publicists, set designers, and writers. The chairman of the conference was a radical young painter with a fighter's build and a broken nose named Herbert K. Sorrell, a man of earthy, warm integrity who commanded great respect among the studio back-lot workers. The studios took note of Sorrell as a man to remember, and he was. Eight years later he led a strike against IATSE domination of back-lot workers that was the bloodiest, most violent confrontation ever seen in the movie kingdom.

At the conference it was pointed out that writers were responsible for 8.2 percent of movie costs but that the technical end was responsible for 17.4 percent, stars and principals accounted for 22.7 percent, miscellaneous costs 23.2 percent, and general overhead 18.7 percent. In other words, the biggest cost drain seemed to be the producers' pockets. By blaming progressives for the loss of Italian markets, slowdowns, and unemployment, and by accusing them of communist tactics, the studios hoped to discredit them not only in the unions but throughout the industry.

Charles Katz, lawyer for both Harry Bridges and Jeff Kibre, said that the Communist Party played a constructive role during this period by trying to caution people such as Kibre against moving too rapidly. The CP was concerned that any gains the progressive unions might make would be lost because of the internal rebellion the studios were trying to foment, to turn the rank and file against their more radical brothers.

Over the next few years, the progressives of the IATSE, like those of the SWG, the Anti-Nazi League, and the Joint Anti-Fascist Refugee Committee, were all accused by the forces of reaction of being front organizations. "The term *front group*," said Elizabeth Spector, "is not a Party term. It was a derogatory term devised by outside elements. Organizations such as the Joint Anti-Fascist Refugee Committee had goals that were also desirable to the CP and the progressive majority, and most active progressives were involved in the antifascist movement. In any organization that the CP participated in, they worked solely for the aims of the organization. Over a period, Party members might have become dominant individuals, but they weren't using the organization to mask goals of the CP. The Party felt that, by working with other people on what there was agreement about, there was a chance to influence thinking."

On April 12, 1937, the NLRB decided that the movie industry was indeed engaged in interstate commerce but would not make a final ruling on the Screen Writers Guild until further testimony and arguments could be heard. Meanwhile, nearly all of the industry's labor groups, encouraged by the ruling, were clamoring for NLRB elections—particularly the IATSE Progressives. But no decisions about these elections could be made until after the additional SWG hearings, scheduled for May, and the board's final decision, to be announced by June. In the meantime, news of the labor unrest in both Los Angeles and San Francisco was disturbing enough for the NLRB executive secretary, Nate Witt, to visit California in March 1938.

When Witt arrived in Los Angeles, he was visited by representatives of several different unions. Representing the Screen Writers Guild were Lillian Hellman, Dashiell Hammett, and Donald Ogden Stewart. Witt remembered that Hellman talked a lot of politics and was "immersed in the minutiae of it, but not really on top of it." He thought Stewart, though charming and funny, hardly seemed like a tactician. Of the three, Hammett was the one Witt respected as being the most politically astute.

Witt found that Towne Nylander, director of the regional NLRB, and William Walsh were the subject of much complaint. Cases had been lying around the regional office for a year with no action. There were many suspicions about the two, but it was impossible to find out whether Nylander and Walsh were on the payrolls of the producers, were corrupt, or were merely ambitious. But after Witt's visit, a close watch was kept on the Los Angeles Regional Labor Board, and the suspicions turned out to be not far from wrong.

Hollywood denizens continued to be swept up in a delirious frenzy of activity. Between antifascist work and union organizing, with all their related activities, there was practically no time for work. This united-front period was suffused with excitement for left-wingers, and many people joined the Communist Party at this time. "Politics was the only thing my father liked in Hollywood," Sam Ornitz's son Arthur recalled. "Without politics it was just a small provincial village where he could make a living."

The sense of being insiders that the Party members had at this time was a valuable tool in recruiting people who had hitherto remained fellow travelers. "I was having a party," recalled Bobby Lees, "and Paul Jarrico followed me into the john. He asked me if I had ever thought of joining the Party. And I said, 'Who joins the Party?' And he said, 'Everyone in your living room, including your collaborator.' I must say that another reason I joined was that from 1939 on, the Party was right on everything, calling all the shots. Within the Party, I had more of a social than a political function. I had no fights with anybody. I had a big house. I was sort of a common denominator; I kept everything friendly."

"I joined the Party for a little while," recalled Roy Huggins. "They gave you meaningless things to read—nobody would know what it meant until somebody told you the Party line. Everyone was unembarrassed by the changes in the Party line, even though it created occasional absurdities. I believed, for a while, that the Party was the only force capable of counteracting this country's trend toward reaction and isolationism. But I couldn't stay in. Lapsed Catholics make bad communists—it's too much like the Church. I would have remained better off as a fellow traveler."

In Hollywood, politics pervaded the air like some heady perfume. At the writers' hangouts—Musso and Frank's, Lucye's, the CineGrill Bar, the Trap, even in the gambling dens of Eddie Nealis's Clover Club—people wondered if the Loyalist forces would be able to hold off the fascists and protect the road to Madrid. Of all the places writers congregated during the late thirties, the bookshops seemed the most popular. And just because liquor wasn't served, that was no reason not to hang out there. People brought their own.

The Stanley Rose bookshop, right next to Musso and Frank's on Hollywood Boulevard, was favored by the higher-paid, less political writers. The principal activity at Stanley Rose's was drinking, and the back room was filled with couches occupied by such legendary Hollywood drinkers as Gene Fowler, Horace McCoy, and William Faulkner. Stanley Rose was, according to several writers, a self-styled con man from Texas with a passionate devotion to literature. Peddling books in the writers' buildings at the studios, Rose became intimate with the underside of Hollywood life. He knew everyone and everything and subsequently became a literary agent. Beyond its political function, the bookshop was a social center, almost a café in a town that was sadly lacking in cafés. The shop had a club, called the Book of the Day Club, which sponsored monthly lectures by writers such as Christopher Isherwood, Aldous Huxley, and Bennett Cerf. Sometimes as many as a hundred people would crowd into the little back room.

It was a time when the lines were clearly delineated between writers and producers, and the Left was clearly in favor of the writers. The bookstore people became particularly close to the writers as time went on, and grew sensitive to their situation in the studios because they used to make so many book deliveries there—ten times a day to Paramount, twice a day to MGM—and they would hear from angry Guild members the latest tactics the companies were using against the writers.

"I remember," said Stanley Rose, "on Christmas Eve 1938 my assistant and I were in the car, working late delivering Christmas books. We were angry because the studios were trying to cut wages again because of the slowdown in production, and we were saying how unfair it was to writers like Trumbo and Stewart. And then we got hysterical, realizing how angry we were for Trumbo and Stewart when we were only making eighteen dollars a week at the bookstore."

The bookstores were among the few places where writers from different studios and different income brackets could mingle. The geographic distances between the studios, and their feudal structures within the little kingdom, tended to create such intense boundaries that generally Fox writers knew only other Fox writers, and MGM people saw only colleagues from Culver City. The economic hierarchy in the studios was such that highly paid writers saw little of the lower-paid ones, and the famous writers' tables in the commissaries were filled with the big names and were gazed at longingly by the little writers. The Moss Harts, George Kaufmans, and their kind, the ones known as the "glamour boys," were actually rather removed from the Hollywood scene in general, and from the struggle of the Screen Writers Guild in particular. Their sojourns in Hollywood were never long enough to engage them in any political activities, apart from the occasional fund-raisers.

These fund-raisers were another route in the late thirties by which the barriers between writers could be broken down. To raise money for antifascist causes, committees like the Anti-Nazi League and the Motion Picture Artists Committee (MPAC)—president, Dashiell Hammett, vice-president, Sylvia Sidney—were founded. At these fetes, regardless of how politically Left someone was, the known and the unknown actor and writer could—for a contribution to the people of Loyalist Spain or struggling China—meet nearly everyone worth meeting in Hollywood.

One such benefit, sponsored by the Motion Picture Artists Committee at the home of Mr. and Mrs. Ira Gershwin, was hostessed by Eve Arden, Fanny Brice, Miriam Hopkins, Luise Rainer, Gale Sondergaard, Dorothy Parker, Jean Rouverol Butler, Dorshka Raphaelson, Mrs. Sidney Buchman, Mrs. Jay Gorney, and Karen Morley. With accomplishments that included the purchasing and equipping of eighteen ambulances for Hemingway to take to Spain and the raising of $1,500 at a benefit dinner for Medical Aid to China, the MPAC claimed that "to many people in many parts of the world, the MPAC's achievements have been the most vital of any created in Hollywood."

At the center of the romantic excitement about the war in Spain was the Abraham Lincoln Brigade, a volunteer unit of Americans who went to Spain to aid the Loyalists. By February 1937, three thousand volunteers had sneaked across the French-Spanish border to help defend the road to Madrid. Screen writer Alvah Bessie and Jim Lardner, the brother of Ring, Jr., actually went to Spain with the Lincoln Brigade, and four whole blocks of Hollywood were closed off for a money-raising bazaar for the brigade volunteers. Almost half of the brigade were killed, including Lardner's brother, and it came as a great shock to people in Hollywood. As romantic as they were about the war in Spain, it seemed a cause in which they could believe but one that they would not be hurt by. The deaths of the volunteers brought the combat uncomfortably close to home.

Apart from the shock of the deaths in Spain, the morale in Hollywood remained splendid. It was a great time to be prosperous, young, and progressive in the movie kingdom. You could buy a used Pierce-Arrow sedan for

Alvah Bessie, 1939, was a member of the Abraham Lincoln Brigade in Spain.

$500 and install your ménage in a three-bedroom farmhouse on an acre of land in fashionable Brentwood, near Leland Hayward and Margaret Sullavan, for only $19,500. You could live better than nine-tenths of the nation yet remain, through political activity, intimately connected to the pulse of humanity.

The optimism of the progressive community was reinforced and apotheosized by an event that allowed them to feel the power of the united front by actual participation. The event was the *Hollywood Citizen News* strike in June 1938. The strike grew out of the petty political opportunism of its publisher, "Judge" Harlan Palmer. (He had once been a justice of the peace and liked the title.) Palmer had been a reformer-liberal until 1938, and had run for district attorney as a reformer and lost. Whether it was his political defeat or his antagonism toward the American Newspaper Guild (which, with NLRB backing, had negotiated a new contract with him and then, when he petulantly refused to sign it and fired three of his top ANG staff members, went on strike), Judge Palmer shed his "liberal coat," as he called it, and became an overnight reactionary.

Palmer found himself totally without support. Labor and the Left were on the side of the strikers, as was the grass-roots community. The big newspaper owners like Hearst and Chandler (of the *Los Angeles Examiner* and *Times* respectively) were pleased at the chance to squeeze the troublesome Palmer out of business. His previous praise of Russia and labor had alienated them, as had his presence as a staunch, small businessman in a fraternity of conglomerates.

Hearst personally ordered the *Examiner*'s managing editor to make contributions to the strike fund, and the response throughout the Hollywood community was overwhelming. On the first day of the strike the picket lines were bolstered by members of the SAG and the SWG led by Robert Montgomery, Frank Capra, and Philip Dunne. The longshoremen rallied to the lines, and the CIO, particularly the radical CIO-based Non-Partisan League, jumped in after them. Among the eight members of the state legislature who came to the strike were radicals John B. Tenney and Sam Yorty (later mayor of Los Angeles), the only two state assemblymen to protest Roosevelt's embargo on munitions to Spain. In those glorious moments, nobody could have predicted that within three years these two would be the leaders of the reactionary State Un-American Activities Committee.

To the grass-roots left-wing community, which had suffered terrible persecution under the repressive regime of police captain William "Red" Hynes (who, with his Red Squad, had ruled Los Angeles like an S.S. elite, conducting periodical purges of "Reds" and "Pinks" in such fields as teaching and the clergy), this was a chance to join in a protest whose celebrity picketers would preclude the use of Hynes's usual tactics of tear gas and clubs to break up left-wing demonstrations.

Little Jewish ladies from Boyle Heights in shawls and laden with food-filled shopping bags for the strikers found themselves rubbing shoulders with the well-coiffed upper-crust ladies from the League of Women Voters. Attorneys from the National Lawyers Guild came down, and Herb Sorrell of the painters' union talked his impassioned strike talk. The wedding of such disparate elements captured the imagination of Hollywood's intellectual community.

The strike reached its high points on Saturday nights, when the picket lines would move from the back street off Hollywood Boulevard, where the *News*'s offices were, right onto the boulevard, the most visible place to be on any Saturday night in Los Angeles. By nine o'clock the street in front of Grauman's Chinese Theater would be filled with two to three thousand people. It was like a carnival with gimmicks, booths, and costumes. Money poured into the strike fund from every source. The strike lifted everybody . . . except the *Citizen News*.

It destroyed Harlan Palmer. With his political hopes dashed and his union against him, Palmer became a hysterical inversion of his former liberal self. He signed a contract, and the strikers—who numbered only about fifteen —went back to work. Palmer became a paranoid recluse and his paper was left a crippled shell, functioning in its final years as a reactionary house organ for Tenney and the Un-American Activities Committee.

The strike had its rewards in several spheres. It helped to reunite the remnants of the End Poverty in California organization behind Culbert Olson, who was elected governor on the Democratic ticket in 1938 under the slogan "United Front Against Fascism." It helped to sweep out the L.A. Police Department and get progressive mayor Fletcher Bowron elected. It strengthened the progressive element of labor in Los Angeles. Spiritually, it exhilarated everyone who had participated. It was the dream of the New Deal become a reality, symbolizing a common spirit and concern. Nobody wanted to look for flaws in the triumph. But the strike would not have been so successful had it not been for the support of the larger papers, glad to destroy the competition.

The exhilarating local events in the summer of 1938 could not mask the fact that the impact of the world situation on Hollywood was becoming more and more noticeable. The influence was, of course, obvious in terms of social life, for the fund-raisers for Spain and China continued. Less immediately obvious, though more dangerous, was the influence of the European situation on the product being manufactured in Hollywood's dream factories.

Mussolini had formed a motion picture triple alliance with Berlin and Tokyo and had issued a list of ten "don'ts" to the Hollywood studios desiring an Italian market. At the top of the list was "Don't ridicule dictators." Charlie

Chaplin's *Modern Times* had already been banned in all three countries for its merciless satire of fascism, which Il Duce found as offensive as movies that gave criminals Italian names or made light of marital relations (two more of the "don'ts"). Furthermore, Mussolini's campaign for a fecund society to bring forth hordes of healthy little fascisti precluded his acceptance of any films that questioned the rectitude and necessity of bringing children into the world. If Hollywood was going to do business with the Japanese, the Germans, and the Italians, it was going to have to concentrate on bland escapist fantasy.

The month of June was marked by a shocking national drought in product as exhibitors across the country suddenly found themselves without films to show. New York theater owners were in a panic as they faced the prospect of closing their doors for the summer months. Everybody had his own explanation of the product shortage. Warner Bros., one of the few studios with a major hit (*The Adventures of Robin Hood*, starring Errol Flynn), claimed that the other studios were holding back their good pictures for the autumn, hoarding the gold during the natural summer box-office drop-off.

The fault was partially that of the exhibitors, who had been offering bigger and better double features in an effort to lure the movie-going public away from the low-cost excellence of WPA theater and the constantly improving fare on the radio. With all of the "A" pictures used up, they were left with a short supply and lower-quality merchandise.

Curiously enough, it seemed that everyone had forgotten, or neglected to draw the conclusion, that a product shortage might be the inevitable result of the slowdown in production and the paring of the work force that the studios had effected in the winter of 1937–38. The only ones who seemed to remember were those troublemaking labor agitators with their "direct line to the Kremlin." In June 1938 the *Daily Worker* published a series of articles entitled "Who Owns the Movies—Who Owns You?" in which they charged the producers with exaggerating conditions in order to "beat down salaries":

> Company by company, Hollywood is dominated by the same vicious banking circles that have collaborated on capital's "sit-down" strike and sabotage in steel, public utilities, automobiles, railroads, and in the light and heavy industries. . . . Furthermore, the story of the sad financial plight of the studios is an exaggerated tale to forestall a pending federal investigation into the monopoly practices of the Hollywood magnates. . . .
>
> The total profits for the Hollywood producers for 1937 totalled approximately $40,000,000. It is apparent, on the basis of the financial reports of the companies, that there was no reason for the wholesale dismissal of hundreds upon hundreds of film workers from the ranks; or for the disgraceful wage cutting; or for the amazing lull in studio pro-

duction which was one of the most important phenomena in Hollywood during the past winter season.

That phenomenon, which amounts to Hollywood's version of finance capital's acknowledged "sit-down strike," caused almost a 40% cessation of picture production on the studio lots, and was one of the major factors in the producer-made panic that is now afflicting the film capital.

W. W. Wilkerson, articulating the producers' point of view in his *Hollywood Reporter,* found it convenient to blame the lack of product on writers who were fighting instead of writing:

> What has this great industry done to all of you that you must throw down your work, march in picket lines, go into frenzies about the injustice that is done to you, pack into meetings with speechmaking, arm-waving, searching for the power to kill the very business that has made many of you rich, most of you luxuriously comfortable, and has given all of you homes, motorcars, pleasant surroundings, and the finest opportunity ever offered to anyone to progress? What's wrong with this business that breeds such discontent among its creators?

The producer-power establishment was aghast when the National Labor Relations Board had ruled, on June 7, 1938, that the screen writers were indeed employees under the provisions of the Wagner Act, defining an employee as a worker who has no control over his or her final product, functioning in an industry engaged in interstate commerce. A certification election was specified for June 28 in which the writers would be able to vote for the organization they wished to represent them—either the Screen Writers Guild or the Screen Playwrights.

The SWG had, a month earlier, reorganized its corporation, making it the Screen Writers Guild, Inc., a California corporation affiliated with the Authors League of America; this offered greater protection for personal liability than the previous corporation, which had been a California branch of the ALA, a New York corporation. The complete local autonomy of the reorganized Guild was intended to quell, once and for all, the hysteria about Eastern domination.

The NLRB ruling had been a stunning, ecstatic victory for the Guild, whose membership had been growing that spring while the power of the SP seemed to be waning. The NLRB had already recommended the invalidation of the prior Screen Playwrights contract with the studios, and writers were leaving the SP for the SWG "like shits leaving a sinking rat," as Dalton Trumbo put it.

By June the Screen Writers Guild had 75 percent of the town's working writers on its roster. Unfortunately, only a small percentage of Guild members were working at any one time, and the NLRB had ruled that only writers working as of June 4 would be eligible to vote in the election, which meant that a sizable portion of Guild members couldn't vote, while nearly all of the SP's remaining members were considered eligible since they were under studio contract. So in the weeks before the election, the feuding organizations were zealously recruiting members, each hoping for as large a vote as possible.

Frances Goodrich recalled the afternoon of the NLRB ruling: "There was that funny party up in Dash's [Hammett's] rooms at the Beverly Wilshire Hotel—it was a big suite that had been occupied by the President of Mexico, or some shah, something like that. It was a big place and Dashiell Hammett was about six foot two—as you got off the elevator and looked down the hall, he was standing in the doorway, and even he looked like a little boy because the place was so huge. Everybody was coming up there and ordering a drink, getting people to come in there and talk, getting them to join the SWG. Lillian Hellman came out of a room where she'd been talking to a writer named Talbot Jennings, a big writer at MGM who did some additional dialogue for Shakespeare in *Romeo and Juliet*. And poor Lillian came out of the room and said, 'Well, if I get Talbot Jennings to join this thing, somebody's got to pay for the abortion.'

"Dottie Parker was in another room talking to a writer named Everett Freeman, trying to get him to join the Guild, and he said he didn't think any creative writer should belong to a union," added Albert Hackett, "and Dottie simply could not stand that and she lost her patience. 'That sonofabitch, telling me that *he's* a creative writer! If he's a creative writer, I'm Marie of Rumania.' "

Wilkerson was not to be gracious about the triumph of the recalcitrant writers. He continued to shriek in the *Hollywood Reporter* that between internecine warfare and meddling in issues such as Spain and China, the writers were forgetting their job—to write movies.

The International Alliance of Theatrical Stage Employees agreed with the producers that the NLRB had no right to classify the screen writers as employees. Two weeks before the writers' certification election, at a national meeting in Cleveland, IATSE president George Browne presented a petition to the NLRB asking it to withdraw all protection from Hollywood's creative guilds and asking the AFL to withdraw charters and other support it had given to "so-called guilds, falsely parading as labor organizations," labeling them a "mockery on organized labor which creates dangerous resentments over their pretensions to be classed in the ranks of American labor."

Browne predicted a swelling in IATSE jurisdiction that would increase its nationwide membership from 60,000 to over half a million. Willie Bioff, whose boldness remained despite the publication of his rather seamy credentials, ominously stated, "We expect to be in Hollywood within the next two or three weeks, at which time we will insist on our jurisdiction. This includes everything and everyone that goes into the making of motion pictures, from actors, writers and directors . . . up and down. . . ."

SWG president Dudley Nichols immediately took out a full-page ad in the *Hollywood Reporter*:

> The IATSE is a very real menace . . . writers will find themselves in a boss-ruled union overnight if they stand alone. . . . IATSE can never take over writers if writers stand shoulder to shoulder with the actors' and directors' guilds, and these guilds stand with the SWG and not with the SP. Therefore, a vote for the Playwrights, or a vote for no representation at all, is a vote for the IATSE.

A mass meeting was held at the Hollywood Athletic Club to further defy the IATSE. Dudley Nichols opened the meeting by saying that the IATSE and the producers were in collusion. John Howard Lawson stated that the producers were determined to gradually but definitely scale down salaries until they were at the same level as those of newspaper writers and that no writer, regardless of how high his salary, was in any position to stand alone. It was a rousing meeting, Lawson's voice echoing through the auditorium, punctuated by the sound of smacks as he plunged his fist into his palm. Franchot Tone brought a pro-SWG message from the Screen Actors Guild; Lewis Milestone, Rouben Mamoulian, and Willard Van Dyke brought the greetings and congratulations of the Screen Directors Guild. The air grew hotter with excitement each time another respected member of the movie industry threw support to the SWG.

John Bright recalled making a speech about the domination of the IATSE gangsters and said that he was listened to with considerable respect because "they assumed I had that kind of savvy, since I had been a crime reporter in Chicago. I knew about Bioff and Browne before they came to Hollywood, from the days they first became personages through their connections with the rackets."

SWG vice-president Charles Brackett read a long policy statement calling for the cooperation of all studio labor groups, though the Guild was against affiliation with either the AFL or the CIO at this time. This policy statement was unanimously upheld by the four hundred writers in attendance.

An article in the *Motion Picture Herald* on June 11 discussed the IATSE convention in Cleveland. The Screen Playwrights, furious that the IATSE statement would also hurt them, since they agreed with the producers that screen writers could not be classified as employees, held their own bitter meeting at the Beverly Wilshire. They were damned if they would help the NLRB accomplish this election. They refused to show the labor board their membership lists so that it could be determined who was eligible to vote. The producers claimed that the NLRB election was illegal and that if it took place, it would be without their assistance. And they refused the board's request for

lists of writers under contract. The Screen Playwrights was ultimately pressured into joining the Screen Writers Guild in presenting its roster.

In the weeks until the election, open letters and accusations appeared in the trade papers. The charges that political activism interfered with movie production were followed, shadow-style, by innuendos about the left-wing conspiracy to wreck the industry. The IATSE adopted a resolution to fight propaganda in motion pictures "glorifying any other form of government than that of the U.S., which might weaken our faith in democracy." The sentiment was both antifascist and anticommunist, quoting the *Daily Worker*'s exhortation that Hollywood make movies of "the kind that carry the message of international security and peace"; the *Motion Picture Herald* inferred that meant "the Communist kind."

Blockade, a Walter Wanger production, with a script by John Howard Lawson, had just been released by United Artists, and this Spanish Civil War saga, sympathetic to the Loyalist cause but less an active polemic than a temperate appeal to the conscience of the world to stop the bombing of civilian populations, was under siege. Catholic priests denounced the film from their pulpits, the Knights of Columbus in Omaha, Rochester, and other cities succeeded in either barring or delaying the film's release in local theaters, and the Boston city council, joining protesting Catholic laymen, asked the mayor to ban the picture.

The reaction was wildly out of proportion to the film's statement, which was too mild to serve any propagandistic purpose.

Screen writer Frank Nugent, then a reporter and critic, wrote in the *New York Times* on July 6, 1938:

> The haste with which [the film's] opponents clamored for its withdrawal, for its boycott, and for other punitive measures is dangerously symptomatic of a growing appetite to suppress any opinion running counter to one's own. . . . Most of us have been urging Hollywood to descend occasionally from its cloud-tipped mountainpeak, look at the world beneath, and make some comment upon the contemporary scene. If every bold producer who does so is to be repaid by misinterpretation, picketed theatres, and abuse, it is obvious that the road from the mountain will be closed for good.

"If a picture as neutral as *Blockade* can run into such opposition," wrote *The Nation*, "what hope is there for freedom or maturity of expression in Hollywood-made movies?"

While *Blockade* was breaking box-office records in London, it opened in New York at Radio City Music Hall and was picketed by Catholic clergy and laymen.

John Howard Lawson had become Hollywood's *bête rouge*, and the producers who hated his union-organizing and political activism, as well as the IATSE, which despised his watchfulness and his alliance with radical labor leaders such as Harry Bridges and Jeff Kibre, were ready to attack anything he was associated with. Lawson had collaborated with Budd Schulberg on a script based on correspondent Vincent Sheean's *Personal History*. Walter Wanger, the film's producer, wrote a letter to Secretary of State Cordell Hull telling of how spies had tried to invade the studio during the production of this "pro-democratic work"; because of intense pressures, Wanger postponed his plans to film the script. The Sheean project was shelved indefinitely, and producers at all of the studios became very wary of any project that in any way involved politics.

As the NLRB election drew closer, the venom grew more toxic. The *Hollywood Reporter* wrote: "You ladies and gentlemen who are gumming up the works with your speechmaking and lust for power, drop Hollywood and its industry and take a boat for London, for Rome, for Paris, or even Budapest." To come right out and call the Screen Writers Guild communist would be libelous, and besides, its chief officers, Dudley Nichols and Charles Brackett, were among the most highly respected workers in Hollywood, and both were politically unimpeachable.

MGM was the pivotal studio in the writers' war. It employed twice the number of writers as the next largest studio. Neither the Screen Writers Guild nor the Screen Playwrights had a clear majority there, since there was a large group of nonaffiliated writers. The SP and the producers were leaning heavily on the independents to join their side, and the SP campaign barely bothered with any other studio, since it looked as if the SWG could carry all of them.

A big surprise, at this time, was the discovery that short-subject film writers would be considered full-fledged writers, eligible to vote in the election. This was both a shock and a revelation, since their in-between status had kept them out of both the SWG and the SP. "When it had been determined that the lowly shorts writers counted in the election," said Bobby Lees, "we became important because we controlled so many votes. There were thirty-nine short-subject writers at MGM. John Lee Mahin started wooing the shorts department, and it was like Delta rush."

Three polling places were set up for the June 28 voting: the Roosevelt Hotel's Singapore Room, for employees at Paramount, RKO, Columbia, Walter Wanger, Goldwyn, Monogram, and Armour; 3855 Lankershim Boulevard for Warner Bros., Universal, Republic, and Trem Carr personnel; and the council chamber at Culver City Hall for those at MGM, 20th Century–Fox, Selznick, and Hal Roach studios.

Prior to the voting, writers were sent affidavits, which were to be notarized, on which they were to indicate if they had been under contract on June 4, and where. The producers, meanwhile, erecting obstacles with perverse ingenuity, had refused to put up the posters announcing the time, place, and details of the election.

Nevertheless, by the time the registration polls closed on Saturday, nearly 350 writers were signed up.

While a Screen Writers Guild rally was being held on Monday, election eve, in the Blossom Room of the Roosevelt Hotel, Hollywood was buzzing with talk of the visit that eight heads of major studios had paid to the White House the previous Saturday afternoon for an audience with President Roosevelt. FDR's pleasant reception had soothed the executives' anxieties about the proposed inquiry into the industry's monopolistic practices, and the writers in town couldn't help wondering aloud if it was mere coincidence that had brought Loew's head, Nicholas Schenck, to Hyde Park the previous Wednesday, accompanied by a delegation bearing a sizable check. Schenck claimed that he had gone there on an unrelated errand and that the check was for charity.

On Tuesday, the polls opened at noon. The first vote had already been cast by screen writer Robert Ardrey, who had dropped his absentee ballot at Towne Nylander's office on his way out of town on Thursday. Each organization had checkers at the polling booths, ready to contest unauthorized voters. Frances Goodrich took a particular delight in being the SWG watchdog at the Culver City Hall location. Just as Jean Harlow's mother was about to drop her secret vote into the ballot box, Goodrich stopped her and yelled, "Challenge!" Mrs. Harlow wailed. "Doesn't anyone know me around here?" as if being the mother of a top MGM star automatically made her a writer.

The Screen Playwrights was also being contentiously vigilant. Robert Benchley, the small, round, blue-eyed humorist whose *Treasurer's Report* had led to a score of other Benchley shorts (including *The Sex Life of the Polyp*), was challenged by the SP, but he dropped his ballot in the box determinedly, snorting, "The hell with you, you Knickerbocker Grey!"

The Screen Writers Guild swept the studios. Billy Wilder remembers that the writers were hanging around the Roosevelt Hotel, waiting for the results. He came in from the NLRB office, where he had been an SWG counter, and as soon as he walked in a cheer went up, because they knew, just from looking at his face, that the Guild had won. The vote was more than four-to-one in favor of the Guild.

The producers hadn't realized how conducive the secret ballot would be to pro-Guild sentiment. The years of threats and intimidation had only emboldened the scribes once they were shrouded in protective anonymity. Even at MGM, the vote for the Guild ran two-to-one over the SP. The closest voting was at Paramount, where the Guild squeaked by with a lead of only three votes.

"The Screen Playwrights made the mistake of not courting young writers," commented Milton Sperling. "They forgot it wouldn't be a class vote, but a democratic vote. The SP were more interested in quality than in quantity when it came to the writers. They were interested in the status of their members, not their number. They made a lot of enemies."

To the great pleasure of the Screen Writers Guild, an NLRB ruling required all producers to post the election results throughout the studios. The day after the elections, however, the SP had conceded nothing.

"Regardless of today's elections," claimed John Lee Mahin in an open letter to all screen writers published in the *Hollywood Reporter*, "no writer will be forced to join any organization."

Then he dragged out statements made by Nichols and Lawson at the SWG meeting two weeks earlier, in which Nichols had said, in response to Wilkerson's denunciation of writers' involvement in politics, "Who can name any great writer in the history of literature who did not take sides as best he dared in the important causes and conflicts of his day?" Mahin countered this statement by making the claim, once again, that the Screen Playwrights believed that writers as a group should concern themselves only with professional problems. Raising the bogeyman of "vague" (i.e., left-wing) politics, Mahin said that the SWG would coerce people into joining, and he called the NLRB a purely administrative body with "possibly fallible members." The SP was going to take the case to the Supreme Court if necessary, and Mahin again denounced Nichols's accusation that the SP was a company union.

The day after the election, NLRB counsel William Walsh claimed that the Screen Playwrights contract with the studios was valid and could not be nullified by the certification. The Screen Writers Guild had, he said, won only the right to operate that five-year Code between the SP and the studios, which had until April 1942 to run. The Guild was, however, entitled to arbitrate credits under the Code.

Suspicions that had been raised when Nate Witt visited the L.A. regional office that Nylander and Walsh were sympathetic to the studios had now been inadvertently confirmed by Walsh. Nylander, looking disheveled, raged at his associate, who left soon after to become chief counsel to the producers. Nylander knew he was ruined. He issued a statement that no member of his local staff had the authority to render an opinion on the validity of the Screen Playwrights contract.

One by one, the producers filed protests with the NLRB, asserting that their rights had been violated. Nylander wanted no more hand-to-hand combat in his regional office, so he sent the argument straight to Washington.

It seemed as if the Screen Writers Guild had lost in winning, and the producers felt pretty cocky about stuffing defeat into the jaws of the writers' victory. But on July 20, their triumph turned to terror. A blockbusting anti-trust action was filed against Paramount, Loew's, RKO, Warner Bros., 20th Century–Fox, Columbia, Universal, and United Artists. The suit would drag on for ten years, but at its end it would necessitate the dissolution of the

Motion Picture Technicians Committee
P. O. BOX 2765, HOLLYWOOD   **SEPTEMBER 15, 1938**

TO ALL IATSE MEMBERS
Greetings:

Once the truth behind the headlines involving the I. A. — The charges of company unionism, bribery of officials, the return of autonomy . . .

You fellow members of the IATSE have all read the charges which have been filed with the National Labor Relations Board against Bioff, Browne and the producers' association.

The formal accusation has been made by Jeff Kibre of Local 37 that Bioff took $100,000 graft from Joseph M. Schenck, president of the producers' association, in return for which the IA locals were turned into company unions which have been going through the motions of collective bargaining.

Anybody who thinks that the IA locals are not company unions or that their members have ever enjoyed the production-distribution-exhibition concentration that had centralized the powers of the studios into a monopoly. It was the first time that the economic sovereignty of the little kingdom had ever really been under siege, and in some irrational way the producers held the writers responsible for this situation.

Then, in September, Jeff Kibre filed a complaint with the NLRB formally accusing Bioff and Browne of receiving a $100,000 grant from the producers' association. Over the next few months, evidence was produced that the International Alliance of Theatrical Stage Employees, threatening producers with a shutdown of all the projectionists, had extorted between $25,000 and $50,000 from each studio. There was testimony describing suitcases filled with cash brought to Bioff and Browne's IATSE suite at the Warwick Hotel in New York. Joseph M. Schenck had been the policy maker, the industry spokesman who had made the deal with Bioff.

The producers claimed that they had been victims of extortion, but their payments had also been part of a deal to keep IATSE wages low and stable during the years of great gains for labor. The matter ended with Schenck, Bioff, and Browne in jail and increased executives' hatred for the radical leadership of Kibre, Lawson, and others whom they felt had been responsible for putting one of their leaders in jail, thus disgracing the entire industry.

For the first time it seemed that the kingdom's rulers could not control what was happening to their world. They firmly believed that this assault had been brought on by sabotage within the kingdom, which had weakened it and actually invited invasion from the outside world. "You've taken your trade problems into the open and the public has become your judge on matters it can never understand," mourned the *Hollywood Reporter* on June 18, 1938. The heads of the industry were tough, brutal businessmen who believed in revenge. And they knew who was responsible for what had occurred. All they had to do was look to the Left.

7

There was a great flurry of activity as the industry attempted to return to normal, and by the autumn of 1938, an all-time high in production was slated, with seventy films rolling at once. There was a renaissance in short subjects, now that the double bill had proved a drain on the supply of features. The movie companies acknowledged the fact that their European markets were steadily and irrevocably eroding, and they accepted the presence of radio in American life as a power that had made a definitive assault on movie-going.

Nevertheless, too much time, energy, and prestige had been consumed in Hollywood's civil wars. The public faith in the motion picture industry had to be repaired, if not restored. The year 1939 brought forth such a host of triumphant cinematic achievements that despite *Gone With the Wind*'s sweep of the Academy Awards, it hardly seemed fair to choose one top film when the competition included *Stagecoach, Mr. Smith Goes to Washington, Wuthering Heights, Ninotchka, The Wizard of Oz,* and *The Hunchback of Notre Dame.*

Ironically, *Gone With the Wind* was a consummate example of the sort of treatment that the writers had been protesting since they had first organized, for this film went through writers and discarded them with astonishingly cavalier extravagance. Even F. Scott Fitzgerald had been called in for two weeks of work on the project, to perfect Rhett and Scarlett's first stairway scene. In a way, this was a perfect symbol for the situation in which the Screen Writers Guild now found itself, for despite the outward appearances, as far as writers were concerned very little actually had changed.

"The Screen Writers Guild faced a very discouraging time after the NLRB election," recalled Ring Lardner, Jr. "We had discovered that getting the right to be bargaining agents didn't give us bargaining *power,* and writers were still not close enough to the actual process of production to make an effective strike."

On August 8, 1938, a reply came from the National Labor Relations Board in response to Towne Nylander's forwarded list of producers' protests. The reply stated quite simply that the Screen Writers Guild had been certified as the collective bargaining agent for writers in the motion picture industry and that unless the producers wanted to be in violation of the Wagner Act, they had to start negotiating a contract with the Guild. So a month later, the producers and representatives of the Guild began bargaining. Two small committees and their lawyers sat down at the negotiating table, and the Guild insisted on having a reporter there to note down the proceedings. They did not expect the battle to be an easy one.

The first negotiation session took place at the Beverly Wilshire Hotel. Representing the producers were Darryl Zanuck, Eddie Mannix, and B. B. Kahane and their lawyers, who included Homer Mitchell and Mendel Silberberg. The writers present were Charles Brackett, who headed the committee, Donald Ogden Stewart, Anthony Veiller, and their counsel, Leonard Janofsky.

Janofsky said that it must be understood that the Screen Writers Guild was the exclusive bargaining agent for writers in Hollywood, to which Zanuck replied that the whole reason for getting together was to try to reach an agreement and to avoid technical and legal questions that had kept writers and producers apart for so many months. "We don't want lawsuits," said Zanuck. "We don't want technical questions that will take us years to decide."

Janofsky replied that the Guild wouldn't discuss anything until it was accepted as the exclusive bargaining agent. The writers left the room to caucus, and one hour later Janofsky returned and said, "Unless you see it our way and recognize that we are the exclusive bargaining agents for writers, there is nothing further to discuss."

Zanuck reiterated his claim that it was a technical point, whereupon the writers walked out. Kahane later called Anthony Veiller to tell him that he thought Janofsky had acted stupidly in walking out of the meeting. But the writers felt they had no other choice. "Most of the other members of the committee were shocked by the producers' intransigence," said Stewart, "but I wasn't. After all," he joked, "the other writers had never been run over before." (He was referring to the fact that he had been hit by a car nearly two years earlier, an event which some said had addled his brain and accounted for his leftward political shift.)

The stonewalling at this first negotiation session was so blatant—particularly the producers' claim that they couldn't violate the contracts they already had with the Screen Playwrights—that the Guild filed an unfair labor practice charge against the producers. When the Screen Playwrights asked the producers for certain amendments to its contracts, the Guild threatened to file another protest with the NLRB and warned the producers that violations of the Wagner Act were punishable by both fines and imprisonment, adding that any further negotiations between producers and the SP would call for aggressive action by the SWG. The Guild was ready to get an injunction against any more changes in the existing pact between the producers and the Screen Playwrights.

The hostilities between the SWG and the producers flared again when contract renewals were signed. The SWG's board had instructed Guild members to sign contracts when renewals were offered but to attach a rider stating that they were signing under protest with reference to the clause requiring arbitration by the Screen Playwrights of any disputes over screen credits. Mary McCall, Jr., discovered this provision when she checked in at MGM. She objected to signing her new contract unless that clause was eliminated, but the executives refused and told her that if she didn't want to sign, there were plenty of writers who would and who would be friendly to the Playwrights. McCall came before the SWG board to give them this bit of bad news, and it was then that the letter rider was drawn up by Janofsky and approved by the board. The rider was sent to all company heads by writers who signed new contracts or renewals. The companies, however, didn't care.

Henry Myers, who had written "The Screen Writers' Marching Song," deleted the SP arbitration clause when he received his contract at Paramount. Half an hour later, his agent called him, telling him he was endangering himself because he was putting the executives at Paramount in a situation in which they might be sued by the SP. Myers finally agreed to sign his contract with the clause in it, but he insisted it be shown that he was doing so under protest.

The NLRB had assigned a special attorney, Bernard L. Alpert, to handle the Guild's complaints of unfair practices and the producers' refusal to recognize an NLRB certification election, but the Christmas holidays and the work backup made it obvious that no action could be expected until early 1939. So the writers settled back and waited.

While they waited, the arbitration mechanism on credits was still controlled by the Screen Playwrights. When Paramount released a film called *The Lady's from Kentucky*, with screen credits given to Malcolm Stuart Boylan, Sy Bartlett, and Olive Cooper (the last two SWG members), Boylan, a member of the SP, protested, and the SP arbitrated the credit. Boylan was awarded exclusive credit. Anger was building again. The bitter writer dispute was far from over.

That Christmas, progressives in Hollywood and around the country were disturbed by anticommunist tactics that HUAC chairman Martin Dies was using in his climb into the national spotlight. A few months earlier one of his committee members, J. Parnell Thomas, had announced that the Federal Theater

Hallie Flanagan, 1938. She was appointed director of the Federal Theater Project after receiving her master's in theater at Radcliffe and serving as production assistant to George Pierce Baker at his 47 Workshop. J. Parnell Thomas, chairman of HUAC: "Practically every play presented under the auspices of the National Theater Project is sheer propaganda for Communism or the New Deal."

Project was a hotbed of communism and was infested with radicals from top to bottom. Dies claimed that the communists were using it to present propaganda plays and to distribute propaganda in government books, pamphlets, and art works.

The progressives knew that Dies was attempting through his attacks to discredit the New Deal, since he linked New Deal and communist propaganda to the Federal Theater Project. Dies called Hallie Flanagan, head of the project, to testify before his committee, and he told her that plays propagandizing fair labor relations were not making proper use of government funds.

Dies further attempted to discredit New Deal forces by claiming that the Democratic candidates for governor, lieutenant-governor, and senator of California—Culbert Olson, Ellis Patterson, and Sheridan Downey—were in the pocket of the Communist Party. Upton Sinclair, whose tattered End Poverty in California remnants had gathered into the Olson coalition, filed an affidavit just before New Year's Day 1939 to register his belief that he had been smeared by the Dies Committee: "[The reactionaries] find it a cheap and easy method to discredit all advocates of economic reform by calling them Communists."

"Dies had a great deal of support from the AFL," recalled Dorothy Healy, "because the AFL was interested in whatever help Dies could give them in breaking the CIO. The main battleground was between the New Deal and the Republicans—and don't forget, the Republicans made big political gains in 1938. Hearst supported Dies's campaign to remove Harold Ickes, FDR's Secretary of the Interior, attacking Ickes for membership in such subversive organizations as the American Civil Liberties Union."

Ickes, who along with Secretary of Labor Frances Perkins and the NLRB, had come under vicious attack from Dies, labeled him "the outstanding zany in our political history." Telegrams also poured into Frances Perkins's office from friends in Hollywood, led by Sonya Levien, applauding her condemnation of Dies. At the beginning of 1939, there was a coalition of liberals and the Left against Dies, whom they hoped would become a laughingstock and discredit himself.

This did indeed seem a possibility. In the committee report published at the beginning of January 1939, one of Dies's star witnesses, J. B. Matthews, a former communist, testified that "the Communist Party relies heavily upon the carelessness or indifference of thousands of prominent citizens in lending their names for its propaganda purposes. For example, the French newspaper *Ce Soir*, which is owned outright by the Communist Party, recently featured hearty greetings from Clark Gable, Robert Taylor, James Cagney, and Shirley Temple. . . . . None, I hope, is going to claim that any one of these persons in particular is a Communist. The unfortunate fact, however, remains that most of them unwittingly serve, albeit in this slight way, the purposes of the Communist Party. Their names have a definite propaganda value which the party is quick to exploit." Dies pointed out in his report that "the above testimony by Mr. Matthews has never been denied and in fact was admitted by some of the screen stars mentioned."

Dies came to Hollywood in 1938, at which time two angry stars, Fredric March and his wife, Florence Eldridge, countered the accusations of Party activity made by John Leech, a former Communist Party secretary turned informer. "We bought Communist stamps on the corner of Hollywood and

Humphrey Bogart before Chairman Martin Dies (Democrat, Texas) of the House Un-American Activities Committee; James Stedman, committee investigator, and Robert E. Stripling are at center. A committee secretary is at left. August 1940.

Vine," said Florence Eldridge, ridiculing the charges. "That would have been like choosing to visit Broadway and 42nd Street to carry on one's conspiracies." Dies issued a statement to the press clearing the Marches of any charges.

"When Dies came to Hollywood," remembered Maurice Rapf, "he made the mistake of pointing the finger at Shirley Temple. He got a little bit discredited in the industry, except for that group of ex–Screen Playwrights and a few right-wing actors, producers, and directors, who'd later become the Motion Picture Alliance for the Preservation of American Ideals." Dies and J. Parnell Thomas had stumbled on a principle that would become a religion to them in the postwar years: the propaganda value of Hollywood names.

Dies even inspired the comic talents of Donald Ogden Stewart, who wrote a skit called, "When Martin Comes," which Stewart and Dorothy Parker performed in 1940 in L.A.'s Philharmonic Hall. The skit ended on a serious note, because as biting as Stewart's ridicule was, the danger was palpable. Parker closed with this speech:

> The people want democracy—real democracy, Mr. Dies, and they look toward Hollywood to give it to them because they don't get it any more in their newspapers. And that's why you're out here, Mr. Dies—that's why you want to destroy the Hollywood progressive organizations—

because you've got to control this medium if you want to bring fascism to this country . . . we're grateful to Hollywood for our jobs and we're grateful for the opportunity it gives us to speak for American democracy.

When the additional hearings opened before the National Labor Relations Board in March 1939, several things were immediately established. The counsel for the major studios claimed that they recognized the Screen Writers Guild as the exclusive bargaining agent and that a committee consisting of Darryl Zanuck, Eddie Mannix, and Hal Wallis was ready to negotiate with the Guild. On March 9, the NLRB trial examiner recommended the invalidation of collective bargaining contracts between the Screen Playwrights and the producers.

The hearings, which were expected to continue for several weeks, promised the development of sensational testimony on charges by the SWG that producers had used coercion to break up the organization. Sheridan Gibney, a member of the SWG's board, told the *New York Herald Tribune* that the action had been brought by the NLRB itself and not by the Guild, because the producers had refused to recognize NLRB jurisdiction over the motion picture industry. The fact that the move had come from Washington indicated that one of the questions to be determined was that of the power of the NLRB and its right to compel recognition of the Screen Writers Guild as the sole bargaining agency. The producers were threatening to take the matter to the Supreme Court, once again testing the constitutionality of the Wagner Act as it applied to the movie industry.

The writers welcomed this renewed battle. Though it promised to be long and full of fireworks, members of the SWG felt that their struggle was about to be crystallized and that matters affecting the future of the motion picture industry would at last be thrashed out in open court.

The producers' awareness of the seriousness of their position was probably the reason for their quick acknowledgment of the SWG on the second day of court proceedings. They hoped that either the case would be dismissed, based on their sudden acquiescence to the Guild, or that this recognition would at least enable them to stall and to rally their forces. Homer Mitchell, the attorney for Paramount, asked to know the accusations against the producers in advance, so that they could prepare their witnesses and "call them back from Europe if they are away."

The producers did not get a dismissal. What they got was only a two-week postponement to give the parties a chance to work out their differences. The SWG was asking for a guild shop and an end to union busting, provisions for junior writers, a minimum wage scale for writers, and protection of rights to film stories in that new medium that was being perfected—television. Other matters to be aired included interference by executives and studio employees with script material and the studios' frequent practice of engaging writers to submit story treatments on speculation. The writers' negotiating committee was composed of Brackett, Stewart, Philip Dunne, and Janofsky. Writer Anthony Veiller, former member of the negotiations committee, had resigned from the Guild to accept an executive position with Paramount. The producers were represented by Zanuck, Hal Wallis, and Mannix, with attorneys Homer Mitchell, Alfred Wright, George Cohen, and Mendel Silberberg.

The last meeting during the two-week postponement for negotiations ended in a deadlock. The producers offered the writers a flat seven-year contract with a 70 percent guild shop the first two years and 80 percent the third year. Writers would be prohibited from working during layoff periods. Charles Brackett called the producers' offer a "seven-year surrender of freedom."

The Guild demanded an immediate 80 percent guild shop, an agreement of not more than two years, and the right of the writer to material produced during layoff periods. A membership meeting of the SWG was held, the proposal was turned down, and Guild witnesses were prepared for the beginnings of the explosive complaint hearings.

The producers opposed the reopening of the hearings on the grounds that the SWG had twice broken off negotiations, and they claimed that the unfair labor practice situation had been eliminated by their recognition of the Guild as the exclusive bargaining representative for all film writers. They agreed to cancel the present contract with the Screen Playwrights as soon as a contract with the SWG had been signed. In the meantime, the SP continued to arbitrate credits, favoring their members with solo credits at the expense of SWG members.

Because of the deadlock, the objections of the producers were overridden and the NLRB complaint hearings reopened. As it turned out, the producers would have been wiser to settle for the Guild's demands, because the testimony that was to come out over the next few weeks was embarrassing, if not damning. Timid, frightened writers who had everything to lose suddenly grew bold and went out on a limb to testify. Witnesses came forth recounting all the horror stories of the Guild's attempt to affiliate with the Authors League of America, the formation of the Screen Playwrights, and the time of terror afterward.

"Francis appeared before the NLRB," recalled Elizabeth Faragoh about her husband. "We'd only recently returned from New York. He was physically small, and terribly frightened, but his voice boomed out with tremendous authority. Later on they said he was wired to Moscow—he was so authoritative, talking about the rights of writers. But, of course, he wasn't wired to Moscow . . . just very brave. It took a lot of courage to carry the SWG struggle through. In that time, we were full of the youthful, brazen feeling that it was all very dangerous, but we'd win. We had not been terrorized yet, the way we were later, after the war."

Francis Farragoh was an executive officer of the Screen Writers Guild in 1935.

Sol Wurtzel of 20th Century–Fox, Eddie Mannix, and Jack Warner all professed ignorance of the meetings held at their studios in 1936 at which screen writers had been warned against the ALA amalgamation. The producers were very cool and controlled. They weren't about to give anything away. It was left to Grover Jones to confirm the fact that the screen writers had not been imagining the whole struggle with the Playwrights. During the testimony, open hostility broke out between Jones and Janofsky.

"I am not a crook," shouted Jones furiously. "You asked the same lousy questions the last time and looked upon me as a crook." Losing control, Jones then said, "Our whole desire was to create an organization that would bust up the other, lousy, communistic outfit, if that is what you are trying to get at."

The specter of the Red menace hung heavily over the hearings. When the producers weren't claiming that they had never intimidated anyone, they and the SP were accusing the SWG of operating with a direct line to Moscow. When Dalton Trumbo testified, he told the story of his interlude with Harry Cohn and of all the attendant intimations of a blacklist.

A Mr. Feston, for the producers, faced Trumbo—small, wiry, tensed for battle in the witness box.

FESTON: Are you a member of the Communist Party, Mr. Trumbo?
TRUMBO: No, I am not.
FESTON: Have you ever been?
TRUMBO: I have never been.

Eight years later, Trumbo went to jail for his refusal to answer that same question. Only then it was asked by the House Un-American Activities Committee (HUAC) and it was asked in the atmosphere of exploding postwar anticommunism. Eight years later, Trumbo was a member of the CP, and his refusal to answer the question hinged on his belief that he was protected by the First Amendment's guarantee of freedom of speech and belief and that HUAC had no right to interfere with his constitutional protections. Eight years later, Trumbo was asked, "Are you now or have you ever been a member of the CP?" but he was asked another question first: "Are you a member of the Screen Writers Guild?"

But in 1939 the progressives were not frightened, as they would be later, because rabid anticommunism had not yet become the dominant trend in American politics. For people such as James Kevin McGuinness and his pistol-packing drinking buddies, a gun was part of a man's pioneer heritage. Dangerous creatures lurked in the outskirts of Hollywood—bobcats in Topanga Canyon, Reds in Beverly Hills. Howard Emmett Rogers reputedly had a gun with two silver bullets, one for his wife, one for himself, to be used in the event of a communist takeover. John Lee Mahin had rifles lined up on his walls the way most people have books. They thought of themselves as a kind of vigilante army, a core of forewarned cynics, unheeded by the community that made movies and closed its eyes to danger.

The progressives had lumped the "Four Horsemen" and their group with Dies, "the outstanding zany in our political history," and figured they would all befoul and discredit themselves with their wild accusations. But in June 1939, to the profound dismay of every left-winger and New Dealer in the arts, Dies succeeded in having the funding withdrawn from the Federal Theater Project. By 1939, the end of FDR's social reform was already in sight—his proposed defense budget was larger than the one proposed for public works, and he was turning his attention away from the internal policies of the New Deal toward the worsening situation in Europe.

Eddie Mannix was a vice-president at MGM.

The Federal Theater debate on the floor of the House of Representatives on June 16, 1939, was a frightening display of reaction that lumped progressivism in art with pornography. During the final minutes of the debate, Congressman Everett Dirksen listed Federal Theater plays—none of which he had seen—that seemed both communistic and pornographic to him: "*A New Kind of Love*. I wonder what that can be. It smacks somewhat of the Soviet. Then there is *Up in Mabel's Room*. There is an intriguing title for you . . . *Did Adam Sin?*, *Lend Me Your Husband*, and *Just a Love Nest*. . . . Now if you want that kind of salacious tripe, very well, vote for it, but if anybody has an interest in decency on the stage, if anyone has an interest in real cultural values, you will not find it in this kind of junk. . . ."

Over one thousand unemployed theater workers in Los Angeles had been saved by the Federal Theater Project, and it had fostered exhilarating cooperation with the artistic community and the universities, particularly UCLA. Now that was all gone. The Guild's involvement in the project gave detractors one more reason to cry "Red" at the Guild, and they might have, had it not been for the fact that Emmet Lavery, an active SWG member and the head of the Los Angeles play bureau of the Federal Theater Project, was a lawyer and an ardent Catholic who was highly respected in the Catholic community.

The charges of "communist propaganda" and "salacious tripe" leveled against the Federal Theater Project only reinforced the frightening trend so evident in the public and industry reaction to *Blockade*. It was an issue that writers like Donald Ogden Stewart, Vincent Sheean, and Dorothy Parker were devoting greater concern to in the League of American Writers (LAW), and it was the question of content and writer responsibility to which they addressed themselves at the Third League of American Writers Congress at Carnegie Hall in June 1939. The crowded meeting featured such antifascists as Thomas Mann, Edward Beneš, Louis Aragon, and Sylvia Townsend Warner, as well as a host of notable American literati.

Dorothy Parker, speaking on "Sophisticated Verse—The Hell of It," remarked:

> . . . Something happened to the light verse writers. . . . It may have been the result of the World War . . . or it may have been the effect of Miss Edna St. Vincent Millay and that doubly burning candle of hers. Anyway, we grew dashing and devil may care . . . and boy, were we proud of our shame! When Gertrude Stein spoke of a "lost generation," we took it to ourselves and considered it the prettiest compliment we had. . . . I think the trouble with us was that we stayed young too long. We remained in the smarty-pants stage—and that is not one of the more attractive ages. . . . And when we finally came to and got out it was quite a surprise to find a whole world of human beings all around us. . . . I think the best thing now about writers is that they grow up sooner. They know you cannot find yourself until you find your fellow men—they know there is no longer "I"; there is "we".

Vincent Sheean closed the meeting with these moving final words on the aim of the Congress:

> The division between a literature of the cultivated and privileged class and a literature existing for the whole people is disappearing; and although there will probably never be a time when special artists do not exert their efforts for special and limited appreciation, the consciousness of social change has affected writers as much as any other group of workers, and inflicts upon most of them a passionate desire to find their right place in relation to the life of their times. . . . I can hardly bring myself to believe that the celebrated ivory tower, of which we have heard so much, ever contained many tenants. Retirement from life has been the recourse of some few spirits unsuited to struggle, but even there, if we examine, we shall find a curious preoccupation with the fate of mankind. . . . The progress of brotherhood becomes important to us from

the moment we understand our relation to it, and we exert our effort as writers and as human beings toward its acceleration. This brings us at once into a field of ideas which used to be labeled, with some distaste, as "political," and therefore outside the proper realm of a proper writer. . . .

Without surrender of the particular character of our work as writers, we thus take part in associated and related efforts of every progressive force wherever it may be found, in or out of the factory or field, political parties, trade unions, universities, and thus in the whole life of our people.

. . . It was a German writer, Erich Franzen, speaking at the Congress in behalf of thousands of writers and intellectuals now in exile from Fascist countries, who cried: "If people would only listen to those whose boat has run aground, history would have no chance of repeating itself." That is a big if; there is much to discourage his hope that the writers of this country will profit by the mistakes of other lands. There is much to indicate that perhaps every country must experience its own burning of the Reichstag before it discovers that those flames have been used to start another conflagration—the burning of the books—in whose sickening glare can be witnessed the crumbling of all defenses for culture, democracy, and human rights. By the time American writers have realized the real "war aims" of the manufacturers of national prejudices and Red scares, perhaps they themselves will have joined in exile those fellow writers "whose boat has run aground" and they will have contributed their own particular evidence of the unchanging historical pattern of "liberal" blindness, stupidity, and self-deception.

The call to arms applied particularly to the motion picture industry. The LAW Congress advised its members that Hollywood, contrary to public opinion, was not just wallowing in oranges and swimming pools but was also reaching out to its fellow men.

The LAW's exhortation of Hollywood's creative responsibility was echoed by Budd Schulberg. Though he was actually growing more successful and gaining more recognition through his short stories in *Collier's* and *Liberty* than through his film writing, Schulberg echoed the sentiments of most left-wing writers in the movie industry when he wrote an article on "Hollywood's Second Generation" for the *New York Times*. His call for a responsible art form—one whose technical advances were matched by mature content—was particularly interesting in terms of his own situation in June 1939. He had just finished working on *Winter Carnival*, which producer Walter Wanger wanted to shoot at Dartmouth, Schulberg's alma mater; so Wanger had sent Budd and his collaborator, F. Scott Fitzgerald, there to work.*

The collaboration was a disaster, beginning with the bottle of champagne

---

* The collaboration was fictionally chronicled by Schulberg years later in his novel *The Disenchanted*.

B. P. Schulberg gave his son for the plane ride, which Budd shared with Fitzgerald and which precipitated Fitzgerald's return to alcoholism. Fitzgerald represented the "lost generation," which Schulberg admired but by which he was also repelled. It was the wild self-destruction of the Old Hollywood, which Budd had grown up in and from which he was still trying to escape.

"Scott thought of himself as quite a communist at this time," recalled Ring Lardner, Jr., "but the CP wouldn't have permitted him to join even if he'd wanted to since he was considered too unreliable because of his drinking. But he did speak in 'progressive terms.' "

Fitzgerald was too ill during his sojourn in Hollywood to be involved in the SWG's struggle, but he was aware of it, though in *The Last Tycoon* he tended to romanticize Thalberg as the artist struggling with the "factory" orientation of Louis B. Mayer. In that sense Fitzgerald was really projecting himself into the Thalberg character of Monroe Stahr, seeing his own unsuccessful attempt to make it as a Hollywood screen writer as the struggle between the artist and the hack.

As the NLRB hearings dragged on, the catalogue of producer injustices was growing. The Screen Playwrights was shown up as the company union it was, and as the summer of 1939 wore on the producers embarrassedly admitted that the SP was no longer potent in deals between writers and the major studios. Writers coming to the stand were able to testify, along with their agents, that new contracts were being made between writers and producers without any reference to settlement of screen credit disputes by the SP.

It seemed to be a time of triumph, a time of great optimism, a time of coalition. But the dream of harmony ended on the night of August 24, 1939, when the nonaggression pact between the Soviet Union and Germany was announced. It was the beginning of two years of internecine conflict among progressives in Hollywood, as it was across the United States.

"I had joined the *People's Daily World* in 1939, before the pact," recalled Charles Glenn. "Hollywood was my beat—I wrote a column called 'Hollywood Vine.' I'd been in the Party a year or less at that point. I was downtown, near Party headquarters. Suddenly there was this unbelievable announcement, and nobody knew what to think. Paul Cline, the local Party chairman, was suddenly on vacation. Browder wasn't available—he'd skipped town. The switchboard at the *People's Daily World* was flooded. It was a rough thing—it was left to the rank and file to struggle through until the Party had managed to come through with the line."

A few weeks prior to the pact, Earl Browder, the secretary of the U.S. Communist Party, had condemned the speculation of "reactionaries" that the Soviet Union might join hands with Hitler, telling an audience in Charlottesville, Virginia, "There is as much chance of agreement as of Earl Browder being elected president of the Chamber of Commerce."

"The day after the pact," said Bonnie Clair Smith, a staff worker for the Hollywood Anti-Nazi League, "you never saw anything like what hit the League's office. The phones didn't stop, and telegrams of withdrawal poured in. I don't even think the *Daily Worker* came out that day."

"The turmoil in Boyle Heights was something else," remembered Charles Glenn. "The known Reds were in hiding—afraid to stick their heads out of doors because the Old Country Jews, the ones who had fled Hitler, would have torn them apart."

Glenn was a Midwestern WASP who considered Boyle Heights an exotic world. He would go to the Center Cafeteria to see friends and watch the arguments—communists on one side, socialists on the other, shouting at each other, but with the enjoyment of Talmudic argument. However, the day after the pact, there was no enjoyment.

"The Center Cafeteria was a hornet's nest," he said. "It took a long time for the bitterness of the pact to wear off. With the Russian Jews it did, but with the Western European Jews it was difficult. For some of them it never wore off."

Orthodox Jew Michael Blankfort had rejected his religion and become pro-Soviet after visiting Russia in 1929. "In those years," he said, "I believed that anti-Semitism was an evil function of capitalism and imperialism— finding someone at whom to direct anger. I thought that in a socialist world, anti-Semitism would disappear. At that time, I didn't think of the Soviets as anti-Semitic and I didn't think, 'How do we feel as Jews?' I thought, 'How do we feel as socialists?' The pact was looked at in political terms."

"The intellectuals were going crazy," recalled Charles Glenn. "There were a lot of people close to the Party who got their first big disillusionment with the pact. It began to alienate the sympathetic liberals like Helen Gahagan Douglas." Indeed, Helen Gahagan and her husband, Melvyn Douglas, were among the first to resign from the Hollywood Anti-Nazi League when it ceased being anti-Nazi.

Arthur Ornitz remembers his father defending the pact with steadfast loyalty. But Sam Ornitz had complete faith in Stalin. Arthur remembers questioning his father after the mid-thirties Moscow trials, and Sam, who had read every page of the transcripts, defended them. Sam Ornitz really did believe that Stalin was going to make the world a better place. He was like so many naive communists in Hollywood, who too eagerly accepted the myth of Russia's universal humanity.

"Sam Ornitz was a highly educated, very talented man who was better informed than most people," recalled Paul Jarrico. "He was up-to-date on all kinds of things and loved to pontificate, loved to share his information, and was a good speaker—and he was fearless. Of course, later on he was terribly embarrassed about the role he had played during the pact. He was very proud of being a Jew, but he kept denying that there was any anti-Semitism in the

Soviet Union or in Eastern Europe, and he *really* denied it until the evidence became irrefutable. And then he was humiliated because he'd stuck his neck out. I mean, he was widely respected, but in the Left Jewish community he was *loved.* If you said to a good rank-and-file cloak-and-suitworker, 'They've got anti-Semitism in that workers' fatherland of yours,' he would say, 'No, it's not true. Sam Ornitz says it's not true and he knows, he's an intelligent man, he's an educated man, he's a cultured man.' So he had prestige which he put on the line, and brother, he really suffered. He really was angrier than almost anybody I know about the 1956 revelations—he suffered more personally, more deeply himself."

"The Stalin-Hitler pact had no effect on me whatsoever," commented Allen Boretz, who had joined the Party in 1939, before the pact. "The Soviet

Helen Gahagan Douglas, c. 1940. After quitting Barnard College to become an opera singer and making her career as an actress, she was elected to Congress in 1944 and was defeated for re-election in 1950 by Richard Nixon.

Union had to live, and if they saw a conspiracy in the West to demolish them, they would sign with the devil. As Churchill said on the other side, I would make a pact with the devil, when they criticized him for later being an ally of the Soviet Union. Russia had to survive. Great Britain had to survive, and when you have to survive you pull knives or shoot guns or get brass knuckles, do whatever you have to do."

The rationale of the Stalin-Hitler pact as a nonaggression rather than as a mutual-aid agreement was the rationale that American communists accepted. After all, Madrid had fallen to the fascists on March 28, 1939, and on April 1, FDR had recognized Franco. Whether or not this was a move to woo Franco away from Hitler and Mussolini, the communists argued, this too was a move to buy time and, further, the pact was essential for Russia's salvation because the United States would have gladly sacrificed Russia to the Nazis.

One week after the pact, Hitler invaded Poland. England and France took up the cause of the Poles, and two weeks later Russia also invaded Poland, meeting the Nazis in the middle of the country. The CP line was that the Russian invasion of Poland was a humanitarian act undertaken to safeguard the rights of Polish workers. The war by England and France against Germany was not a fight against fascism, according to the Party line, but just another imperialist war between capitalist nations. It was the responsibility of the American CP, therefore, to oppose American entry into the war.

In her autobiographical study of her days in the CP, *A Fine Old Conflict*, Jessica Mitford recalled:

> . . . the American CP, in what we considered a hopelessly wrong-headed response to the Nazi-Soviet pact, was in full opposition to the war, its spokesmen appearing on platforms with isolationists and America Firsters under the slogan "The Yanks Are Not Coming."
>
> In our view, the pact was an inevitable outcome of the Munich betrayal and the intransigent refusal over the years of the Western democracies to respond to the unremitting Soviet effort to establish collective security against Nazi aggression. The role of the Communists in the Western countries, then, we believed, should be to press for vigorous prosecution of the war against the Axis powers—instead of which they were denouncing it as an "imperialist adventure."

Friends split over the pact. Robert Benchley, Dorothy Parker, Donald Ogden Stewart, and Herman Mankiewicz were suddenly very cool to each other. Benchley couldn't understand how Stewart and Parker could have been so blind to the Communist Party, and Mankiewicz, who had already been cranky over SWG matters, became downright abusive.

A year later it was indeed awkward for the progressives, who had so thoroughly denounced Charles A. Lindbergh and Senator Burton K. Wheeler (who claimed that the movie industry was being run by foreign-born warmongers), to find that suddenly these two archreactionaries were on the same side as the communists in America. The Hollywood Anti-Nazi League, which had earlier boasted such broad-based support that even Harry Warner contributed several thousand dollars to their fight against Hitler, foundered in the stormy political waters following the pact. When people asked why the League didn't attack communism, the communist members of the Anti-Nazi League found themselves giving the weak reply, "Because it was organized to fight fascism."

Sam Marx, then story editor at MGM, complained in a meeting of the Anti-Nazi League that "communism was the same as fascism," and he was drowned out with boos and hisses. Writer Harry Tugend recalled returning to Hollywood from the 1939 World's Fair (where the Soviet Pavilion proclaimed Stalin's world of the future) to find that the Anti-Nazi League had been replaced by a new organization, the American Peace Mobilization, which was dedicated to opposing U.S. entry into the war in Europe.

On behalf of the CP (covertly) and the American Peace Mobilization

At far right, director Herbert Biberman (*The Master Race*, *Salt of the Earth*), who, under contract at Columbia (he came to Hollywood in 1935 after studying drama at Yale and working for the Theatre Guild) as an actor and director, was a founding member of the Hollywood Anti-Nazi League and was later jailed as one of the Hollywood Ten.

(overtly), Sam Ornitz and Guy Endore began a series of lectures on the world situation at the First Unitarian Church in downtown Los Angeles under the rubric "The Hollywood Peace Forum." The Hollywood Peace Forum's officers included chairman Herbert Biberman, vice-chairman John Wexley, and secretary-treasurer Guy Endore. Endore, who was a brilliant pamphleteer, wrote several pamphlets for the antiwar cause that were passionate and not unconvincing. In one of them, titled *Let's Skip the Next War*, he called for "NO WAR FOR THE USA BUT A HOUSE AND LOT FOR EVERYONE!"

By June 1940, the Nazis had conquered Poland, Denmark, Norway, Luxembourg, Holland, and Belgium, and they were in France. Even some devout Party members, reading of the nightmare in Europe, could not rationalize "humanitarian America" staying out of a war against Hitler. Nevertheless, when Donald Ogden Stewart was compiling the collection of speeches from the Third LAW Congress, he was advised by the CP that inasmuch as Vincent Sheean had recently attacked Stalin and the pact in *The New Republic*, he should omit Sheean's speech from the book. Stewart refused.

As people who were unhappy with the rationale over the pact left the Party, those who stayed home, of necessity, became more dogmatic than ever. Granville Hicks, educator and author of *I Like America*, disassociated himself from the Party in disgust and made public his displeasure in *The New Republic*:

> If they had only admitted their ignorance, the CP of the USA would be intact today. But instead they insisted that the Soviet-German nonaggression pact was the greatest possible contribution to peace and democracy and offered anything that came into their heads as proof. . . . Only one conclusion could be drawn: If the Party leaders could not defend the Soviet Union intelligently, they would defend it stupidly. . . .

The Stalin-Hitler Pact suddenly brought into sharp focus the distinction between Party members and fellow travelers. It also served to focus many of the dissatisfactions that already existed in the Communist Party. For it would be naive to assume that the period of antifascist activity prior to the Pact was one of complete harmony within the CP. Disagreement was implicit in the very nature of writers, and the attempt to gather them into one body where they would have to cope with such things as dogma (the party line, with its numerous twists and turns) and discipline (the submission of their will or instincts to what the Party felt was in the best interests of communism) was bound to result in dissension.

As early as 1937, John Dos Passos had broken with his comrades from the New Theater days. He denounced Russia's role in Spain, claiming that the Communist Party would not dole out arms to non-CP Loyalist units, and that "the Russians had come to Spain fresh from the purges of Trotskyites at home. . . . The blockade forced the Republicans to buy their arms through the

Communists. With the arms came Communist control and the disintegration of the revolutionary parties opposed to Franco . . . and defeat." Nearly twenty years later, looking back on the Spanish situation in his book *Spain: Rehearsal for Defeat*, he wrote: "The dreadful paradox of the Communism of the 30's was that it still managed to use the aspirations of the world's disinherited to justify power for its own sake, attained through massacre and murder on a scale unimagined since the days of Attila and Genghis Khan and Russia's own Czar Ivan."

"The problem with writers, individualistic creatures that they are," commented Charles Glenn, "is that they don't like leaders." The few leaders they did follow were members of the Communist Party and seemed stronger, more sure, and less ambivalent than the average writer.

"Budd [Schulberg] got Fitzgerald to say that he thought he was a communist," said Maurice Rapf, "and persuaded Dorothy Parker that she should be more organized about her left-wing activities. You see it was also, in a way, true of Don Stewart, but although he, like Dottie, had developed Left sympathies generally, they hadn't read the Marxist stuff as diligently as Budd and I had. Hammett, of course, had, and when you could get him sober, he sort of knew what he was talking about theoretically. I respected and looked up to all these people, but not really politically. Politically, I found that somebody like John Howard Lawson seemed to make a good deal more sense."

As leader of the Hollywood Communist Party, Lawson was loved, hated, and even, by some, pitied. "Jack was the father figure who answered every question, laid down the rules, was the court of last appeal," remembered Sam Moore. "He was a smooth guy, liked to laugh and drink—he was an organizational powerhouse, but I got to dislike him as an organization member."

Lawson was known for being both brilliant and dogmatic. One of his favorite expressions was "We've got to look into this further." There were some who considered him a little too square, too doctrinaire, but there were Party members who considered the whole Party too square and doctrinaire. The Hollywood CP was, after all, made up of a bunch of Hollywood screen writers, who were far from being the basic rank and file.

Paul Jarrico was one of Lawson's most vocal critics, and after Lawson got out of jail in the fifties, Jarrico and his brother-in-law writer Michael Wilson wrested control of the Hollywood CP away from Lawson. "I'm sure," said Jarrico, "that if Jack were told by the Soviets to criticize them, without missing a beat he'd have said, 'Well, you know, the way the Soviets treat dissidents is really criminal.' " Jarrico, like others who tangled with Lawson, felt that Lawson participated in intellectual crimes against his fellow Party members. "Now Lester Cole," said Jarrico, "was not an intellectual and was not equipped to deal with complicated problems. But in Lawson's case, his dogmatism defeated him as an intellectual, as a person, and as an artist. He was an intellectual without introspection."

Dorothy Healy felt that Lawson and V. J. Jerome bore the responsibility for the sort of cultural sectarianism that hurt the Party. "Lawson was a tragic figure. He was a man of talent and ability, but he was struggling so hard to prove he was not a petty-bourgeois intellectual. Everything he'd write he'd submit to dozens of people for comment. . . . Look, the minute you join an organization you must surrender some individuality. But it is just as crucial to retain most of that individualism."

There were those for whom Lawson was an almost mythical, all-knowing figure. Milton Lubovitsky was in the Party literary group. He had admired Lawson since he was a kid, and he thought Lawson had the greatest mind in Hollywood. "Most of the Party fights were ego battles," he recalled, "but Lawson was the only non-ego in the bunch. He was truly brilliant."

Michael Blankfort commented that he once saw Lawson coming out of the dentist's office when he was going in. "I was shocked," he said, "that Jack would have trouble with his teeth. He seemed to be beyond the frailties of humankind. It was like seeing Lenin going to the can.

"Jack Lawson loved the people en masse," added Blankfort, "and Sam Ornitz loved them individually. I think Sam always felt it was a little unfair that Jack held more of a position of leadership than he did. Jack was more of a leader and Sam more of a teacher. But Jack was so rigid, so didactic, it ended up making a lot of people resent him."

"I wouldn't call him intractable," said Fred Rinaldo. "In fact, I think he sometimes muddled his conclusions with too many opinions. But what a power. He could give a ten-minute speech and sway an entire audience. He gave himself to the cause utterly. He was an incredibly organized thinker."

Sam Ornitz, too, was known as an extraordinary speaker who could "charm the birds out of the trees." His spellbinding narrative talents kept him working even when his poor screen-writing credits put his talent as a scenarist into question. Both Ornitz and Lawson were described as men who did their best work before they came to Hollywood and then never again had the time or energy to take away from politics to devote to their art.

"I tangled with Lawson," said Paul Jarrico, "because I was, in Party terms, a reformist, a revisionist, a right-wing opportunist, and he was, in Party terms, and certainly in my eyes, an infantile leftist, a sectarian sonofabitch.

"You should also understand," Jarrico continued, "that at this time Lawson was still a friend of mine despite our political differences—I mean we would sometimes be at each other's throats politically and still be concerned with each other's welfare. There was a certain amount of grudging respect that people in the CP had for each other even when they were opposed to each other."

Budd Schulberg, for a variety of reasons, found his own enthusiasm for the Party diminishing around the time of the Stalin-Hitler Pact. He noticed that this was the time that more of what he called "apparatus people," which

Screenwriter Sam Ornitz (*Miracle on Main Street, The Hit Parade, It Could Happen to You,* and twelve others) served on the executive board of the Screen Writers Guild.

was to say CP functionaries, moved in on the Hollywood Communist Party.

"I think," he said, "the real Eastern bosses, the Eddie Mannixes of the Party, started to move in at the time of all the problems with the Nazi-Soviet alliance. I still have a paper I wrote when I was in the Party. I wrote a little essay which I read at the meeting attacking the Nazi-Soviet pact, and I wrote fifteen reasons why I thought the pact was wrong. I thought we were going to argue those things out and discuss them. I thought I might even change their minds. But I didn't realize at the time that the Party was far more centralized than it was democratic. By then, they felt that the Hollywood CP had become quite important. They were greatly interested in the money that would come from the members of the Party, who would give ten percent of quite large incomes. With that much money coming in, it became something they felt they should take over."

Schulberg's troubles within the Party were also artistic. A number of his stories, including the sketch for *What Makes Sammy Run?*, had been published, and Schulberg found the Party hostile to his aesthetic pursuits.

"Long before any difficulty I got into for writing *What Makes Sammy Run?*," he said, "I was told that these stories were too realistic, they were too depressing, decadent. During these years, 1937 to 1939, I would say I was still in favor of the immediate issues as the communists seemed to be following them. By 1939 I was definitely backsliding. I was trying to avoid as many meetings as I could and as many responsibilities as I could. Most of the people I was seeing were writers. Some of these writers might have been strongly opposed to the Party. Some perhaps had not even heard of the Party.

"I had quite a bit of trouble by that time with Lawson. I'd worked with Jack and I admired him, but I had trouble with him over the book, even over the right to write the book. We were under pretty tight Party discipline, and you couldn't just sit down and write a book. You actually had to ask permission of the Party to write the book and to take time off from your other assignments. I believe that the one who felt most strongly at the time was Richard Collins. He disapproved strongly of my attitude toward writing and toward the communists. But I wanted to write my book, so Jigee and I just got in the car and left. We didn't ask permission, we just left and went to Vermont. Now it seems like the most normal thing one can do, but at that time it seemed like a very daring act."

The argument over proletarian literature and over what was considered the Party's dictatorial approach to literature alienated some. James T. Farrell attended one meeting of the League of American Writers and resigned, dubbing it the "League against American Writing."

Richard Rovere was one of the fifties' strongest critics of the left-wing's influence on literature, writing that the "cultural tone they established was deplorable because it was metallic and strident. Communist culture was not aristocratic; it was cheap and vulgar and corny. The left-wing writers of the thirties sought their heroes among working stiffs and bloodied Negroes and their plots in ghettos and slums."

Rovere did not seem to include in his description the better novels that the left wing sought to emulate, novels like John Steinbeck's 1939 best seller, *The Grapes of Wrath*. There were those, like Schulberg and Rovere, who felt that the Party was inimical to art. There were others, like Ring Lardner, Jr., and Dalton Trumbo, who felt that the Party, by providing an intellectual framework and stimulating company, enhanced their lives, both as creators and as people.

The Stalin-Hitler Pact also resulted in growing tension between the left wing and the rest of the Screen Writers Guild. Intrinsic to this tension was the whole concept of writer responsibility. It was particularly evident on the

Left to right: Louise Rapf, Richard Collins (*Song of Russia, Thousands Cheer*), Virginia (Jigee) Schulberg, Budd Schulberg (*Winter Carnival, On the Waterfront, A Face in the Crowd*).

board, between those writers who felt that the SWG was strictly a union and should concern itself only with union matters and those who felt that the Guild had a responsibility to larger goals.

Laurence Beilinson had refused to become the Guild's attorney when it reorganized in 1937, and he claimed it was because the communists on the board had forced the issue of amalgamation, which split the Guild, though he had advised them that it was ill advised. He hated the factionalism. "It was wrecking my life," he said, "to stay up every night and listen to all this nonsense. John Howard Lawson was the leader of the communist group on the board. They would try to railroad the meetings."

"There's no question," said Jean Butler, "but that the most devoted early members of the Guild were from the Left—the most passionate, the most devoted, the most directed. They were willing to stay late, whereas the conservatives couldn't abide a meeting that lasted more than two hours."

"At the time when I was most involved with the SWG, I was not yet a member of the Party," recalled Fred Rinaldo. "But on issues about whether or not the union should discuss the world political situation and take stands, we were dealing with matters of war and peace, and any union worth its salt is concerned with foreign policy."

"I remember one board meeting," said William Ludwig, "where we had to censure the top echelon of the Guild at that time. I think it was during the Nazi-Soviet pact, and we used to meet in the firetrap on Cherokee. We had to censure the top echelon for picketing—I think they were picketing down at the docks at San Pedro, picketing the loading of scrap iron bound for Europe or Japan—you know, this was when the communists were shouting, 'The Yanks are not coming.' Now, as individuals they had every right to do that, but in statements to the press they all identified themselves as officers and board members of the Guild, which made it look as though it were an official SWG action. We had to censure them for that because the Guild had to take a nonpolitical stance."

Apparently this divisiveness within the Guild suited the purposes of the producers. The cancellation of the Screen Playwrights contract was formally announced on Valentine's Day 1940, a few months after the studios had reported themselves ready to negotiate with the SWG on the basis of a minimum contract running five years instead of seven, which was at least approaching the Guild demand of a contract to run no more than two years. The NLRB complaint petition closed, quietly, in the autumn of 1939, with the producers ready to make concessions in various forms to the Guild. The struggle had dragged on long enough. By the end of 1939, the SP was purely vestigial, a little band that refused to join the other members who had gone over to the Guild.

And the producers were still hostile to the Left, whom they felt had precipitated the whole struggle. They saw the divisiveness that had been sparked by the Stalin-Hitler Pact and turned it to their own purposes to gain time and power in the contract negotiations. The producers' lawyers told the SWG's lawyer (by that time Robert Kenny was negotiating for the Guild) that Communist Party members were not acceptable to them at the bargaining table. The board was divided, but one thing was obvious—they wanted to get a contract. Finally, for the sake of the Guild, Lawson and Stewart resigned from the committee. Lawson was unpopular, but Stewart was beloved. The board accepted these demands, which the producers were using as another stalling tactic, but they gained a psychological advantage—if in bargaining the opposition says it has the first demand, this gives the next demand to the other side.

"What a crew it was, at those first sessions," recalled Boris Ingster. "Mary McCall and I were both very militant, very demanding. Dore Schary was the statesman who would say, 'Let us reason together. Let's not get excited.' Mannix was the consummate actor. He'd flare up, get theatrically angry, and Schary would play the part of the pacifier. The other producers would get so furious they would really go insane—for example, Y. Frank Freeman—the silver-haired, elegant anti-Semite who ran Paramount—who'd shake his hands and scream, 'I'll go back to selling Coca-Cola first!' "

The only group for which the Stalin-Hitler Pact seemed a godsend was Dies and his committee. Suddenly, he seemed not quite so big a fool as he had appeared to be, and his questioning of CP secretary Earl Browder drew forth the admission that Browder had traveled on false passports. That sent Browder to prison for two years.

The political scene had been thrown into confusion by the pact, and it was nowhere more evident than in California, where the fragile coalition of the Left and the liberals who had united under Governor Olson was destroyed by the conflicts the Pact generated. By late 1939, numerous former Olson supporters had joined with right-wing Democrats and Republicans in charging that the State Relief Administration, largely composed of left-wing supporters whom Olson had appointed, was infiltrated by communists and other subversive elements. A Relief Investigating Committee was set up in 1940, chaired by Assemblyman Sam Yorty. From the outset, the committee was referred to as the "Little Dies Committee." In 1941 it was reorganized to include members of both the California state senate and assembly in a joint fact-finding committee, the State Un-American Activities Committee.

Chairman of the joint committee was Yorty's former radical soulmate, Jack B. Tenney. This was the same Tenney who had addressed a rally of the Hollywood Anti-Nazi League in August 1939, at which the dissolution of the Dies Committee was demanded. *Hollywood Now*, the publication of the Hollywood Anti-Nazi League, had reported Tenney's words in its issue of August 26:

California State Senator Jack Tenney before HUAC, 1947.

> Fellow subversive elements, I have just heard that Mickey Mouse is conspiring with Shirley Temple to overthrow the government and that there is a witness who has seen the "Red" card of Donald Duck. When the Dies Committee stoops to calling President Roosevelt a Communist, and says that Mrs. Roosevelt is a front for subversive elements, then I think the rest of us should be flattered to be put in that category.

Tenney had further claimed that Dies's Hollywood Red scare was merely a smokescreen under which union busting was carefully concealed.

This was the same Tenney who had so gallantly marched with Yorty on the *Citizen News* picket lines; the same Tenney who had co-authored, with Yorty, a resolution requesting President Roosevelt to revoke the embargo on the shipment of arms to the Spanish Loyalist forces, a resolution which had been presented at the 1939 legislative session.

Tenney's change in position began around the time of the Stalin-Hitler pact. There is no single answer to what transformed Tenney and caused him to shed his "liberal coat," as Harlan Palmer had been so glad to do. One possibility was that Tenney, as president of Local 47 of the American Federation of Musicians, had been considered corrupt and was defeated for reelection in December 1939. Tenney blamed the defeat on "communistic" elements in his union. Another possibility was pure political ambition. Tenney was a large, flaccid, pasty-faced, unremarkable man, a poor public speaker, a man singularly lacking in what later political analysts would term "charisma," and he carefully chose the winning side.

Whatever prompted his decision, Tenney gave himself to the Right, heart and soul. By 1941 he was writing to Hearst: "As Chairman of the fact-finding committee on un-American activities, created by the 1941 California State Legislature, I wish to congratulate . . . you on your courageous campaign of withering publicity against subversive elements in the state and nation."

In the autumn of 1940, Tenney was the leading sponsor of a bill designed to ban the Communist Party from the ballot. It passed in both the state senate and assembly, only to be declared unconstitutional two years later. But Tenney was definitely a political comer. His passionate anticommunism ultimately blended so smoothly with anti-Semitism that he ran for vice-president of the United States in 1952 with Gerald L. K. Smith, another anti-Semite.

"Tenney," recalled Dorothy Healy, "was a typical opportunist—involved with labor 'because it pays.' He was a radical while it helped him. He took Yorty to meetings with the Party to discuss certain things, such as how we could help him get elected to the presidency of the musicians' union."

Just prior to his election he had come down so hard on the International Alliance of Theatrical Stage Employees, attacking them for corruption, that he was criticized by conservative assemblymen for violating democratic principles. Two years later he was climbing into an ideological bed with IATSE leaders, attacking communism in Hollywood unions. When his investigations first began, according to NLRB executive secretary Nate Witt, it was the impression in Washington that the Tenney Committee was the instrument of the California employers, which was also assumed to be true of the congressional "Big Dies Committee." But by 1941, Tenney and Dies were in, and Witt was out.

"Ben Margolis [a progressive lawyer] and I made it a habit," recalled Charles Katz. "If Tenney spoke someplace on a Monday night, we'd schedule a speech in the same place Tuesday night. Ben was a great speaker and Tenney was terrible. We put in a great deal of work trying to get him out."

"He'd issue one of his annual reports," claimed Pauline Lauber Finn, membership secretary of the SWG, "and have some limelight, but he never got the publicity of the House Un-American Activities Committee in Washington. He was a fool, and he couldn't handle the press; he was definitely not a power. Most of the bills he introduced weren't passed, or if they were, they were later declared unconstitutional."

Between 1941 and 1949, Tenney's committee spent almost $80,000 on investigation and sessions looking into communist activities in California without ever sending so much as one communist to jail.

In terms of the damage Tenney did, the assessment seems to be correct that the Left and the liberals underestimated him. He was a drunkard and a buffoon, but he kept the spirit of Red-baiting and undercover investigating alive and kicking in the California state legislature.

Tenney's chief source of opposition came from Robert Kenny, champion of the underdog, who emerged as the most intelligent, enlightened liberal politician of that period in California, holding office as state senator and state attorney general and as head of the National Lawyers Guild. He and his opponent were frequently confused—in name only—and when once asked, "Are you Tenney of the Little Dies Committee?" he replied, "No, I'm Kenny of the little guys committee."

Kenny was a truly beloved figure, a "Merry-Andrew" type, as he was called by Carey McWilliams, a progressive writer whose guiding political principle was justice. Kenny defined a progressive as "a man who is afraid to be a Democrat and ashamed to be a Republican," and he had the knack of bringing opposing factions together. This was undoubtedly why he was asked to become the Guild's negotiating lawyer in 1940, a position that kept him flying back and forth between Hollywood and Sacramento.

Two incidents in the life of Kenny seemed to have contributed to his sensitivity and sense of justice. One was his disability—his right arm had been dislocated and permanently crippled at birth, though most people forgot about it immediately and he was considered quite a ladies' man, despite his portly, cherubic looks. The second incident was the indictment of his father, a bank officer, who, with a colleague, was accused of collusion in a land-fraud deal. Kenny was a child at the time, but at his father's insistence his aunt compiled a thirty-page scrapbook of clippings from the trial. Even though Kenny's father was cleared of the charges, he wanted the clippings saved so his son could see, in later years, how easy it was to accuse a man of dishonesty and what he had to endure to be exonerated.

Tenney and Kenny were political opponents throughout the forties, particularly when it came to radical writers. Their opposition climaxed at the end of the decade when Tenney was feeding the House Un-American Activities Committee information about the communist activities of the Hollywood Ten and Kenny was one of the Ten's defense lawyers.

Kenny was outraged by the "Little Dies Committee" from its inception. When Tenney's assembly resolution calling for additional funds for his "Little Dies Committee" came to the floor of the California senate, Kenny offered an amendment stating that the committee should receive no hearsay testimony, that persons called before it should be given the right to cross-examine their accusers and to object to hearsay testimony, and that if hearsay testimony were received, it wouldn't be privileged under California libel laws. The amendment would have prevented the committee from being used as a privileged sanctuary for those who smeared individuals and organizations but then escaped legal liability for untrue accusations. Kenny could muster only four votes for his amendment, and he ended up casting the only "no" vote on the final adoption of Tenney's resolution. Later in that session of the legislature, Tenney obtained the passage of the Subversive Organization Registration Act, known as the "Little Voorhis Act." Kenny argued that the act was unconstitutional, but his protests were overruled.

It was obvious that there was a serious reactionary movement going on in California. It was the time of deportation delirium, when people such as Harry Bridges were being threatened with deportation. The Smith Act, passed in late summer 1940, called for the registration and fingerprinting of all aliens. The divisiveness was threatening the 1940 presidential campaign, and on March 15, 1940, Harold Ickes came to San Francisco to bring harmony to the warring Democratic factions. The right wing of the Democratic Party was involved in a movement to recall Governor Olson, and it was extremely difficult to obtain any cooperation among the divided liberal forces.

This was part of a more pervasive reaction against progressivism that was going on across the country. In 1940, Roosevelt was reelected by a substantially smaller margin than in his other two campaigns. The Smith Committee had been set up to investigate the NLRB and the supposed communist connections of Nate Witt and Donald Smith. In 1940, Roosevelt decided not to reappoint Warren Madden to the NLRB, and Witt, who became the focal point of the anti-NLRB attack, resigned. To Witt, the resignation was a logical part of the cycle of opposition to progressive agencies. After the public outcry from the employers and the constitutional attack by the Liberty League lawyers, the next step was the attack on how the agency was run, the attempt to discredit the agency by accusing its administrators of every sin from incompetence to communism to drunkenness.

The left wing in Hollywood remembers the Stalin-Hitler Pact period as a distinctly unhappy, tension-filled time. Ring Lardner, Jr., recalled having trouble finding work in the studios. The social activity that had been involved in the Spanish Refugee Committee days and the days of the Anti-Nazi League was circumscribed. It was not quite as joyous to be a member of the Communist Party now as it had been in 1937 and 1938. Party members suddenly found themselves suspect, coolly received by their liberal friends, who looked with disfavor on their new pacifism. The request of the producers' negotiating team that Stewart and Lawson be removed from the bargaining table was symptomatic of the shrinking world that communists in Hollywood suddenly found themselves living in during the years of the pact.

The writers' responsibility to fight fascism, which had been championed in a rather bellicose form during the 1939 League of American Writers Congress in New York, was translated at the 1941 Writers Congress into the writers' responsibility to fight against war. "In 1935, 1937, and again in 1939, we declared our indissoluble ties with the American people," read the opening statement.

> We proclaimed our unalterable conviction that reaction and its wars are the greatest enemies of a free and flourishing culture. . . . We had warned of the consequences of non-intervention in Spain, of aid to the aggressor in China, of appeasement in Munich. Today, these consequences are tragically apparent. WE HAVE WARNED THAT AMERICA MUST BE DEFENDED NOT BY INVOLVEMENT IN THIS WAR, OR BY STEPS TOWARD DICTATORSHIP, OR BY PURSUING A COURSE OF IMPERIALIST EXPANSION, BUT BY PRE-SERVING PEACE AND EXPANDING DEMOCRACY ON THE ECONOMIC, POLITICAL AND CULTURAL LEVELS.

In Hollywood one of the LAW's primary activities was setting up the League of American Writers School for Writers, which began in 1940. A student could study screen writing there with such respected Hollywood scribes as Michael Blankfort, David Hertz, Boris Ingster, Paul Jarrico (nominated for an Oscar at the age of twenty-four for his script of *Tom, Dick and Harry*), and Donald Ogden Stewart (awarded an Oscar for his script of *The Philadelphia Story*); the history of the American stage from the Civil War to the present, with John Howard Lawson; playwriting with George Sklar; non-fiction writing with journalist and travel-writer Cedric Belfrage; and motion picture analysis with Wolfe Kaufman and Meyer Levin (critic and author of *The Old Bunch*). The short story was taught by Irwin Shaw. Lawson also taught a course in the history of American literature in which attention was given to "the lesser-known aspects of our literary history, the development of newspapers and magazines, contemporary documents, economics and social theories." Lawson would attempt to "utilize this cultural heritage for a better understanding of the social and aesthetic problems of our own period." It was really another way of presenting a Marxist study group of American literature without the onus of the Party. Twelve sessions cost $18.

"The League of American Writers," recalled Fred Rinaldo, "filled a special purpose during the pact." Rinaldo, with his partner Bobby Lees, taught a screen writing course at the LAW school. "There had to be some area in which writers could push the antifascist front and far-left issues; there had to be some outlet for these concerns which would have been divisive had they been brought into the SWG. The LAW ended when the war began. But the LAW school proved such a good idea that it outlasted both the LAW and the pact."

When he first came to Hollywood, Carl Foreman was getting $85 a month from the WPA on the Federal Writers' Project and was given a scholarship to the LAW school. At that time, he says, he was on the fringes of the Party, and the LAW school served primarily an educational function for him. His first term was a loosely structured lecture course. In his second term he had a course with Lester Cole and Robert Rossen. The third workshop was with Dore Schary, whose encouragement kept Carl in Hollywood. After the third term, when Foreman was unable to get more scholarship money, Schary paid his way. Foreman later wrote *Home of the Brave, High Noon*, and *The Guns of Navarone*.

The League of American Writers was also active in sponsoring two publications during the period of the Pact: a magazine called *Black and White*, which later became *Clipper*, a West Coast review. Though the circulation never exceeded a few hundred, *Black and White* featured contributions by Donald Ogden Stewart, Ella Winter (Stewart's second wife and the widow of Lincoln Steffens), Carey McWilliams, and Haakon Chevalier (who translated Malraux). When the magazine became *Clipper*, the editorial board included Sanora Babb (short story writer and wife of cinematographer James Wong Howe); Cedric Belfrage; Meyer Levin; and Lester Koenig (a dedicated jazz buff and writer who later became a record producer).

Black and White's transformation into *Clipper* coincided with its becoming the organ of the LAW, giving the magazine a more political direction. The contributors to *Clipper* included John Steinbeck, Gordon Kahn, Sam Ornitz, and Theodore Dreiser, and there was movie criticism by Belfrage, Levin, and Lewis Jacobs. There was also a healthy channeling of material from students at the LAW school to the magazine as submissions were encouraged.

"For me," recalled Wilbur Needham, one of the magazine's original editor-contributors, "the best measure of our success was the virulent condemnation that Martin Dies gave us in his annual report as head of HUAC. He gave us six columns of artfully contrived vituperation, innuendos, and cleverly twisted half-truths. Evidently our little magazine had begun to count on the American scene."

Perhaps the happiest cultural experience that transpired during the pact was the collaborative effort of several New York expatriates with a left-wing orientation in a musical called *Meet the People*. It was one of the first theatrical musical comedies to originate in Hollywood and then move to Broadway, and the only successful one. With music by Jay Gorney ("Brother, Can You Spare a Dime?"), lyrics by Edward Eliscu, dances by Danny Dare, book by Henry Myers, and direction by Mortimer Offner (who had co-scripted several films for Katharine Hepburn, including *Sylvia Scarlett* and *Alice Adams*), it also featured contributions by writers such as Ben and Sol Barzman, who had been successful a year earlier with a pro-labor musical called *Labor Pains*.

Meet the People was an exhortation to Hollywood to come out of its cocoon and realize what was going on in the rest of the world, a variation on the theme of Hollywood's responsibility to produce works of mature content that reflected the times. Those who worked on it considered it the only successful collaborative creative experience of their lives.

AN
INTIMATE
TOPICAL
MUSICAL
REVUE

*Step out
and*
"MEET
THE
PEOPLE"
at the
MANSFIELD
THEATRE
47th ST. WEST OF B'WAY

It began with a Sleeping Beauty, Hollywood, peacefully dreaming away, serenaded by lullabies, while war, strikes, and starvation go on around her. Finally a prince comes and stabs her with a large pin, which wakes her up, and he tells her to come on out and "meet the people." Sleeping Beauty then watches the world, a very funny left-wing perception of it, unfold before her eyes. There were musical numbers such as "They [the fascists] Can't Get You Down" and a hilarious bit of musical nostalgia for all the exiled European talent in Hollywood, called "That Mittel-Europa of Mine," which included such lyrics as:

> Times are slack, so give me back
> that mittel Europa of mine.
> Every night, gemütlichkeit
> In that Mittel-Europa of mine.
> I shot grouse with Oscar Straus
> And lived upon women and wine.
> Ausgezeichnet, Donner Wetter
> Life was perfect—even better
> Than a Schubert operetta
> In that Mittel-Europa of mine.

There was also a dance between Hitler and Stalin that showed Hitler with a knife in Stalin's back and a knife in Stalin's hand at Hitler's back. But the waltzing dictators apparently upset the Party so much that the number was dropped.

The first showings, at the two-hundred-seat Assistance League Playhouse, were so successful that the show quickly moved to the Music Hall Theater, with Michael Blankfort's cousin, Henry Blankfort, as stage manager. The show introduced and helped launch the careers of several performers, including Jack Gilford, Nanette Fabray, Danny Dare, and Nancy Walker.

"The big shock about *Meet the People*," recalled Charles Glenn, "was that Hedda Hopper went for it big. It didn't matter that it was left-wing. She enjoyed it, and even though she was a big Red-baiter, she kept coming back to see it. She hated commies, but she knew what she liked."

When Budd Schulberg returned from Vermont just prior to the publication of *What Makes Sammy Run?*, he did not find Hollywood a happy place to be. Though he and Jigee plunged back into the creative left-wing scene, and both volunteered in January 1941 to work on the LAW's Exiled Writers Committee, the climate grew progressively colder for Budd. *Sammy* came out in March, and it is hard to understand how a book that so enraged the producers could equally enrage the Party. And the producers were indeed enraged.

"My father had read the manuscript while I was in Vermont and he wrote me a letter saying he thought it was a fantastic book, but he asked me not to publish it. He said I would be ostracized and not allowed back in town again, and how would I live, how would I survive? He recommended putting it in a drawer and doing another novel and establishing myself, and then, later on, when I was strong enough economically in that world [Hollywood], to do the book.

"Then when *Sammy* was published, L. B. Mayer was in a rage, just in a *rage* about the book, and so were Sam Goldwyn and many others. Mayer and my father had been fighting almost since the early studio days twenty years before. Mayer took this out on my father and said, 'I blame you for this. God damn it, B.P., why didn't you stop him? How could you allow this? It's your fault.' And my father, although he had tried in a way to stop me, said 'Louis, how can I stop him? It's a free country. You are still supposed to have freedom of the press.' And Mayer said, 'Well, I don't care. You should have stopped him, and I think it's an outrage and he ought to be deported.' And he meant it. And my father laughed and said, 'Deported? Where? He was one of the few kids who came out of this place. Where are we going to deport him to? Catalina? Lake Helena? Louis, where do we send him?' And Mayer didn't think it was funny and he said, 'I don't care where you send him, but deport him.' "

The producers' vituperation was, at least, understandable. *What Makes Sammy Run?* had created a thoroughly reprehensible, craven character and shown how Hollywood was the perfect environment in which someone like this could rise to the surface, like poisoned cream. The book had also closely chronicled the events of the Screen Writers Guild's attempt to affiliate with the ALA and the producer-backed cabal to break it with the Screen Playwrights (called, in the book, the "Association of Photodramatists"). Schulberg saw what happened to the men he admired in Hollywood, including his own father, who was quickly joining the ranks of the little kingdom's forgotten men.

B. P. Schulberg had experienced steadily declining success since leaving Paramount in 1932. In 1938 he had gone to work for David Selznick, whose mentor he had been, but he continued to gamble away his money, and he was disliked by the other producers. By 1949 Schulberg senior was a thoroughly shattered man, broke and unemployed, who took out an ad in *Variety* addressed to "The Top Executives of the Motion Picture Industry":

> As most of you know, I have devoted a third of a century to our industry . . . yet at this time, when the industry demands and requires a fixed habit of production economy, it seems I can't get a job. . . . Must we always wait until a productive pioneer is found dead in some obscure Hollywood hotel room [as D. W. Griffith had been] before you reflect upon an "indifferent and forgetful industry"?

There was little response to the ad, and Schulberg died a few years later.

Given his experience of the ruling side of Hollywood and what he put into *What Makes Sammy Run?* on that subject, it was not surprising that Budd Schulberg was attacked by the likes of Mayer and Goldwyn. But it was the bitter, vindictive attack of the Party that was unexpected and so thoroughly disillusioning for him. Its primary objection to the book was that it was anti-Semitic, which was one of the objections of the producers and of others who were not in the Party. Richard Maibaum recalls that he was one of the ones who objected to the anti-Semitism in *Sammy* when an earlier version of it had appeared as a short story in *Liberty* magazine. "I didn't think it was right to show a grasping, movie-industry Shylock at a time when the Nazis were shoving Jews into ovens. But I told Budd to change the name of the narrator in the story from Al Manners to Al Manheim," Maibaum said. "At least it wasn't quite so bad to have this Jewish bastard described by another Jew."

There were bitter arguments in the Party over the book. Schulberg was accused not only of anti-Semitism but of slandering progressive forces. Schulberg himself felt it clearly was a progressive book, on the side of the union and against the bosses, and that Sammy Glick was an example of a would-be boss, if he had played his cards right.

Charles Glenn knew Schulberg and had bumped into him one day at Larry Edmund's bookstore. A great admirer of Schulberg, Glenn asked Budd if he could read the galleys of the book, and Budd agreed.

"I jumped the review date by a few weeks," recalled Glenn. "I thought the book was good, and I didn't think it was anti-Semitic. I gave the book a rave review. Then I got a call from Madeleine Ruthven to come over. She'd slapped my wrist before for recruiting on her turf, but I went over there and spent the most tortured hour and a half I'd ever spent. I had to retract, they said. Lawson was there, and he said I'd have to write the retraction myself. I said, 'If that's the way you feel, you write a letter and I'll publish it as an article and I'll answer it and we'll have a discussion.' And they said, 'No, no discussion, just write the review.'

"I was young enough in the Party then that it was still like a church. I have never ceased regretting the retraction. Ten years later I still wanted to apologize to Budd, but I didn't have the guts, and by then Budd had used me as his cop-out. As bad as I felt, I knew I'd feel worse if I had to consort with a stool pigeon."

Glenn's first review had said that "while it doesn't qualify as the great American novel, it's still the best work done on Hollywood." His second review read, "Recently, I wrote a review on Budd Schulberg's book, *What Makes Sammy Run?*. I said it was the story of a Hollywood heel and could be regarded as *the* Hollywood novel. On the basis of quite lengthy discussion on the book, I've done a little re-evaluating, and this helps me emphasize the points I've tried to make here. . . ." Ultimately criticizing Schulberg's picture

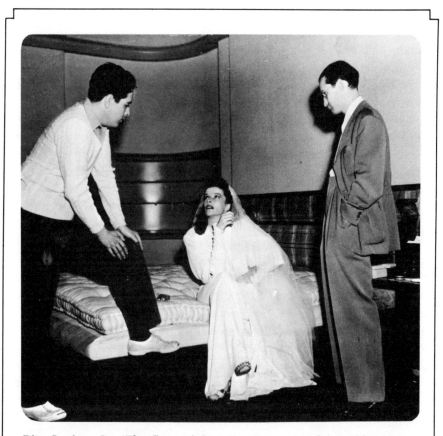

Ring Lardner, Jr. (*The Cross of Lorraine, Tomorrow, the World!, Laura, Forever Amber*), with Katharine Hepburn and Michael Kanin, 1941, on the set of *Woman of the Year.*

of the SWG's struggle, Glenn concluded, "Some day the story of the Guild will be thoroughly told, well dramatized, and done in all the shades of gray which entered the picture, not on the plain black and whites drawn in the Schulberg book."

Ring Lardner, Jr., recalled, "There was a meeting of Party members called expressly to discuss *What Makes Sammy Run?*. I think Richard Collins and I, or maybe it was Paul Jarrico and I, were defending *Sammy* against quite a few other people who said it was implicitly anti-Semitic. There had been some discussion when the book came out, and some individuals had expressed some criticisms to Budd personally, and it was decided that we should talk this out, and my recollection is that arbitrarily six or eight writers were asked to Herbert Biberman's house to listen to Budd's feelings about his book, his side of it. And I had two separate feelings about it: one was that it was ridiculous to have this kind of discussion after a book was published, that you really couldn't expect any writer, particularly a young writer with his first novel just published, to really accept this sort of criticism, and that it could only result in alienating him. But I also happened to agree with the main thesis, that of criticism. . . . There was a similar discussion many years later about the movie *All the King's Men*, with Robert Rossen, after the movie had been completed, and there again the result of the discussion was to drive Rossen out of the Party."

The hostility in Party circles toward *Sammy* may have been predicated on Budd's refusal to let the Party have any direct participation in the writing of the book, despite Lawson's suggestions and desire to influence the work. Perhaps one of the reasons the Left reacted so bitterly was that *Sammy* really articulated the covert anti-Semitism of the Left in its struggle against the producers in the industry, although the anti-union activities and worship of money that would make the producers more willing to make deals with a gangster-controlled union than with an incorruptible one could be ascribed to class rather than ethnic differences. *Sammy*, coming as it did in the middle of the Stalin-Hitler pact, aroused the defensiveness of the Party, out to prove that it was not anti-Semitic, though it was linked with Hitler in a nonaggression alliance.

It is difficult to say which came first, Schulberg's drinking or Jigee's promiscuity, but Jigee's admirers were still legion. It was rumored that Lester Koenig, who had shared a house with her and Budd for a while, had briefly been involved in an affair with her. Fitzgerald had met her during the filming of *Winter Carnival* and had been fascinated by her, just as everyone else was. And while she was still married to Budd, she had become involved with writer Peter Viertel, the great passion of her life. Friends said that Jigee claimed to have left Budd because of his drinking. She couldn't stand drinking or weakness of any sort. She was athletic and never drank or got sick, although she did chain-smoke.

Jigee's sister, Anne, said that Jigee and Peter were better matched than Jigee and Budd. Jigee and Peter had a competitive kind of relationship. She could outshoot him, outride him, outfish him. He fancied himself quite an outdoorsman, but she could even outski him.

"I think she fell for Peter Viertel simply because he was so gallant—for surface reasons," said Paul Jarrico, one of her circle of admirers. "I once asked her, 'What did you see in Viertel?' and she said, 'He gave me a horse. We were riding, and I liked his horse, and the horse liked me, and he said, "It's yours." ' "

Arthur Laurents, a friend of Jigee's, wrote a play in 1945, *A Clearing in the Woods*, an abstract, psychological drama in which a romantic, egotistical young woman delves into her past, confronting troubling memories of herself, her father, and the men in her life. Her name is Virginia, and the three sides of her personality are called Nora, Ginna, and Jigee. The play is like a gestalt exercise, with the character broken down into its component roles.

It is uncertain how close to the truth about Jigee the play really is. However, it was Schulberg's testimony before HUAC in 1951 that was his final divorce—from Jigee and her friends, from the ideology that had disappointed him, from the artistic community that had demanded his obedience and then reviled him. Schulberg was the professional disenchanted. His reactions were symbolic, sweeping, irrevocable gestures. In writing and publishing *Sammy* he systematically dissociated himself from the Party and the industry. Though he finally left the Party over the episode with *Sammy*, and though a further hope that failed was Virginia, who turned into his nightmare of Jere in *The Disenchanted*, the final wrench was his testimony before HUAC. It was in his testimony that he repudiated the life he had once led and grimly, almost proudly, announced, "Some others run, too."

The inscriptions in his books are, perhaps, the most interesting comment on Budd Schulberg. He seems to continually be congratulating his friends for being so different from the people he writes about. In the flyleaf of the Butlers' copy of *Sammy* he wrote, "To Hugo and Jean—thank God the Butlers outnumber the Glicks," and to Samson and Dorshka Raphaelson he wrote, "To Rafe and Dorshka, whose life together is such a happy refutation of the Hallidays" (the Fitzgeralds in *The Disenchanted*).

By the summer of 1941, it seemed quite evident to the leaders of the motion picture industry that the United States was heading toward war. Roosevelt's preparedness plan had begun in 1940, and the two-ocean navy was a reality. In September Senator Burton K. Wheeler of Montana called for a preliminary investigation to see if a full-fledged probe was called for in Hollywood, since, he charged, the foreign-born, warmongering producers who ran the industry were making films calculated to drag the United States into the war in Europe. They were doing this, he claimed, at the behest of the New Dealers. As evidence of the Hollywood stake in British victory, he pointed to the Anglo-American cooperation of studios such as MGM, which was turning out such co-productions as *A Yank at Oxford* in conjunction with the Denham studios in Britain. Former presidential candidate Wendell Willkie refuted the charges, and Wheeler was made to look a fool. Instead, there was the possibility that the war would give a boost to the economy of the nation and to the movie industry.

One valuable effect of the imminence of war was the final working out of a contract between the producers and the Screen Writers Guild. The negotiations had been dragging on, and by May 1941 the SWG was fed up, so they used the only weapon they had—the threat of a strike. A $50,000 war chest was raised for use in the event of a strike, but a strike vote was deferred pending another meeting between the negotiating teams of writers and producers. SWG president Sheridan Gibney, however, promised that if the negotiations were not acceptable, a strike vote would be taken.

"The negotiating committees met at the Brown Derby," recalled Dore Schary. "Boris Ingster, Mary McCall, Jr., Charlie Brackett, Ralph Block, and Sheridan Gibney were there for the SWG, and the producers and their attorneys. All of the big guns were there. We talked, had dinner, and then sat down. Mendel Silberberg, who was a very sharp lawyer, said, 'We want to reach an agreement with you. This country might go to war; the studios might be closed.' And everyone couldn't help remembering the 1933 wage cut. So Bob Kenny said, 'Call for a recess,' and we did, and we talked, and when we came back we said to the producers, 'You're right.'

"Sheridan Gibney, who was a very gentle, soft-spoken man, said, 'Because of the unstable situation, we think it best if you recognize us and make an agreement with us in principle. Agree to at least an eighty-five percent guild shop. And there's no reason to say that once the crisis is past we can't settle on a permanent minimum wage. But for the duration of the crisis, we think you should institute a minimum wage of at least $120. [Under a prior six-month agreement in 1940, which had expired in April 1941, the minimum was $50.]

"And Harry Warner got up and turned to his men and said, 'Is that all they want?' and Gibney said, 'We think, under the circumstances, it's fair.' And Warner turned to his men and said, 'That's all they want . . . those dirty communist sons of bitches . . . they want to take my goddamn studio, my brothers built this studio. I came here from Europe . . . my father was a butcher . . .' and he let out a string of obscenities I wouldn't dare repeat, calling us all sorts of wild names and screaming.

"Well, we were stunned. We didn't even get angry, because we were watching a man who was obviously getting blown out of his head. And I must say the other producers knew it, because two of them got up, Y. Frank Freeman, who was then the president of the Association of Motion Picture Producers, and Eddie Mannix. And they each took an arm of Harry Warner's, and their backs were toward us so they kind of carried him out, and he was still screaming, 'And furthermore, you dirty commies,' and they took him out to the parking lot, and there was an absolutely dead silence. After a couple of minutes, Silberberg asked for a recess. So we went into a corner and Bob Kenny said, 'You got them, I guarantee it. No matter what we said, Warner won the fight for us.' And I said, 'You're as crazy as Harry Warner.'

"So then we were called back to the bargaining table, and Silberberg said, 'Gentlemen, we regret that Mr. Warner cannot rejoin us. He wasn't feeling well. But we've discussed your proposal, and we find it acceptable.'

"So we had our first SWG contract."

The contract was accepted, in principle, by the SWG membership by a unanimous vote of five hundred. The contract was to be written permanently as soon as the war contingency was resolved. On June 18, 1941, nine years after the Guild had organized, they had their first contract. The agreement, to be effective for seven years and subject to reopening after three years, included provisions for an 85 percent guild shop for three years and then a 90 percent guild shop, and minimum pay of $125 per week for all writers, including shorts writers, which would be effective one year after the contract was signed. Also, minimum periods of employment were assured, layoffs were controlled, and arbitration was provided for, with the Guild in control of screen credits. Speculative writing was outlawed, and it was proclaimed that all writers had the right to attend sneak previews of their own pictures.

Although it would not be a reality until the contract was signed, the final settlement of $125 for a minimum wage was regarded as one of the most important points won because of the treatment of the low-bracket screen writers at the studio. With the knowledge that everybody wanted to be a screen writer, the studios had made it a practice to hire unknowns for anywhere from $30 to $50 a week. There was even a classic case of the producer who promoted his secretary to writer; the next day, she came to the studio and found her name on the door of her new office; and on payday, instead of the $60 she had been receiving as secretary, she got $40 as a scenarist.

The writers were elated by this victory. Four days later, on June 22, 1941, Hitler attacked Russia. The Stalin-Hitler pact was at an end, and everyone in Hollywood breathed a sigh of relief.

"I remember it was a Sunday afternoon," recalled Allen Rivkin, "at Sidney and Beatrice Buchman's in Bel Air, and Lilly Hellman walked in dressed all in white. She was somewhere between ecstatic and furious, and I don't know if she was kidding or serious, but she said, 'The Motherland has been attacked.' "

Donald Ogden Stewart recalled his reaction to the news in his autobiography, *By a Stroke of Luck*:

> I was driving alone. . . . It was a beautifully clear, calm, star-filled night, and I was listening to some dance music on my radio. . . . Suddenly the music stopped. After a moment, "We interrupt this program to tell you that this afternoon the German armies invaded the Soviet Union and a state of war now exists"—I listened, and I unexpectedly began to cry. Not with pity for the Russian people. I wept with joy and relief. I was once more on the "right" side, the side of all my old friends. Now we were all fighting Fascism, or, at least, fighting it in Germany and Italy. It was

one of the happiest nights of my life. I could continue believing in my remote dream, the country where the true equality of man was becoming a reality under the philosophy of Marxism and Leninism and the leadership of the great Stalin.

"With the invasion of Russia," commented Robert Kenny, "the left wing returned to its good behavior. The various factions seemed to melt together—Bundles for Britain and Finnish War Relief shook hands with the American-Russian Friends group, the members of the Hollywood Peace Forum were once again on the 'A' list of Hollywood parties, the social life that had been so wonderful in Hollywood resumed.

State Senator Jack Tenney's investigation of communist activities in musicians' Local 47 backfired when his witness, Sam Alpert, testified that all the alleged communist activities committees had been organized with Tenney's complete knowledge when he was in the union and had been used to help elect Tenney president of the union. *Variety* ran the headline, "Commie Purge Backfires—Witnesses Linked to Tenney." Postcards began to pour into Tenney's office after the 1941 session of the state legislature bearing the message "Roses are red/violets are blue/Yorty is through/and so are you."

Senator Wheeler was further discredited with a massive campaign by the League of American Writers. Exhorting writers and readers around the country to protest the activities of the America First committee (and what a relief it was to be rid of that strange bedfellow) with telegrams to D. W. Clark, chairman of a Senate investigative subcommittee, and telegrams to their local newspapers, the LAW said:

> Under the guise of keeping this country out of war, a group of senators, whose position has been revealed to be pro-Nazi in effect, is endeavoring to keep anti-Nazi films from being shown to the American people. These senators, while pretending to investigate whether an investigation of the film industry is needed, are smearing everything progressive and anti-Nazi which has come out of Hollywood. The National Board of the LAW believes this Senate Committee which is directly attacking free cultural expression in our country is a major menace to the unity of the American people in the struggle against Hitlerism. . . .

The fight against anti-Semitism escalated. On October 17, Robert Noble, the organizer of the Friends of Progress, announced, "The Jews are trying to get us in this war. They control the motion pictures and the newspapers. . . . I do agree with . . . Mr. Hitler." The reaction was so violent in the movie community that even Tenney, who still said he didn't consider America First a subversive organization, grudgingly agreed that he thought we should aid Russia in the fight against Hitler.

On November 18, 1941, the Neutrality Act was revised and signed by FDR, and permitted armed American merchantmen to carry cargoes to belligerent ports. While the Nazis were attempting a complete encirclement of Leningrad, trying to cut Russia's second city off from all contact with the outside world and to isolate its defending armies, American war materiels were bound for Russia, two hundred freight-car loads shipped over 5,000 miles. There was even a growing unity among American labor organizations as the CIO repudiated John L. Lewis and his isolationism and united behind FDR.

On Sunday, December 7, 1941, the Japanese bombed Pearl Harbor, and on December 8 the United States entered World War II.

8

There was probably no place in the country as overwhelmingly affected by the war as Hollywood, and as little inconvenienced by it. The proximity of Los Angeles to Pearl Harbor was, of course, disconcerting, and the Angelenos feared that they too would be bombed. On December 8, the day after Pearl Harbor, there were blackouts all over town, barbed wire in the L.A. harbor district, and the mournful wail of air-raid sirens piercing the night. By the time Congress had declared war on Germany and Italy, as well as on Japan, the Women's Ambulance and Defense Corps in Los Angeles was a full-fledged operation, and to build public morale they gave demonstrations, with the women showing how they would spring to action during a gas attack.

There were people so terrified of an attack by Japanese planes that they sold their houses or simply left for inland safety. Suddenly real estate in the Pacific Palisades was cheap. There were others who felt that the danger was not from Japanese planes but from sabotage within. Lockheed and North American Aviation, the two largest airplane factories in California, were right in the midst of Los Angeles, the important commercial port of San Pedro was just a stone's throw away, and U.S. Fort MacArthur stood on Point Fermin. Public fear that Californians of Japanese descent would be disloyal was epidemic in the state, and in the first two months after the bombing, 110 Japanese were rounded up and placed in temporary detention camps. Hollywood's awareness of the roundup grew as, one by one, all the Japanese gardeners and household help disappeared.

On Wednesday, December 10, Los Angeles had its first complete blackout. People in Hollywood were at dinner, lifting fork to mouth, when the sirens began. The next instant a voice over the radio announced, "This is the Fourth Interceptor Command. Unidentified planes in the sky. Complete blackout ordered immediately."

The voice droned on, repeating the message over and over again for a half hour, and the very repetition had an ominous effect. People poured out of restaurants, eager to get home, and watched with fear and awe as Hollywood blacked out by degrees—Musso's, the Brown Derby, the Beverly Wilshire . . . a slow dimming until somebody pulled the main switch and everything became pitch-black. All of Beverly Hills was completely dark, except for the Christmas trees in the middle of the streets at intersections. Eventually those too were dark. It was eight o'clock at night, and it felt like the end of the world.

People lucky enough to find their cars were greeted by policemen out in force to prevent headlights from being turned on. Only the blue glare from the cellophane-covered lights of doctors' cars and other emergency vehicles penetrated the darkness, and cars crawled along like blind insects. Many people were caught wherever they happened to be when the alarm sounded and had to stay there until after midnight, when the all-clear was given.

"The night of that false alarm we were sure the Japanese were going to bomb L.A.," recalled Fred Rinaldo. "Barrage balloons went up, and you heard the antiaircraft guns firing. At the League of American Writers we were in the middle of classes, but we had prepared the basement for the eventuality of a bombing. We moved everyone downstairs and continued classes. At the time, it seemed damned organized and heroic, us in the basement and the air-raid warden on the roof."

There was great fear, but there was also a new sort of exhilaration, one of being caught up in something bigger than any individual. "The greatest thing that could have happened to this nation was Japan's taking the initiative and attacking us," Sonya Levien wrote to a friend in England. "It has solidified this country as nothing else on earth could have done. The funniest thing was listening in over the radio to the isolationist senators. They were falling all over themselves calling for immediate and direct action."

Elizabeth Faragoh also recalled the sudden complete concentration that the war elicited. "The poker games had stopped. There was no more time. And we stopped reading fiction. We read only newspapers and tracts. We were so absorbed in what was going on in the world, things seemed so crucial, that anything even remotely frivolous was decadent."

The country was suddenly obsessed with "enemy alien" proclamations. The 1942 *Authors League of America Bulletin* asked its subscribers:

Have you ever collaborated on any piece of work with a person who is now an enemy alien? Are any rights in any of the literary properties you own shared by someone in an enemy-held country? If you have any work which falls into one of these categories you will be unable to sell it or any part of it in America. Yet if you have a movie sale which is being held up because of such a situation there is a way in which you can make the sale at once. Communicate with the Alien Property Custodian. He will take over the interest of your collaborator, accept any fees, and hold them for your partner until after the war.

This situation was particularly shocking in Hollywood, which was filled with European refugees, many German or Austrian, who had fled from Hitler. The White House was deluged with mail from anti-Nazi refugees such as Thomas Mann and the Viertels, pointing out that many of those categorized as "enemy aliens" were among the first and most prescient critics of the governments that the United States was now battling. The result of this pressure was that many German and Austrian nationals were spared the fate of the Japanese immigrants and Americans of Japanese descent. It was shocking to the refugees to watch as civil liberties were blithely dispensed with in the interest of national defense.

But the war was the best thing that could have happened to the movie industry. After the triumphant box-office sweep of 1939, which culminated in *Gone With the Wind*, 1940 had been a relatively bad year. Foreign markets had continued to shrink, and block booking had been outlawed. By the end of 1940, the box office take was one-third less than the previous year's.

And then the studios began gearing up for the war. There had been rigid economy drives in the industry and the tension of a tightened belt. Whatever caused it, 1941 was a good year for movies, and box-office receipts began to mount. It was a year that produced such films as *Citizen Kane, How Green Was My Valley, The Lady Eve*, and *Sergeant York*. The studios, aware of war's proximity, had been preparing, so that nearly every studio had a war picture in production or ready to be released. Movie attendance increased astronomically throughout the war because gas rationing forced people to stay close to home. Also, there was no better place to go for entertainment and escape than the local movie theater. People went as many as three times a week, and the bills changed just as often.

Furthermore, in this era before TV every movie was coupled with a newsreel, and people were desperately hungry to know what was going on in the outside world. Short subjects were serving both as a training ground for young writers and directors who were being groomed for features and as a funnel for information to the U.S. public. Shorts were made that taught women how to make the best use of their rations in cooking for a family, and the national paranoia about sabotage, particularly with the surge of people working in defense plants, was reinforced and dealt with in shorts such as *Don't Talk*, which employed the "loose lips sink ships" idea to warn workers not to discuss their business where it might be overheard by saboteurs and fifth columnists.

"E for Effort" signs flew above the movie studios, which were giving themselves completely to the war effort. Production in Hollywood was more crucial than production in some industries, because it affected morale. Movies were sent to the camps where men and women in the armed services were stationed, and by 1943, 630,000 enlisted personnel were seeing Hollywood movies each night.

Hollywood set the tone for the American look, formulating style almost as the palaces of old had formulated court style, and the people who flocked to the silver screen nightly saw a world of patient, waiting women; chipper, energetic factory girls; snappy secretaries; eager chorus girls; and every variety of human being who was, underneath, capable of being touched by the larger picture—the war. The sacrifice of the woman Bogey loved to her resistance-fighter husband in *Casablanca* epitomized the wartime spirit. And the movies transmitted the wartime look—curly hairdos, padded shoulders, knee-length skirts, bright red lipstick.

Hollywood was responsible for rendering the war comprehensible to the home-front audience. It created stereotypes of villains—the vicious Nazi ("Ve haff vays of making you talk"), the evil, brutal "Jap." It also created stereotypes of heroes: war films depicted the army as a veritable Noah's ark of ethnicity—a Jewish soldier from Brooklyn, an Italian GI, a tough palooka with an Irish name, whose differences in background become irrelevant in their united war effort. In Robert Walker's role of Private Hargrove the movies created the quintessential green GI, and he was among the easily identifiable symbols of humanity that proliferated in films of that period—a legion of understanding but gruff sergeants; sympathetic and lovely Red Cross nurses; wise, tender, waiting families; and suffering European victims of the Hun.

Movies such as *The Mortal Storm, Foreign Correspondent, Escape, Nazi Agent, Hangmen Also Die*, and *Man Hunt* were filled with passionate antifascism, while *Jane Eyre, That Hamilton Woman, Edison, the Man*, and *Pride and Prejudice* took audiences a million miles from the war into a world of hoop skirts and elegance of days gone by. Movie audiences could either be diverted from the war or experience it vicariously. But one thing was evident —Hollywood was one of the major morale boosters for this country during the war.

Hollywood's talent also mobilized for victory in other ways. Three days after Pearl Harbor, the Hollywood Victory Committee, operating out of Beverly Hills, was organized as a clearinghouse for the volunteer war efforts of all Hollywood talent. The "soldiers in greasepaint"—performers from stage, screen, and radio—toured hospitals, USO camps, and fighting fronts and sold War Bonds in fevered drives. The Victory Committee was chaired by actor Kenneth Thompson, with director Mark Sandrich as vice-chairman and MGM publicity head Howard Strickling as secretary. The board also featured people such as James Cagney, Howard Estabrook, and Eddie Mannix.

The Actors Committee was a coalition that included Charles Boyer, Bette Davis, Joan Blondell, Cary Grant, John Garfield, Bob Hope, Ginger Rogers, Merle Oberon, Rosalind Russell, and Adolphe Menjou, who, although

BALLOT FOR ANNUAL ELECTION OF OFFICERS AND EXECUTIVE BOARD
SCREEN WRITERS' GUILD, INC.

Wedenesday — November 10, 1943 — 8:15 P.M.

The following candidates have been selected in accordance with the Guild Constitution, ARTICLE XI, Section 1. Also, in accordance with the Constitution, ARTICLE XI, Section 3, "Nominations may be made from the floor, or in the case of mail ballots, additional names may be written in."

OFFICERS

PRESIDENT (vote for one)

☐ MARY C. McCALL, JR.
☐ ....

SECRETARY (vote for one)

☐ TALBOT JENNINGS
☐ GLADYS LEHMAN
☐ ....

VICE-PRESIDENT (vote for one)

☐ LESTER COLE
☐ ALLAN SCOTT
☐ ....

TREASURER (vote for one)

☐ HUGO BUTLER
☐ JANE MURFIN
☐ ....

EXECUTIVE BOARD

Vote for *twenty-one* (21). Be sure to include in this number the names of the four candidates you have selected as officers. The eleven candidates receiving the highest number of votes, together with the four officers, will comprise the regular members of the Executive Board. The six candidates receiving the next highest votes will be alternate Board Members.

☐ ROBERT ANDREWS	☐ TALBOT JENNINGS	☐ LEO TOWNSEND
☐ HUGO BUTLER	☐ MICHAEL KANIN	☐ KARL TUNBERG
☐ MARTHA CHAPIN	☐ GORDON KAHN	☐ BRENDA WEISBERG
☐ LESTER COLE	☐ ROBERT E. KENT	☐ JOHN WEXLEY
☐ RICHARD COLLINS	☐ RING LARDNER, JR.	☐ ....
☐ MARC CONNELLY	☐ EMMET LAVERY	☐ ....
☐ OLIVE COOPER	☐ GLADYS LEHMAN	☐ ....
☐ MORGAN COX	☐ MELVIN LEVY	☐ ....
☐ DELMAR DAVES	☐ MARY C. McCALL, JR.	☐ ....
☐ WALTER DE LEON	☐ HORACE McCOY	☐ ....
☐ JAY DRATLER	☐ JANE MURFIN	☐ ....
☐ KEN ENGLAND	☐ FRED NIBLO, JR.	☐ ....
☐ LEWIS R. FOSTER	☐ MAURICE RAPF	☐ ....
☐ SHERIDAN GIBNEY	☐ BETTY REINHARDT	☐ ....
☐ MORTON GRANT	☐ STANLEY ROBERTS	☐ ....
☐ F. HUGH HERBERT	☐ WALDO SALT	☐ ....
☐ JAMES HILTON	☐ ADRIAN SCOTT	☐ ....
☐ MICHAEL HOGAN	☐ ALLAN SCOTT	☐ ....
☐ ARTHUR HORMAN	☐ GEORGE SEATON	☐ ....

Your ballot should be cast at the meeting, unless you are not present. You may vote by mail, or you may use the enclosed proxy form. If you vote by mail or if you cast your own ballot, please note the following instructions:

After marking your ballot, put it in the enclosed blank envelope and seal the same. Enclose this sealed envelope in the addressed envelope, write your name on the outside of the addressed envelope, in the space provided therefor. THE BALLOT WILL NOT BE COUNTED UNLESS THE VOTER PLACES HIS NAME ON THE RETURN ENVELOPE ADDRESSED TO THE PROXY COMMITTEEE.

IT IS NOT NECESSARY TO USE A PROXY FOR THE ELECTION OF OFFICERS, BOARD MEMBERS, OR THE CONSTITUTIONAL AMENDMENT. IN THE EVENT THAT YOU ARE UNABLE TO ATTEND THE ANNUAL MEETING, YOU MAY VOTE BY MARKING THE BALLOTS AND MAILING THEM INTO THE GUILD OFFICE IN TIME TO REACH THE PROXY COMMITTEE NOVEMBER 10, 1943.

he had been Hitler's guest at the 1936 Olympics in Berlin, had transferred his devotion to the American cause.

The material for these patriotic efforts was being provided by the Hollywood Writers Mobilization (HWM), a group organized within a week of the Pearl Harbor bombing. Its first chairman was Francis Faragoh, and Pauline Lauber Finn became its executive secretary. The HWM was not structured in the same way as was the Screen Writers Guild. It had officers and meetings, but there was no constitution or by-laws. It was, theoretically, a pool of writer talent to fill the needs of the Hollywood Victory Committee and of the government, and shortly after the Mobilization was formed, a delegation was sent to Washington to tell the government that the talent of the Guild was at its disposal. The members of the HWM were interested in doing anything they could for the war effort, from writing camp shows to writing political speeches.

The war period was an extremely interesting one for the Screen Writers Guild and for labor in general. All of the factional in-fighting was abandoned for the larger good. Labor agreed to a no-strike pledge for the duration of the war, and the atmosphere was such that on the Monday following Pearl Harbor, the U.S. Supreme Court reversed a contempt citation against labor leader Harry Bridges. It was a seeming honeymoon for every element in America. Russia was our ally.

The communists, fellow travelers, liberals, and right-wingers threw aside their differences and pitched in. Every group wanted to do all it could. By the beginning of 1943, 215 members of the SWG were serving in the armed forces. Those who remained in Hollywood devoted themselves to adjusting to such problems as the manpower shortage and conservation of materials, and, with the sudden upsurge in production and the conscription of so many, they found themselves busier and more fully employed than ever before.

A labor-management committee composed of six writers and six producers was set up, in conjunction with the Motion Picture War Advisory Board, to study the question of manpower in terms of draft deferment for writers. The committee was selected after a lengthy debate over who was best qualified to judge a writer's ability (and replaceability)—the producer, the writer himself, or a committee of his peers. And after a survey, the committee came to several conclusions: Of the writers at that point employed in the industry, 85 percent were men, of whom 35 percent were vulnerable to the draft. That meant that unless requests for deferment were made and granted, 18 percent of the male writers employed would be drafted. It also meant that among the 15 percent of employed writers who were women, there was a greater possibility of expanded employment.

The committee then made a tentative outline of writer categories for war production:

1. capable of translating complex technical information into screen terms (training films)
2. adept at dramatizing social-historical information (educational films)
3. adept at giving emotional power to ideological concepts (morale)
4. physically equipped to accompany film-making units into action (combat films)

Paul Jarrico, one of the writers on the manpower survey committee, was repelled by the whole process. "Writers who didn't want to fight wanted to prove how crucial they were to the war effort, and I was embarrassed by the idea of propagandizing the war effort and not being involved in the war. So I shipped out in the merchant marine as a direct result."

Although there were writers who were quite content to be useful on the home front and avoid the horror of battle, there were others who tried to enlist and found they were unacceptable. The ones who were over thirty-eight were too old to be drafted. But there were anxious, healthy young men who tried and tried to get assigned to active duty and who were rejected each time. The rejections had nothing to do with health or age: they had to do with politics. The FBI and the War Department had assigned a classification to people whose politics they considered dangerous. There were dossiers filled with listings of meetings attended, rallies addressed, and moneys contributed that read like a road map of the left wing in the thirties, charting the landscape from popular front to the Stalin-Hitler Pact. And on those dossiers were the letters PAF—Premature Anti-Fascist.

"I couldn't get into any of the services I wanted to get into," recalled Maurice Rapf. "I never was drafted. I tried to get into various units of the Industrial Sound Division of the navy; the OSS; the Marine Corps photographic unit. I always got turned down. They'd always say it was my eyes or something. But we knew it was political. And they always asked me the question 'Are you a member of the Communist Party?' and I always denied it, which I shouldn't have done. They probably would have accepted me, but we were underground and I couldn't admit it. . . . By 1941, once the war had started and we were allies of the Soviet Union and people weren't even very anticommunist, it was the perfect time for the CP in Hollywood to have surfaced. It should have—there were so many respectable, good people in the CP that it was a shame you had to hide it. It always seemed to me that the whole underground thing was idiotic. I hated it at the time—to lead a dual life all the time, not to be able to tell your best friends that you're a communist. It was awful."

"I was in the Coast Guard during the war," recalled John Bright. "I volunteered for officer's candidate in every branch of the service involving combat, which I wanted, and was turned down on the grounds that I was a

SCREEN WRITERS' GUILD, INC.

1655 NO. CHEROKEE AVE., HOLLYWOOD 28, CALIFORNIA

AFFILIATED WITH AUTHORS' LEAGUE OF AMERICA, INC.

E D I T O R I A L

WHO is loyal to America? What is this new loyalty? All writers who respect their profession should ask these questions. We should give thought to the sharpening attempts of legislative committees and those who use them to put into uniform the expression of opinion. For writers are the first to feel these pressures against the civil liberties of all Americans.

Those who would stifle the interplay of opinion in a free democracy recognize that writers as a group are the most articulate custodians of the traditions of tolerance, democracy, and the freedom not to conform. So it is important that we examine with all possible clarity, and answer with all the intelligence and courage we can muster, these questions: *What is the standard of this new loyalty? Is it conformity: the blind or forced acceptance of the political and economic opinions of a few ultra-conservative manufacturers, newspaper owners and politicians?*

These are poignant questions today. They are coming home with swift insistence to Americans loyal to the America of Jefferson and Lincoln, of Emerson and Thoreau, of Roosevelt and Willkie.

It is not a passing fancy that caused the Los Angeles County Supervisors to classify as dubious if not subversive the Authors' League of America, with which the Screen Writers' Guild is affiliated. It is not personal idiosyncrasy that causes Jack B. Tenney to smear constantly our Guild, other writer organizations and individual writers. It is not playful whimsy that causes the Motion Picture Alliance for the Preservation of American Ideals to brand as premature antifascist. So I joined the Coast Guard, and I was assigned to writing training films, morale films, industrial incentive films."

"I enlisted in the air force when the war came," recalled actor Lionel Stander, "but I was listed as a premature antifascist, in red on my file, so I never went into action. [The gravel-voiced Stander was reported to have filled a few seconds of dead screen time, waiting for an elevator, by whistling "The Internationale."] Most of the guys with that PAF classification got impossible jobs. I worked at Mitchel Field in Long Island, and I never saw action. I had a pilot's license. I was supposed to go to Canada to join the Royal Canadian Air Force, but then Roosevelt declared that they needed everyone with a pilot's license. So I couldn't go to Canada and I couldn't get called up here, either."

When Dorothy Parker wanted to become a war correspondent, she couldn't get a passport; she, too, was considered a premature antifascist. Ring Lardner, Jr., found he was unable to get into combat. Wherever he applied, he was turned down. The Office of War Information (OWI), the Marine Corps, the Office of Strategic Services—all nearly enlisted his services and then, after a security check, refused. The only branch in which he could enlist was the Army Signal Corps, where he worked for a few months on the training-film program in Astoria, Queens.

Interestingly enough, Budd Schulberg was able to get a commission in the navy, and he enlisted in 1943. By that time, he and Jigee were separated. In 1942, she had flown down to Mexico, where he was working on a film, and informed him that she wanted a divorce. She was in love with Peter Viertel and she was going to marry him.

The news of Jigee's impending divorce resurrected hope in the breasts of many of her admirers. Ring Lardner, Jr., proposed to her—which, he humorously remarked, didn't sit well with the wife he was still married to. Her adoring circle began to swarm around her again, and it was even rumored that John O'Hara flew out from New York to propose to her. But she was waiting for Peter.

Jigee was now living in a large, elegant house on Stone Canyon Road in Bel Air and spending a great deal of time at the Mayberry Street salon of her future mother-in-law, Salka Viertel. During this period she had little interaction with the Communist Party, apart from friends such as Lardner. Peter Viertel was not a communist, though his family was of a sympathetic fellow-traveler cast, and Jigee had always been bored by the tracts and dogma. She would occasionally throw open her house for a benefit for something like the *People's Daily World*, but she was no longer the active Marxist she had once been. It certainly made no difference in terms of her social life, because there was such a proliferation of organizations with benefits and fund-raisers: the Hollywood Canteen, the Hollywood Writers Mobilization, Russian War Relief, bond drives, the Red Cross, and on and on.

But even more exhilarating than the sense of being involved in a nation-wide struggle while retaining a privileged aura was the new political harmony in Hollywood. It was truly a honeymoon for the Communist Party. For the first time in its history, the CP's aims were in concert with the American political consensus.

"I'd never seen such incredible unity in Hollywood," sighed Fred Rinaldo. "We all rushed to the papers in the morning to see if Stalingrad still stood. I remember a war mobilization rally sponsored by [L.A.] Mayor Bowron where Eliscu, Gorney, and Myers [of *Meet the People* fame] sang, 'Have you heard/Of a note/That General MacArthur wrote/All about our courageous Russian army. . . . ?' The spirit was incredible. There was never anything like that time in Hollywood, before or since."

This climate actually fostered an upsurge in the number of people who now joined the Communist Party, a harmonious trend which had begun with the termination of the Stalin-Hitler Pact. The seeming consensus of Left and Right would indeed have made this the best period, if such a thing had been possible, for the Party to come up from underground. But the intense absorption in the war effort worked against any move that would have created political divisiveness, and the woods were still full of anticommunists who continued grim mutterings about subversion throughout the war.

One of the people who joined the Party during this period, and who was to be among the ten who later went to jail for their political activities, was Dalton Trumbo. Trumbo had been active all along in the Screen Writers Guild, so much so that he had been asked, in the NLRB hearings, if he was a member of the Communist Party. Though Trumbo has said he joined in 1943, Paul Jarrico claimed to have recruited him during the time of the Pact, a period in which the Party was in disfavor—which would not have been inconsistent with Trumbo's tendency to fight on the side with two strikes against it. Whether he joined at that point or not, his pacifist statements, articulated in his antiwar novel *Johnny Got His Gun*, coincided with the antiwar activities of the CP during the period of the Pact. And once he joined the Party, he became one of its most active workers and one of its most prominent figures.

"Of all the characters I knew on the left," recalled Jarrico, "Trumbo was certainly the most original, the most flamboyant, the most unique. He was an extraordinary man. I got to know him in 1938 when we had offices next to one another at RKO. We were both working on 'B' pictures—his was *Five Came Back*. You had to turn in five pages every day and have the script finished in six weeks. I found this very difficult, so I put in long hours. But Trumbo never seemed to work. He'd come in with word games, or some political news, or he was drinking, or working on some fantastic thing. And I'd start to worry about him, playing around for five weeks. But then, the sixth week, the typewriter would go nonstop, and he'd have a brilliant, first-rate script. He did his work in his head, and at the end of five weeks he'd be ready

Screenwriter Sidney Buchman (*The Sign of the Cross, Holiday, Mr. Smith Goes to Washington, Here Comes Mr. Jordan, A Song to Remember*) came to Hollywood in 1931 after attending Columbia and Oxford and working for a year in London as an assistant director at the Old Vic. In 1953 he was cited by HUAC for contempt of Congress.

to write. He was a fabulous bullshitter, and that, unfortunately, sometimes also extended to his work. He was so facile he could put anything across. He was a highly talented man, and he had a marvelous gift for self-publicizing. He chose the unpopular side; he was a renegade, a maverick. I remember when I first got to know him. One night, after a Guild meeting, he took me to the bakery he used to work in. He was just beginning to make it as a screen writer, and he still had a number of cronies at the bakery. But already he was romanticizing the work he'd done there; already he was turning it into something mythological, larger than life."

When Trumbo and his family were living in town during the war period, away from their isolated ranch, their house was the center for a stream of people and meetings. One wonders how, with the CP, the SWG meetings, the Hollywood Writers Mobilization, the various organizational activities, and his writing career, Trumbo managed to have time for a family. He always liked to be in the middle of everything, to have life spilling and tumbling around him. Trumbo exerted a significant creative and political influence over some of his younger colleagues—Lardner, Hugo Butler, and Ian McLellan Hunter. Hugo Butler called Trumbo "The Knight," and they were his "squires." To many of the younger Party members, Trumbo became a mentor figure in lieu of the older, more doctrinaire, more difficult Lawson.

For the writers on the left who remained in Hollywood, their task was to do as much as they could for the war effort, in everything from the Hollywood Writers Mobilization to the Screen Writers Guild. A day or two after Pearl Harbor, an emergency SWG board meeting was called. Everyone met in the offices on Cherokee Street, during a blackout, and the seriousness of the situation was indicated by the fact that it was the first board meeting called at which everybody showed up. The president of the SWG was Sidney Buchman, one of Columbia's top writers, who had written one of Frank Capra's most successful films, *Mr. Smith Goes to Washington*. On that black December night, the first thing the Guild did was to send a telegram to Roosevelt stating that it was at his disposal. The next issue was the contract negotiations. The so-called left wing on the board wanted to freeze the negotiations for the duration of the war.

"The board was split over the proposed freeze," recalled Richard Maibaum. "The Left figured it was wartime, and it was shoulder to shoulder with the Russians, so there could be no labor problems. They were afraid that there'd be a strike if we didn't get the contract signed the way we wanted, even though the writers' minimum hadn't been fixed yet. The Left wanted to sell out the minimum wage for writers to help Russia. The executive board was split, and there was a terrible argument. Lawson, Chodorov, Lester Cole, and Ralph Block all wanted the freeze, and the conservative board members —Harry Tugend, Claude Binyon, Mary McCall, Jr., Charlie Brackett, Sheridan Gibney, and I—were all opposed to it. The vote was six to six, and Buchman sided with them, with the Left."

Harry Tugend recalled that he said, " 'Wouldn't it be nice if the boys came home and found a contract?'—meaning our members who were already in uniform. But the Left wanted to freeze that contract. So I proposed an amendment that, before we proposed the freeze, we'd listen to what the producers had to say. The amendment won by one vote."

"So we walked into the producers' meeting," said Maibaum, "and let them talk first. And Mannix said, 'We've been screwing around long enough. We won't give them the world, but let's give them the minimum wage.' This was the $125 dollars a week. And Mannix then said, 'There's a war on. So let's sign this goddamn contract and make pictures for the boys.' We were all ecstatic except for the left-wing board members, who sat there, with the freeze proposal in their pockets and egg on their faces."

The minimum basic agreement was finally signed in 1942, establishing the foundations for all future negotiations between writers and producers. The writers had been the first of the creative talent groups to seek a minimum working agreement and the last to succeed in negotiating one.

Once the Guild had its contract, the business at hand became completely oriented toward the war effort. In addition to the Hollywood Writers Mobilization, there were other channels for the writer in wartime. The League of American Writers, whose president in 1941 was Dashiell Hammett and whose vice-president was Erskine Caldwell, sent a communication to American writers on December 8, the day after Pearl Harbor, supporting the president and Congress and urging the immediate declaration of war against Germany, Italy, and their satellites.

Calling on all American writers to put their training, talent, and devotion at the service of the country, the LAW suggested that writers contact Archibald MacLeish in the Office of Facts and Figures in Washington, Garson Kanin, motion picture consultant on civilian morale at the Office of Emergency Management, also in Washington, a host of other government agencies, and private service organizations such as the USO Camp Shows in New York.

In addition, the Authors League of America had formed the Writers War Board, a small, unpaid group that received volunteer assistance, whose purpose was to serve as liaison between the writers of America and the government departments that wanted jobs done. Writers were also assigned war-related duties through the studios. Nat Perrin, for example, was at MGM during the war, and though he never joined the HWM, he wrote war-bond speeches for Norma Shearer and Robert Young.

It was obvious that despite the wartime mobilization, there still were—and there would continue to be—tensions between the Right and the Left. One of the big issues that separated the Left from the rest of the Hollywood Writers Mobilization was the so-called second front. The Left began agitating for the opening of a second front as early as 1942, and their big concern was that Russia not be sacrificed and worn out in Europe.

Producer John Houseman, who at that time was devoting most of his energies to the Office of War Information in Washington, was also active in the HWM, and he recalled that Robert Rossen, then a rising young director, was a vocal supporter of the second front and urged the Mobilization to come out in support of it. "Jack Lawson," remembered Houseman, "was more circumspect, more realistic about the possibilities of the second front being opened before Churchill and Roosevelt were good and ready."

Circumspection aside, it is also likely that Lawson was reluctant to push any issue that threatened to split either the SWG or the HWM during that period. The relief of being united in a joint effort after the deadly isolation of the pact period and the true dedication that everyone felt for the war against fascism kept these tensions at an all-time low. It is likely that Lawson, being a rigid adherent to the Party line, was aware that in any organization that had both communist and noncommunist members—organizations that would later be called "fronts"—the Party members were frequently those with the dedication to work the hardest. "You could always tell the Party people," said Lester Pine, then an aspiring song writer, "because they were the four shmucks putting up the chairs and sweeping up and doing everything nobody else in Hollywood would deign to do."

Lawson was still stung by the memory of being forced off the SWG contract negotiating committee, and he did not want to create a repetition of those circumstances. If the Party was going to do its utmost, divisiveness had to be avoided. It was an attitude summed up by Francis Faragoh in an address to the participants in the Hollywood Writers Mobilization—the radio, screen, and newspaper writers guilds and the contributing writers, readers, publicists, cartoonists, and song writers who formed part of the army of creative workers. Their duty, he informed them, like that of the army at the front, was to their nation and their allies. There would be "no room for the defeatist, the cynic, the special pleader for partisan politics, the appeaser, the diversionist."

The first motion picture unit of the Army Air Forces was established in 1942. The position of the creative person in Hollywood was undergoing a change. Over the course of the next three years, 228 films were produced—educational films, orientation films, special psychological testing films. It was a cooperative set-up, with no credits listed.

The writers in Hollywood were amused at the sudden paradox. Never had their services been more highly valued, and never had they been so anonymous, albeit willingly. In a situation that certain cynics compared to Marie Antoinette's playing at being a dairy maid at her palace at Versailles, many of Hollywood's screen writers, directors, actors, and technicians volunteered to produce training films at "Fort Roach." The army had requisitioned the Hal Roach studios, posted sentries around the grounds, and made the denizens of Beverly Hills and the Hollywood Hills make their beds, sweep their floors, and salute. A furlough meant an even wilder than usual night at Musso's.

"Bobby Lees and I," recalled Fred Rinaldo, "made some OWI shorts, in the quartermaster corps, which Colonel Frank Capra produced [Capra's "Why We Fight" series was the apotheosis of motion picture propaganda to come out of the United States during the War]. We did one called *Substitution and Conversion*, which David Miller directed. Miller had no military training, but they made him a captain. They couldn't let a man direct unless he was at least a captain." The ranking in war was not much different for Hollywood people than the ranking in the studios. You could take the army out of Hollywood, but as far as movie people went, you couldn't take Hollywood out of the army.

"Early on in the war," said Michael Kanin, brother of Garson and collaborator with Ring Lardner, Jr., on *Woman of the Year*, "we all said, 'What can I do?' Lardner was an old newspaperman, and so Ring and I said we'd undertake to put out a publication about this organization of writers who could best give their talents and skills by writing about or for the war.

"To get the government information for this publication, we went through friends of Ring's in Washington and contacted the executive office of the president, the Office of Emergency Management, which was run by H. R. Washburn at that time, in the division of information of the OEM. At first we called it the OEM Writers Mobilization, then the Hollywood Writers Mobilization, after Washburn said, 'We regard screen and radio writers as most important in supplying national defense information to millions of people.' So we put together this publication—the official publication of the HWM—called *Communique*. We had fantastic talent to draw from: Vic Parch doing illustrations, Robert Ardrey and Phil Dunne writing articles."

Kanin was aware of the political coalition that the Hollywood Writers Mobilization represented but only dimly aware of his collaborator's politics. "The communists in Hollywood at the time of the war were very active in the HWM," he said, "but everybody was. There was no control of the HWM or the SWG by the communists, as was later claimed. Throughout most of our involvement, I had no knowledge of Ring as a CP member. I never asked him point-blank, and he never solicited me for the Party. It was a productive collaboration between us, but it didn't last all that long. You see, when you write as a team, people think one of you does the thinking and one does the typing. I think we each wanted to assert ourselves as individual writers. There was also a marked difference in style, living and writing style, between Ring and myself. We'd agree to meet on a Monday, say, and each do three scenes.

So I'd come in at nine o'clock every morning and work all day and go home at five o'clock in the evening. All week, each day, no Ring. And then, about four o'clock on Thursday, Ring would show up with a couple of Benzedrine and a bottle of Scotch and would lock himself in his office until he had finished his scenes. He couldn't get himself to work without a deadline hanging over his head."

It quickly became apparent to writers that the war was going to change every aspect of their lives. Not only would their talents be utilized in extracurricular activities for the war effort, but the entire writing marketplace, from films to fiction, was changing. Kenneth Littauer, who had been fiction editor of *Collier's* and *Woman's Home Companion*, joined other popular-magazine editors in a published symposium that explained how the war was affecting their editorial policy.

"What is to take the place of the gay, frivolous love story which was in demand as recently as two months ago we don't yet know," claimed Littauer in January 1942. "But even the most frivolous fiction dealing with the contemporary scene must at least take cognizance of the fact that a war exists and that the attitudes and actions of characters in stories are necessarily affected by the dislocation at every level."

While acknowledging that stories of military operations would now find an easier market, Littauer expressed his fear of writers' becoming repetitive and using only servicemen as heroes, rendering both the very old and very young, who were ineligible for the army, also ineligible for romance. Graeme Lorimer, editor of the *Ladies' Home Journal*, expected fiction to reflect the war. "As there are more men in uniform and more men and women concerned with defense in contemporary America, it should be so in fiction. Basically, the *Journal* story will still be concerned with the fundamental emotions of men and women."

However, Herbert R. Mayes, editor of *Good Housekeeping*, felt that fiction should have "as little as possible to do with the War." He believed people wanted a good escapist read. Several publishers at this time were also requesting that authors permit them to melt down the plates of their books for bullets. The writers wanted to know if the rights in that case would revert to them.

The Screen Writers Guild proclaimed that "the writer's wartime usefulness depends on the scope of his knowledge and his skill as a propagandist . . . the needs of war writing cannot be met by shallow slogans, noisy drumbeating and patriotic clichés."

Suddenly, the position articulated by the Left and by the League of American Writers—the exhortation for "fighting words," the declaration of the writer's responsibility to fight fascism—became the conventional wisdom. The concept of propaganda took on a greater significance than ever before, and the potential for progressive influence on motion picture content also loomed larger. The significance of content at this time was attested to by two movements, one overt, the other secret. The overt manifestation was the fathering of the first Hollywood Writers Mobilization Writers Congress, co-sponsored by UCLA. The secret manifestation was in the Communist Party Writers' Clinic.

The issue of motion picture content had become more and more important since the inception of talking pictures. There was a saying in Hollywood, "If you've got a message, send it by Western Union"; but the movement against fascism and the growing sense of the movies' place in the campaign against repression rendered that adage meaningless. This sense of the power of the medium was always linked to censorship, and in a 1938 Report on Self-Regulation in the Motion Picture Industry, Will Hays said:

> The industry has resisted and must continue to resist the lure of propaganda in that sinister sense persistently urged upon it by extremist groups. . . . Entertainment is the commodity for which the public pays at the box office. Propaganda disguised as entertainment would be neither honest salesmanship nor honest showmanship. . . . If entertainment and recreation are what 85 million people weekly seek in American motion picture theatres, and they do, so much the better for the screen and the universal public which it serves.

During the Cold War attack by the forces of reaction and the House Un-American Activities Committee on communist infiltration of the movie industry, the communists in Hollywood were accused of trying to influence motion picture content. Dalton Trumbo, on the witness stand before HUAC, produced twenty scripts in which he defied the committee to find propaganda. Did they expect to find Party doctrine stuck into scripts like raisins in a cake? The process of showing how ridiculous the fanatical reactionary assessment of CP propaganda in films was resulted in a denial of the profound philosophical concern on the part of the Left with motion picture content. The left wing in the movie industry understood that artistic choices have a political context, that artistic choices have social reverberations. If a writer saw a way of making a senseless piece of fluff into a more thoughtful, socially conscious piece of entertainment, that writer was pleased. One thing those writers tried to do was to portray blacks as human beings with the potential for more than menial occupations. An ironic result of this was the sudden death of butler and chauffeur roles for black actors. "Man, you gotta write me in," Canada Lee begged Allen Boretz. "The hell with dignity—write me a shoeshine boy. Baby, I'm starving."

These left-wing writers understood the basic link between form and content, and writers' clinics dealt not just with theoretical constructs but with issues of structure, climax, characterization. The studio gave their writers little in the way of a theoretical education; it was the writers' clinics that offered them the chance of learning to write better.

The Writers' Clinic of the CP in Hollywood was organized formally just after Pearl Harbor. A series of meetings was held to determine how such an operation should function, and the duty of the Writers' Clinic, it was declared, was to produce not just better movies but better writers.

With all the postwar talk about how communists were trying to take over the industry and spread Red propaganda, what was obscured was the fact that the CP's concerns with content and craft placed it among the most reverential practitioners of the movie art. The respect of CP members for Hollywood and the motion picture medium seems to have been equaled only by such studio heads as L. B. Mayer, who thought his pictures were the voice of America. The writers in the CP clinic were not those eager to gather up some quick money and head back to New York. They were not the writers who were cynical and businesslike and just did their jobs. These writers were consummate artistic idealists who had a noble vision of the motion picture as a meaningful work of art.

There was a divergence of point of view within the Writers' Clinic between the humanists and the historians. The historians wanted to know *who* the people in a story were and asked how they got that way. Theirs was an absorption in tradition—they wanted to know *why* people were who they were. The humanists, on the other hand, argued more for story, for people in conflict with antagonists, and looked less for the historical forces that had formed their characters. These two groups saw different elements of a script as having greater importance, but both groups agreed that the construction of a script grows out of character and situation. It is neither mechanical nor formulaic.

The clinic participants were constantly examining their own methods and asking questions that stimulated a great deal of discussion and self-criticism. Among the general questions discussed were queries such as, When one permits plot and characterization to be shallow, is this an indication of lack of respect for Hollywood and pictures? Can a full and satisfactory story of men be told with no attempt to integrate women into the story? Is the love relationship central or just diverting, and hence dispensable at will?

The clinic dealt with all writers equally. One week it would deal with a studio screenplay that Richard Collins and Paul Jarrico were working on called *Boy Wonder*; the next week it would deal with an original screenplay by John Howard Lawson; the next week with adapting John Bright's play *Brooklyn USA* for a studio screenplay; and in other weeks with junior writers, plays, documentaries, radio programs, adaptations, and original scores and scripts.

The writers' clinics seem alternately like rather dull, stately exercises in theoretical examination of content and exciting discussions of the implications of certain themes. The criticism was often harsh and graceless, but the writers asked for it, and they rarely found such concentrated examination of their work elsewhere.

"The Party was helpful," recalled Carl Foreman. "I don't know if it was at the LAW schools or in the Party discussions, but I was learning about form and content."

"The point was," said Ben Barzman, "you tried to make socially conscious pictures within the restrictions and limitations of the mass medium."

Therein lies the core and the paradox of the whole issue of left-wing content and propaganda in movies: no matter how radical a writer was, movies were—and still are—an art by committee. There is a long process from the inception of a script to its realization on film, and, along the way, a script goes through the hands of those who are looking for commercial values, not political ones. No matter how much doctrine a Paul Jarrico might have infused into a script, unless it was palatable to the movie-going audience, Louis B. Mayer would not let it go on film.

The right wing also tried to influence content on occasion. Nat Perrin remembers doing a Red Skelton comedy whose plot dealt with three murders. In the original script, Perrin had a taxi driver who was murdered for trying to form a taxi drivers' union. James Kevin McGuinness, his executive producer, read the script and said, "No, the taxi driver gets murdered because he refused to join the union." Perrin would not change it, and the script went to what he calls the MGM Supreme Court—either Mannix, Mayer, or Benny Thau. When the ruling came down, it was in Perrin's favor.

Furthermore, the producers would change content to suit their purposes or to make the ideology more palatable. The film *Hangmen Also Die*, which John Wexley wrote in conjunction with Bertolt Brecht and which was directed by Fritz Lang, originally contained a scene of people in a concentration camp with Jewish stars on their arms. Wexley says that the film was cut until the Jewish parts were barely recognizable—"You blinked and they were gone." He attributed such editing to the desire of the producers not to touch on sensitive Jewish subjects.

The films that were later accused of being outright CP propaganda—like *Mission to Moscow*, scripted by Howard Koch, *The North Star*, written by Lillian Hellman, and *Song of Russia*, by Richard Collins and others—were written at the studios' behest during the period when Russia was the ally of the United States and the Hollywood Bowl was overflowing with members of the community who were eager to contribute to Russian War Relief. The problem that arose later, during the Cold War, was that the ideology of the films could not be changed, though the national policy had shifted.

Although the Party's approach was dogmatic, it nevertheless trained a group of writers to take nothing in a script for granted. Even if a writer

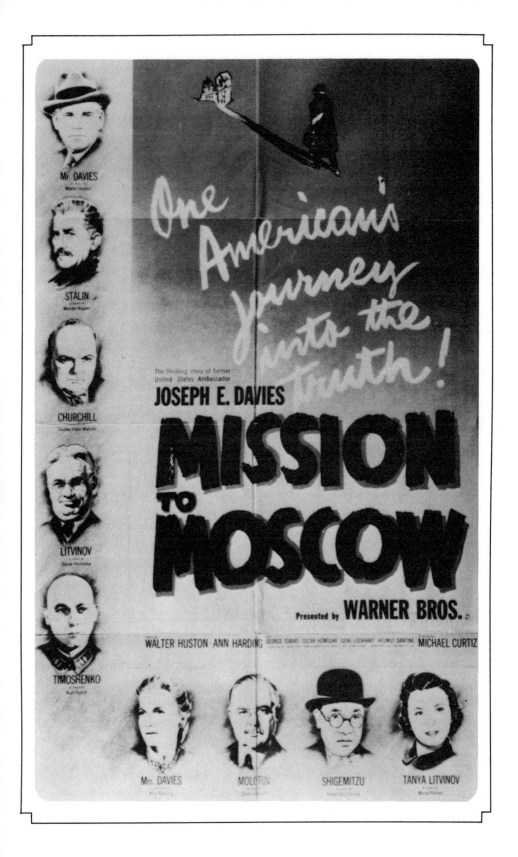

Westbrook Pegler. As syndicated columnist for the Los Angeles *Examiner*, he wrote on September 22, 1953: "I wish it were possible to lock up all those who have invoked the Fifth, and to put them into concentration camps as austere as the Arizona State Prison, where relatively harmless and morally stupid animals of the common sort must drink water from the john if they get thirsty in the dead of summer nights in the desert."

formed in this process rejected the Party's notion that the individual product must be subjected to group unity, that writer would still be made aware of themes. It seems beyond question that the Party did more for the writers than the writers did for the Party. In fact, this applied to many of the people in the Party, writers or not: they got more from being in the Party, in terms of a social context, a sense of purpose, and intellectual stimulation than the Party actually got from them in terms of money and help in effecting a class revolution in this country.

The trend that had emerged most viciously with Martin Dies's attack on supposed communist propaganda in the Federal Theater Project was continued through the ministrations of such people as syndicated columnist Westbrook Pegler and California State Senator Jack Tenney. As early as August 1943, Pegler attacked the motion picture industry as being a hotbed of subversives, and the various guilds joined the SWG in protesting against not only Pegler but all of the industry smear-mongers. Even the conservative Talbot Jennings pointed out, at a Guild meeting, that those people who refused to join in the protest against Pegler would eventually be "forced by events" to join in a campaign to defend the industry.

Part of Pegler's venom toward the Screen Writers Guild and toward the industry was on behalf of Hearst. In March 1942, a League of American Writers meeting in Los Angeles focused on the subject of "The Fifth Column in America." Dudley Nichols, Sam Ornitz, and Robert Kenny were the primary speakers. Nichols attacked "unconscious fifth columnists and those who fight this war without fighting for its objectives of a better life. . . . To express doubt as to the war's outcome is dangerous." Sam Ornitz directed his criticism toward Hearst, claiming that Karl von Weigand, a Hearst foreign correspondent, was suspiciously close to German and Japanese fascist circles. Kenny attacked "idle machines, men, and materials, all of which work for Hitler."

That these statements and others like them were being made under the auspices of the League of American Writers and that many of them were directed against Hearst enraged the right wing in Hollywood and around the country and were countered by the ongoing charges that the LAW was a communist-controlled organization. Attorney General Francis Biddle, in fact, attacked the LAW school in 1942, claiming it was communist-dominated, and his cudgel was eagerly grabbed up by Senator Tenney when he launched an attack against the Hollywood Writers Mobilization and its proposed writers' congress at UCLA.

The Hollywood Left, by 1943, had grown accustomed to Tenney as a right-wing, publicity-seeking communist-hounder who saw the Red menace as the answer to everything unusual that transpired in California. In January 1943 he was appointed chairman of an American Legion committee to investigate the Japanese relocation camps, and by November he was insinuating that the communists were inciting the Japanese and that the War Relocation Authority's handling of the internees was lax enough to call for the army's intervention and control. The anti-Japanese hysteria of that time guaranteed that statements such as Tenney's would find their way onto the front pages of the daily newspapers, particularly the Hearst and other conservative presses.

In August 1942, over a hundred Mexican-Americans were arrested after the murder of José Diaz, who had been killed in a brawl resulting from gang rivalries in Los Angeles. Known as the Sleepy Lagoon case, it was given wide and sensational publicity. It was a classic example of public hysteria incited by newspaper headlines, and in June 1943 there was full-scale rioting between the Mexican-American gangs and servicemen in Los Angeles. The press referred to these as "zoot suit" riots, placing the onus of incitement on the Mexicans rather than on the servicemen who invaded their neighborhoods spoiling for a fight.

The members of the Hollywood left-wing community were horrified by these events, and many of them participated actively in the Sleepy Lagoon Defense Committee. Two pamphlets—now legendary as examples of eloquent protest against injustice—were written on behalf of the Sleepy Lagoon defendants, one by Dalton Trumbo, the other by Guy Endore. In June 1943 Tenney's State Un-American Activities Committee held a public hearing in Los Angeles for the proclaimed purpose of determining if the communists had deliberately fostered the "zoot suit" rioting and the racial disturbances of that summer.

The National Lawyers Guild had been active in the defense of the Chicano youths, and Tenney attacked it as a communist front covering the Party's agitation of minority groups in Los Angeles County. Tenney further attacked the CP press for charging that Mexican youths in the United States were being subjected to police brutality, race discrimination, segregation, and humiliation. The chief lawyer for the Sleepy Lagoon defendants was Ben Margolis. Leading figures in the National Lawyers Guild were Carey McWilliams and Robert Kenny. When Tenney launched his attack on the Hollywood Writers Mobilization Congress, one of the proposed segments of the program against which he protested most violently was a panel on minority groups to be led by McWilliams.

In 1941 the Authors League of America and the Screen Writers Guild had held a congress of writers on the campus of UCLA at which the chief preoccupation had been with problems of craft. Two years later, the HWM joined with UCLA to co-sponsor another kind of writers' congress. By this time there was no longer any debate about the writer's social function. The war had made that, in the words of John Howard Lawson, "a matter of elementary duty and terrible urgency." The intent of the congress was to build for a closer association between writers and scholars, a separation that the congress deemed artificial. The combined efforts of writers and educators were directed not just toward the end of the war and how they could help hasten it, but toward a postwar world and their place and function within it. For many of the writers in Hollywood, it was impossible not to be totally involved in the war effort.

The UCLA people were entranced by the whole experience of their involvement with the Hollywood Writers Mobilization. Suddenly, they were included in Hollywood dinner parties on Saturday nights. Breakfast merged into lunch, and dinner was like one big continuous party, full of glamour and intellectual stimulation. One of the representatives from UCLA who became most closely involved with the HWM was the respected professor of psychology Franklin Fearing, who was on the HWM Congress steering committee, along with Gustave Arlt and Ralph Freud from the university, authors Marc Connelly and James Hilton, and Stephen Longstreet, Emmet Lavery, and John Howard Lawson from the movie industry. Fearing was considered a social-educational radical at UCLA, and one of his prize students was Sylvia

Jarrico, whom he encouraged to do research for her thesis into the nature of motion picture content. Fearing was a very intelligent man, but by his own admission politically naive, and he really had no sense of the political implications of his involvement with this group. For him it was simply the high point of his life.

"I remember," Sylvia Jarrico recalled, "that one time, in a meeting, Fearing made some abstract comment, and Sam Moore said, 'You gotta watch yourself around these academic guys.' Fearing was just tickled to death at being a kind of interesting, complex, academic figure to these people he so admired."

In the initial planning phases of the conference, Marc Connelly and Ralph Freud were appointed the congress's co-chairmen, with Francis Faragoh the treasurer and Robert Rossen assisting from his position as head of the Hollywood Writers Mobilization. One of the first issues the planning committee faced was getting rid of any factionalism. As Marc Connelly said at a planning meeting in May 1943, the issues at hand were greater than any political party, and the question was not one of the Democrats versus Republicans but of liberalism versus reaction.

Writer Allan Scott suggested that panels on censorship be included in the program and that the theme of the congress, in relation to motion pictures, be "unconscious fascism." (Although the conference was designed to deal to a large extent with motion pictures, radio and print media were to be included as part of an attempt to break down the barriers between the east and west coasts.)

The congress was to be ambitious, prestigious, and progressive. It was just the sort of thing that would distress the forces of reaction—it was just the sort of thing that was trying to counteract those forces.

Jack Tenney set his two most valuable investigators, Thomas Cavett (who once insinuated himself into the home of Lincoln Steffens to spy on a gathering there) and Richard Combs, to ferret out the "truth" behind this announced writers' congress. Tenney's investigators returned to him convinced that the Hollywood Writers Mobilization was being promoted and controlled by the communists. Combs told his superior that the congress was designed to involve many prominent and innocent people and, with the prestige of the university, to give impetus and direction to developing the communist line through the unwitting participation of known noncommunist intellectuals. The congress was being attacked in its most vulnerable area—academe.

Approximately one month before the congress was to take place (after more than six months of planning by the Hollywood Writers Mobilization and UCLA), Tenney had his investigators present the information they had collected about the HWM to UCLA president Robert Gordon Sproul. A week later, Tenney followed this up with a fifteen-page report on the history of the

HWM movement and an outline of the background of the principal "instigators."

"Tenney's attempt to separate the university from the writers' congress was bolstered by the fact that he could intimidate the university professors," recalled Pauline Lauber Finn. "Their jobs were on the line, and they were that much more vulnerable because of Tenney's effect, as a state senator, on the university's board of regents."

Dr. Sproul immediately called a press conference and stated that the approval for the congress had been granted by his representative on campus, Dean Gordon S. Watkin. Watkin said that the initial recommendation that the university participate in the congress had come from members of the English department, who, Watkin said, "are competent judges of the educational value." Tenney claimed that the issue of academic freedom was being raised to divert the attention of the public from real issues. His attack seemed farfetched enough to be discredited, and he looked even more ridiculous when the HWM announced that messages from President Roosevelt and Wendell Willkie were to be read at the opening of the congress. It was also announced that the OWI would film the affair "as part of a documentary picture to be shown our fighting men overseas and in Allied countries," to depict the war on the home front.

By this point, Tenney's pride was inflamed. He was determined to get the congress canceled. Tenney called Dr. Sproul and demanded that he cancel the congress. Tenney offered Sproul the specter of his immediately convening his State Un-American Activities Committee and subpoenaing the principal instigators of the congress in order to reveal their "true characters and affiliations."

By this time, Sproul and the university had realized that any further direct communication with Tenney would be even more dangerous, so Sproul made no reply to Tenney's offer except through the newspapers, and preparations for the congress continued. The liberals and the radicals figured Tenney had been put in his place by Sproul's dignified disdain, and Tenney jokes proliferated around town. Tenney's wounded pride was salvaged in an article in the *Hollywood Citizen News*, which quoted him extensively, giving him a hero's laurels. As a result of the article, the council of the American Legion adopted a resolution calling for an investigation of the faculty of UCLA. Tenney had also slipped the *Citizen News* a few references to a fanatical smear text called *Sinister Shadows* by Edwin Marshall Hadley, published in 1929 by Tower Press. It claimed to be an exposé of communist infiltration in the faculties of American colleges and universities, and one of those listed was UCLA dean Gordon S. Watkin.

The *Westwood Hills Press*, another of Los Angeles' conservative organs, printed the accusation gleaned from the *Citizen News* in banner headlines: "DEAN WATKIN A COMMUNIST, SENATOR SAYS." Tenney, of course, protested mildly that he hadn't said that; he had merely said that Hadley's book said it.

An outraged Dean Watkin denied the charges. "It is utterly fantastic," he declared. "I am not a communist and I have never voted the communist ticket. If I had, I wouldn't mind saying so. The fact is, I am a nonpartisan."

Tenney was a clever disciple of Martin Dies. He had learned the power of a good fight in the press. He let the newspapers carry on the charges and countercharges for the next few days, and then, on September 27, four days before the congress was to convene, he declared that the UCLA *Daily Bruin*, the campus newspaper, followed the Communist Party line.

Tenney did not quote any of the inflammatory material he cited, so it was impossible for anyone to really gauge the seriousness of the *Daily Bruin*'s articles, which were frequently in a lighthearted, college humor vein. He also acted as if the United States were at war with Russia, although 1943 was the year that Russians were depicted as glorious allies in *Song of Russia, Mission to Moscow*, and *The North Star*. However, Tenney's statements had the desired effect. Assemblyman Chester F. Gannon sent out messages from the legislative seat in Sacramento branding the members of the congress radicals and insisting that Sproul cancel the congress.

It was at this point that the question of academic freedom was raised and Tenney declared that the issue was a diversion. "In my opinion," he claimed, "teachers and professors in publicly supported institutions are subject to the direction of their employers, the taxpayers, as those directions are made manifest by the taxpayers' representatives. If the teachers and professors do not like their instructions in this regard, they may exercise 'academic freedom' in a school or college established and financed by themselves and not by the taxpayers." Tenney knew he was striking at the heart, which was the pocket-book, of the university, invoking the sacred name of the taxpayer.

Now the controversy took on a truly Alice in Wonderland quality. The article Tenney chose to cite in support of his claim that *Daily Bruin* student writers were influenced by communists was an innocuous bit of college humor entitled "Sex Like a Drink of Water":

> Next to a revolution, the thing which makes life most worth living is sex. Sex is what gives true liberals the clear head and body which allows them to devote themselves to a revolution.
>
> Conservatives are sexually frustrated. This is why they turn all their efforts toward business and thus oppress the mass of the people. If they would recognize the importance of sex they would become kind and decent since they would realize how much they have in common with the masses.
>
> Sex is wonderful. It's here to stay.

The *Los Angeles Daily News* picked up on the item with humor, heading its story about the controversy "Sex Enters Dispute Over Writers' Meet" and concluding with the statement that "just what connection sex has with the congress was pretty vague."

Sproul, who was fed up by this time, announced on the eve of the congress that it was "clean" and he would personally address the opening session.

The ugliness of the preceding weeks was almost forgotten in the triumphant four-day congress at UCLA. It was one of the most prestigious literary academic gatherings of the war period, and its intent was so patently patriotic that the participants could only wonder, or laugh, at Tenney's attempts to block it. Dr. Sproul did open the congress, with an address that began,

> Out of the tumult and the shouting of the papers and the politicians, we welcome the Writers Congress of 1943 to the comparative quiet of the groves of academe of the Los Angeles Campus of the University of California. . . . From the very beginning of the planning, months ago, a conscientious effort has been made to free the Congress completely from party labels of any kind, subversive or otherwise, and to eliminate from the program any partisan political or ideologically controversial issues. . . . We of the university have joined with the Writers of America in this Congress to avert a common danger, to destroy a common menace in the threat of a totalitarian new order, and to build for a finer America in the happier world of the future.

The congress drew the participation of more than 1,500 writers and scholars, who paid five dollars a head to hear speeches such as "The Responsibility of the Industry" (Darryl F. Zanuck), "The Director's Point of View" (Edward Dmytryk), "The Function of the Radio Dramatist" (Arch Oboler), "The Exiled Writer's Relation to His Homeland" (Thomas Mann), and "The Psychological Analysis of Propaganda" (Paul Lazarsfeld and Robert K. Merton) and panels on minority groups, propaganda, and different technological aspects of the media.

The writers in the congress were galvanized. The workers were examining the means of production, and the assembly line could never be the same. The editorial board of the congress was a mixture of radicals such as John Howard Lawson, liberal-conservatives like Emmet Lavery and Marc Connelly, Professor Franklin Fearing, and James Hilton. They all helped collect the proceedings of the congress into a book that was published by the University of California Press in September 1944. When it was reviewed in the *New York Times*, M. McNeil Lowry wrote, "The screen, radio, publicity, songwriters and cartoonists of the nation have made a solemn declaration of their responsibilities and in effect served notice on the entertainment industry that they are about to take over Hollywood."

In the studio executives' offices it sounded like revolution, but they understood that it was all part of the war effort. To Senator Tenney, war or no war, it *was* revolutionary. The congress had embarrassed him by not being canceled at his behest, and Senator Tenney was a man who didn't take defeat lightly. He now began his investigation of the Hollywood Writers Mobilization in earnest.

Just after the UCLA writers' congress, another educational-humanistic experiment was begun that would arouse the investigatory zeal of Chairman Tenney in the years to come. This was the People's Education Center (PEC), a nonpartisan, independent institution whose goal was to provide a bridge between labor and learning. It came into existence as the League of American Writers' school, which had outlasted the League, was dissolving.

The People's Education Center offered studies in history, in culture, and in the problems of various ethnic groupings within the community, such as blacks, Chicanos, and Jews, in addition to courses in the arts, which included writing workshops like those the LAW had conducted.

One of the things the PEC found out was that the blue-collar workers were so tired from their day's travails that they did not want to go to school at night. So the main student body was mostly composed of white-collar workers along with professionals. The PEC had an enrollment of from 350 to 650, with a higher percentage of women than men. Most of them came from the west side of town, from Echo Park to Santa Monica.

The People's Education Center was doomed after being attacked as a Communist Party front organization in the 1945 Tenney Report. In 1948 it went out of existence, merging with the California Labor School.

9

Nineteen forty-four was a crucial year for the nation and for Hollywood. Roosevelt was facing the stiffest opposition he had ever encountered in his unprecedented bid for a fourth term as president, and the forces of the entertainment industry, which had learned so well the extent of that industry's persuasive powers, were to be singularly influential in getting him reelected.

It was also the year that the supposed harmony between Right and Left in Hollywood turned dissonant. The coalition had been held together by the war, the way a flimsy marriage might have been held together for the sake of the children, but the charade was impossible to sustain, even for the sake of national unity. Two significant events occurred in Hollywood in 1944 in this regard: the dissolution of the Communist Party and the formation of the Motion Picture Alliance for the Preservation of American Ideals.

The U.S. Communist Party was formally dissolved by its head, Earl Browder, and was replaced by the Communist Political Association (CPA). Browder, hoping to perpetuate the good-fellowship of the wartime period, revised the Party line and turned the organization into a more educationally oriented, progressive coalition with American liberals. The trouble with the Browder line, for some of the hard-line Party people, was that it no longer seemed that there was any Party. It seemed instead like part of the mainstream. Regardless of any embarrassment about the Party line, the result of the Browder line was that in 1944 the membership of the CP, or CPA, reached an all-time high of eighty thousand in this country.

At the same time, another organization was also being formed—the Motion Picture Alliance for the Preservation of American Ideals. The group elected Sam Wood, the millionaire director who had successfully neutralized on screen all the antifacist elements of *For Whom the Bell Tolls*, to be its president. Chairman of the executive committee was James Kevin McGuinness, who by then was an executive producer at MGM and had lost none of his reactionary zeal since the death of the Screen Playwrights. First vice-president was Walt Disney, who, in 1941, had successfully fought a strike by his underpaid cartoonists, claiming that he would close his studio down and sell toys rather than meet the Cartoonists Union's demands. Second vice-president was Howard Emmett Rogers, and the executive committee also included Rupert Hughes. The riders may have been a little older, but "The Four Horsemen" were back in the saddle, ready to don their armor and go into battle for the forces of reaction.

As had been the case with the Screen Playwrights, the Alliance's strength was concentrated mainly at MGM. The most celebrated film star among the group's supporters was Gary Cooper, who was known as being one of the most politically naive reactionaries in Hollywood. During the late thirties he had gotten caught up with Arthur Guy Empey's Hollywood Hussars, a reactionary vigilante army that was preparing, with the help of guntoters like McGuinness, Victor McLaglen, and Ward Bond, to do a little housecleaning in their community—their targets, preferably, anyone slightly pink. Cooper's agent had pulled him out of the Hussars. Other supporters that the Alliance claimed to have were Clark Gable, Barbara Stanwyck, Irene Dunne, and Spencer Tracy.

The Motion Picture Alliance's statement of principles was published the day after its founding meeting, in a full-page, two-color ad in the *Hollywood Reporter*. The Alliance announced, "We find ourselves in sharp revolt against a rising tide of Communism, Fascism, and kindred beliefs. . . . We resent the growing impression that this industry is made up of, and dominated by, Communists, Radicals, and crackpots. . . . We want no new plan, we want only to defend against its enemies that which is our priceless heritage. . . ."

The bellicose bluster of the ad helped to compensate somewhat for the disappointment the Alliance had experienced the night of its inaugural session, when it found the attention of Hollywood and the press elsewhere. The competition was Vice-President Henry Wallace, who addressed two audiences that evening—first a dinner sponsored by the Free World Association at the Beverly Hills Hotel and then a "Win the War" mass meeting staged by the AFL, CIO, and railroad brotherhood unions at the Shrine Auditorium, where members of the various screen guilds were prominent among the thousands of industry workers. Wallace stole all the main headlines and wire-service coverage with his attack on the sort of "free enterprise" that meant "freedom for freebooters."

The newspapers had been enthralled by the gathering at the Free World Association dinner, which was attended by such Hollywood celebrities as Rosalind Russell, James Cagney, Dudley Nichols, and the president of the Motion Picture Academy, Walter Wanger, who took the occasion to aim the

M.P.A.

THE MOTION PICTURE ALLIANCE

for

THE PRESERVATION OF AMERICAN IDEALS

STATEMENT OF PRINCIPLES

> *"We, even we here, hold the power and bear the responsibility. We shall nobly save, or meanly lose, the last, best hope on earth."* — Abraham Lincoln.

We believe in, and like, the American way of life; the liberty and freedom which generations before us have fought to create and preserve; the freedom to speak, to think, to live, to worship, to work and to govern ourselves, as individuals, as free men; the right to succeed or fail as free men, according to the measure of our ability and our strength.

Believing in these things, we find ourselves in sharp revolt against a rising tide of Communism, Fascism and kindred beliefs, that seek by subversive means to undermine and change this way of life; groups that have forfeited their right to exist in this country of ours, because they seek to achieve their change by means other than the vested procedure of the ballot and to deny the right of the majority opinion of the people to rule.

In our special field of motion pictures, we resent the growing impression that this industry is made up of, and dominated by, Communists, radicals and crack-pots. We believe that we represent the vast majority of the people who serve this great medium of expression. But unfortunately it has been an unorganized majority. This has been almost inevitable. The very love of freedom, of the rights of the individual, make this great majority reluctant to organize. But now we must, or we shall meanly lose "the last, best hope on earth."

As Americans, we have no new plan to offer. We want no new plan, we want only to defend against its enemies that which is our priceless heritage; that freedom which has given man, in this country, the fullest life and the richest expression the world has ever known; that system which, in the present emergency, has fathered an effort that, more than any other single factor, will make possible the winning of this war.

As members of the motion picture industry, we must face and accept an especial responsibility. Motion pictures are inescapably one of the world's greatest forces for influencing public thought and opinion, both at home and abroad. In this fact lies solemn obligation. We refuse to permit the effort of Communist, Fascist, and other totalitarian-minded groups to pervert this powerful medium into an instrument for the dissemination of un-American ideas and beliefs. We pledge ourselves to fight, with every means at our organized command, any effort of any group or individual, to divert the loyalty of the screen from the free America that gave it birth. And to dedicate our own work, in the fullest possible measure, to the presentation of the American scene, its standards and its freedoms, its beliefs and its ideals, as we know them and believe in them.

THE OFFICERS		EXECUTIVE COMMITTEE	
President	Sam Wood	James K. McGuinness, Chairman	
First Vice-President	Walt Disney	Borden Chase	Cliff Reid
Second Vice-President	Cedric Gibbons	Victor Fleming	Casey Robinson
Third Vice-President	Norman Taurog	Arnold Gillespie	Howard Emmett Rogers
Secretary	Louis D. Lighton	Frank Gruber	Harry Ruskin
Treasurer	Clarence Brown	Bert Kalmar	Morrie Ryskind
Executive Secretary	George Bruce	Rupert Hughes	King Vidor
		Fred Niblo, Jr.	Robert Vogel
		George Waggner	

first dart at the newly formed Alliance, saying that although he was "no defender of homegrown Communism," the members of the Free World Association did not intend to let themselves be "misled by the familiar Hitler line by which Communism is made the bogey."

The only satisfactory coverage the Motion Picture Alliance found was in the Hearst press (no surprise, since Hearst was one of their biggest backers, in terms of both money and publicity), which devoted columns of quotes and editorials speculating that the Alliance would root out such progressive sentiments in films as those inspired by the Hollywood Writers Mobilization Writers Congress at UCLA held the previous October.

A few days later, the Motion Picture Alliance took advantage of a midweek news lull in Hollywood to issue a series of statements about the organization's purpose. The *Citizen News* delightedly reported the words of Alliance president Sam Wood, who proclaimed that the organization was "for everyone in the Motion Picture industry, regardless of position. . . . None of us are 'joiners,'" Wood told the press. "None of us are professional organizers or 'go to meeting types.'" (This was a deliberate contrast with the left wing.)

Wood explained that the organization was assembling because "those highly indoctrinated shock units of the totalitarian wrecking crew have shrewdly led the people of the United States to believe that Hollywood is a hot-bed of sedition and subversion, and that our industry is a battleground over which Communism is locked in death grips with Fascism. . . . We intend to correct that erroneous impression immediately and to assure the people of the United States that . . . Hollywood is a reservoir of Americanism and that those forces which have presumed to speak in the name of our industry and under the geographical identity of Hollywood, have been acting under false pretenses and that we repudiate them entirely."

The sort of climate that was becoming prevalent in Hollywood is perfectly illustrated in this situation described by William Ludwig, an SWG steward at MGM at that time. "I remember one really startling day which began when two writers—and I will not mention their names—came into my office. As they came in, one of them locked the door, and I asked them what it was about. They said that they had been observing me and watching me carefully and they felt I was very good material, and they gave me an invitation to join the CP. I said that I didn't think it was for me, I wasn't the kind of fellow who liked to be told what to think before I had a chance to figure out what I wanted to think. And then I went to lunch.

"After lunch, King Vidor, for whom I'd written *An American Romance*, came in, and he wanted to talk to me, and he wanted me to join the Alliance for the Preservation of American Ideals. I said, 'What are they for, King?' and he said, 'We're against this and against this and against this, and especially against the communists.' I said, 'I know what the Alliance is against, but what are they *for?*' And he said, 'What do you mean?' I said, 'King, I have made up my mind that I'm not going to join things just because they are against something. I want to find, if there is such a thing, something that's *for* what I'm for. What is your organization *for*, King?' There was a long pause, and King said, 'I'll have to talk to Sam Wood about that,' and he got up and left the office."

"I used to tell them all," recalled Mary McCall, Jr., "that when the revolution comes, you can put me up against a cellophane wall and shoot at me from both sides."

It was a period when people were being solicited by both the Right and the Left, and the seeming security of the CPA period brought people to Party meetings who might never have gone otherwise.

"That is the period when I thought it would have been relatively easy for the CP to surface," recalled Maurice Rapf. "There were open meetings held during that time—that is to say, the communists invited noncommunists to come to the meetings to talk about some of the same problems. The lines were down, but it was still underground, and that's where a lot of noncommunists got into trouble. Some of the people who were there became informers later on, and they accused people of being communists who really weren't—the visitors—along with the genuine communists. There was a very large CP membership in Hollywood by that time. I mean *real* membership. As to whether anybody ever signed anything—I have often wondered what you use as a test of whether people are members of the Party or not. I would suppose it has to do with whether or not they paid dues and took orders from their groups."

"We were always on drives to get people into the Party," recalled Allen Boretz, "and an awful lot of people got into the Party during the Browder period that *never* should have been Party members. And out of this came the ones that really finked. I mean, we succeeded in getting many more people into the Party during the war who would never have become Party members earlier."

In March 1944, the Motion Picture Alliance did something that was always deemed a cardinal sin and a last resort in Hollywood: it brought the outside world into industry matters that that world could never understand.

The Alliance went to Washington to plant a missive with Senator Robert Rice Reynolds of North Carolina, which the senator promptly slipped into the *Congressional Record* of March 7, 1944. It was a calculated move on the part of the Alliance, which was hoping that the senator would read it aloud to the Senate and thereby give them publicity. Instead, he merely slipped it into the record under the title "Our Own First."

The Alliance's letter began by calling the senator (who was already on the warpath against "Reds") the Nostradamus of the twentieth century—a tribute to his powers of foreseeing the future. The letter continued:

> The very fact that such outstanding representatives of the decent, patriotic American element of the Motion Picture Industry felt it compulsory to organize to combat the "totalitarian-minded groups" working in the industry for "the dissemination of un-American ideas and beliefs" is proof that such groups have [existed] and do exist in the industry. Otherwise, men of Rupert Hughes' and Fred Niblo's and Walt Disney's intelligence would not feel it or find it necessary to organize the decent, patriotic element of the industry to combat them for the welfare and safety of the American people.

Variety on March 15 claimed that its criticism of the action was that the Alliance should "either . . . help drive into the open the undesirable element within the picture industry which is claimed is there, or . . . put an end to this ambiguous Hollywood name-calling. Nor does *Variety* mind reiterating its opinion that the whole thing has a pro- and anti-Roosevelt foundation. . . ."

Senator Reynolds, founder of the *American Vindicator*, which became the *National Record*, was the author of many anti-alien measures proposed in the Senate from the mid-thirties to 1944, and to him the Alliance's letter seemed to express admiration for his foresight in sponsoring such attacks on "aliens of un-American ideology."

The Alliance was jockeying the producers into a position in which they would have to capitulate to some sort of investigation to remove the label of communism that had been pinned on the industry.

On April 21, 1944, Dies Committee sleuths appeared in Hollywood in response to the Alliance's charges. "I remember," said Pauline Lauber Finn, "that just around this time Bob Kenny took me to a meeting at Fox of high-level industry executives who were concerned by the coming of Dies to Hollywood. I was there representing the Hollywood Writers Mobilization. Sheridan Gibney was there representing the Screen Writers Guild. The producers wanted to send some 'honest brokers' to Washington to appease the committee. The guilds wanted to have a big show of strength to refute the charges of the Alliance and the Dies Committee. The Alliance opened the door for HUAC, and then the reactionaries began casting about for some CP informers to make their picture complete."

Ambivalent as the attitude of the producers was toward the Alliance—and men like Selznick were taking every opportunity to criticize it and Tenney—there were indications that some in the industry would acquiesce in its campaign.

When the Dies Committee investigators were being hosted in fine style in Hollywood, the Alliance escalated its activities in the industry to prove to the Washington Red-hunters how severe was the problem they faced. At a meeting of the Chamber of Commerce, the Alliance expanded its drive to enlist the rank and file of "good citizens of the industry." The highlight of the evening was an appearance by Captain Clark Gable of the U.S. Air Force, trim and resplendent in his uniform, who said: "I recently left a place where there are no Communists and no anti-Semites, and I hate to see anything like Communism enter into the home front. The boys are getting very violent, sitting around and talking about home. They expect to come back and find what they left, and that's not Communism."

The capacity audience (most of them there undoubtedly for the Washington dignitaries) included Barbara Stanwyck and Gary Cooper.

Next, Howard Emmett Rogers outlined the history of the "communist plot" in Hollywood, saying that character assassination was the favorite weapon used against those who spoke out against left-wing machinations in the industry. He said such persons had been accused indiscriminately of being anti-Semitic and fascist, regardless of their racial heritage. The five individuals in the country doing the most to fight communism, Rogers said, were Eugene Lyons (author of *Red Decade*), David Dubinsky, columnist George Sokolsky, Max Eastman, and Benjamin Gitlaw, all of whom were Jews. In fact, Rogers added, the editors of the country's most outstanding Jewish newspapers had been accused of being anti-Semitic. "What chance have you got against people who can twist things around like that?" Rogers asked.

("Rogers came up to me one day," said Donald Ogden Stewart, "and said, 'You commies accuse me of being anti-Semitic, but I'll tell you something nobody in this whole town knows. My wife is Jewish.' And I looked at him, thinking, My God, the poor woman has been forced to hide it all these years, living with this bastard, and I told him, 'That proves my point.' ")

Rogers concluded with the statement "The Communists constitute a small minority, but they work like termites."

The progressive community in Hollywood fought back. A meeting was sponsored by the Screen Writers Guild in May 1944, attended by representatives of thirty-eight organizations, to discuss the aims and character of the Motion Picture Alliance and to lay the groundwork for a mass meeting. This meeting, which took place in June, was the first open, industry-wide meeting in the history of Hollywood. Its objectives were to reinforce guild and interunion activity for the war effort and to prevent the curtailment of screen freedom, as well as to repudiate the Motion Picture Alliance.

Just prior to the meeting, Martin Dies proclaimed:

> Hollywood is the greatest source of revenue in this nation for the Communists and other subversive groups. . . . Two elements stand out in this category—the making of pictures which extol a foreign ideology—propaganda for a cause which seeks to spread its ideas to our people and the "leftist" or radical screenwriters. . . . Many of them, perhaps in the belief they are aiding a cause they could not even give an intelligent explanation of if called on to do so, slyly and cleverly insert these "leftist" ideas

into their screenwritings. . . . In my opinion, if it is worth anything to the [motion picture executives], they will do well to halt the propaganda pictures and eliminate every writer who has un-American ideas.

It was rumored that the Motion Picture Alliance was so thrilled by Dies's understanding of their work that they offered him $50,000 a year to become their director.

The mobilization against the Alliance, organized by the Emergency Committee of Hollywood Guilds and Unions, consisted of such groups as the Screen Cartoonists Guild, the Screen Office Employees Guild, the Screen Publicists Guild, the Society of Motion Picture Film Editors, the Story Analysts Guild, the Brotherhood of Carpenters and Joiners, the Conference of Studio Unions, and the Brotherhood of Electrical Workers, as well as members of the Hollywood Writers Mobilization, the Hollywood Victory Committee, and the SWG and other talent guilds. At the Emergency Committee's mass meeting, Walter Wanger characterized the Alliance as a "stimulant to disunity"; Sidney Buchman, now a producer at Columbia, said that the Alliance's unsupported charges of "subversive activities" in films were a threat to Hollywood management and labor alike; and Mary McCall, Jr., president of the Screen Writers Guild, flatly accused the Alliance's members of union-busting intentions. "We don't believe union busting is an American ideal," she declared.

James Hilton declared that the British people had not found Hollywood films subversive, and he called for further cooperation between English and U.S. film industries and workers. Telegrams and messages of support were read by the meeting's chairman, Emmet Lavery (who had written such popular wartime films as *Hitler's Children* (1943) and *Behind the Rising Sun* (1943), from Orson Welles, Rita Hayworth, Dore Schary, and others who had been unable to attend.

Following the discussion, the delegates voted to continue operating the Emergency Committee for two years as the official council of Hollywood guilds and unions. Resolutions constituting its program for action called for declaring "undeviating loyalty to the President"; cooperating with producers in reabsorbing returning Hollywood servicemen and women; combating all disunity groups; extending the freedom of the screen now and in the postwar period; and giving wide publicity to the Emergency Committee's activities.

Representatives from the committee were among the most active that summer in organizing Hollywood for Roosevelt. Hearst and the forces of reaction solidly backed Thomas Dewey, the Republican candidate; the Motion Picture Alliance headed the Dewey-for-President movement in Hollywood. Two of Hollywood's most interesting women in the political-creative community found themselves on opposite sides of the fence. Helen Gahagan Douglas, the Democratic nominee for Congress from California's 14th District, spoke at the Democratic National Convention in Chicago, while Congresswoman Clare Boothe Luce gave a stirring address to the Republican Party at their convention, also in Chicago.

Helen Gahagan Douglas, who had been a national convention delegate for Roosevelt in the 1940 campaign, countered reports of growing Republican strength in California, telling *Collier's* in September 1944: "There's not going to be any Republican trend out here. . . . This state is going Democratic, and nobody knows it better than Governor [Earl] Warren, who gently withdrew as the Republican Vice-Presidential nominee because he knew how the wind was blowing."

There was also a movement within the intellectual Republican community away from that party toward Roosevelt. Author Marcia Davenport made a speech at an election rally for the Book Industry Committee for Roosevelt in which she explained the reasons why she, an independent Republican, was going to vote for him. She stated that it was the prime responsibility of writers and publishers to make clear to others the nature of all "reactionism": "One big trouble with the Republican Party today is the fringe around it of men and organizations and ideas not to be trusted. If I felt like being flippant, I could call it the lunatic fringe. But I cannot think of the worst proponents of reactionism and isolationism in the United States as harmless lunatics."

Including in this fringe newspaper publishers Robert McCormick and Frank Gannett, Senator Gerald Nye, Senator Hiram Johnson, Congressman Hamilton Fish, Senator Wayland Brooks, and right-wing spokesman Gerald L. K. Smith, she declared that they weren't good Americans and they were supporting the Republican ticket:

> They aren't good Americans specifically because if they are allowed to run rampant with their isolationist, nationalist, divisionist, racist, and other reactionary ideas, they will land us in WW III even faster than we got into WWII. . . . Democratic reactionaries have not been numerically and politically powerful in Congress. And upon the re-election of President Roosevelt, they would not hold positions of such powerful influence as Chairman of the Senate Foreign Relations Committee, the Senate Committee on Appropriations, or the House Committee on Rules, and the probable speakership of the House of Representatives. You all heard President Roosevelt last Saturday warn voters away from any political package on which they appear. . . .

She concluded by saying that Dewey had lost the support of one of the real leaders of the only good kind in the Republican Party—Joe Ball.

It quickly became obvious that the Democratic Party in Hollywood had enormous resources in the creative community. By the end of October, the

Hollywood Democratic Committee (HDC) had spent only $75,000 on campaign activities, with the bulk of their donations coming in terms of free talent contributions. The head of the Hollywood Democratic Committee was George Pepper, a violinist, who had been an early opponent of Jack Tenney's in the musicians' union.

At that time, the Hollywood Democratic Committee had only Hollywood industry people as members. Hannah Dorner, head of the newly formed Independent Citizens Committee for the Arts, Sciences, and Professions (ICCASP),* a group of Eastern intellectuals based in New York and dedicated to the reelection of Roosevelt, argued that if the HDC were a national organization, it would be more important. Orson Welles came to several HDC board meetings and finally, shortly after the election, persuaded the board to change its name to the Hollywood Independent Citizens Committee for the Arts, Sciences, and Professions (HICCASP).

Ellenore Bogigian, at that time a member of the California Democratic Central Committee, recalled: "I saw the Democratic Party as an avenue for change, politically, in the country, so I couldn't see the point in wasting the name-recognition of the Hollywood Democratic Committee."

The political-creative coalition for Roosevelt in Hollywood was powerful. Bobby Lees made a United Auto Workers Roosevelt campaign film that was animated by John Hubley. Writers such as Dalton Trumbo and Albert Maltz wrote political speeches for Edward G. Robinson and others. According to Bogigian, the communists were not active in the Hollywood Democratic Committee, although for several years John Howard Lawson had written parts of the Democratic platform approved by the State Democratic Central Committee.

"The majority of Democrats wouldn't have liked it if they'd known," said Bogigian. "They would have said, 'Don't we have people who can write as well?' The point was . . . we didn't. But the platform wasn't communist. It just happened at that time that the aims of the Communist Party were the aims of the progressive consensus. The platforms were reformist. They didn't use terms like *capitalist* or *proletariat.*"

Dorothy Healy agreed that the Party was not deeply involved in Democratic or liberal politics. "We never understood," she said, "a Bob Kenny or a Willkie. We couldn't know the strength of Democratic tradition as it revolved

---

* The objectives of the ICCASP were: (1) through a program of enlightenment and political action to promote and cultivate the continuance of the democratic way of life in the United States and among the peoples of the world; (2) to ensure a just and enduring peace when it occurred; (3) to promote a program in which the resources of the nation would be organized to provide full employment and a decent standard of living; and (4) through the arts, sciences, and professions to enlighten the members of the public on matters relating to social, economic, and political policies of the United States.

around bourgeois democratic concepts, so we didn't understand the significance of it. It's something that didn't lend itself to easily stereotyped syllogisms."

Nevertheless, there were those who were convinced that the change of the Hollywood Democratic Committee to the Hollywood Independent Citizens Committee for the Arts, Sciences, and Professions was a CP tactic to gain control of the Democratic Party. "When the Communist Party couldn't have their way," recalled Nat Perrin, "when the HDC wouldn't follow the Party line, they thought they'd change the organization around and give it a new name. But for a while the Left was quite good with money raising and activities for the Democratic Party, especially in the Roosevelt 1944 campaign."

Factionalism and in-fighting evaporated, however, in the last-minute frenzy to reelect Roosevelt, and the combined talents of the Hollywood community united under Norman Corwin to produce a special election-eve broadcast that was one of the most successful uses of the media to influence the public politically. Corwin was, at that time, the leading figure in American radio, known as a dramatist as well as a commentator. He had produced a popular "Bill of Rights" radio program in 1941 and was known for a rather lyrical approach to humanitarian issues. He was often criticized, both by members of the Party and by the intelligentsia, for what they called "Norman Corwin poeticism" and "sentimental common-man populism." Nevertheless, he hit the right spirit at the right time.

His election-eve broadcast was one of the broadest, most audacious canvases that had ever been presented on radio. Corwin has said that he agreed to take part in the broadcast only if he were totally free to do as he pleased. Paul Porter, who was to become head of the Federal Communications Commission after the election, wrote a letter to Corwin in September 1944 stressing the need to emphasize domestic rather than foreign policy, since the Republicans, at this late stage of the war, would not have done things very differently from the way Roosevelt did.

Corwin decided to go for several things in the broadcast. He would show how Dewey had sought to disenfranchise the soldiers and deprive them of their vote in the election. And he would show that Roosevelt's support came from the people—$13 million from 13 million people who each had contributed a dollar. This would be contrasted with Dewey's support—$13 million from one man, oil baron Joseph Pew—and the big-money boys would be shown to be the antiunion boys. Then there would be a look at the horror of bygone days. James Cagney, Groucho Marx, and Keenan Wynn would sing "In the Good Old Hoover Time . . . ," which would melt into a version of "The Old Red Scare It Ain't What It Used To Be," pointing up the communism scares of 1936, 1940, and 1944 "used with such distinguished lack of success by Dewey and the Republicans" in Corwin's words. There would also be a broadside launched against the racism of Dewey and the Republicans, with E. Y. Harburg composing the "Free and Equal Blues," an attack on the racism of the Red Cross's not wanting to give white soldiers plasma from nonwhites. Criticizing the "international metabolistic cartel," Harburg exhorted, "Tell Hitler and Goebbels, circulation is global."

Prior to the broadcast, the script was shown to Roosevelt, whose only comment was "Can he do all this?" Corwin's big decisions were not to pussyfoot with the opponent, to come right out and say "Dewey, phooey." Testimonials were used for the first time in a political campaign—spots such as "I'm a farmer, and I'm voting for Roosevelt," and "I'm an Italian GI, and I'm voting for Roosevelt." Humphrey Bogart narrated a segment that used a train motif: "I'm on the train for Roosevelt. All aboard for the Roosevelt special." An expert in doubletalk gave an example of Dewey's kind of doubletalk. And, of course, there was a galaxy of stars on the program, every leading Democratic thespian in Hollywood from Bette Davis to Olivia de Havilland to Paulette Goddard. At the last minute, Jimmy Durante, who was to have participated in the broadcast, was scared off by the sponsors of his radio show, but it turned out to be a good thing: the Republicans had bought time after the show, and because of Durante's pulling out, the broadcast ran short and there were several filler minutes of dreary organ music and most people went to bed. Corwin's name was not announced during any part of the show.

The results were astounding. An estimated 1 million votes were swung to Roosevelt by the broadcast, and California sported the largest Democratic landslide in the country. In a letter to Paul Porter, Corwin thanked him for the "heroic and ingenious job you did clearing the show with the networks, and for that you have a place, not only in my heart, but in the history of the progress of American radio." Corwin then launched into a gleeful description of the response to the broadcast the next day in Hollywood:

> The stars, the studios, the agencies, Romanoff's, Chasen's, and the Players, were all abuzz with it; Tallulah Bankhead kissed my hand; Groucho Marx was reduced to gaglessness; Durante looked uncomfortable and solemn the day after the show; reactionaries like Howard Emmett Rogers grudgingly admitted it was an effective broadcast; Hedda Hopper passed me in a huff; Nunnally Johnson offered me a piece of International pictures. . . .

The power of radio, so clearly demonstrated by the Roosevelt broadcast, was very much on the minds of writers, as it had been for years. And it was with a certain instinct for media power that they began their investigations of television during the war. The advent of commercial television had been delayed by the war, but as early as 1937 it had loomed as a possibility that was of grave concern to American writers. In the spring of 1937, the Authors League of America was agitated by reports that a move had already been made by the Du Ponts and the Rockefellers to take over RCA enterprises and build up a giant amusement corporation that would dominate the radio, television, and motion picture fields. RCA was, at that time, making some television broadcasts and was expected to get in on the ground floor when TV emerged from its experimental stage. Both the Du Ponts and the Rockefellers were heavily committed in RCA, which in turn had a controlling interest in RKO, in addition to its ownership of NBC. The ALA, viewing this situation with alarm, concluded in April 1937: "The author's position is totally insecure with such corporations. The author is faced first with choosing between selling only on the terms offered or not selling at all. Their bargaining power is infinitesimal. A manuscript is a commodity. . . . Whether authors wish it or not, they are regimented by the industries which buy their products and will be increasingly so."

By the middle of the war, television receivers had been placed in police stations, high schools, and other public meeting places where defense volunteers, such as air-raid wardens, auxiliary police, and fire watchers, assembled and received instructions. Dramatizations of actual air-raid incidents staged by wardens in the studio were one form of presentation, along with chalk talks and cartoons and on-camera demonstrations.

"During the war," said Michael Kanin, "I remember being led to some apartment, in a side street of the Hollywood Hills around Yucca, and there in the middle of the apartment, in this dark room, was a television. The following night there was a meeting of the Guild's board of directors, and I told the board about this box: 'You just have to see it to be impressed, but it's going to have an enormous impact on our lives.' It sounded outlandish, coming out with this during the middle of the war, but the SWG appointed a committee of one to investigate television—me. I called Milton Merlin from the Radio Writers Guild, and then people from other guilds and unions assigned representatives to this group, the Affiliated Committee for Television."

In July 1944, the committee began functioning with Curtis Dean as its acting chairman. Among its first projects were programming experimental television broadcasts, putting together a comprehensive course of study for UCLA, and organizing a circulating library. The committee's aims and purposes were the reemployment of guild member veterans; assistance to creative artists in making the transition from educational to commercial television at the end of the war; the fostering of understanding between different groups working on the common problems of television; and the structuring of lectures, research, courses of instruction, and a study of the economic problems that television would bring about. The SWG members on the committee included Michael Kanin, Boris Ingster, and Maurice Rapf.

"The committee lasted through part of 1945," recalled Kanin, "but then war activities were so involving that the guild and union involvement in the committee dwindled away from lack of support. The report was taken to Dean Knudsen at UCLA, who used it in an investigation the school was making of expanding their communications department. A few years later, when TV burst on the movie industry, I felt that we did at least give the guilds and unions some insight into what was coming. But if not for the war, the writers would have been in a much stronger position to cope with television."

The only truly bitter note during that exhilarating autumn of the Roosevelt campaign was the two days of Tenney Committee hearings on the Hollywood Writers Mobilization Congress. On October 12, 1944, a meeting was called by John Howard Lawson at the home of writer Paul Trivers for those subpoenaed by Tenney. Included were Lawson, Trivers, Marc Connelly, Francis Faragoh, Albert Maltz, Ralph Freud, Waldo Salt, Pauline Lauber Finn, and Mischa Altman of the musicians' union.

"Years later," recalled Finn, "after having testified before Tenney, I watched McCarthy, and it was incredible—the same verbiage, attacks, chanting. They were cut from the same mold. Tenney was physically similar to McCarthy, too—beefy without being fat. From the time Tenney attacked the Mobilization, factionalism set in. It got worse when he subpoenaed members of the HWM and even worse when he began publishing his reports."

There was an obvious undertone of anti-Semitism, as well as anticommunist smear tactics, in the Tenney hearings, and it surfaced quite blatantly when Lawson took the stand:

"Lawson. Pen name or legal name?" asked investigator Richard Combs.

"Legal," replied Lawson.

Combs insisted that Lawson's name had been changed.

"What was your father's name?" Combs asked.

"His name was Simon Levy, but he changed it before I was born," said Lawson, obviously getting angry.

When Combs claimed that his questioning was innocuous, Lawson called his procedure "grossly improper."

Senator Tenney stepped in to agree with Combs. "This is the one committee in California that has fought very diligently against anti-Semitism and other racist prejudices and intolerances," he said.

"I differ with regard to the record," said Lawson.

Tenney's line of questioning was basically a review of the points he had made when he had tried to prevent the writers' congress from taking place in 1943—that it was a communist-controlled front organization whose derivation was from the communist-controlled League of American Writers.

By the time the Tenney Committee's report on the hearings came out in

1945, in a printing of fifteen thousand copies, the state senator had managed to smear nearly everyone associated with the HWM Congress, along with the people involved in the People's Education Center, some of whom were also members of the Mobilization. As a matter of fact, Tenney said in his report: "There is good reason to believe that this Communist front is an offshoot of the writers congress held on the campus of UCLA."

One of Tenney's notable achievements was that Frank C. Davis, an assistant professor at UCLA and a teacher at the PEC, lost his university job, after which he became director of PEC. As an ultimate result of Tenney's attacks, there was a hearing by the state's board of equalization that threatened to take away the nonprofit tax status of the school.

Tenney's attack on the People's Education Center was prefaced by a quotation from J. Edgar Hoover's 1944 commencement address at Holy Cross College, in which Hoover claimed that the American communists had

Emmet Lavery, president of the Screen Writers Guild, testifying before HUAC, October 29, 1947. His play *The Magnificent Yankee* and the screenplay he wrote from it were based on Francis Biddle's biography of Oliver Wendell Holmes, Jr. His other film credits include *Hitler's Children* and *Behind the Rising Sun*.

developed an elaborate Marxist school system directly controlled by V. J. Jerome. The heat was on the PEC, though people tried to dismiss the charges as ridiculous. Ben Barzman remembers once being followed by sheriff's men into the parking lot of the school. They were obviously Tenney's men. During the blacklist period, when Barzman was in Paris and asked why his U.S. passport had been taken away, he was told that it was because he had worked at the PEC. Barzman got furious. "That's ridiculous," shouted Barzman, "I just volunteered. I never even got paid." "Of course not," was the reply. "You were a communist."

"If you want to complain about front organizations," said Sydney Dawson, a left-wing intellectual who succeeded Frank Davis as head of the PEC, "the money was generally lousy. The people in HICCASP made twice what the people in PEC did."

The threat of Tenney didn't seem so terribly ominous at the beginning of 1945, however. Roosevelt had been reelected; the HWM, despite some factionalism, was still together; and Democrats and progressives in Hollywood laughed at Tenney for attacking such distinguished liberals as Dudley Nichols for being part of a communist front.

Robert Kenny had also been forced to answer charges of radicalism, but he had told the public: "I did vote against the bill outlawing the Communist Party, but my opponents tell only half the truth when they fail to point out that the state Supreme Court has unanimously agreed with me that our Constitution does not permit such a measure."

The measure had, of course, been introduced by Tenney. It seemed that time and again when the reactionaries had attacked the liberals, branding them and their activities communist-inspired, all it took was the truth to show that the Tenneys of the world wallowed in half-truths. The attack of the Tenney Committee on the PEC and the HWM was a sign, argued the members of the Left, that cohesiveness and decisiveness among the various organizations were more crucial now than they had ever been.

It was an odd time. Victory loomed closer and closer. The thoughts of the American people were turned toward winning the war, with a peripheral worry about the coming peace. Under the leadership of the SWG's new president, Emmet Lavery—a Catholic liberal who, it was thought, would deflect some of the criticism and the charges of radicalism being leveled against the Guild—SWG members had begun to question the entire issue of the returning veteran and his place in the industry, and what the writers' responsibilities would be in the postwar world. With characteristic ironic contrariness, the year when Hollywood began to contemplate the peace was the year when the war really began there.

10

The death of Roosevelt in April 1945 and the end of the war in September coincided with a growing reaction in this country that emerged, full-blown, as the Cold War. In Hollywood, the coalition of Right and Left that, for the sake of the country, had been formed, albeit with misgivings, for the duration of the war split apart with a ferocity that was seemingly more intense for having been repressed for four years.

In the midst of such growing opposition, the American Left—and particularly the Left in Hollywood—adopted a course that, in light of external circumstances, could only be viewed as naively optimistic, deliberately myopic, or tragically self-destructive. At a time when the gains labor made during the New Deal were being slowly but steadily eroded, when new legislation and forms of censorship were being introduced that were aptly and fearfully labeled "thought control," when Hollywood itself was being attacked legislatively and economically, the Left manifested an unwitting complicity in the process, which ultimately destroyed them.

The issue that finally ended up splitting the Screen Writers Guild politically was not, as one might have expected, an international issue, but rather an industry labor matter. It was the outcome of the struggle that had existed since the late thirties, when Jeff Kibre's United Screen Technicians Guild, a rival organization, had struggled against the domination of the corrupt International Alliance of Theatrical Stage Employees. It was Kibre who had been largely responsible for the charges and the investigation that had ended with Willie Bioff, George E. Browne, and Joseph M. Schenck in jail, and the industry hadn't forgotten. Kibre, the labor troubleshooter, the man in the leather jacket, became too notorious and controversial to function effectively within the unions. In 1939, with the United Screen Technicians Guild uproar,

Kibre made a deal with the unions and the producers: to effect settlement of the dispute, to get everyone back to work, he would leave the industry. He had been forced to move with a round-the-clock bodyguard from 1937 to 1939, until he was finally blacklisted out of the industry.

It has been claimed that Kibre, because of his notoriety, was forced to use fronts in the industry to take positions that he couldn't possibly espouse without discrediting them, because anything he said by the late thirties was branded "Red" by the producers and the trades and the Hearst press. Also, Kibre had no constituents, as leaders of more integrated guilds did, and his directives aroused suspicion.

"Kibre was the official communist in the Hollywood trade union movement," said Fred Rinaldo. "He never really stayed in one place long enough to take root, so he never got a following. He was the man in the leather jacket who would pop out of nowhere, assume a leadership position, function as a troubleshooter, and disappear."

One man who did have a following was a former boxer named Herbert Sorrell who in 1942 had been business agent of the Motion Picture Painters Local 644 after the successful strike which he had helped to organize against the Walt Disney Studios. Sorrell founded the Conference of Studio Unions, a coalition of five dissatisfied AFL locals (the Screen Cartoonists Guild, the Screen Office Employees Guild, Film Technicians Local 683, Machinists Local 1185, and Motion Picture Painters Local 644). These groups had originally been overlooked by the IATSE because they were small numerically and their efforts to organize independently had been unsuccessful. By 1945, the Conference of Studio Unions (CSU) had nine member unions, including the powerful carpenters' local, and it represented nearly ten thousand workers in the motion picture industry. In a town of symbols, the CSU stood for honest democratic trade unionism. It would only be a matter of time before it was destroyed. The IATSE sensed it as a growing threat and, because Bioff and Browne were in jail, sent in two new troubleshooters who were to become powerful and lethal in Hollywood—Roy Brewer, an officer of the Motion Picture Alliance and international representative in Hollywood of the IATSE, and IATSE president Richard Walsh.

The IATSE had a friend in Sacramento who was just as eager as they to discredit Sorrell. Jack Tenney was now, according to the Motion Picture Alliance for the Preservation of American Ideals, the IATSE, and the Hearst press, the voice of reason and justice in California, and in his 1945 report he listed Herb Sorrell among the Red and the damned:

> Herbert Sorrell is an officer in the Studio Painters Union, A. F. of L. He has persistently followed the Communist Party line. He subscribed to the Communist Party publication, the *People's Daily World*. Leaflets distributed in July of 1940 listed Sorrell as an officer in the American

Peace Crusade, a Communist Organization. He also appeared as an endorser for Mrs. LaRue McCormick, Communist Party candidate for State Senator, in a paid political advertisement in the *Los Angeles Times*, November 2, 1942.

In March 1945, the war continued in Europe and the Pacific. It was one month before the death of Roosevelt, one month before the slow process of purging his New Deal. On March 12, Local 1421, a member of the CSU, went on strike on behalf of the set decorators, for whom they claimed exclusive bargaining rights. The Society of Motion Picture Decorators had voted to affiliate with Local 1421 as early as October 1943, and the producers had been notified of the change in affiliation and the desire of 1421 to negotiate a new contract for the decorators when the old one ran out in January 1944. But, by using all the dodges of wartime worries that were so convenient, the producers somehow didn't get around to negotiating that contract, and suddenly, in mid-August 1944, an IATSE union, Local 44, declared that it had jurisdiction over the decorators. It was clearly a tactic used by the producers

Herbert Sorrell, far right, head of the striking Committee of Studio Unions. Representative Carroll Kearns from Pennsylvania (center), chairman of the House subcommittee investigating Hollywood's labor problems.

to fight against any extension of the power of the CSU in place of the IATSE. Angry haggling went on for the next several months, and finally Local 1421 filed a strike notice, which brought the War Labor Board into the negotiations. The War Labor Board decided in favor of the CSU-affiliated Local 1421, but the producers continued their delaying tactics until 1421, in desperation, went out on strike.

The Left was divided over whether or not to support the strike. On the one hand, the IATSE was undoubtedly corrupt, and the CSU was striking a blow against the producers for honest trade unionism. On the other hand, the United States was still at war, and honoring labor's "no-strike" pledge to Roosevelt meant aiding our Soviet allies.

"I opposed Jack Lawson's adherence to the no-strike pledge," recalled Bonnie Smith, who had left the Anti-Nazi League to work with the CSU. "There comes a point when the Red position isn't the best position for the worker."

Jean Butler agreed. "I was so irritated that the Left wouldn't take Sorrell's position. He had so much morality on his side."

"There was dissatisfaction within the CP with the no-strike pledge, even before the CSU strike," recalled Elizabeth Spector. "When it came to workers on strike, I thought we should support them and not condone what they did at North American [Aviation, Inc.]. There was a terrible disturbance when Roosevelt sent the troops into the North American strike. And the county executive committee of the Party kept flip-flopping—one week there'd be excitement and tremendous support for the strikers, and the next week they'd be agreeing that Roosevelt was right to send in troops, because after all it was wartime."

"I was against the no-strike pledge," recalled Lionel Stander, "but that's because I was a militant trade unionist, not a Party person. I was lefter than the Left. The communists considered me undisciplined, an infantile leftist."

The IATSE, like the Left, ceremoniously proclaimed their adherence to labor's no-strike pledge, deploring the activities of Local 1421. Nevertheless, IATSE president Richard Walsh let the producers understand that if negotiations with Local 1421 were completed, every movie projectionist in every theater in the United States would take a walk. As far as the producers were concerned, they had their choice of a bunch of unhappy communist set decorators or dark screens.

"Does that mean that the producers' fear of an IATSE threat is greater than their respect for the federal government?" asked the president of Local 1421, Frank J. Drdlyk. The answer was without question "yes."

In June 1945, publisher Carl Hovey, husband of screen writer Sonya Levien, wrote to Secretary of Labor Frances Perkins, "I hope you will come to the Coast. Not that it is any inducement, but you could look on at one of the most virulent strike wars in history. We have our own ideas about the right and the wrong of it and not much hope that the right will come through. (Right stands for Left in this case.)"

For those who later accused the CSU of being communist-controlled, the simple fact that they were striking in wartime, without the complicity of leftists from the more intellectual circles, like the Screen Writers Guild, should have been enough to exonerate them. However, the strike continued, without the assistance of the Left or the tacit assistance of the SWG. There was escalating violence and bitterness on the picket lines. But the Left had major problems of its own by the spring of 1945.

Roosevelt was dead, and the United Nations conference was taking place in San Francisco, now that the war in Europe was over and the end of the war in the Pacific seemed close at hand. There was already marked disagreement within the Hollywood Writers Mobilization about whether or not that organization should be continued. There were those who believed that the desire of the HWM to go on, now that the war was ending, was evidence that it was controlled by communists who wanted to use it as a front organization. The crunch came, and the meetings of the HWM went through the period of smaller and smaller meeting rooms that was so symbolic of a dying organization in Hollywood.

The San Francisco Conference had been beset with problems right from the beginning. There was a fight about letting the Argentinian delegation into the United Nations; there were two Yugoslavian delegations (Drazha Mihailovich and Tito), and they were each trying to frame the other with sex scandals; and the paparazzi were scurrying around with their flashbulbs popping away.

"The cynics predicted that the U.N. conference held the promise of later splits," recalled Elizabeth Spector, "but I was optimistic, like so many people. I wanted the harmony of the war to continue. And then, in the middle of the conference, came the Duclos Letter."

The Duclos Letter was the published treatise of Jacques Duclos, the leading French theoretician of the Communist Party, in which he declared Earl Browder a heretic and labeled his attempts to create a more liberal coalition counterrevolutionary. Duclos denounced the renunciation of revolutionary values implied in Browder's Communist Political Association and the dissolution of the American Communist Party. This event caused grave confusion on the Left, particularly during the limbo period of the next few months, during which they watched Browder and his CPA tossed out of the CP and William Z. Foster instated as head of the U.S. Communist Party.

Dalton Trumbo had just returned from writing speeches for the U.S. delegation to the San Francisco Conference. Hugo Butler was home on leave for the weekend from Fort Orde, and the talk was all about the Duclos Letter.

"There was one all-night session between Hugo and Trumbo," recalled Jean Butler, "that lasted so long I finally fell asleep on the couch. At about two a.m. I woke up and Trumbo was saying, 'It comes down to this—either Lenin was right and Browder was wrong, or Browder was right and Lenin was wrong. I prefer to believe that Lenin was right.' And I thought, 'Oh dear,' and rolled over and went back to sleep."

"I knew people from the New York Party," said Abe Polonsky, "and though I'd left the Party to go into service, almost as soon as I got back they asked me to let them use my home for a meeting on the Duclos Letter. There must have been one hundred people in my living room. And of course the FBI was outside, writing down license-plate numbers.

"I thought the Duclos policy was absurd—ramming an arbitrary revolutionary policy down the throats of the American communists. There was good talk and some opposition. It was a surprise to see people resisting the Party line and a shock to see it driven down their throats.

"At last I got up and told the head of the group it was absurd, and somebody jumped up and said I should be expelled. I wasn't even a member anymore. But the people who weren't part of the Hollywood community didn't understand that they were helping to destroy an important part of human relations. Everyone voted for what the Party wanted."

The Hollywood Communist Party had remained important in the eyes of the national leadership. After the Duclos Letter, when Foster took the helm of the reconstituted national CP, he was sent out to Hollywood.

"Even the national Party leaders were swayed by the glamour of Hollywood," recalled Elizabeth Spector. "I remember when Foster came to town, after Browder was out of the Party, there was a meeting at Trumbo's house so that the people there could meet Bill Foster. Foster was a big fan of Western movies. As soon as a Western came on, just looking at the opening shots, he could tell you all the credits. Foster was unhappy at that meeting because there were no Western stars there, and he had hoped to meet some.

"When the Browder line became the Foster line, it was an extremely traumatic experience. The feeling that something was wrong had been building up. Before the shift, Carl Winter, who was the CP's L.A. chairman, came back and reported to the Party functionaries' meeting at the Olympic Auditorium. It was a disorderly meeting—people in the audience spent most of the time in the foyer talking, and you couldn't hear Winter inside. There was an expression of real disquiet concerning the Party line."

The sudden blanket imposition of this latest shift in Party doctrine alienated many members of the left-wing community. Party members were expected to adhere to the Duclos line, and any deviation was branded "internal renegacy."

Even some of the Party's most supportive members agreed with critics like Abe Polonsky, who said: "The madness which is inherent in revolutionary parties which enables them to survive also forces them to destroy the strength in individualism."

Dorothy Healy, who became secretary of the Party after the announcement of the Duclos Letter, agreed: "There is a tragic vulnerability to revolutionaries who don't challenge, who don't think. It's necessary to have a certain level of faith or acceptance among those who are going to follow a certain line, but in the long run it's better to have thinking, challenging people. It's like that story about the woman who comes to a psychiatrist convinced that she's dead. And the psychiatrist says to her, 'But suppose you bleed. Do dead people bleed?' 'No,' says the woman. So the doctor pricks her finger, she bleeds, and she looks up at him and says, 'Oh! Dead people do bleed.' "

"When the Party finally died," said Charles Glenn, "it wasn't just because of external forces. It died of its own intransigence."

In August 1945, in the midst of the chaos, the arguments, and the infighting, the atom bomb was dropped on Hiroshima. The war was over, but not in Hollywood. The CSU strike continued; however, the end of the war meant a shot in the arm for their cause, because it ended labor's no-strike pledge. The Left began to push for support of the strike, particularly the Left in the Screen Writers Guild, and the Guild then divided, Right against Left, with the Right adhering to the stated Guild policy of not taking any political stance or side in any dispute and the Left claiming that it was the Guild's responsibility to support the strike.

"Jack Lawson and others felt that we should lend every moral and, if possible, financial support to the trade-unionist brothers who were on the picket line," recalled SWG president Emmet Lavery. "And my personal position, and that of the majority of the board, was, 'It's not our fight.' And then Jack ingenuously wanted to offer a resolution one night that we compensate any member of our Guild who might get hurt on the picket line if, out of the goodness of his heart, he went to try and do something."

The SWG board at that time was composed equally of conservative liberals such as Oliver Garrett, Helen Deutsch, F. Hugh Herbert, Emmet Lavery, Sheridan Gibney, Howard Estabrook, and Frank Partos; radical progressives like Harold Buchman, Richard Collins, Gordon Kahn, Leo Townsend, Ring Lardner, Jr., and John Howard Lawson; and liberals like Michael Kanin and Frances Goodrich and Albert Hackett and William Pomerance, a radical trade-unionist.

The Guild, though divided over the issue of whether or not to support the strike, remembered what it was like to be ignored by the producers in a jurisdictional controversy. They tried to use their rather dubious muscle to influence the producers, if only to get them to negotiate with the strikers. The Guild sent a wire to the producers in September, and the producers' representative, Mendel Silberg, told the SWG's lawyer, Morris Cohn, that a tradepaper announcement of the wire had been damaging to writer-producer relationships. Nevertheless, Cohn was empowered by the Guild to arrange a meeting with Silberberg so that the producers and the Guild could discuss a strike settlement and negotiations with Local 1421. The producers weren't supposed to know that the writers intended to meet with the strikers first.

Divided over the issue of picketing, the SWG, as a union, was inclined to respect picket lines. And as writers, they could do their work at home while seeming virtuous and not crossing the lines. But no formal letter could go out to the Guild's membership encouraging this action, because it would violate the minimum basic agreement with the producers.

Then, suddenly, in the midst of the intellectual caviling, a far more serious issue required attention. The producers wanted to empower the persons replacing the strikers—in other words, the strikebreakers—to vote. A National Labor Relations Board certifying election was to be held for the set decorators, as had been held for the SWG seven years earlier, and the NLRB was hearing arguments to decide whether people replacing the strikers could vote. If the NLRB decided in favor of the strikebreakers, the Wagner Act would be effectively nullified. The SWG had Morris Cohn phrase a resolution opposing this and sent it off to the NLRB.

In general, the strikers were growing more optimistic, despite the facts that the strike was past the six-month mark, the CSU members were broke, and the organization's treasury was depleted. In addition, on September 12, labor representatives convinced the city council to vote down Councilman Meade McLanahan's proposed ordinance that would have forbade picketing in Los Angeles, and that seemed a promising sign. But the strike dragged on, and Sorrell decided to single out Warner Bros. for mass picketing in order to break the unified resistance of the studios. On October 5 the picketing began, and three days later it was met by the goon squads of Los Angeles Sheriff Biscailuz and his deputies.

"You can't imagine how shocking it was," recalled screen writer David Robison. "It was the first bloody strike since the war. The Burbank police were there, the goon squads; there was blood all over the streets. After all the spiritual violence the producers had done, the strike now became permeated with physical violence."

Roy Brewer of the IATSE claimed that the violence was started by the Left. He said that Harry Bridges sent goons down from San Francisco. There were others who also said that the strikers had precipitated the violence out of desperation, that it had come from a bitter carpenter who said, "Give me four hundred people, and I'll close down Warner's." While angry strikers turned over cars, metropolitan police armed with automatic rifles arranged themselves along the street opposite the Warner Bros. autogate. A picture of the scene there in October 1945 looks like something nobody expected ever to see in Hollywood, except possibly on the screen. Milling police wearing hard hats watch strikers sitting at the Warner Bros. gates carrying posters saying, "We demand our jobs and contracts."

Emmet Lavery, Howard Koch, and Gordon Kahn went to see what was going on and reported what they had witnessed to the SWG—the fire hoses, the tear gas, the vicious, random violence against the picketers. Telegrams protesting the NLRB's delay in settling the strike were sent to President Truman, Secretary of Labor Lewis Schwellenbach, Senator Robert Wagner, the NLRB, and State Attorney General Robert Kenny. Another telegram was sent to Eric Johnston, head of the Motion Picture Producers Association, urging the producer to sit down with the strikers.

The screen writers had good reason for respecting the picket lines now— fear of bodily harm. Yet the Guild could still not instruct its members to stay away from work. On Sunday, October 7, a mass meeting took place at the Hollywood Legion Stadium.

"Herb Sorrell completely captured that meeting with a warm, witty speech in which he condemned people who 'covered the fact that they'd lost their pants by wrapping themselves in the American flag,' " recalled Karen Morley, who had been active in trade unionism all over the country. "I later found out that Herb Sorrell's warm, witty words had come from Dalton Trumbo's pen."

On Monday morning, fifty picketers were injured when the goon squads charged their lines. Lester Pine recalled that morning at Warner Bros.:

"I was just a kid at the time of the strike. All I knew was they were trying to get recognition for the good craft unions in the industry, so I joined the picket lines. I was in the SWG, an associate member I think, but I wasn't even working at the time.

"Across the street there was a big assortment of guys who all looked like Charles Bickford. Especially the leader. They were tough sons of bitches, had wire cable and other things like that in their hands. They charged at us and hit the line broadside from across the street. They beat the shit out of people."

Lester Cole proposed that the SWG take the position that the spirit of the minimum basic agreement had been broken by Warner Bros.' violations of civil liberties. He didn't want any writers to work there until the strike was settled. Cole's opponents pointed out that such an action might result in the destruction of the SWG. But Cole and the progressives argued that this was the destruction of progressive trade unionism in Hollywood. If the Conference of Studio Unions were destroyed or weakened, the Screen Writers Guild would be more vulnerable to the IATSE.

"The SWG was pussyfooting as a union," recalled David Robison. "Emmet Lavery was very formal, noncommittal. The SWG was a frightened little union and it chickened out on all counts. The SWG should have helped another progressive union."

The NLRB's decision was not an easy one, but on October 16 the board found in favor of the CSU and Local 1421. On October 18, the Screen Writers Guild drafted a resolution that called for the producers to promptly abide by the decision when the official NLRB certification was announced. The Guild also called for the return to work of all employees who had struck, back to the positions they had held before the strike.

In their resolution, the Guild claimed that by using delaying tactics, by insisting that a jurisdictional dispute still existed, the producers were creating a lockout. If the producers didn't restore employees to their jobs, if they didn't recall the workers and reaffirm recognition of the unions and contracts as soon as the official certification was announced, the SWG promised, the Guild would call a membership meeting to "take action" to meet the crisis. The producers would have to honor the NLRB decision or they would find themselves with a new strike on their hands. The SWG was also considering whether there was anything they could do about Columbia Pictures' cancelation of John Howard Lawson's contract for his activities at Warner Bros. during the strike.

The writers gathered the support of the Hollywood Council of Guilds and Unions and stuck up for the Screen Publicists and Screen Office Employees guilds certified by the NLRB. And again they warned that the producers' defiance of NLRB certification was a big enough threat to provoke action within the other guilds.

Finally the NLRB ruled for the CSU, and the producers had to give in. Though the producers had backed down, the CSU's victory seemed somewhat Pyrrhic after eight months without work, and the struggle had only whetted the producers' and the IATSE's appetites for vengeance.

There was an uneasy feeling in Hollywood. This wasn't the way it was supposed to be with the war over. There was supposed to be harmony, unity, joy. But the only unity was created by archreactionary Gerald L. K. Smith. He had come to Los Angeles to make a series of anti-Semitic speeches, and he united the Hollywood community the way no other issue, labor or political, could have.

"Smith was a broad barn," recalled Ellenore Bogigian. "The Mobilization for Democracy was a big coalition to protest Smith, and there were members in the group like Walter Wanger, Bette Davis, and Frank Sinatra."

"I've never seen a picket line like the one the Mobilization had against Smith," recalled Fred Rinaldo. "There were four square blocks of people, four abreast."

"The truth was," said Bogigian, "that people turned out because Smith was such a terrible fascist, but you couldn't convince the activists that that was the reason, that the coalition was because Smith was an anti-Semite. Again, the Left misread the signs and thought it was their own organizational power that had rallied these masses of people."

The UCLA writers' congress had made it clear to the Hollywood community what the Hollywood Writers Mobilization instinctively felt—that after the war, the entertainment industry could never be the same. To perpetuate the concerns articulated at the congress, a group was formed, composed of Hollywood people and academics, to found a magazine called the *Hollywood Quarterly*. Its editors were Samuel T. Farquhar, John Howard Lawson, Franklin Fearing, Kenneth MacGowan, and Franklin P. Rolfe. The assistant editor was MacGowan's protégée, Sylvia Jarrico. On the advisory committees were such people as Ralph Beals, Emmet Lavery, Howard Estabrook, Sidney Buchman, Edward Dmytryk, Alexander Knox, Jay Leyda, Dudley Nichols, Ben Maddow, Florence Odets (Clifford Odets's wife), Abe Polonsky, Abe Burrows, John Houseman, and Orson Welles. Though a great deal of the *Quarterly*'s fire was stolen by the SWG's own magazine, *The Screenwriter*, edited by Dalton Trumbo, which began to publish almost simultaneously, the beginning of the *Quarterly* was an auspicious event in intellectual circles.

Published by UCLA, the *Hollywood Quarterly*'s first issue came out late in 1945. The writers and educators involved in the *Quarterly* knew that movies, radio, and the new toy, television, were going to be important factors in the creation of the postwar society. The magazine featured analyses of wartime activities in film and radio, movie and book reviews, technical articles, essays on the psychological implications of movies, and discussions of craft, but always, running through all this, was an undercurrent of conscience. The writers were concerned about their responsibilities to the world, but they hadn't lost sight of their struggle for rights within the studio system. The CSU strike had emphasized how frail union independence really was.

Morris Cohn, counsel for SWG and chairman of the Los Angeles chapter of the National Lawyers Guild, was an expert on censorship and literary properties, and he wrote on "The Author's Moral Rights," a code employed in Europe that considered the artist's work an extension of his or her personality and concerned itself with protecting that work from distortion by middlemen. This was an obsessive concern of screen writers, who were suffering under the very factor that had enabled them to unionize under the Wagner Act—the fact that they had no control over their final product, with which the studio could do as it liked.

The doctrine of moral rights didn't apply to writers as employees. Even though the Senate in 1935 had passed an amendment to the copyright act that recognized moral rights, the thrust of this assertion was undermined by another section of the amendment, which claimed that "the necessary editing or adaptation for publication, film or broadcast, should not be regarded as a violation of moral right." Moral right was recognized in name only, and even so, the amendment never passed in the House. The Duffy Bill, enacted in 1936, didn't even pay lip service to moral right. Its concern was more in the line of *droit de seigneur*. The point that Cohn ultimately made, in his series of articles, was that if movies and radio sought to become media for sincere work from America's great writers, then the public had to be made to see that the work of these artists deserved the greatest protection. Creators could not make significant social statements if their words were edited. Cohn's articles were accompanied by Lester Cole's account of how a "happy ending" was tacked onto his script for *Blood on the Sun*. Cole detested the ending and thought it a fraud; it was embraced by the studios and praised by Hearst.

It was news to nobody that Hollywood was a fiefdom run by studio executives, but the sort of regulation that Cole was dreaming of, which would have protected screen writers and their material, appeared as a nightmarish inversion in the form of increasing censorship legislation in Congress and increasing attempts to repress freedom of expression in Hollywood.

The threat of censorship had been increasing since the end of Roosevelt's administration. In the autumn of 1945, while the CSU strike raged in Hollywood, HUAC Committee Chairman John Rankin, who had replaced Martin Dies, called for the scripts of several well-known liberal radio commentators, which he chose to analyze. Shortly thereafter, two of those commentators, Hans Jacob and William Gailmor, were dismissed by their stations. Congressman Emanuel Celler accused the committee of "seeking to out-Dies the original Dies Committee. Unfortunately, even if its hunted and hounded victims emerge vindicated, people will not be properly informed, and the truth will not catch up with the lies."

Rankin weakly replied that the scripts of conservative commentators like Drew Pearson and Walter Winchell were also being examined, and he answered his opponent with more than a modicum of vengeance, referring to Celler as "that Jewish gentleman from New York."

Encouraged by the success of Rankin, Jack Tenney also continued his own campaign. In 1946 he escalated his hearings, and his two prime focuses were the communist influence at UCLA and the communist influence of the People's Education Center, and the relationship between the university and the PEC. UCLA was already having problems by the end of 1945: during the CSU strike, a group of students had joined the picket line carrying banners identifying themselves as being from UCLA. As a result, when a state assembly subcommittee under the chairmanship of C. Don Field investigated the violence at Warner Bros. during that bloody October, one of the hearings was held on the UCLA campus, with Provost Clarence Dykstra and members of the faculty and student body called as witnesses. At this hearing, questions were asked concerning faculty members who had lectured at the People's

Education Center, and evidence was given to show that some students at UCLA were members of American Youth for Democracy, the campus Communist Party group.

The result of the hearing was that in December 1945, the regents of the University of California passed resolutions to the effect that faculty and students must have prior written permission before engaging in any off-campus activity which conveyed the impression that they represented the university. On January 5, 1946, this resolution was replaced by another stating that "any member of the faculty or student body seeking to alter our American government by other than constitutional means or to induce others to do so, shall, on proof of such charge, be subject to dismissal." It was in essence the first loyalty oath to hit the university system in California.

Tenney thus had the backing of the regents, as well as that of the IATSE and the Motion Picture Alliance, when he renewed his investigative hearings in January 1946. He launched the new hearings with the announcement that he had switched his party affiliation and had become a Republican. He knew that the Motion Picture Alliance had financed the Dewey campaign in 1944, and 1946 was an election year. So with the headlines Tenney was garnering from his hearings and the enormous financial resources of the Alliance, which he assumed he could count on (as a newly baptized Republican), Tenney had every reason to be optimistic and perhaps a bit more zealous than usual.

Tenney questioned six UCLA professors, primarily about the connection with the People's Education Center, of which one of them was a board member and at which several of them had lectured. Then Tenney called the beleaguered Dr. Dykstra and questioned him extensively about the *Hollywood Quarterly*. Tenney denounced John Howard Lawson as being one of the editors of the *Quarterly*, invoking the litany of the writer's communist affiliations, and then questioned Dykstra. He didn't think Dykstra himself was a communist, merely a fool, a dupe, a tool of the Party, which was using him and the university as "window dressing" for their infiltration of education and culture.

Tenney augmented his attacks on the *Hollywood Quarterly* and the university with claims that the Mobilization for Democracy was under communist control.

John Houseman in *Front and Center* stated: "A glance at [the *Hollywood Quarterly*'s] contents during its brief life will show the absurdity of the charge. There is no doubt that Jack Lawson, as one of the party's cultural leaders on the West Coast, welcomed the creation of such a publication. . . . It remained an earnest, rather mild magazine—part professional, part academic and sociological. It created no major stir and exerted not the slightest influence on the filmmaking of its time. Yet it remains the first serious cultural publication in which members of the motion picture industry were collectively involved."

Herb Sorrell appeared and resolutely declared that he was not a communist. He so swore under oath. Tenney also called Samuel Farquhar and questioned him about the CP's influence on the editorial policy of the magazine. Farquhar claimed that he was on the editorial board to "see that nothing subversive was run in the magazine."

Tenney's information about the communist conspiracy at that time came from three sources—his own files on individuals and groups, which he had been keeping since 1939; data from the committee's investigators, including people like Charles Backsy, a former treasury agent who claimed to have infiltrated the radical hotbed of Lincoln Steffens's home up at Carmel; and information received from HUAC and other federal and state investigative agencies. In addition, he had a supremely diligent clipping service to handle his material, which consisted of subscriptions to such subversive publications as the *People's Daily World* and the *Daily Worker*, as well as a great deal of organizational paper. Tenney had his committee agents become members of progressive organizations, such as the HWM, the PEC, and the Mobilization for Democracy, so that he had access to such juicy mailing-list materials as letterheads, pamphlets, announcements of meetings, and so on. And, of course, his agents went to just about every political meeting held in Los Angeles.

Richard Combs was particularly dear to his boss. Tenney described him by saying that "his smooth clever method of examination and suave manner were persuasive in wresting from hostile witnesses the answers they did not want to give. . . . He had a sense of the dramatic."

Tenney's tactics were responded to with anger, horror, and amusement by the progressive community. The *Beverly Westwood Reporter* for March 1946 featured an essay contest on "Why I Hate Jack Tenney." The essay, not to exceed one hundred words, was to be accompanied by the top of a copy of the bright red Tenney report. "The judges are to be Dr. Frank Davis [the PEC director who had lost his job at UCLA], Dr. Clarence Dykstra, and Herb Sorrell. The prizes will include a copy of *Mein Kampf* autographed by Tenney, and two tickets to the celebrated comedy, *The Tenney Follies*. Consolation prizes will be an unused copy of the United State Constitution and subpoenas to the next committee hearings."

The effect of the Tenney Committee became more measurable as time went on. One of the results of the hearings was to take away some of the broader-based support of the PEC and to make it more radical in orientation.

While the PEC was pushed toward the left by the Tenney investigations, the *Hollywood Quarterly* became more conservative. "I had originally been asked to join the board of the *Quarterly* because I was considered more literary than most, having taught English at City College," recalled Abe Polonsky. "I'd become a forceful person in the Party by that time, because I had trade-union experience. I had international experience, I'd been in the war. The *Hollywood Quarterly* was a good magazine. It wanted to be better but was forced into an academic bind. It never got to the heart of what films were about. It couldn't survive the attack on radicals in the university and in Hollywood."

By 1947, Lawson and some of the more radical people were off the *Quarterly* board, though Polonsky remained, as did Sylvia Jarrico. The magazine announced a new general policy, which was basically an excision of all political content from its pages. The Hollywood Writers Mobilization was no longer involved, having "transferred its interest in the periodical to a group of directors, writers, actors, producers, and other craftsmen in motion picture and radio work who share a common interest in the techniques of those fields and their social, educational, and aesthetic functions." By 1951, all contact with Hollywood was more or less broken off, and the magazine assumed the title *Arts and Communications Quarterly: A Journal of Film, Radio and TV*. Finally, Sylvia Jarrico resigned rather than sign a university loyalty oath, necessary to remain on the magazine.

"Sylvia didn't want to fight," remembered Abe Polonsky, who also severed his connection with the magazine. "She'd seen the joy of these academics in the magazine, knew their fear and their anguish, and just couldn't bear to force the confrontation. She was sympathetic to frightened people. So am I."

One of the saddest, most bewildered victims of the Tenney attacks on the Mobilization and the *Hollywood Quarterly* was Franklin Fearing. By the end of 1948, Tenney's catalogue of subversive fronts had been incorporated into the attorney general's list of subversive organizations, and a frightened, desperate Fearing wrote a letter to John Houseman, a friend from the HWM:

> Like yourself and others, I had been naive enough to assume—until it went on the "list," that in contributing my small talent to the HWM, I was making a tiny contribution to the war effort. It seems that other citizens also thought the Mobilization was a patriotic, rather than a subversive agency. But it seems that this was all the result of a huge swindle. The U. S. Government, Canada, the Guild, and the Community Chest were all taken in by those clever reds.
> As you know, locally we had gotten so that we more or less took Tenney in stride. I, at least, never dreamed that the Tenney report would be taken over by the attorney general. . . . I have more or less resigned myself to carrying the Mobilization around my neck like the well-known albatross for the rest of my life. . . .

Fearing was naive enough to suggest to Houseman that the leaders of the Mobilization—Robert Rossen, Howard Koch, and Emmet Lavery—petition the attorney general for removal of the Mobilization's name from his list. He had no idea that Rossen or any other members of the Mobilization were communists. To him, it had just seemed like the greatest adventure of his life.

People in the arts had long been disturbed by Tenney's attacks. His snide insinuations that linked them to the supposedly promiscuous rantings of the Left Wing were a discomfiting echo of the condemnation of the Federal Theater Project for producing communist-inspired plays that were "salacious tripe." But what was even more frightening was the trend in national publications and government along lines that Tenney was merely echoing. Roosevelt's New Deal had spread a progressivism that included a profound respect for art. But the administration and climate of reaction were emerging not only as anti-Roosevelt, but also as anti-art. Westbrook Pegler wrote:

> Singing and acting are so absurdly overrated as arts, now that performers are allowed familiarities with their betters, that few of us bear in mind the origins of these poor trades, above which the current celebrities never rise, however we fawn upon them. . . . A singer emits certain sounds from the neck, causing sound effects by the expansion and contraction of certain muscles and by regulating the flow of air. . . . The actor utters recitations written for him by a writer; he bawls, whimpers, or whispers, and stands here or there according to minute directions after long and patient instructions.

One of the most tragic aspects of the destruction of the Left in America and in Hollywood was the way in which it countered the growing repressions of government and the press with small repressions of its own. An example was the so-called Maltz controversy. During the war Maltz had worked on several films that were highly respected, including *This Gun for Hire*, *Destination Tokyo*, and *Pride of the Marines*. Maltz had been quite active in the League of American Writers and was a hearty advocate of the writer's responsibility to fight fascism.

"Albert was a rather humorless man who took causes in which he was involved very personally," recalled Paul Jarrico. "He threw himself into causes, especially that of getting Europeans out of fascist-controlled countries before the war."

In February 1946, Maltz published an essay in *The New Masses* titled "What Shall We Ask of Writers?" in which he analyzed a writer's responsibility to his muse and to his political affiliations, and questioned the myopia of viewing art solely as a weapon. "I have come to believe," he wrote, "that the accepted understanding of art as a weapon is not a useful guide, but a straitjacket." However, it was generally thought in the Party that "unless art is a weapon, like a leaflet, serving immediate political ends, necessities and programs, it is worthless or escapist or vicious."

Maltz felt that the Party should stop judging works of art on the political lineage of the writer. He felt that James Farrell's work shouldn't be dis-

Screenwriter Albert Maltz (*This Gun for Hire, Destination Tokyo, Pride of the Marines*) attended Columbia and Yale and won the 1938 O. Henry Prize for Best Short Story. In 1947, Maltz was cited for contempt of Congress and black-listed. He later emigrated to Mexico, where he wrote scripts that were sold on the black market—among them, *The Robe*.

counted because he was a Trotskyite. Aesthetically, Maltz had embodied the literary equivalent of the Browder line, and the Party pounced on him with such anger that he did, in fact, seem like a Browder surrogate.

"Albert Maltz was a philosophical idealist," recalled Fred Rinaldo. "There was not a materialist bone in his body. He was willing to accept any good writing without judging the content as to whether it was good or bad for the working class. The Party never accepted it."

"Maltz was the victim of a dialogue which had been going on between the Hollywood Party and the CP for years," said Abe Polonsky. "The Hollywood Party resented intervention from New York on the issue of writing and thought New York [the center of the Party] was programmatic, formalized, and fundamentally incorrect on the application of radical politics to artists. Party politics were a drag to people in Hollywood who were more radical in the human sense. Back East they carried on the radicalism, while in Hollywood we suffered the idealism. What was going on was outrageous, but it was an old outrage. That's why we thought the New York reaction to the Maltz article was too heavy. It was out of line."

The New Masses carried attacks on Maltz's position for the next couple of issues, which were penned by Samuel Sillen, the editor, novelists Michael Gold and Howard Fast, and William Z. Foster. Two meetings were held in Hollywood, a week apart. At the first, Maltz was attacked for his position. At the second, he recanted and changed his position.

The first Maltz meeting was held across the street from Abe Polonsky's house, in actor Morris Carnovsky's basement. Over fifty people were present. Some New York people came, including Sam Sillen. Among Maltz's most violent attackers were Lawson and Robert Rossen, and the meeting lasted throughout the night.

"Of the people who were defending Maltz," said Polonsky, "there were about four who were doing so actively, including [writer] Arnold Manoff, Johnny Weber, and me. But most of the people, even if they spoke for Maltz, weren't defending him, because to do that was to tell New York to mind its own business."

Sydney Davidson, as the head of the PEC, had been invited to the meeting. "The people who made the most vociferous attacks on Maltz, the ones who had been most rigid on Party-line questions, were the ones who became the worst stool pigeons," he said.

"The point was," emphasized Polonsky, "that Maltz was irrelevant to the meeting. It was a discussion that had been going on for years. Even those who considered themselves most pure in their radicalism felt that the Party was fundamentally incorrect about the applications of radical politics to artists. The Party, while it offered help in trade-union work, couldn't really give the writers any help in their craft."

The postwar period was not the beginning of the process that led to the betrayals of the early fifties. The seeds of these conflicts had been implicit in the Party and the political situation in Hollywood since the thirties. By 1945, the Party no longer had its favorite love object, either. Jigee Schulberg had married Peter Viertel in 1944, and he had returned from the war extremely anticommunistic.

First Jigee left the Party, then she left Hollywood, moving with Peter to Europe. Somehow it seemed a symbol of the way in which the kingdom was disintegrating. By the time Jigee returned, all the magic was gone, and she, too, ended up betraying all that she had represented.

11

The Cold War was becoming a fact. On June 21, 1946, in an address to the Chicago Bar Association, Attorney General Tom C. Clark announced that the United States was the target of "a sinister and deep-seated plot on the part of Communists, ideologists, and small groups of radicals." He said he had discovered a plot to capture important offices in labor unions, to foment strikes, and to raise barriers against the efforts of lawful authorities to maintain civil peace. And he attacked lawyers who had not helped to repress conspiracy by denying conspirators legal services.

Robert Kenny, listening to the speech with horror, would later write, "Clark's speech in June, 1946, was an early warning of the coming witchhunt that was to disfigure our history for the next ten years."

In May 1946, the House Un-American Activities Committee (whose ranking Republican, J. Parnell Thomas, had distinguished himself in the 1939 WPA hearings by asking which WPA payroll Christopher Marlowe was on) had received an additional appropriation of $75,000. This was apparently the committee's reward for obtaining contempt citations in the House of Representatives against sixteen members of the executive board of the Joint Anti-Fascist Refugee Committee (JAFRC) and its executive secretary, Helen R. Bryan. The Joint Anti-Fasicist Refugee Committee was one of the groups that HUAC was convinced was a communist front. What particularly enraged HUAC was the JAFRC's attempts to raise money for the Spanish refugees who had fled their homeland and were now in France. The JAFRC's slogan was "Break Off Relations with Franco," a slogan that was, to HUAC's John Rankin of Mississippi, evidence that the group was an anti-Catholic conspiracy of communists, masterminded by Jews. Rankin was supported in his contention by the fact that the groups that had coalesced to form the JAFRC —the American Committee to Save Refugees, the League of American

Writers, and the United Spanish Aid Committee—had all been on the subversive lists of the Dies Committee.

HUAC charged the JAFRC with being engaged in "political activity of Communists" and distributing material of a "subversive character." The committee subpoenaed the records of the JAFRC, and when access to those records was denied, Rankin cited the executive board for contempt. Included in the excutive board were Dashiell Hammett, Howard Fast, and theatrical producer Herman Shumlin. Both Hammett and Fast went to jail subsequently when the Supreme Court refused to review the case.

The additional appropriations for HUAC did not haphazardly coincide with the fact that 1946 was an election year. Red-scare, pink-smear tactics were one of the major techniques the Republican Party used that year to cast a pall of subversion over the New Dealers who remained in office.

The Hollywood Democratic Party, in the form of the Hollywood Independent Citizens Committee for the Arts, Sciences, and Professions, found it extremely difficult to raise funds for candidates that year. Frank Sinatra, for example, had been attacked in Westbrook Pegler's column for contributing to Roosevelt's fourth campaign and for making a speech for the HICCASP—which so unnerved the singer that his managers found "advisers" to warn him of the political nature of anything he was asked to endorse. People who had previously given lavishly to the Democratic campaigns were suddenly parsimonious, whereas Republicans, particularly in California, found the enormous resources of people like Hearst at their disposal.

California was considered the key danger to the Republicans in the 1946 election. The state had given FDR his greatest majority in 1944 and with it a superb, progressive congressional delegation. A defeat in 1946 for FDR's ideals and the candidates who supported them would, it was felt, result in an unparalleled wave of reaction throughout the country.

The California Democrats were also frightened by the passage in 1946 of some of the most stringent antilabor legislation of this century. What particularly worried progressives was Truman's "work or draft" bill, which was a new version of the Case Bill. In the spring of 1946, the California Democrats in HICCASP were mounting a massive telegram campaign to congressmen and the White House urging Truman to reconsider his bill and urging the veto of the Case Bill.

It was hoped that the Democratic Party in California could be saved by drafting Robert Kenny as the candidate for governor of California. He was to run against the incumbent and successful governor, Earl Warren. Kenny didn't really have a chance, and he knew it. But he was under great pressure from the more liberal and left-wing Democrats to run in the name of party unity. The major issue Warren used against Kenny was that he, Warren, was the best man to protect California from invasion by "Eastern criminal elements."

The involvement of artists in California politics reached a peak that year. The war had taught the creative community the meaning of mobilization. Screen writers like Albert Maltz and Dalton Trumbo wrote campaign speeches for candidates. Artists like Ben Shahn contributed work for political posters. And in the true spirit of resurrecting the New Deal coalition, James Roosevelt, son of FDR, was hired at $25,000 a year to become the executive director of the HICCASP.

"Jimmy Roosevelt was an employee of ICCASP in New York," recalled Ellenore Bogigian, "along with Harold Ickes. And then he came out to California, where he was the executive director of HICCASP and I was the legislative director. He had the office right next to mine, which he moved into with his complete staff. The Democratic primaries were approaching, and all hell was breaking loose. War hero Evans F. Carlson [of Carlson's Raiders], who had been the unanimous choice for senator, withdrew because of poor health, so there ensued a fight between Ellis Patterson and Will Rogers, Jr., who both wanted the office. Sheridan Downey wanted to be governor, but Kenny was drafted. And HICCASP was split over whom to endorse for senator, Patterson or Rogers."

"Everybody who was anybody was active in HICCASP," recalled Joan LaCoeur, then the recording secretary of the organization. "There was this upbeat feeling of power in the support of both the artistic and scientific and the professional communities. Everyone assumed Jimmy Roosevelt would one day be president—there was still this awe of him, based on his father. But he turned out to be one of those gutless, opportunistic wonders. And I really couldn't believe it when I heard him lie. I was absolutely stunned that FDR's son would lie."

The lie grew out of the split in the HICCASP. At that time director John Cromwell was chairman, and vice-chairmen were Colonel Carlson, Olivia de Havilland, Franklin Fearing, Lena Horne, Linus Pauling, Dore Schary, and Frank Sinatra. E. Y. Harburg was secretary and Ernest Pascal was treasurer. The organization was split between support for the more conservative Rogers and for the more liberal Patterson. There was going to be a big fight at the next board meeting, and Roosevelt, whether out of design or by accident, was not going to be able to be there.

"Before leaving town, Roosevelt came out for Patterson, in front of most of the staff of HICCASP," said Joan LaCoeur. "And then, in the midst of the big board fight, he was contacted by phone, and I heard him lie. He said he was for Rogers and had always been so."

In November the entire Democratic slate, including Edmund G. Brown for state attorney general, went down in bitter defeat. Jerry Voorhis lost the congressional race to a young ex-navy man named Richard Nixon. It was part of a national Republican sweep in which many of labor's friends were not returned to Congress. The Democrats who succeeded in weathering the national storm and winning reelection either radically changed their liberal approach to civil liberties and labor or lay low until the wind died down. For the first time in sixteen years, the 1946 election returned control of the House of Representatives to the Republican Party, and from this point on, there was only token opposition to the activities of HUAC.

"I knew the 1946 Kenny slate would lose," said Bogigian. "It was tough to raise money. The national political picture was moving in a different direction from what we expected. People out here in the Democratic progressive group expected there to be a postwar depression to galvanize the public. They didn't expect a postwar boom; they didn't expect to find an electorate that didn't care about the left-wing Democratic platform. There was a time lag— the way things often seem best at the end of an affair. For example, in January 1945 we put on the biggest, most successful legislative conference ever held. And in the autumn of 1945 the Mobilization for Democracy had raised so much money against Gerald L. K. Smith—money piling up on the stage on top of a Nazi flag symbolizing Smith's anti-Semitism—that the Mobilization became a full-fledged organization. We were having this marvelous legislative program, but, actually, nobody could have said by late 1945 that things would continue to be good. The intelligence agencies were busy as hell."

According to activists in the Democratic Party at that time, like Bogigian and Pauline Lauber Finn, the attacks on the Left were really linked with the work of the Hollywood Independent Citizens Committee for the Arts, Sciences, and Professions. Its members were working in politics and using a lot of the same people who were in the Hollywood Writers Mobilization, writers and actors who were designing effective campaign literature and writing speeches. These members of the movie industry were having an effect on politics.

"When the Tenney subpoenas went out," said Finn, "they primarily went out to members of HICCASP. A number of Hollywood writers had ideals about films and took that content-related position, but it really wasn't the hard issue. That wasn't what was giving the right wing trouble. It merely contributed to the fact that the people within the organization became more active, and in campaigns they supported and worked for Democrats overwhelmingly."

The link between the accusations of communism in the industry and the attacks on the Democratic organization in California was particularly obvious when Senator Tenney chose to subpoena Emmet Lavery to testify less than one month before the 1946 elections. Lavery had run unsuccessfully for Congress in the previous election, and he was a good, solid Democrat who was an unimpeachable liberal. His credentials were impeccable—he was a lawyer, he had written *The Magnificent Yankee*, a popular play based on the life of Justice Oliver Wendell Holmes, and he was one of the country's leading

Catholics in the arts. He was subpoenaed as a former president of the Screen Writers Guild. Lavery made Tenney look like a fool, but the charges Tenney made were publicized by the reactionary press.

Lavery began by explaining that his "approach to the field of social action is identical with that of people such as Archibishop Lucey of San Antonio; Bishop Haas of Wisconsin; Bishop Shiel of Chicago. They believe, and I believe, the problem at the moment is to integrate Christian ideals, Catholic ideals, broad virtues of good persuasion in the broad life of a democratic community." Countering the charges of subversive content in the film industry, Lavery said, "I think the Skourases, the Schencks, and Mr. Zanuck . . . are as alert as this committee to not allow Marxian doctrines in pictures." In answer to the charge that the SWG was communist-run, Lavery said, "With respect to [the SWG] time after time the actions and the thinking of 10 or 12 people at the outside—it never gets past 10 or 12—are used to smear the good work of a thousand active members and 400 associate members. . . . We are not a radical guild. We are conservative. . . ."

Tenney then switched his attack to political organizations:

TENNEY: Mr. Lavery—let me point out for the sake of the record—that up through your history in the Hollywood Motion Picture Democratic Committee, which undoubtedly was Communist dominated and inspired—

LAVERY: That, I deny, because I was affiliated with them.

TENNEY: Let me point out to you that Melvyn Douglas and several other people at the time of the Hitler-Stalin Pact resigned from the organization because of its Communist character. Then it became the Hollywood Democratic Committee, the same group, and now it is the Hollywood Independent CCASP, which every investigating committee has looked into and has declared it to be a Communist organization or a Communist front organization.

The press began immediately to construct headlines declaring that the HICCASP, which was endorsing the Democratic slate headed by Kenny (known to the committee as former president of the National Lawyers Guild, which they called another CP front organization), was a communist front organization.

One of the primary sources of Republican support in Hollywood continued to be the Motion Picture Alliance for the Preservation of American Ideals and its blue-collar cousin, the International Alliance of Theatrical Stage Employees. The Alliance contributed substantial funding to the Republican campaign in 1946 and encouraged the Tenney investigations as the bulwark of Americanism in Hollywood. The IATSE's crusade against communist agitators in Hollywood was fed by the conflict between the IATSE and the Conference of Studio Unions, which erupted anew in the autumn of that year. Roy Brewer's strategy and leadership during the strike provided a total victory for the IATSE. One of Brewer's biggest weapons was Red-baiting, making his union seem to be the defender of Americanism.

At the end of the 1945 CSU-IATSE strike, a bumbling effort had been made by the executive council of the AFL (with which both unions were affiliated) to define jurisdictional lines in Hollywood, ostensibly to avert a repetition of the conflict. A three-man committee visited Hollywood, and on December 26 issued a decision whose semantics contained the seeds of a renewed conflict. The CSU's carpenters' union was awarded "all trim and millwork on sets and stages," and the IATSE was awarded "the erection of sets on stages, except as provided in Section One." The multiple possible interpretations of the phrase "erection of sets" inspired IATSE president Richard Walsh to conjure up and charter a new union of "set erectors" who would build scenery and gobble up the carpenters' jobs. The problem posed by this jerry-built union resulted in angry carpenters who continued to work, carrying the dispute to the top level of the AFL and demanding clarification of the fuzzy wording.

On August 27, 1946, AFL President William Green sent Walsh a clarification that left no doubt about the intent of the decision, which was in favor of the CSU. But Walsh wasn't about to give up his set erectors. The IATSE and the producers ignored the clarification, thereby cleverly manipulating a situation in which the carpenters would, for union reasons, be forced to refuse to work on sets where IATSE men were doing their jobs. A strike was inevitable.

The month after the clarification was filled with secret meetings between the IATSE and the producers in which a strategy was formulated to force every CSU member out of his job. On September 23 carpenters were assigned work that was below their seniority or summarily fired with a paycheck. The CSU picket lines went up, and the other guilds within the CSU went out on strike with the carpenters.

"The 1946 strike couldn't be won," recalled attorney Ben Margolis. "The producers in 1946 had decided they were going to break Sorrell, and they didn't care what it cost. Unless the workers went back, they'd starve them out."

CSU pickets massed angrily at the gates of Warner Bros., MGM, and five other major Hollywood lots, and the violence began again. Studio laborers, according to *Time* magazine,

> scattered tacks in the path of movie stars' automobiles, threw coffee in the faces of picket-line crossers, stoned busloads of rival AF of L workers convoyed through their jeering, milling ranks.
>
> The new blowoff came when the studios instituted wholesale firings of carpenters and painters belonging to the AF of L CSU. CSU members had refused to work on sets where producers had handed over disputed

jobs to the competing AF of L IATSE. Neither the jurisdictional squabble nor the producers' inclination to string along with the IATSE faction were new angles in Hollywood's continuing labor war. . . . The CSU [is] led by beefy, belligerent Sorrell. . . . His politics are of the far left; his relations with the CIO chummy. The IATSE once threatened to try him before an AF of L court on charges of being a member of the Communist party, then later dropped the accusation.

"CP member Phil Connelly of the California State CIO and the CIO people supported the CSU against the IATSE," recalled Elizabeth Spector. "The basic craft unions in Hollywood were IATSE, and they had good relations with the producers, so it was virtually impossible to reach the members. They were afraid of their IATSE leaders. There were a few AFL unions— mostly painters, carpenters, and electricians—but they were the old-line craft unions in the AFL, and they never bought the idea of industrial unionism. Sorrell's hope was that the CSU would build a coalition. I don't know if he thought of eventually going CIO."

"My people—the cartoonists, the office workers, and the screen story analysts—wanted to go back to work," remembered Margolis, "but Sorrell said 'You'll have to go through my lines.' Harry Bridges set up a private meeting with Sorrell to try and talk him out of what he was doing."

"The second Hollywood strike destroyed progressive unions in Hollywood," recalled Elizabeth Spector. "They were dragged into the strike when they shouldn't have been. It was throwing more troops into a lost battle. The set designers' guild and the Screen Office Employees Guild were destroyed."

"Sorrell was being fed information and manipulated by the producers," said David Robison. "His problem was that he thought Pat Casey, the studio labor leader, was his friend. He became obsessed with power, and so he got manipulated by the producers. Sorrell thought Casey was passing on privileged information to him. One day Herb got a call from Casey, in his office, and when he hung up Herb said, 'Okay fellas, we hit the bricks tomorrow.' A strike was exactly what the studios wanted."

"It was impossible to convince Sorrell that Casey was using him," agreed Margolis sadly. "He was as honest a man as ever was in the labor movement. And he thought he and Casey could make deals that were in the interest of the workers. But Herb became a kingpin and destroyed the rank and file. The CSU was weakened by divisions, by renegades. Sorrell was totally apolitical and totally lacked leftist grounding. He was a terrible tactician. So the CSU was destroyed and the IATSE took over."

The violence of the strikes and the intractability of the producers, the IATSE, and the CSU produced major divisions and critical splits in the already divided talent guilds like the SWG and the SAG. It was a time of blood, of mass arrests, of mass trials. The producers negotiated with the teamsters' business manager, who nullified a membership vote to support the strike, and the teamsters were instructed to carry busloads of strikebreakers through the picket lines.

Ben Barzman, who was working at RKO at the time, said that during the picketing the studio was turned into a "beleaguered compound," with employees staying there around the clock rather than going home and having to contend with the picket lines. Barzman was honoring the picket lines, but he was given permission by the picket captains to go to his office to get some books. He ran into a waitress from the commissary who told him that since the food was free, underpaid secretaries were wolfing down more chow than two-hundred-pound grips. The strike was precipitating something of a free-for-all inside the studios. When Barzman arrived at his office, he found a bizarre scene—liquor bottles and condoms all over. Those who remained inside the studio were obviously making the most of their internment.

"During the 1946 strike," said Lester Pine, "we were on the lines at RKO on Marathon Street, at the little notch where it joined Paramount. There were a lot of girls on the picket line, office workers and readers, then another lineup of goons appeared. They were carrying lunch pails, and we all knew they didn't contain lunch. When I saw those pails I really got scared about being beaten. I was really relieved when we were arrested before they attacked. Everybody was schlepped onto the police bus, and it was better than getting your brains smashed. I was lucky and managed to get out without a scratch."

"When the second CSU strike broke," remembered John Bright, who had been in the coast guard during the first strike, "I was one of several people who volunteered to be the chauffeur for Herb Sorrell, whose driving license had been revoked—the gangsters had some sort of influence that got it revoked. I became very friendly with him in that period. The SWG did not vote to strike, but there were a few of us, some communists, some not, who supported the strike. I myself was fired from Metro for refusing to cross the picket line. I was doing a very satisfactory job, satisfactory to my producer, Arthur Freed, and a job that I enjoyed. Now there were a few people who had work-at-home clauses, but I didn't have that in my contract. Therefore, people like Donald Ogden Stewart, Dottie Parker, and Alan Campbell, who would not cross the lines, just stayed home. I made no bones about the fact that I wouldn't go through the picket line. I told my producer and said, 'I'm not sick.'

"Well, Louis B. Mayer and Mannix told the producers that any writer not having a contractual clause that he could work at home or out of town and who refused to cross the picket line was fired. Now I was writing a picture for Lucille Bremer, who worked with Arthur Freed, and she loved it and he loved it. Freed called me up and begged me to come to work. Eddie Mannix had said to Freed at a producers' meeting at Metro, 'You've got a man working for you that hasn't been through the picket line—John Bright.' And

Freed said, 'I think he's been ill.' And he tried to protect me with some kind of crap, and Freed called me up and begged me—he said, 'Come through the line once, just once, and Mannix will call off the dogs.' It was a token thing, you see, like naming your neighbors, a token thing. So Freed said to me, 'Can I talk to you, baby?' He was an old Tin Pan Alley song writer and he used those words, called me 'darling,' 'baby,' 'sweetheart.' So I said, 'I'll meet you across the street from the studio. I'll be glad to talk to you, Arthur, but I'm not going in that building under any circumstances. You can put cobwebs on my office door.'

"So he met me in the little coffee shop across Washington Boulevard from Metro. It was filled with strikers and pickets, and Freed and I had it out. He said, 'Please, when this mess is over, I'll get you a straight five-year contract at $2,000 a week—no options. You'll just work for me. I'll show my gratitude.' Because Mayer and Mannix told the various producers and associate producers that it was their ass too, their jobs were at stake if they let writers stay away from the studio.

"But I said, 'I will not do it.' Then he blew up and said, 'You're a goddamned fool, you're just a goddamned fool. Your fucking union isn't supporting the strike. What obligation do you have to support it?' And I said, 'I support the strike, and I will not walk through that picket line. I don't give a shit if every member of the SWG goes through it,' and hundreds were. At first they gathered in little places and talked among themselves in front of the studio, and then they went home. And then, two or three days later, when the pressure was on from their producers, they went through the lines. As a token gesture, of course."

Members of the Hollywood Left were amenable to token gestures, their rationale being that since they were smarter than the executives who set so much store by them, token gestures permitted them to pursue more extensive activities inimical to the powerbrokers. But the history of token gestures in Hollywood culminated in the HUAC three-ring circus in the fifties, and nobody should have been surprised.

"I was the SWG shop steward at MGM," remembered William Ludwig. "During the CSU strike, I had an office right near the entrance of the Thalberg Building at MGM, and one day I looked out the window to see writers leaving the building and going across the street to the parking lot. And then I got a call from Milton Beecher who said, 'What the hell is going on with your writers? They're leaving the building and they're having a strike meeting across the street.' And I said, 'They can't be having a strike meeting, I didn't call any and I'm the shop steward.' And he said, 'They're having it.'

"So I went across the street and some of the left-wing Guild members—subsequently revealed to be Communist Party members—had spread the word that there was to be a writers' meeting across the street relative to the CSU strike, and they had told the painters that we were walking out in sympathy, which would have broken our contract completely. Well, I had to rush across the street. With violent opposition from the organizers of this illegal walkout, I had to harangue our people and make them walk back in through the CSU picket line, and I can well understand why the painters were furious with us, why no explanation, really, satisfied them, but we had to preserve our contract."

Among the noncommunist liberals who marched through the picket lines were Albert Hackett and Frances Goodrich: "Our producer at Paramount wanted us to come through the picket line, and our agent said, 'You cannot subject Mrs. Hackett to this, somebody might spit in her face,' and the producer said, 'She should wear it like a badge of honor.' And story editor Meta Reis was coming to us collecting money each week for the strikers. But we weren't fired. We had a very strong contract."

"I remember during the CSU strike we had several meetings with Ronald Reagan and other people from the Screen Actors and Screen Directors guilds," said Ring Lardner, Jr. "We argued rather sharply about the CSU. I think it was probably unrealistic to think that we could get wide enough support and get the actors, particularly, who were in the AFL—and especially since this was a split between two AFL groups—it was probably unrealistic to think we could get them to support the CSU against the IATSE, and it certainly did result in some isolation of the Left within the guilds."

The factional differences between right and left in the Screen Writers Guild, exacerbated by the strike and charges of various coloration from pink to red at the instigation of the Motion Picture Alliance, affected not only the off-year congressional elections in California but the 1946 executive board elections in the Guild. A coalition of liberals gathered around Emmet Lavery, whom they proposed for reelection to the presidency, as well as various executive board nominees, including the liberal George Seaton and the left-wing Lester Cole and Hugo Butler. A conservative faction, spearheaded by Charles Brackett, proposed an alternate slate with Talbot Jennings for president. The Jennings slate was notably missing the names of any of the writers who had been attacked as having leftist sympathies and activities. Though Lavery was reelected, there was still a great deal of discontent in the Guild, and much of it centered on William Pomerance, the executive secretary of the Guild.

Pomerance, who had gone from being a National Labor Relations Board field examiner to being the business manager of the cartoonists' union, was close to Herb Sorrell and eager for the SWG to cooperate with the CSU strike and honor the picket lines. In the course of the ugly arguments that preceded the election, which had a lot to do with why the Guild should or should not support the CSU strike, Pomerance resigned.

"It seems to me I was active in asking for Pomerance's resignation," recalled Ludwig, "on the grounds that in a situation where we were not party to a strike, it seemed rather disastrous to have our executive secretary serving as a walking delegate for some of the CSU unions. And so Pomerance resigned."

The Screen Actors Guild, as an AFL union, was sharply divided over the subject of whom to support and tried to be a conciliatory body. "The reactionaries called a special meeting to talk about the strike," said Karen Morley. "There were about five thousand actors there, and the goon squads were in the aisles. They were mostly stunt people—the poor darlings. Tell them the Reds are taking over, and they believe it. The meeting opened with a vote of confidence, and the reactionary leadership kept the floor for one hour. Sinatra was there with his goons. Outside, thousands of CSU people were keeping a silent vigil. They were carrying signs that said DON'T WRECK OUR UNION. Sinatra said he'd go through any picket line—nobody would stop him.

"I took the floor on a point of personal privilege. I said the Guild should use its good offices to settle the dispute and not cross the picket lines until after it was settled. The Chair ruled it out of order. The lawyers were called, and they thumbed through *Robert's Rules of Order* and finally made their recommendation, as SAG lawyers, that it was not a legal motion. And Reagan was making speeches about how it was an unimportant jurisdictional beef. He made long, fancy speeches about technicalities like which union was allowed to touch rubber."

There were attempts at conciliatory arbitration offered by the SWG and by the Interfaith Religious Councils, which were leapt at by the CSU and resented by the IATSE.

Alexander Knox was part of the liberal opposition to Reagan, Robert Montgomery, Edward Arnold, George Murphy, and the rest of the conservative SAG leadership. Knox recalled, "Katharine Hepburn, Edward G. Robinson, Paul Henreid, and I felt we had a useful gimmick with four religious organizations, the Jews, Catholics, Protestants, and World Council of Churches, agreeing to the wording of a resolution we wanted to pass. We were trying to haul the board back to a stated position of neutrality, but actors were crossing picket lines and the board position was leaning toward the producers. It was a danger to have so many people on the board who were Metro contract people.

"We were quite serious about getting back to neutrality, particularly with the Hearst and Chandler papers so biased that they actually added fuel to the fire of the strike. And, of course, Reagan, Murphy, and Menjou had already begun their anticommunist crusade."

There was another meeting of the SAG, at the Hollywood Legion Stadium, at which Hepburn, Robinson, and Knox all spoke in opposition to the policies of Reagan and Murphy. At one point Knox imitated Reagan's glibness.

"Reagan spoke very fast," recalled Knox. "He always did, so that he could talk out of both sides of his mouth at once. It was a deliberate attempt to pull the rug out from under Reagan's feet. And then we heard this noise, and it was Reagan's 'bodyguards' coming down the aisle slapping bicycle chains against the chairs. And Franchot Tone jumped up and said, 'Now wait, stop that, call them off.' After the meeting I went over and thanked Roy Brewer for coming, and he said, 'I'll see you run out of Hollywood.' "

"The actors always had the real power to shut the studios down, but somehow they never realized it," said Karen Morley.

The strike dragged on, growing more destructive and more divisive. "Many people in the SWG saw what was happening with the CSU and Sorrell's destructive strike, and they became antiprogressive," said Ben Margolis. "The strike nourished the Motion Picture Alliance and made it more powerful. The Alliance was largely responsible for what Congress did. It was a stimulant to HUAC." The smaller unions that were affiliated with the CSU were shriveling and dying as the months of unemployment impoverished them. Throughout the autumn of 1946, constant attempts were made by outside parties to arbitrate some sort of conciliation between the two factions. Invariably it would turn out that the CSU, by now desperate and losing ground and supporters, would accept the suggestion of arbitration and the arbitrator's decisions, while the IATSE would ignore the suggestions and the producers' claim that they wouldn't interfere in a jurisdictional matter.

In March 1947 Father George Dunne, a Jesuit priest and pro-CSU labor expert (as well as a cousin of Philip Dunne), offered an arbitration proposal that demanded major concessions from the CSU and made it difficult for the producers not to become involved in the settlement. The IATSE again ignored the proposals; the CSU accepted them. And the producers were both rude and brutal in their simultaneous suggestions that the clergy butt out and that they weren't interested in what the proposal suggested. The producers, who had been so gracious to the Catholics' National Legion of Decency and the Breen Office,* and who had always professed such piety, had alienated the Church. Things were getting out of hand, and for the first time the studio executives were convinced that their power was no longer absolute.

In March 1947 President Truman issued his Executive Order No. 9835, which prescribed procedures for the administration of an employees' loyalty program in the executive branch of government. This order was designed to purge all communists and fellow travelers in Washington, and the files of J.

---

* Breen, a well-known Catholic intellectual, was appointed to head the newly created Production Code Administration (PCA) as a means of heading off the boycott campaign against Hollywood films launched by the Legion of Decency the previous year. The film executives agreed not to distribute films without the PCA's seal of approval.

Parnell Thomas's House Un-American Activities Committee were being used not only to check on suspect employees but to help the attorney general in compiling his definitive list of subversive organizations. This postwar fear of internal subversion was a reflection of this country's foreign policy, which, through the Truman Doctrine, sought to contain any possible extension of Russia's influence in Europe—most immediately in Greece and Turkey. It was the same spirit that had prompted Truman's demand in the final stages of the 1946 national campaign that former vice-president Henry Wallace resign as secretary of commerce after his Madison Square Garden speech opposing the administration's "get tough with Russia policy."

John Rankin and Thomas were in their glory. Not only were their files assisting in the purification of the executive branch, but they had subpoenaed Gerhart Eisler, a Party functionary who refused to testify; when Eisler fled to East Germany to avoid prosecution, their charges, they felt, had been substantiated. Their critics were silenced. Better still, the trail of the foreign subversive led to Hollywood, where Eisler's estranged brother, Hanns, was a successful composer. In Hollywood the subversion seemed richer and redder, and the headlines were bigger.

But HUAC was not the first House committee to fish in Hollywood's celebrity-stocked waters. In March 1947, the hearings of a labor subcommittee began in Los Angeles to investigate the IATSE-CSU strike, which was still unresolved. The jurisdictional dispute among the carpenters had been echoed by a similar dispute regarding who in Congress would handle the investigation—Fred Hartley's labor subcommittee or Thomas's Un-American Activities Committee. Opponents of the CSU—principally the Motion Picture Alliance—wanted to turn the labor investigation into a communist purge. Senator Tenney wired Hartley that his own "Little Dies Committee" in California had already revealed the subversive nature of the CSU and Herb Sorrell. Roy Brewer used the communist issue against his opponents whenever possible, and Ronald Reagan was by this time openly denouncing the CSU communist conspiracy whenever he could.

"What the communists wanted to do in terms of the CSU strike," Reagan explained in retrospect, "was to shut down the industry, and when everybody was angry and dissatisfied with their unions for their failures, the communists would propose one big union for Hollywood with everyone in it from producers to grips."

Did that mean industrial unionism? Like the CIO? "Exactly," said Reagan.

Richard Nixon, the freshman congressman from California, was the only member of Hartley's subcommittee affiliated with HUAC, and he was originally designated to chair the Hollywood subcommittee to investigate the strike.

But it was not through the labor probe that the Red probe began. In May 1947 J. Parnell Thomas went to Hollywood and became so obsessed with exposing the communist infiltration of screen content (and so entranced at the idea of its news value) that he turned his attention to the Screen Writers Guild. HUAC's interest in the CSU-IATSE fight was further diminished when Nixon became interested in the case of Alger Hiss. While Nixon was discrediting Hiss, J. Edgar Hoover gave his blessings and his information to the Thomas-Rankin Committee. A full account in Washington of the Communist Party's infiltration of the motion picture industry further focused HUAC's attention on the West. Hoover had been followed on the witness stand by Jack Tenney, bearing 372 pages of information devoted to the communist conspiracy in Hollywood. And, in May, communist experts like Sam Wood and Adolphe Menjou filed through Hollywood's Biltmore Hotel, where the committee's chairman was then esconced.

The CSU-IATSE probe was further deterred from becoming a Red roast by the concern of Jesuit labor expert Father Dunne. Dunne knew that the real issues of the 1945–46 strike would be glossed over if the investigation focused on the "communist conspiracy" rather than on the labor problem in Hollywood. Dunne convinced Hartley to keep the investigation in his own committee, and Hartley instructed Carroll D. Kearns, a Pennsylvania Republican and chairman of a special subcommittee of the House Committee on Education and Labor, to confine the hearings to labor grievances between the IATSE, the CSU, and the producers and to exclude testimony about communism or Willie Bioff's and George Browne's racketeering. This was easier said than done—particularly since just before the committee arrived in Los Angeles, Herb Sorrell was kidnapped. The *New York Herald Tribune* on March 4 carried the story of Sorrell's abduction in Glendale by three armed men, one wearing a policeman's uniform, who beat him and dumped his battered body in the desert.

The labor problem was obviously smack in the middle of the central political struggle in Hollywood, and the allegations were flying from both sides. The studios and the IATSE claimed that the labor unrest was being fomented both by the communist agitators in Hollywood who had infiltrated the CSU and by Sorrell. He was charged the next year with being a communist, and congressional investigators produced an alleged Party card signed by him. He denied the charges. The liberals, the Left, and angry union people like the CSU carpenters' superintendent Oscar Schatte claimed that the racketeers had infiltrated Hollywood labor, stilled the reverberations of the Bioff-Browne scandal, and were fomenting the violence of the strike.

The liberals and the Left anticipated that the blame for the Hollywood strike would be laid on the backs of the Left and the CSU. And their fears were exacerbated by the comradeship of Kearns and the producers, who were chauffeuring him around town in an MGM limousine and keeping him well entertained in the evening.

The issues weren't simple, particularly in terms of the participation of the press. The anticommunist fervor of the country's leading reactionaries, for example, who had long been ready to pounce on Hollywood, did not go hand in hand with sympathy for the gangsterish influence on labor in Hollywood. Westbrook Pegler, who smeared Reds with zeal, had been most active in persecuting and hounding Bioff and Browne. Pegler's philosophy was shared by Irving McCann, the Alabama counsel for the Kearns Committee, who had worked to expose the Bioff-Browne partnership with the Capone mob. It was McCann who, to the delight of Pegler and many union folk, decked the arrogant AFL general counsel Joseph Padway in a dramatic courtroom fist-fight during the hearings. Yet McCann, though incorruptible, was a reactionary exponent of the Taft-Hartley Bill in Congress, and so the liberal and leftist press were anti-McCann and criticized him throughout the hearings.

Kearns was a weak, conciliatory man. He attempted a peaceful settlement of the strike but failed. Six months after his hearings were concluded, in September 1947, the subcommittee mildly condemned the conspiracy between management and the IATSE. But by this time the CSU was broken, beaten, and nearly vestigial; the Taft-Hartley Act had resulted in pleased management and frantic labor, and the Red conspiracy in Hollywood and Washington was garnering all of the spotlight. With the rich and famous accused of subversion, national interest in what was persistently and mistakenly referred to as merely a jurisdictional dispute between some Hollywood carpenters hardly captured the national imagination.

The Taft-Hartley Bill had become law in June, 1947, and it was, to a large extent, a negation of all the gains labor had made under the Wagner Act. The most devastating part of the bill was a reflection of the anticommunist spirit of the times, a clause requiring that any unions requesting an NLRB hearing and certification election have its officers sign noncommunist affidavits.

"We didn't have too many illusions during the CSU strike," recalled Karen Morley, "about how the studio people behaved. But we really weren't prepared for the political onslaught from the reactionaries. The right wing rolled over us like a tank over wildflowers."

In that same frightening March of 1947, when Truman issued his loyalty order and Hoover testified about communist infiltration in the industry, Eric Johnston, president of the Motion Picture Association of America (MPAA), called for more pictures extolling homespun virtues and the American way of life.

Carey McWilliams looked at HUAC's sally into Hollywood with horror, considering it an attempt at censorship and thought-control: "Had there not been a set of quisling-like characters in Hollywood willing to go along with a movement like the Alliance, for whatever reasons, it would have been necessary to have invented the Alliance. Underlying this triple play from Rankin to Hearst to the Alliance and back from the Alliance to Hearst to Rankin were two important considerations. The motion picture industry represents, after all, private enterprise, and even J. Parnell Thomas had to have some excuse for attacking so important, albeit so vulnerable, a segment of American industry. The second consideration had to do with the attitude of the producers. In all of its experience in fending off attacks from without, the motion picture industry never had to contend, prior to the appearance of the Alliance, with a Trojan-horse conspiracy from within."

Referring to Thomas's statement made at the end of May and to his visit to Los Angeles, when he had said, "Up until the present time there has been no inclination on the part of the industry itself to cooperate with the committee in ferreting out these influences," McWilliams remarked on "the additional implication that there had also been too little cooperation in making the 'right' kind of pictures. To bring about this desired cooperation, it was necessary to jockey the producers into a position where capitulation would be accepted as the price to be paid for the removal of a label which had been pinned on the industry by its own quislings and stooges."

When HUAC came to Hollywood, it was greeted by the Alliance and its executive director, Dr. John Lechner. Lechner welcomed the committee and agreed with its analysis of motion pictures containing "sizeable doses of communist propaganda," which included *The Best Years of Our Lives, Margie, The Strange Love of Martha Ivers, A Medal for Benny, The Searching Wind, Watch on the Rhine, The North Star, Mission to Moscow,* and *Pride of the Marines.*

James Kevin McGuinness praised the committee's war on propaganda in movies and called for "films as pure entertainment." "Just think over the number of times you have seen industrialists portrayed on the screen as slave drivers," said McGuinness.

The Alliance was in essence inviting HUAC to impose censorship on the movie industry in the name of American ideals, though the Alliance announced that at the moment it had "no new plan to offer."

Jack Warner told the Thomas Committee that "communists injected 95% of their propaganda into films through the medium of writers," though he personally had never seen a communist and "wouldn't know one if I saw one."

Among the fourteen friendly witnesses who testified behind closed doors, Lela Rogers, mother of Ginger, pointed out that in Dalton Trumbo's script for *Tender Comrade,* he had inserted the subversive line "share and share alike—that's democracy." She considered Trumbo as big a communist as Clifford Odets.

Robert Taylor also testified to the subversive nature of motion pictures in Hollywood. He had, he later said, been naively duped into appearing in *Song of Russia,* which he said was pure propaganda, and he detailed several other scripts that he perceived as being chock full of subversive material.

Taylor's performance behind closed doors was lauded in a Sunday Hearst article that praised him for his courage and quoted his wife, Barbara Stanwyck, who said that he didn't like to read and that even though his hobby was cooking, "he just looks at the pictures and starts mixing," without reading the recipes.

Actor Howard da Silva regarded the list of "condemned" films and remarked, "Communist propaganda? Rankin should live so long. And it can't even be simply that these are good pictures, because they're not all that good. No, these appreciators of outhouse art put their sticky thumbs down on these films because each of them, in one way or another . . . touched on reality. And when you touch reality, you're stamping on their heartbeats—and they see Red."

The thrust toward censorship was a two-pronged attack in Hollywood. One was to strangle creativity through the objective censorship operated by the Breen Office, the Johnston Office, the Tenney Committee, the Thomas Committee, the Hearst press, Pegler, and the Alliance. The second, more insidious, form of censorship was self-censorship, the before-the-fact self-editing of writers and other creators in the industry who found themselves avoiding the controversial, playing safe rather than becoming the target of organized pressures that were growing stronger.

"The communists were determined to get control of the movies," explained Roy Brewer. "In 1945, American motion pictures were the mass media of the world. I didn't feel the communists should be allowed to use the movie industry. The communists developed tactics of hatred, bitterness, and character-assassination. This was not an American trait. It was created by the communists. It was my concern to keep communist individuals from gaining power and control. I don't think anybody who had any concern for the future of America could have done any less. We haven't won the battle yet."

Whether by chance or by design, the visit of the Thomas Committee to Hollywood in May 1947 coincided with a massive Hollywood rally for Henry Wallace in support of his 1948 presidential candidacy. A liberal-democratic coalition called the Progressive Citizens of America, which was affiliated with the HICCASP, had tried to get the Hollywood Bowl for the rally, but their application was turned down. The people who ran the Bowl called the meeting "dissemination of propaganda." So the meeting was held at Gilmore Stadium, and 27,000 people attended. The massive turnout was not surprising. Wallace was extremely popular, one of the last links to the Roosevelt administration, and Truman had lost a great many supporters over his foreign policy. In fact, the polls showed that 24 percent of the registered Democrats in the nation would vote for Wallace over Truman, should Wallace decide to run for president.

The rally's keynote address was delivered by Katharine Hepburn wearing a bright scarlet dress. She declared American culture under attack by Rankin

Left to right: Edward G. Robinson, Henry Wallace (then Secretary of Commerce), and Mervyn Leroy, 1946.

and Tenney and said that their purpose was to create disunity. "The artist," said Hepburn, "since the beginning of recorded time, has always expressed the aspirations and dreams of his people. Silence the artist and you silence the most articulate voice the people have. Destroy culture and you destroy one of the strongest sources of inspiration from which a people can draw strength to fight for a better life."

The crowd went wild. Then Wallace came to the podium and movingly condemned the intolerance in the country and the state. He pointed to Tom Mooney,* in jail for seventeen years, to the 100,000 Japanese-Americans driven from their homes. He cited "a group of bigots first known as the Dies Committee, then the Rankin Committee, now the Thomas Committee—three names for fascists the world over to roll on their tongues with pride. . . . No one who dares praise Willkie's vision of 'one world' is safe from attack."

When Katharine Hepburn entered the MGM commissary the next day, everyone in it stood up and cheered for her speech. She had been so moving, so eloquent, that few realized that her words had been penned by Dalton Trumbo. And while the waves of her colleagues' admiration washed over her,

* A labor leader who was convicted of a bombing in San Francisco in 1916 and served a twenty-three-year prison sentence in San Quentin.

director Leo McCarey, a member of the Motion Picture Alliance, declared in *Daily Variety* that he had decided not to cast Katharine Hepburn in his next picture because of her speech for Henry Wallace.

Wallace gave hope to the liberals in California, and this hope divided them even further. Their attempt to make him the Democratic presidential candidate for 1948 became the third-party movement, the Independent Progressive Party, and it destroyed the last vestiges of progressive unity in the state.

"The third party was senseless," recalled Ellenore Bogigian. "It was almost as though people had lost their senses. There was never any chance for success. When everyone had been engaged in reelecting Roosevelt, some animosities from the Stalin-Hitler Pact had finally been washed away. There was the euphoria of winning the war, but nobody had forgotten the past. In the 1944 election, the people felt that they were the ones who'd put the grand coalition together, these left-wing Democrats, and there was such pleasure from it. In reality, the time of coalition only lasted a short while, but the desire to maintain that condition was wonderfully intense. There were a handful of us left as Democrats for Wallace. The people in the Wallace campaign wanted him to get the independent nomination because he couldn't get the Democratic nomination. I left HICCASP for good when it went along with the third party."

J. Parnell Thomas was well satisfied with his spring visit to Hollywood, and he announced that "90 percent of communist infiltration in Hollywood is to be found among screenwriters." Thomas claimed that he would gather "communist actors, writers, directors, and producers and confront them in public session with the testimony and evidence against them."

In September, he subpoenaed forty-five people in the film industry, whose politics ranged from far right to far left. A United States deputy marshal appeared at the house of each of those called, bearing a bright pink subpoena issued "by authority of the House of Representatives of the Congress of the United States of America." The subpoena commanded its recipient to "appear before the Un-American Activities Committee . . . and there testify touching matters of inquiry committed to the the the same committee . . . and not to depart without leave of said committee. . . ."

Nineteen of the recipients immediately formed a group denouncing the subpoenas and claiming that they would not for any reason cooperate with Thomas's "inquisition." These were the people who were the committee's major targets to begin with, and they were quickly labeled the Hollywood Nineteen and the Unfriendly Nineteen. They were directors Herbert Biberman, Lewis Milestone, Robert Rossen, and Edward Dmytryk; actor-director Irving Pichel; actor Larry Parks; writers Alvah Bessie, Bertolt Brecht, Lester Cole, Richard Collins, Gordon Kahn, Howard Koch, Ring Lardner,

Jr., John Howard Lawson, Albert Maltz, Samuel Ornitz, Waldo Salt, and Dalton Trumbo; and writer-producer Adrian Scott.

The day after the subpoenas were delivered, Hanns Eisler was interrogated harshly and exhaustively by the committee, who made him out to be a conspirator whose very notes were packed with musical propaganda. Eisler's visa had been obtained with the help of some of America's leading literary figures, and he was also supported by Eleanor Roosevelt, but that only increased the anger of the committee against him. A year after his investigation,

Katharine Hepburn with Robert Kenny, former California attorney general, at a rally sponsored by the Progressive Citizens of America in Hollywood, 1947. Four months later Kenny became the lawyer for the Screen Writers Guild.

orders were given to deport Eisler and his wife. They were allowed to leave voluntarily for the newly created German Democratic Republic, where he was accorded the honor and respect he deserved.

At first the Hollywood community responded with indignation to the blanket of subpoenas. The HICCASP had held a widely attended Thought-Control Conference at the Beverly Hills Hotel, which was chaired by Howard Koch and dedicated to the memory of FDR. It expressed with overwhelming unanimity that "there is an alarming trend to control the cultural life of the American people in accordance with reactionary conceptions of our national interest." The keynote address was given by John Cromwell, chairman of the Arts, Sciences, and Professions Council of the Progressive Citizens of America, who stated: "Those who recognize the power of the artist, the scientist, and the educator to awaken people to their dangers have never hesitated to use every means at their command to stifle these gifted and articulate voices, using the great powers of the press, legislative committees—and, of course, name calling."

A Committee for the First Amendment was formed to support the Un-friendly Nineteen and their fight against the Thomas Committee's assault on their Bill of Rights protections. The first meeting, at Ira Gershwin's house, drew all the stars.

"Everyone in Hollywood was there," said Abe Polonsky, "irrespective of their beliefs, political or otherwise. Howard Hughes offered a plane to take members to Washington, and they said, even before he withdrew this offer, 'No, we're going to pay for it ourselves.' There was a meeting at Chasen's, a big party. It was a holiday, because it was a fight for a great cause, and the whole community for that moment was sharing the spirit of the radical com-munity, and they loved it. Don't forget, the protest was a success initially."

Jack Tenney, though somewhat miffed at the national committee's steal-ing so much of his fire, hoped to horn in on some of the national publicity and had announced that the California Un-American Activities Committee would cooperate with the congressional committee in its investigation of Reds in Hollywood.

"We have volumes of information showing wide-spread Marxian leader-ship in the film colony," he told Thomas. And Tenney had been in almost continuous correspondence with Rankin on the subject, with both of his in-vestigators, Richard Combs and Thomas Cavett, conferring with HUAC in-vestigators when they came to Los Angeles. Tenney was acutely aware that as much publicity as he had been able to squeeze out of his hearings would be minimal compared to the coverage the national hearings would get, both on film and over the radio.

"I really never felt any fear in 1946," recalled Sylvia Jarrico, "so I guess I underestimated the dangers. Even when the first hearings took place in

Washington, we were so optimistic. But I remember later on reaching the panic stage, and as I was reaching that advanced state of despair, I realized this is why people commit suicide."

The resources of the HICCASP were mobilized for the defense of the Nineteen. Joan LaCoeur recalled that the organization was totally committed to fighting for the Nineteen, and they arranged a series of rallies at which the "unfriendlies" spoke. Joan's job was to line up the Nineteen backstage, in alphabetical order, and when she reached the S's she encountered her future husband, Adrian Scott.

"Adrian was a vague left-winger," said Joan. "He and Eddie Dmytryk were subpoenaed not because they were important in the Party or because they were big names, but because of *Crossfire* [a picture that dealt with anti-Semitism among soldiers]. Two or three weeks before the subpoenas came out, federal agents came to the studio and demanded to see *Crossfire*. It was totally because of the content that they were subpoenaed."

Paul Jarrico asserted that the reason neither he nor Michael Wilson nor any of the other more active Party people like John Bright figured among the Hollywood Nineteen (they were all later subpoenaed) was because they had done military service during the war. One thing that all of the Hollywood Nineteen had in common was that, for various reasons, they were not in the armed forces during the war. It was far easier, especially just after the war and at the beginning of the Cold War, to attribute subversive activities to those who had stayed at home. Not only was military service at that time an index of loyalty (though during the later waves of hearings it made little difference), but there was greater menace in the notion of subversives working away at home, a fifth column in the movie colony, doing damage while our boys were on the battlefield. Of course, most of the men who stayed at home, particularly the writers in the industry, had joined the Hollywood Writers Mobilization and contributed to the war effort in that way. Some, like Lardner, had tried to enlist and had been turned down. To reinforce the accusation that the HWM was a communist-front organization, and to bolster the contention that the Nineteen were subversives, the Thomas Committee could always rely on the Tenney Committee, which had branded the HWM a front as early as 1943.

The rabid anticommunist columnist George Sokolsky wrote in 1952, "If Mr. X joined the Hollywood Writers Mobilization and I decide for myself that I will not see a TV show that has on it anyone who has joined that organization or written for it, it may be too bad for Mr. X if others reach a similar conclusion. . . . No blacklisting is involved here because Mr. X by his own choice and decision joined the HWM. . . . In the eyes of most Americans, every Communist blacklists himself. . . ."

"When the Nineteen were subpoenaed," recalled Paul Jarrico, "we sent a telegram asking for the support of the most famous members of the literary community—Carl Sandburg, John Steinbeck, William Faulkner, Ernest Hemingway, and others. We didn't receive a single reply."

The subpoenas were, to a large extent, the rock on which several organizations were finally split. The HICCASP split over a motion to make, as an organization, a noncommunist statement that would clear it of the charges made by Tenney and HUAC.

"There had always been a range in HICCASP from the extreme left to the extreme right—people like Trumbo on one side countered by [writer-producer] Don Hartman and Reagan on the other," recalled Joan LaCoeur Scott. "After the 1946 election, the Red-baiting reached such a pitch that people began to quietly withdraw. There was a board meeting and some of the right-wing members wanted to make an anticommunist statment to clear HICCASP. People like Johnny Green and Olivia de Havilland—not strong people, middle-of-the-roaders—began to panic early in the fight. It was decided that if a statement could be arrived at that all could subscribe to, people would stand fast. The idea that a unilateral statement would be arrived at was such an unlikely prospect that everyone agreed. It was decided to appoint a six-man committee representing left and right, with a neutral chairman. They decided that if they could agree on a unanimous policy statement, everybody would stick together, and the prevailing feeling was 'No way.' The committee met for three days and three nights. Lawson and Trumbo represented the Left; Reagan and Hartman represented the Right; Linus Pauling and Jimmy Roosevelt represented the middle; and [writer] True Boardman was chairman."

"Reagan took a leaf from the supposed communist book and organized a fraction," recalled Ellenore Bogigian. "The Left and Right were, at that point, at each other's throats—I remember gruesome meetings. Olivia de Havilland had been meeting with Reagan's conservative fraction, and she got up at some meeting and started disputing Linus Pauling on the issue of the anticommunist resolution. And Pauling drove her to the wall. He was so lucid, such an extraordinary thinker, and she thought of herself as an intellectual. Johnny Green was a sweet man. He said to me, 'I just feel so guilty. I've been attending Ronnie's fraction meetings. How did I ever get into that?'

"At the end of three days, the tripartite committee arrived at a statement they all supported. It said: 'We are not communist, we are not Republican, et cetera,' and, naming every conceivable category, it finished by saying, 'We are an independent organization.' It was an unwieldy, ridiculous statement. They came back to the executive board with it and everybody jumped overboard. They had no intention of abiding by the agreement to support the statement. The board just resigned anyway. This tipped the organization, the middle weakened, the Right resigned. This was how the 'communists' supposedly took over. It was the beginning of the end of the organization. Nobody on the staff resigned, though."

By the autumn of 1947, Jimmy Roosevelt had come out for Truman against Wallace and left the HICCASP, whose energies were devoted then to the cause of the Hollywood Nineteen and later, when it was whittled down, the Hollywood Ten.

The autumn of 1947 also witnessed the major split toward which the Screen Writers Guild had been heading for years. The fight coalesced as the SWG executive board elections neared, and the Right and the Left were divided over several issues. One had been a source of contention for over a year. It was known as the American Authors Authority (AAA) Plan, and it had been proposed by one of the Guild's most conservative members, James M. Cain (who was, according to Samson Raphaelson, "a little scornful of all politics, for civilized reasons"). It took some instruction from Edna Ferber, whose agent, Leland Hayward, had been able to negotiate successfully a contract whereby she leased the rights to her novel *Saratoga Trunk* to the movie industry rather than selling them outright. Cain thought it an outrage that the copyright of all material written for movies was in the name of the studios and proposed that writers lease rather than sell their material outright to the studios. The plan would guarantee that writers share not only in the original profits from their work but in all resales and remakes of their material. It was supported by conservatives like Emmet Lavery and Mary McCall, Jr., as well as by young progressives like Ring Lardner, Jr.

"The Left actually thought the AAA was ridiculous," said Fred Rinaldo, "that there was no way the industry would countenance writers owning their own material. The progressive writers were more interested in the idea of a writers' pool, but that would have been even harder to get support for. So the progressive caucus took up the AAA Plan. They were so concerned with unity that they threw their support to Emmet Lavery and the issues he was pushing."

The major opposition to the plan came from the Right. As with all progressive and protective plans for writers, charges of leftism, dictatorship, regimentation, and totalitarianism against the AAA were inevitable. In Hollywood, any effort of writers to strengthen their position was seen as a communist plot. The conservative Cain was denounced by such former allies as H. L. Mencken and Rupert Hughes as being a communist. Implementing the AAA Plan would have called for the SWG to coordinate with the Authors League of America to get a pledge from members not to make outright sales of material to producers after a particular cutoff date. Louis B. Mayer made a statement that the studios had enough stock holdings of available material to last twenty years, but the whole situation eerily echoed the SWG's attempt to affiliate with the ALA in 1936 and the accompanying charges of communist domination.

Only the King brothers, heads of an independent production outfit, did not join in the hysteria against the proposal to set up a "repository of copyrights" for writers, much as ASCAP functioned for musicians. They agreed with the AAA that the writer should benefit financially from any remakes of his original story and that the sale of motion picture rights should not give the producer the secondary rights of TV, radio, and so on, and they were making individual deals to embody these principles.

One of the problems implicit in the AAA Plan, as good as it was, was that it would have violated the NLRB's certification of the Guild. The SWG was only able to have collective bargaining certification under the Wagner and then the Taft-Hartley acts if its members were employees and not independent contractors. It was a problem of ownership, and the reason the Screen Writers Guild had qualified as a union was because its members *didn't* have ownership, didn't have control of the final product. That, along with the divisiveness the plan itself engendered in the Guild, was one of the reasons it never came to fruition, and James Cain ended up protesting that he had been used by the left-wingers in the Guild, notably by Ring Lardner, Jr.

The second major issue over which the SWG was split was related to the Taft-Hartley Act, which had become law in the summer of 1947. According to the act, for a union to have a certification election under NLRB auspices, its officials had to sign noncommunist affidavits. And the question of SWG board members signing such affidavits sparked astonishing fireworks. Neither of the two Guild members who ended up facing off over the issue was a communist. Philip Dunne, who had written the script for the Academy Award–winning *How Green Was My Valley*, had been chief of production at the Motion Picture Bureau of the overseas branch of the Office of War Information. He had been on the executive board of the SWG for four terms and had served for two years as SWG vice-president. Emmet Lavery had championed the Guild's stance in opposing the Ball-Burton-Hatch Bill, which would have emasculated the Wagner Act, in 1945 and supported the Patman Full-Employment Bill, a progressive measure; by 1947 the Taft-Hartley Act was law, and Lavery wanted only to protect the Guild. In the interests of Guild unity, he wrote a pamphlet entitled *Sitting Out the Waltz* in which he encouraged signing the loyalty oath, saying that it was not illegal to be a communist and that if the Guild didn't accede to signing the oath, it would create a repetition of the climate that had fostered the birth of the Screen Playwrights. Lavery, defending himself in support of the affidavit, talked of "apostles of the last stand, people who turned out to be patriots rather than traitors."

Lavery had reason to be defensive. He was being bitterly attacked by liberals and progressives. The left wing of the Screen Writers Guild had met with Ben Margolis to discuss the legal and constitutional impact of not signing the noncommunist affidavit, and Margolis told the group what they ultimately told the Guild—that although the Taft-Hartley Act did require the signing of loyalty oaths by the union's officers if the group desired the services of the NLRB, the consequences would not have to be faced until 1949, when the Guild's present contract expired, provided that the act were still untested in the Supreme Court. Once the SWG's contract had expired, there was the possibility that a company union might arise to challenge the Guild on political grounds, and if at that time the Guild sought assistance from the NLRB, then they would be required to sign the affidavits.

The liberals attacked the affidavit as "an attempt to divide labor against itself" and to destroy trade unions. Philip Dunne wrote an eloquent response to Lavery's *Sitting Out the Waltz*, in which he called the Taft-Hartley Act a "slave labor bill" and cited Lincoln, Thoreau, and William Lloyd Garrison, saying, "There is a philosophical and historical precedent for defiance of laws which attempt to qualify the basic liberties." He questioned the rush of people like Lavery to surrender civil liberties, and just prior to the Guild's 1947 elections, its board voted nine to five to cross the affidavit bridge when they came to it in 1949.

"I took emotional positions," recalled Dunne. "I was what I suppose might be called a 'pure liberal.' The pure ones were those who never deviated from a pure civil liberties orientation, who never let any party or political loyalty allow them to abrogate the rights of anybody. In that category, I'd put people like Jane Wyatt, the Hacketts, Charlie Brackett, William Wyler. I sometimes, however, found myself in the position of defending people who conceived of civil liberties only for themselves [i.e., the Left]. Lavery was trying to purge the guild of communists. I would have preferred no Party line in the Guild myself, but I wouldn't stand for measures to push them out."

Nevertheless, pushed out they were. There had always been anti-Left members of the Guild, conservatives like Joseph Mankiewicz, and the more right-wing members of the defunct SP who had been absorbed back into the Guild after 1940. However, the conservatives never really gained a foothold on the SWG's executive board until the election of 1947. A group called the All-Guild Committee had formed, composed entirely of conservatives. They asked the left-wing members of the board to resign or not to run again if they wouldn't sign the loyalty affidavit.

"Art Arthur was an active right-winger," recalled Wells Root. "Art felt that *The Screenwriter* was controlled by the left wing. The conservatives caucused sporadically, but without the hard-core political know-how of the Left, whom we assumed were caucusing all the time."

"When we were trying to keep the Guild on a moderate course," said screen writer Catherine Turney, "we used to have secret meetings at Leonard Spigelgass's house. Secret except that everybody came. But we were trying to keep the communists from wrecking the Guild, from getting all their people into the offices. Funny thing was that back in the thirties and during the war, all the people I really admired were on that side, on the Left, like Hellman and the Hacketts."

The All-Guild slate knew that the president of the SWG had to be someone who could unite both factions. Sheridan Gibney was unanimously drafted as the choice for president. He received a telegram at his ranch in Montana from seventy-five SWG members who felt he was the only non-partisan candidate who could lead the Guild through troubled times. But there was bitter opposition for the other offices.

"Spigelgass told me his group hated the communists," said Gordon Stuhlberg, who later became SWG counsel. "They'd pushed them around in the war, and they felt they had to ally themselves with the Right to create an opposing force to the CP in the Guild. There were more Gentiles on the right in the Guild, but the anti-Semitism in the Guild would never be overt. There were too many Jews in the business in high places. The Right had anger. The Left knew *Robert's Rules of Order* and would try to use it to manage a meeting."

"We were determined, the moderates in the Guild, that we would finally clean it up once and for all," said Leonard Spigelgass, "and that we would do it by letting the membership vote between one slate that was clearly non-left and one group that was clearly left. That's why we formed the All-Guild slate. I really shouldn't talk about this, but a group of us put up a little money ourselves to hire a detective, and we had people trailed. We discovered that they got their instructions from Fourteenth Street, back East—Party head-quarters."

Spigelgass, with writing credits that include *I Was a Male War Bride*, thought of himself as Hollywood's answer to Noël Coward. He was also a militant veteran who was fiercely attached to the men he had fought with during the war.

Carl Foreman recalled that "during the executive board loyalty-oath fight, the fights were so bitter, and I stood out against that loyalty oath. And Spigelgass, who had been my commander when I was in his regiment during the war, begged me, crying, not to vote against the loyalty oath. 'It'll ruin you,' he said to me; 'you're throwing your career away.' " There was a special bond between the writers who had served together in the army, which added tension to the political splits that began in 1947.

Sheridan Gibney won the presidency of the Guild unanimously. The political shift in the Guild was apparent in the winners of the other executive board offices. F. Hugh Herbert, George Seaton, and Dwight Taylor were elected as the vice-presidents of the Guild; Arthur Kober and Frances Good-rich did not get enough votes. Arthur Sheekman, one of Groucho Marx's writers, was elected secretary over Stanley Rubin, and Harry Tugend beat Leo Townsend for treasurer. Both Rubin and Townsend were Party members. The board members elected indicated a resounding blow to the Left, with such SWG progressive stalwarts as Frances Goodrich, Hugo Butler, Lester Cole, and Gordon Kahn defeated. And as the SWG shifted toward the Right, the struggles that had once been good-natured harangues became passionate, vicious fights.

"At the end of 1947," said writer Karl Tunberg in a speech to the Commonwealth Club of California in 1951, "the communists had card-carrying members among our offices and on our board. They were never in the majority, but the majority was lethargic and disinterested and busy making money. I know because I was one of the disinterested majority. The communists were clever enough to espouse a number of good, liberal measures, and in opposing them we were frequently open to charges of being reactionary. We stopped their technique of controlling meetings by digging up an obscure provision of the Guild constitution which provided for proxy votes, and we laboriously collected the proxies from people who didn't attend meetings. Communist practice was to bring up measures late at night when most members had gone home. We stopped this by limiting the agenda early in the evening. We threw the rascals out. The history of communism in the Guild is a history of defeat, and today we are completely purged of their influence."

"When you look at the anger and bitterness within the Guild during those years," recalled Stuhlberg, "you must remember the conjunction of events in that period. Television was a reality, and the Consent Decree [which separated the three arms of the industry—exhibition, distribution, and production] severely changed the economics of the industry. On both sides there was unemployment, bitterness, frustration. Your bread-and-butter writers, those people, on the extreme right, being out of work and not quite understanding what had happened, vented their spleen in hostile acts and often blamed the communists for what had happened to them and to the industry."

In a time of a shrinking marketplace, a blacklist was one way of whittling away the competition.

On October 19, 1947, the Hollywood Nineteen sat at the Shoreham Hotel in Washington awaiting word from their lawyers. Their attorneys, Robert W. Kenny, Bartley C. Crum, Ben Margolis, Charles Katz, Martin Popper, and Samuel Rosenwein, were meeting elsewhere in the hotel with representatives of the Producers' Association and their attorneys. The lawyers presented the producers with a brief that challenged the subpoenas and maintained that the Thomas Committee "aims at censorship of the screen by intimidation." The chief reason the lawyers were having the meeting was to ascertain whether or not the producers were behind the statement Thomas had made to the newspapers that claimed that the producers had agreed to establish a blacklist throughout the movie industry.

"That report is nonsense," Eric Johnston claimed angrily. (In 1945 Johnston had become president of the MPAA.) "As long as I live, I will never be a party to anything as un-American as a blacklist, and any statement purporting to quote me as agreeing to a blacklist is a libel upon me as a good

American. . . . Tell the boys not to worry. There'll never be a blacklist. We're not going to go totalitarian to please this committee."

The Nineteen were pleased and relieved, but not totally convinced. After all, there had been blacklists in Hollywood before. As Jack Warner had once said, he didn't need a list, he had the telephone. Hollywood was a town of lists—A-lists, B-lists, good lists, bad lists. Nevertheless, Johnston delivered a statement to the newspapers ("One of our people wrote the Johnston statement," said lawyer Charles Katz), and the hearings began with the ostensible support of the industry against repression.

The members of the subcommittee, under Presiding Chairman Thomas, were John McDowell, Richard B. Vail, Richard Nixon, and John S. Wood,, with Chief Investigator Robert E. Stripling, who had clerked for Martin Dies. Banks of lights and cameras filmed the entrance that Thomas· had been practicing for two days, and the crowd of spectators was overflowing.

The first witness among the friendlies was Jack Warner, who gave a repeat of his springtime performance before the committee in Los Angeles. He was followed by Sam Wood, who trumpeted the need for his Motion Picture Alliance and painted it in full armor on a white horse. Then came Louis B. Mayer, who mentioned the writers he thought were communists—Cole, Trumbo, and Donald Ogden Stewart. His reasoning as to why these writers were communists despite their large incomes was "In my opinion, Mr. Congressman, which I have expressed many times, I think they are cracked."

Next came Ayn Rand, author of the best-selling novel *The Fountainhead*, who testified to the horrors of Russia, which, as a Russian immigrant, she knew to be true, and to the dangers of propaganda in such films as *Song of Russia*, which painted the false portrait of happy, smiling Russians. "If they [smile], it is privately and accidentally. . . . They don't smile in approval of their system."

Then Adolphe Menjou took the stand. Menjou had long been a member of the Motion Picture Alliance and was himself the possessor of enormous dossiers on suspected communists. In his files, for example, was a copy of a pamphlet from a 1946 series of forums called "Counter Attack," which were sponsored by the Hollywood Writers Mobilization to counter the threats of the Alliance and the Rankin-Wood-Tenney committees.* In the pamphlet were listed the speakers, and of the eighteen members of the Mobilization who were on that platform, eight of them were marked "CP" in red pen—Millen

---

* Sam Wood was the first president of the Motion Picture Alliance for the Preservation of American Ideals. Walt Disney, Cedric Gibbons, and Norman Taurog were vice-presidents; Clarence McGuinness was treasurer. On the executive committee were Borden Chase, Bert Kalmar, Rupert Hughes, Fred Niblo, Jr., Casey Robinson, Howard Emmett Rogers, and Morris Ryskind.

Brand, Franklin Fearing, Lion Feuchtwanger, Harry Holjer, Howard Koch, Emmet Lavery, John Howard Lawson, and Dalton Trumbo. In the margin, next to the markings, Menjou had noted, "Marked by Prof. Hook"; this was Sidney Hook, a self-styled anticommunist expert.

Menjou spoke about the Conference of Studio Unions strike, which he claimed was fomented by the communist Herbert Sorrell, and he called himself a well-read expert on all forms of political philosophy and subversion. He was questioned by Nixon, who asked him, "Do you believe the motion picture industry at the present time is doing everything it can to rid itself of subversive influences?" which seemed an obvious response to Johnston's statement about no blacklist. Throughout the hearings, Nixon asked the friendly witnesses if the industry was making serious anticommunist pictures to counter the propaganda in the existing ones.

A deaf old Rupert Hughes testified about the communists in the business and about his canniness in fingering them. "You can't help smelling them in a way." (In 1948 Hughes's nephew Howard became the owner of RKO Pictures and instigated the procedure of removing the names of suspected and accused communists from the credits of motion pictures.)

Then came the star attractions. Robert Taylor attacked Howard da Silva as a left-winger. Taylor said that he would not willingly work with a communist because "life is . . . too short to be around people who annoy me as much as these fellow travelers and communists do."

Morrie Ryskind followed Taylor, claiming that "if [Lester Cole] isn't a communist, I don't think Mahatma Gandhi is an Indian."

Ronald Reagan, Robert Montgomery, and George Murphy all spoke about the blessed lack of communist influence in their guild, the SAG, and mentioned their fight to overcome communist tactics during the CSU fight. Reagan said, "I detest, I abhor their philosophy, but I detest more than that their tactics, which are those of the fifth column, and are dishonest. . . ." Gary Cooper claimed, "I don't know the basis of communism, beyond what I have picked up from hearsay. From what I hear, I don't like it because it isn't on the level."

Then Lela Rogers did a repeat of her springtime song and dance about "Sharing and sharing alike," and Walt Disney, one of the Alliance's proudest members, claimed that the "commie organizations" put him on the unfair list because of his attitude toward Herb Sorrell. He claimed that the communist union organizers had fomented rebellion and discontent among his happy cartoonists. And on that note, the hearing's first movement came to a close.

In the second phase, the unfriendly witnesses were called. The first eleven included Lawson, Trumbo, Bessie, Lardner, Ornitz, Maltz, Scott, Dmytryk, Biberman, Cole, and Brecht. Paul Jarrico speculated on why these, the Hollywood Ten (exclusive of Brecht), were chosen to testify first: Lawson was an obvious choice, since he was well-known as the nominal head of the Party in Hollywood. Trumbo had high visibility, a name, and was big in pamphleteering and political campaigning. Scott and Dmytryk were chosen on the basis of the content of *Crossfire*. Maltz was picked because of his pamphleteering, his content, and the whole *New Masses* controversy. Alvah Bessie, though a small fish in Hollywood, was chosen because he had been in Spain as a member of the Lincoln Brigade, and his organizational associations were quite open. Cole was chosen because of his concern with content and because of the content of his pictures and was an obvious choice because of his position in organizing the Guild. Lardner was a name and had been active in the SWG and in all the other various organizations. Ornitz was the paterfamilias of the Party, and Herbert Biberman had numerous affiliations. And none of them had served in the military.

"From the beginning," said lawyer Charles Katz, "the Ten were agreed on a consistent course of action. There was a discussion of all testifying and answering, and we thought we had a good First Amendment point. The position was decided before we left Los Angeles. There was a lot of discussion before, and a lot of rehearsing on the train going down to Washington. Nobody wanted to take the Fifth. Actually, it seemed less likely to stand up then. It was an early decision, because the Fifth seemed the weakest course to take in terms of maintaining a position within the industry. We wanted to destroy the committee, and it was an objective that seemed realistic at that time."

Another reason that the Fifth Amendment seemed repugnant was that it had been invoked most often by gangsters, and the last thing the Hollywood unfriendlies wanted to do was to provide the committee and the columnists with more ammunition for making connections about "Red racketeering from Moscow" infiltrating the industry.

Eric Johnston was called to the stand to testify about subversive content in the industry. Then Counsel Stripling stated that Edward Cheyfitz, a member of Johnston's executive staff, had communist affiliations. Did Johnston know that Cheyfitz had been a communist and had been named by the old Dies Committee? Johnston did not. He was shaken, and it was, quite possibly, the committee's way of warning him not to be so free with his statements against blacklisting; his own house was not inviolate. And though Cheyfitz came out in the next few days with claims that since leaving the Party in 1939 he had been attempting to expose it, this still was a blow against the industry. What hand the Motion Picture Alliance had in this investigation is uncertain, but Adolphe Menjou's files contained extensive documentation about Cheyfitz's past, and this material may well have been given to HUAC before the investigation began.

In a letter to Menjou concerning Cheyfitz, Edward Nellor, a correspondent from the *New York Sun*, wrote, "He [Cheyfitz] is, in my opinion, the underground director of a large segment of the Communists out in Hollywood. I don't trust him as far as I could throw Louis B. Mayer. . . . I realize that Eric Johnston and his press relations people here in Washington defended Cheyfitz vigorously, but frankly I don't trust him nor do the investigators on the Thomas Committee, who have considerable information on his activities."

Emmet Lavery was subpoenaed, and testified on October 27, 1947, in the middle of testimony by the unfriendly witnesses. He was authorized by the Screen Writers Guild to act as its official spokesman, since he was then the president (Gibney's election was still a month away). The Guild had voted to defend the principle of screen freedom in terms of films and film content. The individual activities of the SWG's members, particularly their politics, were to be relegated to the realm of private, individual matters.

Lavery said that in his testimony he would try only to reflect the Guild's basic operations. However, when he got on the stand he couldn't keep from "lawyering." He did what he thought was the best thing to do. He first mentioned his suit against Lela Rogers, who had accused him on "Town Hall of the Air" of having written a piece of communist propaganda. (Lavery won the suit, in one of the few libel cases where accusations of communism were run to the ground.) Lavery next discoursed at great length about the Guild and about the small amount of communist influence in it. But then he began setting forth his own ideas about film content and about the committee. He gratuitously said that he had appeared before the FBI voluntarily and had offered to put himself and any Guild records at their disposal.

"It would be very easy to show how bad Mr. Stalin is, but the positive virtues of our great American leaders are the thing that the screen should be showing at this time," Lavery said. "And I think that if sincere people come before this committee and say that they think the positive picture of the American life is the better way to do it, that doesn't mean they are less loyal Americans. I think it means they are more vital Americans and they are trying to do it on a deeper and more stable basis than merely a lot of attacks on a potential enemy."

"Mr. Lavery, it is a great relief to have you testify," said Senator McDowell.

"My only concern with respect to this whole proceeding, Mr. Chairman," said Lavery, "is merely that people might go home and think that they have been political martyrs. An election in November which is coming up in our Screen Writers Guild might be seriously affected, and not for the better, if people thought that perhaps government had interfered any more than was necessary in the normal operations of the Guild." (An edited version of Lavery's testimony is included in Eric Bentley's *Thirty Years of Treason*.)

Dalton Trumbo and the other unfriendly witnesses were furious. They saw Lavery's stance as a betrayal, because Lavery "didn't want his appearance to be misinterpreted as a moral stand against the committee's investigation," said Trumbo. "He was impetuous in his desire to answer questions the committee had not even put to him: he was willing to forego any obligation to the constitution and the freedom it protects."

Trumbo, in his *Time of the Toad: A Study of Inquisition in America*, published by the Hollywood Ten in 1949, quoted Lavery's statement to the committee: "I have a piece of information that I would like to put in the record on my own motion, and on my own volunteering, because I am not sure as a student of constitutional law whether the committee does have the authority to demand it of me, but let me break the suspense immediately and tell you that I am not a communist."

"I felt," said Lavery later, "from a tactical point of view as president of the Guild that it would be almost fatal to the Guild to have the same counsel as the so-called Ten. So I was the lawyer. I was admitted to the Bar in New York in 1925, so the [SWG] board agreed, and I chose to testify—there was no reason I shouldn't. I said privately to people, 'You make a big mistake about Parnell Thomas and his committee. The fact that you don't care for the person as a person mustn't shut your eyes to the power of the committee and the subpoena.' And you know now, to this day, there are only a very few people that ever beat the contempt citation. I mean the person who says, 'You don't have the power, and I don't have to testify.' There were very few victors in that situation. All I learned about contempt in law school was that you can't beat it; it's the last vestige of sovereignty, and there's more of it in the House than there is anywhere else in the government."

The Hollywood Ten, however, didn't have any respect for the power of the Thomas Committee and were of the opinion that they didn't have to testify. John Howard Lawson had been the first of the unfriendlies to testify. He asked to make a preliminary statement, of which Thomas read the first line and then rejected it. All that Thomas and his committee were interested in were the answers to two key questions: "Are you a member of the Screen Writers Guild?" and "Are you now or have you ever been a member of the Communist Party of the United States?"

Ben Margolis, one of the attorneys for the Nineteen, thought the committee asked the question about SWG membership first to put people on the spot. If you responded by refusing to answer either of the questions, it made the Guild seem one with the Party. And after all, Lawson had been the Guild's first president.

Lawson's answer to the first question, about Guild membership, affirmed the decided-upon stance of the unfriendlies. "The raising of any question here in regard to membership, political beliefs or affiliation is absolutely beyond the powers of this Committee." He further antagonized his inquisitors by saying, "I am not on trial here, Mr. Chairman. This Committee is on trial before the American people." In response to the question of membership in the Communist Party, Lawson replied: "The question of Communism is in no way related to this inquiry, which is an attempt to get control of the screen and to invade the basic rights of American citizens in all fields."

Lawson, belligerently challenging the committee, was removed from the witness stand by police. In his statement—the one he had not been allowed to read—Lawson said, "In its illegal attempts to establish a political dictatorship over the motion picture industry, the Committee has tried to justify its probing into the thought and conscience of individuals on the ground that these individuals insert allegedly subversive lines or scenes into motion pictures. . . . This is a fantasy out of the Arabian nights."

Dalton Trumbo was even feistier than Lawson. He brought in boxes of scripts and prints of his movies, defying the committee to find subversive content in any of them. He would not answer yes or no to either of the two key questions. "Very many questions can be answered 'yes' or 'no' only by a moron or a slave," he said. By the end of his session, Trumbo, like Lawson, had been cited for contempt. As he was roughly led from the stand, Trumbo shouted, "This is the beginning of the American concentration camp!"

After rousing testimony by Roy Brewer concerning the communist attempt to control the trade unions in Hollywood, Albert Maltz took the stand. Surprisingly, he was allowed to read his statement, which ended with the words "The American people are going to have to choose between the Bill of Rights and the Thomas Committee. They cannot have both. One or the other must be abolished in the immediate future."

Maltz also would not answer either of the two key questions. When asked "Are you a member of the SWG?" Maltz replied, "Next you are going to ask me what religious group I belong to. . . . Any such question as that is an obvious attempt to invade my rights under the constitution."

Just before the next witness, Alvah Bessie, was called, Robert Kenny was summoned to the stand by Thomas. Thomas persisted in trying to find out if Kenny had advised his clients to refuse to testify. Kenny told Thomas, "If there is one thing that is sacred in this country, it is the matter of advice that a counsel gives his clients." Thomas was not unembarrassed.

Alvah Bessie also refused to answer the two questions and was refused the right to read his statement, which repeated the charge made by the *Chicago Times* that "the real object of Chairman Thomas and the reactionary Republican majority of the House Un-American Activities Committee is not primarily to uncover subversive influences in Hollywood. It is to smear New Dealers, and whatever their progressive successors may be called. . . ."

Bessie, too, stood on his constitutional rights and the protections of secrecy of private affiliations. "What is good enough for General Eisenhower is good enough for me," he said. Thomas excused the witness, saying, "If you want to make a speech, go out there under a big tree." And then, after Bessie's dossier was read, both Bessie and Maltz were cited for contempt.

Then came Sam Ornitz—plump, sorrowful, the oldest of the Ten, the guru, worrying if his gentle teachings had led his acolytes toward destruction. He, too, was forbidden to make his statement, which read, "I wish to address this Committee as a Jew, because one of its leading members is the outstanding anti-Semite in the Congress and revels in this fact. I refer to John E. Rankin. I refer to this evil because it has been responsible for the systematic and ruthless slaughter of six million of my people. . . . When constitutional guarantees are overridden, the Jew is the first one to suffer . . . but only the first one. As soon as the Jew is crushed, the others get it. . . . I am struck forcibly by the fact that this Committee has subpoenaed the three men who made *Crossfire*, a powerful attack on anti-Semitism. . . . Is it mere coincidence that you chose to subpoena and characterize as 'unfriendly' the men who produced, wrote, directed or acted in . . . feature-length pictures and short subjects which attacked anti-Semitism and treated Jews and Negroes sympathetically? . . . I ask as a Jew . . . is bigotry this Committee's yardstick of Americanism and its definition of subversive? . . . I must not . . . falter before the threat of contempt, which word sounds like the short way of saying concentration camp."

Herbert Biberman was not allowed to read his statement either. His responses to the committee were interrupted every few words by Mr. Stripling. Biberman was finally prompted to say, "Mr. Chairman, I would be very suspicious of any answer that came out of my mouth that pleased this committee," to which Stripling replied, "I would too." Thomas magisterially pounded his gavel and shouted "Take him away!" to the marshals.

Biberman's statement had said, "This Committee is in the course of overthrowing, not Karl Marx, but the constitutional way of American life." Biberman's dossier was read aloud, and once again Thomas recommended that Biberman and Ornitz be cited for contempt.

Adrian Scott was the next to appear. His statement was also denied a public reading. In it he said: "I would like to speak about the 'cold war' now being waged by the Committee on Un-American Activities against the Jewish and Negro people." He cited the contributions made by some of the men who had been subpoenaed: "Robert Rossen wrote the anti-lynch picture *They Won't Forget*. His latest picture is *Body and Soul*, which treats Negro and Jew with dignity and justice as free men. Howard Koch wrote *Casablanca* and *In This Our Life*. The Negro is treated honestly as a free man. Albert Maltz wrote *Pride of the Marines* and *The House I Live In*. . . . Both pictures exposed anti-Semitism and religious and racial intolerance. Waldo Salt wrote *The Comington Story* for the OWI, an attack on anti-Semitism. Ring Lardner, Jr., wrote *The Brotherhood of Man*, calling for more understanding among races and religions. Herbert Biberman produced *New Orleans*, hailed by the Negro press as an intelligent treatment of Negroes. Lewis Milestone directed *Of Mice and Men*, in which the Negro was handled with dignity. And lest we

The writers, producers, and directors who were subpoenaed by HUAC and cited for contempt of Congress—they became known as the Hollywood Ten—and their lawyers, January 1948: Back row, left to right: Ring Lardner, Jr., Edward Dmytryk, Adrian Scott. Middle row, left to right: Dalton Trumbo, John Howard Lawson, Alvah Bessie, Samuel Ornitz. Front row, left to right: Herbert Biberman, attorney Martin Popper, attorney Robert Kenny, Albert Maltz, Lester Cole.

forget, Nazi Storm Troopers stopped the showing of his anti-war film *All Quiet on the Western Front* in 1939, in Germany. Lester Cole wrote *None Shall Escape*, which exposed Nazi brutality to the Jews. Richard Collins wrote *Don't Be a Sucker* for the armed services. It exposed anti-Semitism and kindred hatreds. Irving Pichel directed *A Medal for Benny*, which treated a Mexican minority with dignity. Will the American people allow this bigoted committee to sit in judgment of these men and their records?"

In answer to the question "Are you now or have you ever been?" Scott replied, "I believe that I could not engage in any conspiracy with you to invade the First Amendment." He was cited for contempt.

Roy Brewer later condemned the progressives for deliberately making films that focused on the weaknesses in the American system, such as poverty, racism, and unemployment, instead of focusing on the wonderful advantages of democracy.

Next came the director of *Crossfire*, Edward Dmytryk. His statement was not read; it too deplored the committee's success "through threats and intimidation, in effectively censoring a screen which has just within the last few years begun to emerge from a never-never land into a dim realization of its responsibilities to the people of this nation and the world." He would not answer the questions. He was cited for contempt.

Lardner, though promised he could read his statement if he answered the questions, never got to do so. "It seems to me," said the handsome, diffident writer, whose wide eyes gazed out from dark-rimmed glasses, "that you are trying to discredit the Screen Writers Guild through me, and the motion picture industry through the SWG and our whole practice of freedom of expression."

Stripling answered, "If you and others are members of the Communist Party, you are the ones who are discrediting the SWG. . . ."

Thomas interrupted, saying, "Are you or are you not?" to which Lardner, grinning, replied, "It depends on the circumstances. I could answer it, but if I did, I would hate myself in the morning," at which the chairman shrieked, "Leave the witness chair! Leave the witness chair!"

In Lardner's statement, he ridiculed the Party card that the committee claimed belonged to him, with the name "Ring L." on it, just as Trumbo had ridiculed the Party card attributed to him with "Dalt T." on it. Lardner said, "It doesn't matter to me what kind of preposterous documents your investigators produce from unnamed sources describing my affiliations under such heavily cloaked pseudonyms as 'Ring L.' . . . Under the kind of censorship this inquisition threatens, a leading man wouldn't even be able to blurt out the words 'I love you' unless he had first secured a notarized affidavit proving she was a pure, white, Protestant Gentile of old Confederate stock."

Lester Cole, the last of the Ten, lasted six and a half minutes before the committee forcibly ejected him. The question of membership in the Guild was responded to with the statement "I believe the reason that question is being asked is that there is an election in the Screen Writers Guild in Hollywood . . ." Cole's statement, which he was not allowed to read, spoke of the history of the Guild, saying, "After years of failure by James Kevin McGuinness, Rupert Hughes, and other of your friendly witnesses to disrupt the SWG . . . a desperate appeal was made to Martin Dies . . . or maybe Martin Dies made the appeal; at any rate, the investigations began. . . . This committee is determined to sow fear of blacklists, to intimidate management, to destroy democratic guilds and unions by interference in their internal affairs, and through their destruction bring chaos and strife to an industry which seeks only democratic methods with which to solve its own problems. . . ." The agreement to cite Lardner and Cole for contempt was so implicit that it required merely nods of the head among the committee members, and the muttered word "contempt."

The last of the witnesses was Bertolt Brecht. Brecht confounded the committee by asking for an interpreter, and he played the foreigner to the hilt, aided by the broadly accented English of his interpreter. Brecht's only connection with Hollywood had been the sale of his story *Hangmen Also Die*, which had been scripted by John Wexley. The committee also did not think Brecht's statement, which chronicled his flight from Hitler, was pertinent to the investigation. Brecht, under questioning, told the committee that he was not a communist. The committee plied him with questions about conversations and

Edward Dmytryk (among the films he directed: *Hitler's Children, Murder, My Sweet, Back to Bataan, Crossfire, Obsession*) was born in Grand Falls, British Columbia. (His father, a Ukrainian truck farmer, worked winters as a local copper smelter.) Dmytryk was graduated from Hollywood High and Cal Tech and at the age of thirty-one went to work at RKO. Albert Maltz on Dmytryk (from a letter to *The Saturday Evening Post*, May 1951): "He believed in many principles until the consequences of those beliefs became painful."

associations that went back over a twenty-year period. Brecht answered the question of whether he had ever applied to join the Communist Party with Lear's wail, "No, no, no, no, no, never!" Then the committee asked if anyone had ever solicited him to join the Party, and Brecht replied that someone had—"Readers of my poems or people from the audiences." But it turned out that Brecht meant in Germany. The committee beamingly let Brecht leave the stand, telling him, "You are a good example to the witnesses of Mr. Kenny and Mr. Crum." The committee didn't realize that to the educated listener, they had just been made fools of.

Brecht's status as a foreigner convinced him that regardless of how much he felt the committee was raping the U.S. constitution, he was not entitled to its protection. So he did not seek shelter in any of the amendments but answered the questions as he saw fit. Soon after, Brecht left for Paris, and stayed there.

No more of the Hollywood Nineteen were called. It was commonly thought that the Hollywood Ten had been triumphant. They had given the committee a run for its money and exposed its fascist tactics so blatantly that it would be bad press for them to go any further. Their headlines had even been rivaled by the Committee for the First Amendment, which sent a star-studded planeload of known non-communist supporters (the only one who was a communist, Sterling Hayden, was unknown to any of the others as such), which included Danny Kaye, Humphrey Bogart and Lauren Bacall, John Huston, Jane Wyatt, and Gene Kelly.

The First Amendment plane came to Washington in the third week of October, just as the Ten were going on trial, and the publicity the anticommittee people got was bolstered by two broadcasts, on October 26 and November 2, directed by Norman Corwin, which used the glittering array of celebrities from all walks of life to support the Ten with the same kind of panache Corwin had enlisted in the 1944 broadcast in support of Roosevelt. The committee was having its publicity tactics thrown back at it, and for the month of November this seemed to be successful—there was a good, solid popular response in the press on the side of the Ten.

A special session of Congress, held on November 24, calling for the appropriation of funds to bolster Europe against the onslaught of communism, provided Thomas with the opportunity he had been waiting for since the last day of the hearings. Choosing to focus first on Albert Maltz, Thomas asked for his citation for contempt. He followed this up shortly thereafter with requests for the citations of the other nine. But Maltz was the test case. Thomas requested that Maltz be cited for contempt of Congress. The debate was bitter in the House, but out of 463 congressmen present, only 17 voted against the citation. The last speech before the vote was taken was given by Richard Nixon. He pointed out that there were only two issues—whether the committee had the right to ask the questions—yes—and whether the defendants had

Norman Corwin, radio writer, CBS producer and director, and author of *We Hold These Truths.*

refused to answer the questions—yes. It was a clear and simple case of contempt. In rapid succession, the other nine were cited for contempt of Congress. The overwhelming majority of Congress voted for the citations.

On that same afternoon, the Motion Picture Producers Association, led by Eric Johnston, reversed its position of a month earlier. The producers had been locked in conference all day at the Waldorf-Astoria in New York, waiting for the word from Congress. When it came, the press lined up outside the hotel suite, to get some response from the ruling powers within. Among the men gathered at the hotel were lawyers F. Barnes, Mendel Silberberg, and Paul McNutt; Eric Johnston; and producers and studio executives Barney Balaban, Nicholas Schenck, Harry Cohn, Joseph Schenck, J. Cheever Cowdin, Walter Wanger, Sam Goldwyn, Y. Frank Freeman, Louis B. Mayer, Dore Schary, Spyros Skouras, William Goetz, and others. The statement they handed out to the press became known as the Waldorf Declaration.

"Eric Johnston was of no help," recalled Dore Schary. "Goldwyn, Wanger, and I were angry at the Waldorf meeting. We proposed to the producers that they organize a council to protect people who were unfairly accused. The position was just terrible."

The statement read as follows:

Members of the Association of Motion Picture Producers deplore the action of the ten Hollywood men who have been cited for contempt by the House of Representatives. We do not desire to prejudge their legal rights, but their actions have been a disservice to their employers and have impaired their usefulness to the industry.

We will forthwith discharge or suspend without compensation those in our employ and we will not re-employ any of the Ten until such time as he is acquitted, or had himself purged of contempt and declares under oath that he is not a Communist.

On the broader issue of alleged subversive and disloyal elements in Hollywood, our members are likewise prepared to take positive action.

We will not knowingly employ a Communist or a member of any party or group which advocates the overthrow of the government of the United States by force, or by any illegal or unconstitutional method.

In pursuing this policy, we are not going to be swayed by any hysteria or intimidation from any source.

We are frank to recognize that such a policy involves dangers and risks. There is the danger of hurting innocent people, there is the risk of creating an atmosphere of fear. We will guard against this danger, this risk, this fear. To this end we will invite the Hollywood talent guilds to work with us to eliminate any subversives, to protect the innocent, and to safeguard free speech and a free screen wherever threatened.

The absence of a national policy, established by Congress, with respect to the employment of Communists in private industry makes our task difficult. Ours is a nation of laws. We request Congress to enact legislation to rid itself of subversive, disloyal elements.

Nothing subversive or un-American has appeared on the Screen, nor can any member of Hollywood investigations obscure the patriotic service of the 30,000 Americans employed in Hollywood who have given our government aid in war and peace.

"I think there was a subconscious cumulative effect in the minds of the community against the Left, which grew with each action the Left took which upset the liberals," said MGM producer Joe Cohn. "The Pact was one of those things. People forget that the left-wingers put Russia first. And the moment you disagreed with the Left you were called anti-Semitic. Nevertheless, in retrospect, there should never have been a blacklist. I feel the way Eddie Knopf does about the blacklist. If a violinist does something wrong, you don't break his violin. You shouldn't deprive a writer of the right to use his tools."

The Monday night after the Waldorf Declaration, the Hollywood Ten, by now all fired or suspended, were asked to join with the rest of the Guild in a meeting at which Eddie Mannix, Walter Wanger, and Dore Schary would explain the producers' position. It was a big showdown, and practically every writer in Hollywood was there.

"When I went to address the Writers Guild, I went because I wanted to," said Schary. Dore Schary was a man so anxious he sometimes had to wear cotton gloves to cover the nervous rashes on his hands. He was given the task of trying to sell the blacklist to his colleagues. He had been one of them. He was the kid from New Jersey who had made good. And now he was reading the death sentence, passed by a congressman from his home state, to a group of angry, disgruntled, ruined men he had known since they had all begun, back in the days when nobody had a swimming pool except the people you saw in the movies.

The producers and their mouthpiece, the *Hollywood Reporter*, called for unity in the industry to save the movie business from divisive politics and from destruction: "For his own salvation each and every member of the industry has been asked to forget . . . that he is a member of a left-wing group or a right-wing group, to forget his politics and unite with his fellow workers . . . in an effort to save this business. . . ."

Schary made his speech, and then Robert Ardrey, who had cast the first vote in the 1938 certifying election, made a statement supportive of Schary. Next Millard Lampell got up and, pointing his finger at Ardrey, began to denounce him. "I used to admire you, I learned from you. . . ." Trumbo jumped to his feet, calling Mannix a liar, Wanger a betrayer, and Schary a thief. The opposition had divided into the two factions, the progressives and the All-Guild slate, and were like two angry rival teams, each cheering for its side.

12

The actual blacklisting of Hollywood writers happened gradually. The Committee for the First Amendment followed the lost-cause shuffle that was so common to dying organizations in a town of rented halls. The CFA had apparently not publicized its purpose as support of the Nineteen and had supposedly only informed the planeload of stars who went to Washington on Sunday, October 26, that its major function was to denounce HUAC and to support the First Amendment and Eric Johnston in his appearance on October 27.

"When the hearings ended," recalled Abe Polonsky, "and Johnston issued the big declaration, the government was putting pressure on the producers—this blacklist is in the interests of our foreign policy, don't go against it. When the Hollywood Nineteen returned from Washington, the Ten with the Nine who did not get called, there was a second meeting at the Gershwins', and it was like the middle of a flu epidemic. Bogart was furious. He was shouting at Danny Kaye, 'You fuckers sold me out,' and he left. John Huston took to the hills shortly thereafter. Finally, there was one last meeting of the Committee for the First Amendment—Willie Wyler was still president, me, Phil Dunne, Millard Lampell, and a secretary. From our huge auditoriums it had shrunk to a little projection room on Sunset. Wyler said, 'Well, I guess it's no use. We oughta fold. But I can continue to say what I wanna say,' meaning he'd make his fight in his pictures. And Lampell pointed his finger at Wyler— he was always pointing his finger—and he said, 'You'll never make good pictures again.' "

The pressure was slowly but firmly applied in the studios. The sympathetic supporters of the Ten no longer wanted to give their contributions in checks. If they continued to give money, it was surreptitiously, in untraceable bills. Somebody turned in Nat Perrin's name for collecting money for the Hollywood Ten on studio time. He was called into Eddie Mannix's office;

every top Metro executive except for Louis B. Mayer was there, including producer James Kevin McGuinness. The producers wanted Perrin to stop collecting money for the subversives. Perrin insisted that by collecting money for the Committee for the First Amendment he was working for the industry. "You're the one who created this smear," he told McGuinness.

"The Alliance people were conveniences for the producers," Perrin said. "They couldn't have hired anybody better. Ever since they first encouraged them to form the Screen Playwrights, that group and then the Alliance created the hysteria in the industry. And then when the producers got hysterical, they offered to go in and clean up the industry."

In December 1947, the SWG engaged the prestigious Washington law firm of Arnold, Fortas, and Porter to represent it in a suit against the Waldorf Declaration, which they considered a breach of contract, and to ask for an injunction against the blacklist. Thurman Arnold, Paul Porter, and Abe Fortas stated in their brief, "It must be the function of the Guild to prove to the association of producers that this kind of subservient industry is not what the American people want. The motion picture industry is not theirs to surrender." As the suit dragged on, Arnold found himself representing a guild that was increasingly divided in its support or abhorrence of the blacklist, and which was becoming more, not less, entrenched.

When asked if, in retrospect, he thought the blacklist was a good thing, Ronald Reagan replied, "I don't believe in depriving people of their livelihood, but the American people made their wishes known."

The producers' breaking of the Hollywood Ten's contracts precipitated seven years of civil litigation, which accompanied the trials of the Ten and the appeals in the hopes of a Supreme Court reversal of the contempt citations. The process was long and financially exhausting, to say nothing of the wear and tear on the emotions and the souls of those involved. Between 1947, when the contempt citations were issued, and 1950, Supreme Court Judges Frank Murphy and Wiley Rutledge died, and the climate in the court became more conservative.

There was the Alger Hiss case. The war in Korea began. Loyalty oaths proliferated in every local and regional government and institution and spread throughout the groves of academe. The Smith Act trials sent Communist Party members to jail as criminals. It was realized that the only safe position to take against the committee was the Fifth Amendment. But by then it was too late, and the Supreme Court declined to review the cases of the Ten. The Hollywood Ten went to jail, and in 1951 another wave of hearings began, in which the leading friendly witnesses were former communists Richard Collins, Martin Berkeley, and, just out of jail, Edward Dmytryk. Soon after came Budd Schulberg and others who had left the Hollywood Party. And the circles of fear and betrayal and blacklisting widened in Hollywood and across the nation. The climate grew so hysterical that, as columnist Thomas Stokes said in the *Los Angeles Daily News*, "a portion of our population is slowly reaching the stage where it blames Communists when it can't find its socks in the morning."

When the Iron Curtain came down in 1946, the tensions within the Left had intensified in response. It was the first time that spies and informers within the Party began to have serious implications.

"We took it for granted that there were informers in the Party," said Dorothy Healy, "but we knew that to ultimately be deceptive as informers they also had to work like hell, so they did some good. We took stool pigeons, we took arrests, for granted. So there was no thought of public exposure. The

At left, Dalton Trumbo (among his credits: *A Bill of Divorcement, Thirty Seconds over Tokyo*) with Richard Collins, 1946. A year later both men were blacklisted. Trumbo emigrated to Mexico; using such pseudonyms as "Marcel Klauber" and "Sally Stubblefield," he worked on a number of scripts including *Roman Holiday*. Collins, in New York, wrote black-market scripts for the next four years. In 1951 he came before the committee as a cooperative witness—and worked openly and steadily thereafter.

only conclusion was that the enemy was working in the ranks. John Leech had been a Party organizer in 1933. He was a dissolute fellow who became an informer. The Red Squad, still conducting periodic purges of supposed communists in the Los Angeles area under police captain Hynes, had found him in a hotel with a woman not his wife, so the story goes, and they threatened to blackmail him if he didn't cooperate. So he became an informer in 1933 or 1934. Rena Vale was also cultivated by the Dies Committee and she wrote an article in the *American Mercury* in the late thirties about the horrors of the Party. There were always informers. It was a class war."

During these terrible times, many Party members looked for help. Though the Party generally frowned on psychoanalysis, they did approve Phil Cohn as a therapist for Party members, because he was on the county committee of the Communist Party.

"Between 1945 and 1947 I must have sent twenty people to Phil Cohn," said Dorothy Healy. "I remember a meeting with Max Silver at which he told me that Cohn was the Party comrade for people with problems. So I had a few meetings with Cohn, communist to communist, where we discussed the problems of certain people."

"Phil Cohn didn't have any legitimate credentials, I don't think," recalled Jean Butler. "But he recruited patients from the Party. He was always dying for Hugo and Waldo Salt to come see him. He said he thought he could help them, and he had his other patients telling them he'd like them to drop by."

"He was a little man, not attractive," said Joan LaCoeur. "I came to him in 1941. My sister referred me to him. You'd lie down on a couch and I suppose the influence on him must have been Freudian. I had such trouble discussing my sex life with him that he used to give me brandy, and after several shots I'd loosen up a little. But I would never have thought of sleeping with him."

"Phil Cohn was the most devastating blow," said Dorothy Healy. "We discovered that he was a conduit for convincing his patients to become informers. In a way, I suspected that Cohn had been a stoolie all along. And even though we took informers for granted, Cohn was a shock."

"Phil Cohn became the number one pipeline for the House Un-American Activities Committee," said Charles Glenn. "There were things brought to people's attention during the questioning that made this obvious."

Among the people who were Cohn's patients and who became friendly witnesses were Richard Collins and fellow writers Sylvia Richards and George Beck.

"Cohn made people feel comfortable about informing," said Glenn. "This was especially unfortunate because it reinforced the suspicion of shrinks which was ingrained in most left-wing people. So the Party made it a rule that one had to leave if one were in analysis, just at the very time that many left-wingers might have been able to derive some comfort from it. What Cohn did was to cut off an emotional escape route for some people who really needed help, during the hearings and afterward."

The question still remains as to why Hollywood capitulated so easily to the blacklist, why the producers were so quick to open the gates to the kingdom so that the armies of HUAC could sweep through.

Roy Brewer, international IATSE representative in Hollywood, saw a logical progression that had paved the way for the crusade against the communists in the industry. He said that when the Communist Party lost the CSU strike, it gave up its efforts to gain control of the unions. Suddenly Party people began to disappear. The CSU was in opposition to the IATSE, which was a militant anticommunist force, and the IATSE put pressure on the studios, as a form of self-preservation, to get rid of the communists. Another factor, as Brewer indicated, was the presence of a "Trojan horse" contingent in Hollywood that was waiting and hoping for the arrival of the committee. Another was the increasing governmental intervention in Hollywood's finances. The committee was aware that through a reconsideration of tax-exemption regulations and tax deductions, it could make Hollywood comply with its aims. And the process of control of Hollywood by the Eastern banks, which had been an operant principle since 1933, was by 1947 quite complicated, since most of the film companies had been absorbed into conglomerate associations—Warner Bros. with J. P. Morgan and Company; 20th Century–Fox with General Foods and Pan American Airways; RKO with United Fruit and National Can Corporation. The movie companies were already quaking under the onslaught of the Consent Decree and television. They couldn't afford to take a position that would place them in opposition to Wall Street, because Wall Street by this time exerted a very large degree of control in Hollywood.

The governmental interest in Hollywood was an obvious opportunity to garner headlines. "HUAC wasn't interested in going after the real members of the Party," said Lionel Stander. "You don't get headlines going after broken-down functionaries. They wanted the Hollywood people."

The publicity was great enough to stir up the fear necessary to a continued war economy. Historians such as Garry Wills have viewed the psychology of the Cold War as a channel diverting the mobilized consciousness of the

American people from hating enemy fascists to hating enemy communists. But psychological trends often have economic rationales, and it was so in this case.

HUAC's seizure of the hub of publicity coincided with the willingness of the producers after the CSU strike to open the movie industry to outside intervention. In an industry that was starting to lose its power as television took hold, an industry that had just come out of its most serious and violent labor disputes, perhaps there was a need to pin the woes on the communists. The tension and the resentment had been there for a very long time. It only took the appropriate climate and the appropriate spark to set the whole house on fire.

Because of Hollywood's support of Roosevelt, the publicity the movie industry offered could also be used in the postwar attempt to eradicate all vestiges of the New Deal era. In time, as the attorney general's lists grew longer and as the taint of subversion crept into everyone's past associations, nearly every Roosevelt-associated progressive organization was labeled a communist front. Hollywood in the postwar period was a useful, if not a compliant, helpmeet in aiding the Republicans in regaining control of this country. In 1947, Harvard professor Harlow Shapley had called witch-hunting "a transparent device for vote-catching in a presidential election eighteen months away." And out of the power shift came some of the leading Republicans who would dominate this country's and California's politics over the next few decades—George Murphy, Ronald Reagan, and Richard Nixon.

"It didn't matter if they proved who was or was not a communist," said Sam Moore. "Some were. But the irony was in their attempt to prove that the Left had a master plan for manipulation of the public. This was ironic and truly ridiculous in light of the enormous manipulations that went on at every level to purge the traces of Roosevelt progressivism from our society. If ever there was a master plan, it was to reinstate the Republicans and terrify the United States with the fear of a foreign conspiracy."

"I cannot get over the idea that the Committee attacked Hollywood for a reason," wrote Dalton Trumbo to Sam Sillen in 1953. "I think it had three reasons: (1) to destroy trade unions; (2) to paralyze anti-fascist political action; and (3) to remove progressive content from films. There must have been some progressive content, some results of progressive action in Hollywood. . . . I think the content of films was better in 1943 than in 1953. I think that anti-fascist films were being made in 1943 and that anti-Communist films are being made in 1953."

It has been estimated that several hundred people in the creative fields of Hollywood were blacklisted. Those who supported the blacklist, like Roy Brewer, claim that the number of communists in Hollywood, possibly three or four hundred, was an irrelevant figure because of the legion of dupes and

Sam Moore with Martin Popper before HUAC, April 1947.

fronts, both knowing and unwitting. "I had to spend hours explaining to some of those who'd been duped by the communists how they'd been manipulated," he said. "I had to explain that the way communists take someone over is they find out what interests a person, and in the course of time they infiltrate every phase of that person's life until their whole life is surrounded, and all their friends, their doctors, lawyers, and teachers are communists, so there's never any doubt but that the communists are 100 percent right."

"They talk about the blacklist and focus on Trumbo," said Elizabeth Spector, "and those people who were able to survive in Mexico, working under the table, working through fronts. But there were hundreds of people who lost their jobs in the industry, secretaries and so forth. I knew one who was thrown out of the studio she'd worked in her whole life, and she developed a terrible drinking problem. For many people the blacklist was the end of their lives."

There were people like Franklin Fearing and scores of other teachers who were destroyed because of their associations—the associations that had seemed so exciting to them. And the ones who remained turned toothless and frightened, producing a generation that was singularly frightened and repressed and lacking in innovation, an academic environment so "normal" and conformist that when it ended it was with the explosive, rebellious rupture of campus turmoil in the sixties, which, interestingly enough, began in Berkeley, in the same state that imposed the first political restrictions on its students and faculty in 1945.

"The number of casualties was low in terms of people actually murdered by the committee, driven to suicide or death like Phil Loeb, Madelyn Dmytryk, or [actress] Mady Christians," said Carl Foreman. "But I know of no writer who didn't suffer so much trauma that it took each of them years to recover."

It was ironic that the film that swept the Academy Awards in 1947, the product of which Hollywood was so proud, was a celebration of the postwar era called *The Best Years of Our Lives*. The Hollywood mythmakers were quick to pay homage to the postwar era, which, for all its problems and inequities, was suffused with the optimistic attitude that the American people would reap the benefits of everything they had fought for.

But 1947 was the year that the tragedy began in Hollywood. It would spread from West Coast to East Coast, leaving in its wake wrecked lives, devastated careers, marriages and families blown apart, friends betraying friends the morning after they had sworn devotion, suicides and bitter early deaths that the unforgiving termed "murder"—a tragedy particularly bitter in light of the national myth that was preparing Americans for the best years of their lives in the better world they had created.

For the survivors of the Hollywood Holocaust, the best years of their lives were the ones they paid for most dearly. The ten years from 1934 to 1944 were years of heady social, political, and creative involvement. The writers were at the center of the activity. Their union struggle reflected the mainstream battles of American labor, and never had there been a more articulate labor force. Their creative talents, adaptable to the campaign platform as well as to the movie screen, could make a difference in the American political process. When motion pictures talked, millions of Americans listened.

The Left was actually something of an anomaly in Hollywood. Its members were considered radical, yet their values were highly traditional ones. For example, in a town noted for cavalier partnering and casual sex, for multiple marriages and legendary affairs, the Party had an almost puritanical streak. "I think," said Paul Jarrico, "that we on the Left in Hollywood didn't align ourselves with people who were careless about marriage. That's why so many of the couples that started out as the young progressives in the thirties stayed married for so long."

The Hollywood progressives, basically an upper-middle-class group, treated women with greater respect in their community than they were treated elsewhere. Jarrico cited the number of outstanding progressive women writers, such as Sanora Babb, Viola Brothers Shore, and Jean Butler; organizers, such as Pauline Lauber Finn and Ellenore Bogigian; and others, like Patsy Moore and Elizabeth Faragoh, who were active in organizing child-care centers for the children of women working in defense plants. There were also women who were important in the Communist Party hierarchy, such as Dorothy Healy, Elizabeth Spector, and Madeleine Ruthven.

"During the period of the thirties and forties," Jarrico said, "many of the wives of radicals, whether writers or not, were young mothers. So many of them didn't have jobs. But there were many women who were wives and mothers and writers, too. Don't forget, these people were making a lot of money, so that women had servants, and they weren't chained to the house and kids."

The Left also evinced more respect for the motion picture as an art form than practically any other group in Hollywood. Their values translated into movie content. The writers tried not to write stereotyped characters of either women or blacks. But this doesn't mean they never wrote in a hooker or a harpie. The political activities of the Left, the organizations they belonged to, the way they treated their wives, their approach to unionization, their feelings about the dignity of the writer, their concern with motion picture content were all of a piece. They all stemmed from a central impulse.

Did the blacklist take them by surprise? Was the Cold War a total shock? There are always warning signs. The blacklist didn't just happen. It was the outcome of forces that had been coalescing for fifteen years. For every action the Hollywood progressives took, there was a reaction. It could be found in the industry, in the government, in the organizations, in the unions. They were not warning signs overlooked. They were separate instances whose impact was dissipated by every lull and gain in Hollywood. But in those years there was an energy that seemed invulnerable, and everybody did indeed believe they were building a better world.

Notes

30. *ready to negotiate.* The committees consisted of the following: Writers: Ralph Block, John Emerson, James Gleason, Dudley Nichols, Waldemar Young. Alternates: Gladys Lehman, Rupert Hughes, John F. Natteford, Steven I. Miller, Courtenay Terrett. Actors: Kenneth Thompson, Ralph Morgan, Richard Tucker, Pat O'Brien, Robert Montgomery. Producers: Irving Thalberg, Darryl Zanuck, I. Chadwick, Henry Henigson, Sol Wurzel. Alternates: Hal Wallis, Larry Darmour, Harry Cohn, Merritt Hulburd.

47. *efforts to recruit them.* "Guild Shop," declared the SWG in 1933, "the ultimate goal toward which we are striving, becomes possible in direct ratio to the degree to which the Guild attains one hundred percent membership among all available screenwriters."

60. *under their control.* All testimony from the NLRB hearings is quoted from transcripts of those hearings.

74. *good guy with the producers.* John Lee Mahin was interviewed by Todd McCarthy and Joseph McBride in the March-April 1980 issue of *Film Comment.* In contrast to the left-wing and pro-union writers who were later blacklisted, Mahin at the age of seventy-nine looked back on a long and successful writing career. The interview stated that Mahin was and is a deeply conservative man. He "unapologetically describes himself as 'an old rightist' and stands by his conviction today even though he is well aware that time has tarnished their aura of rectitude." Mahin lives in a comfortable Bel Air home and is still writing for films and television. To the question "Were you involved with the Screen Writers Guild at the very beginning, in the Thirties?" Mahin stated:

> Yes, at the very beginning. I put money up, a lot of us put money up, and then we found out who was really running the thing, with Jack [John Howard] Lawson and his minions. We used to call him George Washington Lawson, who was going to lead us into a great rebellion but we found out they had other interests: the Party was in there heavy. Then we split and we formed the Screen Playwrights Inc. They called us a company union. Yes, we were a company union, formed by the workers themselves. We were cloak-and-dagger and we found out all the leading, hard-working guys in the Guild were members of the Party. . . . Frankly, we spied on them. . . . But then we couldn't convince a lot of the people that they were, and some said, "Yeah, we agree with you, but you ought to stay within the Guild." We said, "To hell with it. . . . Let's form a

guild where we will welcome them in, but we don't want to be run by them! . . ."

We started to form the Playwrights—156 people—and then it got around to Thalberg and he said, "Now what the hell is this?" We said, "You're going to have to recognize writers sooner or later, Irving, because the Federal Labor Relations Act is coming in. . . . So Irving signed, and we ran writers' problems for four years, until the Labor Relations Board finally came into real being, and the Guild, who greatly outnumbered us because two weeks' work in a studio gave you a voting membership in the Guild, and we required three screenplays or two years' work.

In response to the comment that "there was a lot of bitterness over that power struggle between the Guild and the Playwrights," Mahin said:

Oh, yeah, a lot of people called us fascists, anti-Negro, anti-Jewish, anti-labor—the same old tired jokes they do today. The only thing we were never called, strangely enough, was anticommunist. Why? Now they got a thing called "McCarthyism," which they use any time there's a hint of people not being able to work. Well, McCarthy was a fool. I remember talking to him on the phone, several of us. I got Mayer to speak to him, because I thought he might get some money from Mayer for his next campaign. . . . It was a long cry from fourteen years before. But they speak of that era as the McCarthyite, when McCarthy wasn't even known.

When asked "How do you feel about the events of the blacklist era now?" Mahin answered:

We didn't want the blacklist, but those things happened. It's not our fault that they joined the Communist Party, and I didn't give a damn if they worked or not. I could care less. I used to kid Dalton [Trumbo] and Jack Lawson. I'd say, "You're gonna get in trouble because the American Legion and the Catholic Church are gonna have you blacklisted. . . . You're gonna scare these guys to death and you're gonna get blacklisted." And, by God, they were. *We* didn't blacklist them. Some of them were very good writers.

115. *throughout the industry.* Studio executives were getting their strategy from Kyle Palmer, political news reporter for the *Los Angeles Times,* and behind-the-scenes manipulator in conservative politics in California. Fred Rinaldo described Palmer as "the official unofficial adviser to the producers on labor practices. He taught them how to pattern their union busting against the SWG on the Mohawk Valley Plan. Palmer advised them every inch of the way. L. B. Mayer and he were very close. He was slick, smooth, adorable, charming, had the best wines, gave the best dinner parties, and he had a high power circle of intimates. He made Nixon. He made Reagan. He was behind every invidious action at that time. He operated very carefully, behind the scenes. The reason I know all this is that the sonofabitch was my brother-in-law."

116. *visit California in March 1938.* When Witt went to Hollywood to check on the local office of the NLRB, it was run by Towne Nylander, supposedly intellectual bureaucrat who had a Ph.D. and was constantly reminding people to call him "Dr." Nylander. Witt had planned to go to San Francisco with his wife, meet with Harry Bridges, and then travel to Los Angeles by train. But Nylander suggested that rather than going straight to Los Angeles, the Witts should get off at San Luis Obispo and that Nylander and William Walsh would show them a few of the sights, including Hearst's estate, San Simeon. They had given Witt the erroneous impression that San Simeon was then what it subsequently became—a state historic monument.

Mr. and Mrs. Witt disembarked at San Luis Obispo and were driven, Mr. Witt in front with Nylander and Mrs. Witt in back with Walsh, to the gate of San Simeon. Nylander handed Witt a letter to give to the gate guard. It was a letter of introduction from the general manager of the Hearst newspaper in Los Angeles to the staff supervisor of San Simeon telling him to treat the NLRB party well. When he saw the letter, Witt, feeling like a naive dupe, got angry. Hearst, of course, was smooth and clever and didn't mention unions throughout the day, which featured a sumptuous lunch at the banquet table in the nave hosted by Hearst, with Marion Davies, Buster Keaton, and other glamorous Hollywood denizens as guests. Witt was furious, especially since one of the cases pending before the NLRB involved the Newspaper Guild. Hearst had compromised him in two worlds, publishing and the movies.

116. *no time for work.* The *People's Daily World* began publication on January 1, 1938. "It was an offshoot of the *Western Daily Worker*," recalled Ring Lardner, Jr., "but it billed itself as the voice of expression of the united front. It was really a Party organ. Looking back, it's funny to remember who was on our side in those days. On those original letterheads, we've got the names of [John] Tenney and [Sam] Yorty, among others."

128. *any way involved politics.* Even though Governor Earle of Pennsylvania later overturned the Philadelphia board of censors' ban on the 1937 Joris Ivens–Ernest Hemingway documentary, *The Spanish Earth*, producers and exhibitors worriedly noted the loss of revenue during the months prior to the governor's ruling and acknowledged that it was a bad risk commercially for a film to be so vulnerable to criticism.

133. *first stairway scene.* Fitzgerald was extremely liberal to the Left. One friend reports that when he visited Fitzgerald when he was living in actor Edward Everett Horton's guest house, Fitzgerald was reading *The 14th of May* and the works of Karl Marx. He was very aware of the social dislocation of the capitalist system, and in spite of his aristocratic leanings, his sympathies were increasingly turning left.

160. *in December 1939.* A piano player and organist, Tenney had composed a very popular song called "Mexicali Rose."

163. *fight against war.* The concerns of the Congress were defined as follows:
1. How as writers can we best resist the drive toward war and reaction which threatens our democratic culture?
2. What can we do to extend further help to persecuted writers of other lands?
3. What can we do to restore the WPA cultural projects and transform them into permanent Peoples Art Projects vital to national strength?
4. What new technical developments in the various forms of writing need to be analyzed and evaluated?
5. What measures can we take to combat and surmount growing restrictions on our work as honest craftsmen?

163. *began in 1940.* The school, according to its brochure, "offers to new writers and those who already earn or augment their living at some form of writing, an opportunity to develop latent talent or sharpen technique, at a cost within the means of any serious student. For talented young writers unable to meet even this nominal cost, a limited number of scholarships are available."

189. *"were good and ready."* In his memoir *Front and Center*, John Houseman wrote:

> It would have surprised me to learn, between 1944 and 1946, that the vaguely patriotic activities in which I was engaged as a member of the Hollywood Writers Mobilization constituted political action. Evidently it did—for the Mobilization eventually found its way onto the Attorney General's list of subversive, Com-

munist front organizations and helped to swell the already formidable catalogue of misdemeanors of which I was accused during the Plague Years.

At the time, it seemed innocent enough. The Mobilization had been created early in the war by the Screen Writers Guild to act as a channel between writers and studios—a clearing house for a variety of wartime activities that included the drafting of brief speeches for stars and executives to be delivered at bond rallies, blood banks and Red Cross drives. Its contributions also included theatrical material (especially jokes and comedy routines) to be used for troop entertainment—camp shows, canteens and overseas broadcasts. On the home front the Mobilization collaborated throughout the war years with various domestic information agencies and the War Production Board: it prepared material intended to clarify and popularize the wartime regulations on rationing, price controls and conservation. By then the Mobilization included members of other Hollywood guilds: the cartoonists, publicists, studio readers, songwriters and, to a lesser degree, the Newspaper Guild. But its main creative and financial support came from the Screen Writers, in whose Hollywood office the Mobilization continued to occupy space as long as it existed.

190. *Woman of the Year*. With this script Michael Kanin and Lardner broke a streak of bad luck that had plagued Lardner during the pact period. The script *Woman of the Year* so delighted Katharine Hepburn that she insisted MGM buy it, without knowing who had written it. It was sold for the highest price ever paid for an original screenplay and earned Lardner and Kanin an Academy Award.

192. *Communist Party Writers' Clinic*. All information concerning the CP Writers' Clinic comes from the files of several clinic members who took notes and kept the information over the years. Since some of these people have not openly declared their Party affiliation, their names will not be used. In the actual clinic notes, their names are abbreviated, with only first names or initials used. Whenever Marxism or Marxist is referred to, it is denoted as "M," as in "attaining a M. perspective."

193. *all writers equally*. The best way to understand the workings of the Writers' Clinic is to examine some of their sessions and see exactly how they treated material and what they thought they could do with it. The following examples are taken from actual clinic sessions:

1. In a story of small-town politics concerning a judge, one member of the committee pointed out the reactionary aspects of the treatment—it was based on the theory that the people of the town, which is to say "the people," get the kind of government they want, and it is simply stupidity that allows them to be saddled with evil officials. This minimized the "will of the people" in terms of social change.

2. In a discussion of the screenplay for *Moby Dick*, the question was raised as to how the clinic would approach the task of putting nineteenth-century literature on the screen in 1942. Was it a violation of Melville if the positive elements were stressed and the defeatism omitted?

3. Concerning a remake of *Humoresque* (released in 1946), it was noted that the musician's separation from the people ultimately led to fascism. The group made an effort to get beneath the conception of art for art's sake as it applied to the musician. They made the point that this artistic theory had its roots in political and economic views and was a rationalization of both by the musician. In regard to the story, there was no dramatic opposition to his "art for art's sake" concept in the form of a concept of a "people's music."

4. Concerning attitudes about gangsters, it was noted that too many pictures had shown gangsters as heroes in the fight against fascism. "We know that the gangster and the hoodlum are the natural tools of fascism in this country," said one member

of the group. It was agreed, however, that a scene in the script under discussion, in which the top gangster spoke lucidly of this association of interests (gangsterism and fascism), was unbelievable. It was decided that in the opening there should be an actual physical connection made between fascists and gangsters but that it should be the protagonists who not only discover it but understand and explain its significance.

5. In the discussion of a Civil War studio project, the group felt that the project was a general distortion of historical material to sell fascist ideas. They were particularly unhappy about the treatment of blacks in the script. The question was raised as to whether or not a picture about the Civil War could be written at that time. The point was stressed that history had to be reexamined in terms of historical truths from a Marxist viewpoint. It was decided that should a member of the clinic be given the assignment, an effort should be made to change entirely the point of the story or to turn down the job if the writer could afford to. One writer suggested that many of the speeches, scenes, and ideas could be watered down so that the picture would become innocuous. The writer was attacked on the following lines: (a) there were limits to what the writer was expected to demand of himself as a craftsman; and (b) in the political arena, there was a point at which Party members had to refuse to go along with certain groups, and the same applied in accepting an assignment of this sort.

6. A discussion of one particular play brought up the question of male chauvinism, which was frequently referred to at that time as "the woman question." It was agreed that the group felt it was good to have plays about working women to challenge male chauvinism. Along these lines, an author was criticized for dealing in political generalities and applying these generalities to specific characters. In the case of a particular character, the author maintained that her passivity, her lack of militancy, was portrayed deliberately, that she took on the point of view of the people for whom she worked, that her job was a form of semiprostitution.

7. In a discussion about the problem of sympathetic treatment of a Nazi soldier in a love story about a Nazi and a Norwegian girl, the following statement was made: "It is significant to note that newspaper reviews have sharply condemned this sort of sympathetic treatment of our enemies and have stressed the political importance of what is written today and the danger of sentimentality. It bears out the judgment of the committee, and indicates a fruitful line of discussion as similar problems arise."

8. About a discussion of a play that had been begun before the war, the minutes from the Writers' Clinic of April 5, 1942, show the following comment: "The play was started before the present world situation and consequently lacks the quality of positiveness and life which is needed today. Apart from that, there was a time when dissolution of the middle class was important to examine. Is it now?"

199. *"unconscious fascism."* Robert Rossen suggested that recognition be given to the fact that the forces of reaction were making an attempt to break up the OWI, claiming it was being run by radicals. On June 28, 1943, members of the Screen Writers Guild sent letters to senators Sheridan Downey, Edwin C. Johnson, and Kenneth D. McKellar, Vice-President Henry Wallace, and Elmer Davis, asking them to ensure the continuation of the domestic branch of the OWI and deploring the attempt of Congress to hamstring the usefulness of an important government agency. In 1942, Congressman Dies had launched an attack on Malcolm Cowley, the book editor of *The New Republic*, whom Archibald MacLeish had hired as the chief information analyst of the Office of Facts and Figures. Dies claimed that Cowley

was "one of the chief communist intellectuals of this country" and said that his committee files gave Cowley seventy-two connections with the CP and its fronts. The Hearst press trumpeted these charges in boldface type, and the pressure was so intense that after two months Cowley resigned.

201. *Communist Party line.* "The time has come," Tenney nobly announced, "when the people of California must take definite action to stop its state institutions, and particularly its university, from being used as a springboard for Communist front groups and a sounding board for Communist propaganda.

"Looking over recent issues of the California *Bruin*," he continued, "which is published by the student body on the campus of UCLA, and apparently under the administration of Dr. Gordon Watkin, who appears to be the spokesman for the University of California at Los Angeles, it seems to me that it reads in many cases like the *People's Daily World*, the Communist Party paper for the West Coast, or the *Daily Worker*, official Communist publication in New York City.

"I note in the edition of July 23, 1943, that the paper attacks the American Legion, veterans of the last war, and viciously attacks, throughout its issues, the Americanism of the metropolitan press of Los Angeles. . . . In the issue of Monday, September 23, 1943, we find a vicious attack on the Federal Bureau of Investigation. In the edition of September 20, 1943, we find a reader of the California *Bruin* protesting the policy of the paper in praising and publishing announcements of meetings of the Young Communist League. In the same edition we find an article following the Communist Party line in its policy in commenting on the recent dismissal of Sumner Welles and the policy of the United States State Department in general."

203. *of women than men.* While the conscription of all eligible men tended to change the situation in many of this country's industries, so that women suddenly had a place in the working world—Rosie the Riveter and Swing-Shift Maisie, the girls in the defense plants—the situation didn't change very much in Hollywood. There had always been a number of prominent women in the writing end of the industry, including Frances Goodrich, Mary McCall, Jr., Sonya Levien, Frances Marion, Lillian Hellman, Anita Loos, and Helen Deutsch. And during the war, many of the men were at "Fort Roach" making training films in the Capra unit, so there were plenty of young men around. Hollywood was unlike the rest of the country in that way. However, Hollywood did have some extraordinary woman organizers; two of them were particularly active during the forties—Pauline Lauber Finn and Ellenore Bogigian—and many writers' wives were active in various organizations.

232. *education and culture.*

> TENNEY: Do you think that a magazine published by the university should attack men in this state who are paying big taxes towards the support of the university? It does that in this magazine.
> DYKSTRA: My recollection, Senator, is that the writers are complaining that producers do not use their plays and scripts as they were written, but maul them about and do with them what they please. I don't know that that is an attack on a taxpayer, is it?
> TENNEY: There is a direct attack on a taxpayer. If you read it you will see it. I will be glad to talk to you about it later. Their complaint is that they are not given a free rein in the drawing up of the scripts, and the writers who write these things and the people connected with them plan to use the motion picture industry and the university. . . . We are concerned with individuals who are writers for the direct purpose of indoctrinating people with their philosophy.

233. *"run in the magazine."* Richard Combs asked the witness, "Assume that a front organization such as the HWM . . . as we have reason to believe it is, is a Communist front organization and they wish to divest themselves of suspicion and clothe themselves with dignity and respect, and they could persuade an institution like the University of California to join hands with them in a joint publication of a magazine . . . would it add immeasurably to their prestige?" Farquhar took a breath and answered, a bit dazed, "I think it would, yes."

233. *held in Los Angeles.* Looking back with pride on his hearings, Tenney recalled, "I usually signed the subpoenas in blank, 50 or 60 at a time, and turned them over to Combs. He had them served on those persons he deemed necessary to a particular phase of the investigation."

238. *she had represented.* When the Viertels returned from Europe, their marriage was on the rocks—it had been for a while, ever since they had crossed over to Europe after the war on a ship with Hemingway and his wife, Mary. On the boat, Jigee and Hemingway had an affair. It was said that Jigee had the affair to get back at Peter for an affair he had had with a nurse during the war. Peter took the affair as a grave insult.

In Europe, the marriage disintegrated further. Peter did not want a child, and Jigee had several abortions before finally deciding to have a baby. And while she was in Paris, pregnant, Viertel abandoned her for a model named Bettina. Jigee came back from Europe and had a protracted breakup with Peter that lasted over a period of several years and encompassed a vast circle of adulteries. Despite Viertel's betrayal, she still loved him, and on her return from Europe she was bitterly unhappy. She lived with Peter's mother, Salka, and the child, and tried to pick up the threads of some kind of life. Her passport had been taken away because of her subversive past, and she could not return to Europe. She tried to get a job—as a reader, as a story editor. She worked for Milton Sperling as his story editor for a while. And finally she became a friendly witness.

Some said it was because she had a tentative job offer at the Goldwyn studios but couldn't get the job unless she cleared herself. She explained that she had to testify to protect Peter; although she and Viertel officially separated in 1952, they had not yet divorced.

She testified in a closed session before HUAC in 1956, after most of the hearing frenzy was over, and she did it reluctantly, disheartened. She resisted it for a long time, living with Salka, who would not testify and was violent in her denunciation of "the shits" who did.

"If I hadn't felt strongly about speaking up, I would be in Europe now where life was altogether better for me," she wrote to Ring Lardner in 1956. Peter Viertel, who received a commission from the Marine reserves, was called up on charges before his Marine board and was branded with the stigma of his estranged wife's former activities.

"I couldn't refuse to clear Peter," she wrote. "I couldn't think of any reason why he should suffer because of my thoughts and actions. He would be a more admirable character if he had fought all the charges, but my opinion of his character has very little bearing. . . . It was a near choice for me: either I cleared him, which involved clearing myself, or he signed the papers giving him a dishonorable discharge."

Jigee went to lawyer Martin Gang and prepared a statement that Viertel could read during his hearing. Gang at that point was famous for "clearing" people who wanted to testify, for getting them off the blacklist, and he was referred to by angry progressives as "Torquemada's adjutant."

"The only real glimmer of hope for me," Jigee wrote, "is that Peter is now going to resign his commission and then they might just let the whole thing drop. Peter's lawyer feels the Corps might not accept the word of an ex-Communist who is not entirely an ex.

"I have been in a cold sweat for weeks. And I daresay it will continue. It is odd and terrible to find yourself on the other side. I will lose the only people I really care about as they won't forgive the fact, no matter what the reasons were that brought about the fact. I remember what you said about the motives behind informing. I certainly cannot call what I did patriotic or socially useful, nor is it corrupt because of any material gain involved for me. There is nothing good in it for me. I feel corrupted because it is wrong to present yourself to these creatures, but it is a wrong I think I had to do."

By the time Virginia Viertel testified before HUAC in executive session, the committee had pretty well exhausted the Hollywood lode and had turned to investigating CP activities in northern Ohio. She testified for just over an hour on June 6, 1956, in room 484 of the L.A. Statler Hotel. William Wheeler, the investigator for the committee, questioned her, and Martin Gang was present. She was nervous and chain-smoked throughout.

She said she was born in Beaver, Pennsylvania, on September 3, 1915 (the newspapers said she had been born in 1911). She said she joined the Party in 1936 and left it in 1945. She told of marrying Budd Schulberg on December 31, 1936, and living in the home of Budd's father. She told of the house she had moved to with Budd, which was shared by Leon Becker and Lester Koenig. And she named the names of the young people who had been in the Communist Party with her: Budd, Ring, Trumbo, Robert Rossen, Albert Maltz, Maurice Rapf, and, generally, their wives. She told of flying to Mexico in 1942 to separate from Budd and of their official divorce in 1944.

Clyde Doyle, a member of the committee, asked her, "Why did you come forward and volunteer to come before the Committee?"

She answered, "There are an awful lot of circumstances altogether. I think probably I would have just let it go, because my life is pretty busy, just being a mother, you know, but they know about Peter, certainly—"

She was interrupted by Martin Gang. "Do you want to tell the Committee something to help them in legislating on the problem?" he coached.

"Yes, certainly," she answered. She was asked why more people didn't realize that they were welcome before the committee, and she answered, with a trace of impishness, "I think they often don't know where you are, possibly."

After an hour, the ordeal was over. She was no longer part of Hollywood. She had betrayed the people who were the only ones she truly liked and admired. She had betrayed the good life they had all had together. But testifying didn't help her. Much of her magic had been drawn from the group that surrounded her. And in breaking the magic support circle by testifying, she didn't even have the comfort of the Left. She had no resilience, since she was not truly politically committed. Joining the Party for her had really been a social function.

"When she came back from Europe," said Ring Lardner, Jr., "the glamour was gone. She looked like any other forty-year-old, and much of her physical deterioration was caused by the drinking."

She moved to New York with Salka. There was heavy drinking, drugs, heavier drinking. Salka ended up doing most of the caring for her grandchild.

"I was in New York with Salka," said Paul Jarrico, "and I drove her back to the apartment she was sharing with Jigee. Salka was a woman of principle and had no love for stool pigeons, but she was protective toward Jigee. And when she got out of the car I told her, 'Say hello to Jigee.' And that was the first time, the first time I'd softened toward any of the betrayers, and Salka knew it. She looked back over her shoulder at me and smiled. 'Yes, yes, I'll tell her that, it will make her very happy.' That was in 1957 or 1958. I was not forgiving toward any of the friendly witnesses at the time, but it was Jigee, and she was something different."

In 1959, Jigee was divorced from Peter Viertel. She appeared in court, looking puffy, wearing dark glasses. She was accompanied by Christopher Isherwood, a friend since her early days. Isherwood had worked with Berthold Viertel in England. Jigee was, at that point, alcoholic. There was a bruise on her forehead from falling down.

She had been living in a house on Monte Grigo Drive in the Pacific Palisades and drinking heavily. It was later said that drinking had destroyed brain cells and caused an epileptic seizure. In mid-December 1960, she was smoking a cigarette, as always, and she got up to go to the bathroom, and whether she had a seizure or just dropped the lighted cigarette in her drunken haze, it fell on her nylon nightgown, and she went up in flames.

Jigee was conscious for a week, then lapsed into a coma. She lingered for five weeks. She died at the end of January in Cedars of Lebanon Hospital in Los Angeles.

Many of the people in Hollywood remembered her from the early years there. They lost track of her after she and Peter went to Europe, and they never saw her in her period of decline. She avoided people in the later years and then died before she reached fifty, so she was remembered as a legend.

Virginia never aged in the minds of any of the men who loved her. She became a muse figure of sorts. She has been pointed out in Irwin Shaw's *Two Weeks in Another Town*, Arthur Laurents's *A Clearing in the Woods*, and in the film *The Way We Were*. She was the dark lady of the Left, the basis for the character of April, the heroine in a novel by Ring Lardner, Jr., *The Ecstasy of Owen Muir*, written in prison after the Hollywood Ten were convicted. There the physical description is of Jigee, particularly the coloring and those perpetually flushed cheeks. Whether she was the naked sylph with the dogs in Irwin Shaw's novel or April in Lardner's really doesn't make any difference. When any of those who had loved her read of a woman loved by many men, who never got old, but continued to haunt them in death as in life, they thought of Virginia, who had been as full of promise as those golden years, the best years of their lives, when a better world still seemed possible and the Communist Party appeared the best vehicle to achieve that better world.

241. *"had always been so."* "The board of directors was locked in a knock-down, drag-out fight, and it was a tie," recalled Ellenore Bogigian. "John Cromwell broke the tie by voting for Patterson. So we came out for Patterson, but there was never any unity in HICCASP again. Dore Schary had called me two days before the big board meeting and said, 'All hell is breaking loose in the studios over this endorsement. Who really cares if HICCASP makes an endorsement? I suggest we don't have a vote.' And I said to him, 'We have to endorse a full slate.' Schary recommended double endorsement."

250. *Father George Dunne.* Ronald Reagan in *Where's the Rest of Me?* gives his version of the story: "[Father Dunne] took to the air waves and blasted the SAG and all opponents of the CSU eloquently and with vigor. The papers reported also that he appeared on the platform at CSU rallies. George Murphy and I decided he must be the victim of a snow job. We knew he had never been exposed to the Guild side of the controversy, and he was saying some pretty harsh things about us. We called

and asked if we could see him, and then went down to the university one evening, armed with our records. We were a little taken aback when he introduced us to his lawyer, and coldly informed us he had asked the lawyer to sit in on our meeting. It was a short meeting. The next night he was back on radio kicking our brains out. But not for long; someone else began to teach political science and he was on the other side of the country."

280. *saw in the movies.* In *Heyday*, Dore Schary wrote:

> I suggested to Scott, Dimytryk, and Katz that I believed that they could keep the majority of public opinion on their side by avoiding the histrionics of those members of the Ten who had preceded them to the stand. I told them that if I were a Communist or accused of being one and had decided to invoke the First Amendment, I would get on the stand, quietly, say I would not answer any question concerning my political beliefs, and add that while I was aware my refusal might place me in jeopardy in the minds of the committee, I believe the First Amendment protected me. . . . Katz insisted I was naive. Perhaps I was. However, even now I am convinced that if the ten men had taken the course I suggested, the disaster that followed the hearings would not have taken place, despite Hedda Hopper, Westbrook Pegler, and the Motion Picture Alliance for the Preservation of American Ideals, which was the wordy title dreamed up by strong right-wing opposition in Hollywood.

Appendix I
Selected Filmographies

*	one of the Hollywood Nineteen
**	one of the Hollywood Ten
AAn	Academy Award nomination
AA	Academy Award
WGAAn	Writers Guild of America Award nomination
WGAA	Writers Guild of America Award
NYFC	New York Film Critics Award

Alvah Bessie (b. 1904)**

1943 *Northern Pursuit*, co-scr
1944 *The Very Thought of You*, co-scr
1945 *Hotel Berlin*, co-scr; *Objective Burma*, story, AAn
1948 *Smart Woman*, co-scr

On November 24, 1947, Bessie was cited for contempt of Congress and later sentenced to one year in prison. On his release, he found it difficult to obtain even black-market writing assignments, since his screenwriting credentials were not so firmly established as those of other blacklisted writers. Hired by union leader Harry Bridges, for five years Bessie wrote and helped publish the weekly newspaper of the San Francisco Longshoremen's local. For twelve years, he ran lights (beginning at $80 a week) at San Francisco's the hungry i and continued to write, publishing *Inquisition at Eden* (1965), in which he reappraised the congressional investigations of the 1940s; *The Symbol* (1967), a novel based on the life of Marilyn Monroe, which he adapted for TV; and *Spain Again* (1975), covering his collaboration as screenwriter and actor on the Spanish film *España otra Vez* (1968).

Herbert Biberman (1900–1971)**

1935 *One Way Ticket*, dir
1936 *Meet Nero Wolfe*, dir
1938 *King of Chinatown*, story
1944 *Action in Arabia*, co-story, co-scr; *The Master Race*, story, co-scr, dir; *Together Again*, co-story
1946 *Abilene Town*, prod; *New Orleans*, co-scr, co-prod

On November 24, 1947, Biberman was cited for contempt of Congress and sentenced to six months in prison. Blacklisted along with his wife, actress Gale Sondergaard, who also refused to testify about her political affiliations, he went into business while she sold real estate. In 1954 Biberman directed *Salt of the Earth*, which was financed by the International Union of Mine, Mill, and Smelter Workers and focused on the living and working conditions of a group of New Mexican miners who go on strike. Union projectionists protested screenings of the film, which was shown in only one New York theater and ten others in the west, receiving rave reviews. Voted the year's best film by the French Motion Picture Academy and winner of the top prize at Czechoslovakia's Karlovy Vary Film Festival, it did not go into general release in the United States until 1965.

1969 *Slaves*, co-scr, dir

Michael Blankfort (b. 1907)

1935 *The New Gulliver* (USSR; animated feature), English lyrics
1939 *Blind Alley*, co-scr
1940 *Adam Had Four Sons*, co-scr
1941 *Texas*, co-story, co-scr
1942 *Flight Lieutenant*, scr
1948 *An Act of Murder/Live Today for Tomorrow*, co-scr; *The Dark Past*, co-scr
1950 *Broken Arrow*, scr, AAn, WGAA; *Halls of Montezuma*, story, scr
1952 *Lydia Bailey*, scr; *My Six Convicts*, scr
1953 *The Juggler*, scr from his novel, co-prod
1954 *The Caine Mutiny*, addtl dial
1955 *Untamed*, scr
1956 *Tribute to a Bad Man*, story, scr
1957 *The Vintage*, scr
1966 *The Plainsman*, scr

Blankfort was blacklisted for a time and his passport withdrawn. Summoned by HUAC, he testified that he had never been a member of the Communist Party, though he had supported activities promoting social change. Over the years he has continued to write, publishing several novels.

Ralph Block (1889– ?)

1926 *The Canadian*, co-production ed; *The Show Off*, supervising ed; *So's Your Old Man*, production ed
1928 *The Blue Danube*, assoc prod; *Celebrity*, prod; *The Cop*, prod; *Let 'Er Go Gal-*

legher, assoc prod; *Man-Made Women*, prod; *Power*, prod; *Show Folks*, prod; *Skyscraper*, assoc prod; *Stand and Deliver*, assoc prod

1929   *High Voltage*, supervisor; *His First Command*, assoc prod; *The Office Scandal*, prod; *The Racketeer*, assoc prod; *Rich People*, assoc prod; *The Shady Lady*, prod; *This Thing Called Love*, assoc prod

1930   *The Arizona Kid*, story, scr, dial; *Officer O'Brien*, assoc prod; *Scotland Yard*, prod; *The Sea Wolf*, scr

1934   *I Am a Thief*, co-story, co-scr; *Massacre*, co-scr

1935   *In Caliente*, from his story "Caliente," with Warren Duff; *The Melody Lingers On*, co-scr, co-dial; *The Right to Live*, scr

1936   *Boulder Dam*, co-scr; *Nobody's Fool*, co-scr

1940   *It's a Date* (remade as *Nancy Goes to Rio*, 1950), co-story

1945   *Patrick the Great*, co-story

In 1939 Block received a special Academy Award, a plaque, on behalf of the Motion Picture Relief Fund, as its first vice-president.

Allen Boretz (b. 1900)

1938   *Room Service* (also the basis for *Step Lively*, 1942), from his play with John Murray; *Trouble for Two*, addtl dial

1942   *It Ain't Hay*, co-scr

1944   *Bathing Beauty*, co-scr; *Up in Arms*, co-story, co-scr

1945   *The Princess and the Pirate*, co-adapt

1947   *Copacabana*, co-scr; *It Had to Be You*, co-story; *Where There's Life*, co-scr

1948   *My Girl Tisa*, scr; *Two Guys from Texas*, co-scr

1949   *The Girl from Jones Beach*, from his story "Fargo Girl"

Bertolt Brecht (1898–1956)*

1922   *Die Insel der Traenen/The Isle of Tears* (Ger), from his short story "Robinson auf Asuncion," with Arnott Bronnen

1931   *Die Dreigroschenoper/The Threepenny Opera* (Ger; remade in 1963 [Fr/W Ger]), from his play

1932   *Kuhle Wampe/Whither Germany?* (Ger), co-scr

1943   *Hangmen Also Die*, co-story, co-scr, uncredited

In October 1947 Brecht testified before the committee, denying that he had ever applied for Communist Party membership. He left the country within hours after his testimony, settling in East Germany.

1954   *Das Lied der Ströme/Song of the River* (E Ger; documentary), co-lyrics

1955   *Herr Puntila und sein Knecht Matti* (E Ger), co-scr from his play

1958   *Die Mutter/The Mother* (E Ger; filmed as performed onstage by the Berliner Ensemble)

1960   *Mutter Courage/Mother Courage* (E Ger; filmed as performed onstage by the Berliner Ensemble)

1965   *The Shameless Old Lady/La Vieille Dame Indigne* (Fr), from his short story

1974   *Galileo* (Br/US), from his play

John Bright (b. 1908)

1931   *Blonde Crazy*, co-story, co-scr; *The Public Enemy*, co-story, AAn; *Smart Money*, co-scr

1932   *The Crowd Roars*, co-scr; *If I Had a Million*, co-scr; *Taxi!*, co-scr; *Three on a Match*, co-story

1933   *She Done Him Wrong*, co-scr

1936   *Girl of the Ozarks*, co-story

1937   *The Accusing Finger*, co-scr; *John Meade's Woman*, co-story; *San Quentin*, co-story

1938   *Frankie*, co-scr

1939   *Back Door to Heaven*, co-scr

1940   *Glamour for Sale*, story, scr

1942   *Broadway*, co-scr; *Sherlock Holmes and the Voice of Terror*, co-scr

1945   *We Accuse* (documentary), commentary

1948   *Close-Up*, co-scr; *Fighting Mad/A Palooka Named Joe*, scr; *I Walk Alone*, co-adapt; *Open Secret*, addtl dial

1949   *The Kid from Cleveland*, co-story, co-scr

1951   *The Brave Bulls*, scr

To avoid a HUAC subpoena, Bright emigrated to Mexico, where he wrote black-market scripts; films of this period include *Rebellion of the Hanged/La Rebelión de los Colgados* (1954, scr, as "Hal Croves") and *Mexican Trio*. In the 1960s he became reader–story editor and literary adviser for comedian Bill Cosby's production company, Campbell-Silver Cosby.

Sidney Buchman (1902–1975)

1927   *Matinee Ladies*, co-story

1931   *Beloved Bachelor*, dial; *Daughter of the Dragon*, dial

1932   *If I Had a Million*, co-scr; *No One Man*, adapt, dial; *The Sign of the Cross*, adapt, dial; *Thunder Below*, adapt

1933   *From Hell to Heaven*, co-scr; *Right to Romance*, co-scr

1934   *All of Me*, co-scr; *Broadway Bill*, co-scr, uncredited; *His Greatest Gamble*, co-scr; *Whom the Gods Destroy*, co-scr

1935   *I'll Love You Always*, co-scr; *Love Me Forever*, co-scr; *She Married Her Boss*, scr

1936   *Adventure in Manhattan*, co-scr; *The King Steps Out*, scr; *The Music Goes 'Round*, story; *Theodora Goes Wild*, scr

1937   *The Awful Truth*, co-scr, uncredited; *Lost Horizon*, co-scr, uncredited

1938   *Holiday*, co-scr

1939   *Mr. Smith Goes to Washington* (remade as *Billy Jack Goes to Washington*, 1978), scr, AAn

1940   *The Howards of Virginia*, scr

1941   *Here Comes Mr. Jordan*, co-scr, AA

1942   *The Talk of the Town*, co-scr, AAn

1943   *Sahara*, co-scr, uncredited

1945   *Over 21*, scr, prod; *A Song to Remember*, scr, prod

1946   *The Jolson Story*, co-story, uncredited

1948 *To the Ends of the Earth*, co-scr, uncredited
1949 *Jolson Sings Again*, story and scr (AAn, WGAAn), prod
1951 *Saturday's Hero*, co-scr, WGAAn

Buchman testified before the committee in 1951, and he invoked the First Amendment; while he offered to talk about himself, admitting to his former membership in the Communist Party, he refused to name others. In 1953 he was found guilty of contempt of Congress and fined $150, receiving a one-year sentence, which was suspended due to a legal technicality. After his conviction Buchman went abroad, becoming a permanent expatriate while maintaining ties with Hollywood as a writer and independent producer.

1961 *The Mark* (Br), co-scr, co-prod
1963 *Cleopatra*, co-scr
1966 *The Group*, scr, prod
1972 *The Deadly Trap/La Maison sous les Arbres* (Fr/US), co-scr

WGA Laurel Award, 1965

Hugo Butler (1914–1968)

1936 *Arsene Lupin Returns*, contribution to treatment
1937 *Big City*, co-scr
1938 *A Christmas Carol*, scr
1939 *The Adventures of Huckleberry Finn*, scr; *Society Lawyer* (made in 1933 as *Penthouse*), co-scr
1940 *Edison, the Man*, co-story, AAn; *Wyoming*, co-scr; *Young Tom Edison*, co-story, co-scr
1941 *Barnacle Bill*, co-scr; *Free and Easy*, contribution uncredited
1942 *The Omaha Trail*, co-scr; *A Yank on the Burma Road*, co-story, co-scr
1943 *Lassie Come Home*, scr
1945 *The Southerner*, adapt
1946 *From This Day Forward*, scr; *Miss Susie Slagle's*, co-scr
1949 *Roughshod*, co-scr
1950 *Eye Witness* (Br), co-story, co-scr; *A Woman of Distinction*, co-story
1951 *The Big Night*, co-scr; *He Ran All the Way*, co-scr; *The Prowler/The Cost of Living*, co-scr
1952 *The First Time*, co-story, co-scr

To avoid a HUAC subpoena, Butler emigrated to Mexico. His films there include two co-written pseudonymously and directed by Luis Buñuel—*The Adventures of Robinson Crusoe* (1953) and *The Young One/La Joven* (1961, as "H. B. Addis")—and two semidocumentaries: in 1956, as "Hugo Mozo," Butler co-wrote the screenplay and partially shot *Torero* (Robert Flaherty Award, Venice Film Festival); in 1958 he directed and co-wrote the story and screenplay for *Los Pequeños Gigantes/¿Cuán Alto es un Gigante?*, shown on NBC-TV in 1960 as "How Tall Is a Giant?" Because of the blacklist, his work on the screenplay for Columbia's *Cowboy* (1958) was uncredited.

1962 *Eva*, co-scr
1963 *A Face in the Rain*, co-adapt; *Sodom and Gomorrah* (US/Fr/It), co-scr
1968 *The Legend of Lylah Clare*, co-scr

James M. Cain (1892–1977)

1934   *She Made Her Bed*, from his story "The Baby Is in the Icebox"
1938   *Algiers*, addtl dial
1939   *Stand Up and Fight*, co-scr; *When Tomorrow Comes*, story; *Wife, Husband, and Friend* (remade as *Everybody Does It*, 1949), from his novella *Career in C Major*
1940   *Money and the Woman*, from his novella *The Embezzler*
1944   *The Bridge of San Luis Rey*, co-scr; *Double Indemnity*, from his novella; *Gypsy Wildcat*, co-scr
1945   *Mildred Pierce*, from his novel
1946   *The Postman Always Rings Twice* (remade in 1981; also filmed as *Le Dernier Tournant* [Fr, 1939] and *Ossessione* [It, 1942]), from his novel
1956   *Serenade* (loosely remade as *Interlude*, 1957), from his novel; *Slightly Scarlet*, from his novel *Love's Lovely Counterfeit*

Lester Cole (b. 1904)**

1929   *Painted Faces*, acted
1930   *Love at First Sight*, acted
1932   *If I Had a Million*, co-scr
1933   *Charlie Chan's Greatest Case*, co-adapt
1934   *Pursued*, co-scr; *Sleepers East*, scr; *Wild Gold*, co-adapt
1935   *Hitch Hike Lady*, co-scr; *Too Tough to Kill*, co-adapt; *Under Pressure*, co-scr
1936   *Follow Your Heart*, co-scr; *The President's Mystery*, co-scr
1937   *Affairs of Cappy Ricks*, scr; *The Man in Blue*, scr; *Some Blondes Are Dangerous*, scr
1938   *The Crime of Dr. Hallet*, co-story, co-scr; *The Jury's Secret*, story, co-scr; *Midnight Intruder*, co-scr; *Secrets of a Nurse*, co-scr; *Sinners in Paradise*, co-scr
1939   *I Stole a Million*, story; *Winter Carnival*, co-scr
1940   *The Big Guy*, scr; *The House of the Seven Gables*, scr; *The Invisible Man Returns*, co-scr
1941   *Among the Living*, co-story, co-scr; *Footsteps in the Dark*, co-scr; *Pacific Blackout*, co-scr
1942   *Night Plane from Chungking*, co-scr
1943   *Hostages*, co-scr
1944   *None Shall Escape*, scr
1945   *Blood on the Sun*, scr; *Men in Her Diary*, adapt; *Objective Burma*, co-scr
1946   *Strange Conquest*, co-story
1947   *Fiesta*, co-story, co-scr; *High Wall*, co-scr; *The Romance of Rosy Ridge*, scr

On November 24, 1947, Cole was cited for contempt of Congress and later sentenced to one year in prison. Suspended without pay by MGM after the Waldorf meeting, he sued Loew's, Inc. (the studio's parent company) for conspiracy to blacklist and breach of contract; though he won at trial level, the decision was reversed on appeal and the case was dropped. Cole worked as a cook and sold story ideas to studios pseudonymously, including that for *Chain Lightning* (1950). In 1965 he scripted *Born Free* under another name and has since lectured in American colleges.

1965   *China!* (documentary), asst prod
1967   *Inside North Vietnam* (documentary), editorial consultant

Richard Collins (b. 1914)*

1937   *In Old Chicago,* contribution to treatment
1939   *Rulers of the Sea,* co-story, co-scr
1940   *One Crowded Night,* co-scr
1941   *Lady Scarface,* co-story, co-scr
1943   *Song of Russia,* co-scr; *Thousands Cheer,* co-story, co-scr
1946   *Little Giant,* co-story

The blacklisting of Collins began in 1947 when Warner Bros., where he had been earning up to $1,500 a week, refused to give him work. From 1947 to 1951 he wrote black-market scripts and worked in the pattern business in New York. In April 1951 he became the fourth cooperative witness to testify before the committee. Hired by independent producer Walter Wanger to write *Riot in Cell Block 11,* Collins worked steadily after its success.

1953   *China Venture,* co-scr
1954   *The Adventures of Hajji Baba,* scr; *The Bob Mathias Story,* story, scr; *Riot in Cell Block 11,* story, scr
1955   *Cult of the Cobra,* co-scr; *Kiss of Fire,* co-scr
1957   *My Gun Is Quick,* co-scr
1958   *The Badlanders,* scr; *Spanish Affair,* story, scr
1959   *Edge of Eternity,* co-scr
1960   *Pay or Die,* co-scr
1968   *99 Women,* story

Edward Dmytryk (b. 1908)**

1930–39   film editor; films include *Only Saps Work* (1930) and *Ruggles of Red Gap* (1935)

directed, unless otherwise noted:

1935   *The Hawk*
1939   *Television Spy*
1940   *Emergency Squad; Golden Gloves; Her First Romance; Mystery Sea Raider*
1941   *The Blonde from Singapore; Confessions of Boston Blackie; The Devil Commands; Secrets of the Lone Wolf; Sweetheart of the Campus; Under Age*
1942   *Counter-Espionage; Seven Miles from Alcatraz*
1943   *Behind the Rising Sun; Captive Wild Woman; The Falcon Strikes Back; Hitler's Children; Tender Comrade*
1944   *Murder, My Sweet*
1945   *Back to Bataan; Cornered*
1946   *Till the End of Time*
1947   *Crossfire,* AAn; *So Well Remembered* (Br)
1949   *Give Us This Day/Salt to the Devil* (Br); *The Hidden Room/Obsession*

On November 24, 1947, Dmytryk was cited for contempt of Congress and sentenced to six months in prison; after the Waldorf meeting, he was fired by RKO. In September 1950, from prison, he made a statement maintaining his belief in refusing to cooperate with the committee while denying that he had ever been a Communist Party member. Dmytryk testified before the committee in April 1951, citing as his reasons for doing so the North Korean invasion of South Korea and the espionage trials of Alger Hiss and Judith Coplon. The only one of the Ten to recant, he named twenty-six others.

1952   *Eight Iron Men*; *Mutiny*; *The Sniper*
1953   *The Juggler*
1954   *Broken Lance*; *The Caine Mutiny*
1955   *The End of the Affair* (Br); *The Left Hand of God*; *Soldier of Fortune*
1956   *The Mountain*, and prod
1957   *Raintree County*
1958   *The Young Lions*
1959   *The Blue Angel*; *Warlock*, and prod
1962   *The Reluctant Saint/Cronache di un Convento* (It/US), and prod; *A Walk on the Wild Side*
1964   *The Carpetbaggers*; *Where Love Has Gone*
1965   *Mirage*
1966   *Alvarez Kelly*
1968   *Anzio/Lo Sbarco di Anzio* (Br), English-language version; *Hamlet* (produced for West German TV, 1960), presented; *Shalako* (Br)
1972   *Bluebeard* (Hung), and co-story, co-scr
1975   *The Human Factor* (Br/US)
1976   *He Is My Brother*

Carl Foreman (b. 1914)

1940   *Bowery Blitzkrieg*, co-scr
1941   *Spooks Run Wild*, co-story, co-scr
1942   *Rhythm Parade*, co-story, co-scr
1945   *Dakota*, story
1948   *So This Is New York*, co-scr
1949   *Champion*, scr, AAn, WGAAn; *The Clay Pigeon*, story, scr; *Home of the Brave*, scr, WGAAn
1950   *Cyrano de Bergerac*, scr; *The Men*, story and scr, AAn, WGAA; *Young Man with a Horn*, co-scr
1952   *High Noon*, scr, AA, WGAAn

Subpoenaed by the committee in September 1951, Foreman testified but named no names. In 1952 he went to England, losing his U.S. passport. There he worked on the black market, pseudonymously and anonymously and in 1954, with blacklisted writer Harold Buchman (as "Derek Frye"), wrote *The Sleeping Tiger*. Foreman's passport was returned in 1956, after he denounced himself before a committee of one. The following year his uncredited screenplay (with blacklisted writer Michael Wilson) for *The Bridge over the River Kwai* won an Academy Award; official screenplay credit went to Pierre Boulle, author of the novel on which the film was based, though Boulle could not write in English. In 1958 Foreman established a production company based in London and distributing through Columbia, then signed a three-year contract with Universal as producer-writer, working through his independent New York-based production company, High Noon.

1958   *The Key* (Br), scr, prod
1961   *The Guns of Navarone* (Br/US), scr (AAn), prod (AAn, Best Film)

1963 *The Victors* (Br/US), scr, prod, dir
1966 *Born Free* (Br), prod
1969 *MacKenna's Gold*, scr, prod; *Otley* (Br), prod
1970 *The Virgin Soldiers* (Br), prod
1971 *Living Free*, exec prod
1972 *Young Winston*, story and scr (AAn), prod
1978 *Force Ten from Navarone*, story
1979 *When Time Ran Out*, co-scr

WGA Laurel Award, 1969

Paul Jarrico (b. 1915)

1937 *No Time to Marry*, scr
1938 *Beauty for the Asking*, co-scr; *The Little Adventuress*, co-story; *I Am the Law*, contribution to treatment
1941 *The Face Behind the Mask*, co-scr; *Man of the Timberland*, story; *Tom, Dick, and Harry* (remade as *The Girl Most Likely*, 1957), story, scr (AAn)
1943 *Song of Russia*, co-scr; *Thousands Cheer*, co-story, co-scr
1946 *Little Giant*, co-story
1948 *The Search* (Swiss), addtl dial
1949 *Not Wanted*, co-story, co-scr
1950 *The White Tower*, scr

Because Jarrico was uncooperative in his testimony before the committee, taking the Fifth Amendment, screen credit for work already done on *The Las Vegas Story* (1951) was withheld by RKO president Howard Hughes. With the SWG, Jarrico brought a suit against the studio but lost the case when the California supreme court sided with Hughes. In 1954 he produced *Salt of the Earth* (see Biberman filmography), then expatriated permanently to France.

1969 *The Day the Hot Got Cold/Le Rouble à Deux Faces/El Rubio de las dos Caras* (Fr/Sp), scr
1977 *The Day That Shook the World*, scr

Gordon Kahn (1902–1962)*

1931 *X Marks the Spot*, co-story
1932 *The Death Kiss*, co-scr
1934 *The Crosby Case*, co-story, co-scr
1935 *Gigolette*, story, scr; *The People's Enemy*, scr
1937 *Affairs of Cappy Ricks*, addtl dial; *All Quiet on the Western Front* (rerelease), co-narration; *Navy Blues*, co-story, co-scr; *The Road Back*, co-narration, uncredited; *The Sheik Steps Out*, addtl dial
1938 *I Stand Accused*, scr; *Ladies in Distress*, addtl dial, uncredited; *Mama Runs Wild*, story, co-scr; *Tenth Avenue Kid*, story, co-scr
1939 *Ex-Champ*, story; *Mickey the Kid*, co-scr; *Newsboys' Home*, co-story, scr; *SOS—Tidal Wave*, co-scr
1941 *Buy Me That Town*, scr; *World Premiere*, co-story

1942 *Northwest Rangers*, co-scr; *Tarzan's New York Adventure*, contribution; *A Yank on the Burma Road*, co-story, co-scr
1944 *The Cowboy and the Señorita*, scr; *Song of Nevada*, co-story, co-scr
1945 *Lights of Old Santa Fe*, co-story, co-scr; *Two O'Clock Courage*, addtl dial
1946 *Blonde Alibi*, story; *Her Kind of Man*, co-scr
1948 *Ruthless*, co-scr; *Whiplash*, adapt
1949 *Streets of San Francisco*, co-story

In 1948 Kahn wrote *Hollywood on Trial*, the first account of the committee's proceedings and the Hollywood Ten. He moved to Mexico, then to New Hampshire, writing regularly for *Holiday*, *Atlantic*, and other magazines under the pseudonym of "Hugh G. Foster."

Howard Koch (b. 1902)*

1940 *The Letter*, scr; *The Sea Hawk*, co-story, co-scr; *Virginia City*, co-story, uncredited
1941 *Sergeant York*, co-scr, AAn; *Shining Victory*, co-scr
1942 *Casablanca*, co-scr, AA; *In This Our Life*, scr
1943 *Mission to Moscow*, scr
1944 *In Our Time*, co-story, co-scr
1945 *Rhapsody in Blue*, co-scr
1946 *Three Strangers*, co-story, co-scr
1948 *Letter from an Unknown Woman*, scr
1950 *No Sad Songs for Me*, scr
1951 *The Thirteenth Letter*, scr

For a decade, Koch fought to get work without naming names. As a result of the blacklist, United Artists rejected producer-director Joseph L. Mankiewicz's request to purchase a script by Koch; an advertising agency for "U.S. Steel Hour" refused a play by Koch about Woodrow Wilson; CBS-TV turned down John Houseman when he requested that Koch help him write his new "Seven Lively Arts" series. Though in 1956 Koch, as "Peter Howard," wrote the screenplay for Joseph Losey's *The Intimate Stranger/A Finger of Guilt*, he received no screen credit until the early 1960s, and those were in England.

1961 *Loss of Innocence/The Greengage Summer* (Br), scr
1962 *The War Lover* (Br), scr
1964 *633 Squadron* (Br/US), co-scr
1968 *The Fox* (Can), co-scr, assoc prod

Ring Lardner, Jr. (b. 1915)**

1937 *Nothing Sacred*, co-scr, uncredited; *A Star Is Born*, co-scr, uncredited
1939 *Meet Dr. Christian*, co-scr
1940 *The Courageous Dr. Christian*, co-story, co-scr
1941 *Arkansas Judge*, co-adapt
1942 *Woman of the Year*, co-scr, AA
1943 *The Cross of Lorraine*, co-scr
1944 *Laura*, co-scr, uncredited; *Marriage Is a Private Affair*, co-scr, uncredited; *Tomorrow, the World!*, co-scr

1946　*Cloak and Dagger*, co-scr
1947　*Forever Amber*, co-scr
1949　*The Forbidden Street*, scr
1950　*Four Days' Leave/Swiss Tour* (Swiss), addtl dial
1951　*The Big Night*, co-scr

On November 24, 1947, Lardner was cited for contempt of Congress and sentenced to one year in prison. Having been fired by 20th Century–Fox after the Waldorf meeting, Lardner, on his release from prison, began looking for work even as he joined the fight to abolish HUAC. Anonymously and under pseudonyms he wrote films in the United States and abroad, including the British *Virgin Island* (1959), with Ian McLellan Hunter (as "Philip Rush"), and *A Breath of Scandal* (1960). Writing with Hunter as "Oliver Skeyne," he worked on such British TV series as "The Adventures of Robin Hood" and "Sir Lancelot." His novel *The Ecstasy of Owen Muir* was published in England in the 1950s but did not go into print in the United States until the next decade.

1965　*The Cincinnati Kid*, co-scr
1970　*M*A*S*H*, scr, AA, WGAA
1972　*The Deadly Trap/La Maison sous les Arbres* (Fr/US), co-scr, uncredited
1977　*The Greatest*, scr

John Howard Lawson (1894–1977)**

1928　*Dream of Love*, co-titles
1929　*Dynamite*, dial; *The Pagan*, titles
1930　*Our Blushing Brides*, co-continuity, co-dial; *The Sea Bat*, co-scr, co-dial; *The Ship from Shanghai*, scr
1931　*Bachelor Apartment*, story
1934　*Success at Any Price*, co-scr from his play *Success Story*
1935　*Party Wire*, co-adapt
1937　*The Heart of Spain* (documentary), co-scr
1938　*Algiers*, scr; *Blockade*, story, AAn
1939　*They Shall Have Music*, scr
1940　*Earthbound*, co-scr; *Four Sons*, scr
1943　*Action in the North Atlantic*, scr; *Sahara*, co-scr
1945　*Counter-Attack*, scr
1947　*Smash-Up—The Story of a Woman*, scr

On November 24, 1947, Lawson was cited for contempt of Congress and sentenced to one year in prison. Blacklisted, he emigrated to Mexico, and though he never again worked on films under his own name, during this period he wrote *Theory and Technique of Playwriting and Screenwriting* (1949) and *Film in the Battle of Ideas* (1958). He later taught and lectured at Stanford, Loyola, and other universities.

John Lee Mahin (b. 1902)

1932　*Beast of the City*, scr; *Red Dust* (remade as *Congo Maisie*, 1940, and as *Mogambo*, 1953); *Scarface*, co-scr, co-dial; *The Wet Parade*, scr, dial
1933　*Bombshell*, co-scr; *Eskimo*, adapt; *Hell Below*, co-dial, acted; *The Prizefighter and the Lady*, co-scr

1934 *Chained*, scr; *Laughing Boy*, co-scr; *Treasure Island*, scr
1935 *Naughty Marietta*, co-scr
1936 *The Devil Is a Sissy*, co-scr; *Love on the Run*, co-scr; *Small Town Girl*, co-scr; *Wife vs Secretary*, co-scr
1937 *Captains Courageous*, co-scr, AAn; *The Last Gangster*, scr; *A Star Is Born*, co-scr, uncredited
1938 *Too Hot to Handle*, co-scr
1940 *Boom Town*, scr
1941 *Dr. Jekyll and Mr. Hyde*, scr; *Johnny Eager*, co-scr
1942 *Tortilla Flat*, co-scr; *Woman of the Year*, contribution, uncredited
1943 *The Adventures of Tartu/Tartu* (Br), co-scr
1949 *Down to the Sea in Ships*, co-scr
1950 *Love That Brute*, co-story, co-scr
1951 *Quo Vadis*, co-scr; *Show Boat*, scr, WGAAn
1952 *My Son John*, adapt
1954 *Elephant Walk*, scr
1955 *Lucy Gallant*, co-scr
1956 *The Bad Seed*, scr
1957 *Heaven Knows, Mr. Allison*, co-scr, AAn, WGAAn
1958 *No Time for Sergeants*, scr
1959 *The Horse Soldiers*, co-scr, co-prod
1960 *North to Alaska*, co-scr, WGAAn
1962 *The Spiral Road*, co-scr
1966 *Moment to Moment*, co-scr

WGA Laurel Award, 1958

Albert Maltz (b. 1908)**

1932 *Afraid to Talk*, from his play *Merry-Go-Round*, with George Sklar
1942 *Moscow Strikes Back* (adaptation of the Russian propaganda film *The Defeat of the German Armies Near Moscow*), commentary; *This Gun for Hire* (remade as *Short Cut to Hell*, 1957), co-scr
1943 *Seeds of Freedom* (expanded version of Sergei Eisenstein's *Potemkin*, 1925), dial, contemporary story
1944 *Destination Tokyo*, co-scr
1945 *The House I Live In* (documentary, short subject), scr; *Pride of the Marines*, scr, AAn
1946 *Cloak and Dagger*, co-scr
1948 *The Naked City*, co-scr, WGAAn

On November 24, 1947, Maltz was cited for contempt of Congress and sentenced to one year in prison. Blacklisted, he emigrated to Mexico, where he worked on novels, scripts, and a play. During this period he wrote films on the black market, for reduced fees; one of these was *The Robe* (1953), for which he received no credit. His name was also omitted by Paramount from the credits for the remake of *This Gun for Hire* in 1957. As late as 1960, when Frank Sinatra announced that Maltz would write the screenplay for his film version of *The Execution of Private Slovik*, pressure from such groups as the Hearst press and the American Legion forced Sinatra to cancel the project.

1970 *Two Mules for Sister Sara* (US/Mex), scr
1971 *The Beguiled*, scr, uncredited at his request
1973 *Scalawag* (US/It), co-scr

Lewis Milestone (1895–1980)*

1919–25 editor and scenario writer; films include *This Foolish Age* (1921, asst dir), *Up and At 'Em* (1922, co-story), *Main Street* (1923, asst film ed), *The Yankee Council* (1924, co-adapt), *Bobbed Hair* (1925, scen), *Dangerous Innocence* (1925, adapt), *The Mad Whirl* (1925, screen treatment), *Seven Sinners* (1925, co-story, co-adapt, dir), *The Teaser* (1925, adapt)

directed, unless otherwise noted:

1926 *The Caveman*; *Fascinating Youth*, appeared as himself; *The New Klondike*
1927 *Two Arabian Knights*, AA (Comedy Direction)
1928 *The Garden of Eden*; *The Racket*
1929 *Betrayal*; *New York Nights*
1930 *All Quiet on the Western Front* (rereleased in 1939 with narration), AA; *Hell's Angels*, co-dir, uncredited
1931 *The Front Page*, AAn
1932 *Rain*
1933 *Hallelujah, I'm a Bum*
1934 *The Captain Hates the Sea*
1935 *Paris in Spring*
1936 *Anything Goes/Tops Is the Limit*; *The General Died at Dawn*, and cameo appearance
1939 *The Night of Nights*; *Of Mice and Men*, and prod, AAn (Best Film)
1940 *Lucky Partners*
1941 *My Life with Caroline*, and prod
1942 *Our Russian Front* (documentary), co-dir, co-prod
1943 *Edge of Darkness*; *The North Star/Armored Attack*
1944 *A Guest in the House*, co-dir, uncredited; *The Purple Heart*
1945 *A Walk in the Sun*, and prod
1946 *The Strange Love of Martha Ivers*
1948 *Arch of Triumph*, and co-scr; *No Minor Vices*, and prod
1949 *The Red Pony*, and prod
1950 *Halls of Montezuma*
1952 *Kangaroo*; *Les Misérables*
1953 *Melba*
1954 *They Who Dare* (Br)
1955 *The Widow/La Vedova* (It), and adapt; *King Kelly* (unfinished)
1959 *Pork Chop Hill*
1960 *Ocean's Eleven*
1962 *Mutiny on the Bounty*
1963 *PT-109*, replaced, uncredited
1966 *The Dirty Game/La Guerra Secreta* (It), replaced, uncredited

Samuel Ornitz (1891–1957)**

1929   *The Case of Lena Smith*, story; *Chinatown Nights*, from his novel
1930   *Sins of the Children*, adapt
1932   *Hell's Highway*, co-story; *Secrets of the French Police*, co-story
1933   *Men of America*, adapt; *One Man's Journey*, scr
1934   *One Exciting Adventure*, dial
1935   *The Man Who Reclaimed His Head*, co-scr; *Three Kids and a Queen*, co-scr
1936   *Fatal Lady*, scr; *Follow Your Heart*, co-scr
1937   *A Doctor's Diary*, co-story; *The Hit Parade* (remade as *I'll Reach for a Star*, 1949), co-scr; *Portia on Trial*, scr; *Two Wise Maids*, scr
1938   *Army Girl*, co-scr; *King of the Newsboys*, co-story; *Little Orphan Annie*, co-story, co-scr
1939   *It Could Happen to You*, co-scr; *Miracle on Main Street*, co-story
1940   *Three Faces West*, co-story, co-scr
1944   *Little Devils*, scr; *They Live in Fear*, co-scr
1945   *Circumstantial Evidence*, adapt

On November 24, 1947, Ornitz was cited for contempt of Congress and sentenced to one year in prison. Ornitz was ill with cancer during his prison term. He worked on novels until his death.

Larry Parks (1914–1975)*

acted:

1941   *Harmon of Michigan*; *Harvard, Here I Come!*; *Mystery Ship*; *Sing for Your Supper*; *Three Girls About Town*; *You Belong to Me*
1942   *Alias Boston Blackie*; *Atlantic Convoy*; *Blondie Goes to College*; *The Boogie Man Will Get You*; *Canal Zone*; *Flight Lieutenant*; *Hello Annapolis*; *Honolulu Lu*; *A Man's World*; *North of the Rockies*; *Power of the Press*; *Submarine Raider*; *They All Kissed the Bride*; *You Were Never Lovelier*
1943   *Calling All Stars*; *The Deerslayer*; *First Comes Courage*; *Is Everybody Happy?*; *Redhead from Manhattan*; *Reveille with Beverly*
1944   *The Black Parachute*; *Hey Rookie!*; *The Racket Man*; *She's a Sweetheart*; *Stars on Parade*
1945   *Counter-Attack*; *Sergeant Mike*
1946   *The Jolson Story*, AAn; *Renegades*
1947   *Down to Earth*; *The Swordsman*
1948   *The Gallant Blade*
1949   *Jolson Sings Again*
1950   *Emergency Wedding*
1951   *Love Is Better Than Ever*

Parks became a star with his appearance in *The Jolson Story*. He was the first to testify, though reluctantly, before the resumed HUAC hearings in 1951; even so, he was blacklisted and his contract with Columbia terminated. Parks went into real estate and with his wife, Betty Garrett, appeared occasionally on stage and TV.

1955   *Tiger by the Tail/Cross-Up* (Br)
1962   *Freud*

Irving Pichel (1891–1954)*

acted, unless otherwise noted:

1930   *The Right to Love*
1931   *An American Tragedy*; *The Cheat*; *Murder by the Clock*
1932   *Forgotten Commandments*; *Madame Butterfly*; *The Miracle Man*; *The Most Dangerous Game*, co-dir; *The Painted Woman*; *Strange Justice*; *Two Kinds of Women*; *Westward Passage*
1933   *Before Dawn*, dir; *The Billion Dollar Scandal*; *I'm No Angel*; *King of the Jungle*; *Oliver Twist*; *The Right to Romance*; *The Story of Temple Drake*; *The Woman Accused*
1934   *British Agent*; *Cleopatra*; *Fog over Frisco*; *Return of the Terror*; *Such Women Are Dangerous*
1935   *I Am a Thief*; *She*, co-dir; *Silver Streak*; *Special Agent*
1936   *Beware of Ladies*, dir; *Don't Gamble with Love*; *Down Under the Sea*; *Dracula's Daughter*; *General Spanky*; *The Gentleman from Louisiana*, dir; *The House of a Thousand Candles*
1937   *Armored Car*; *The Duke Comes Back*, dir; *High, Wide, and Handsome*; *Larceny on the Air*, dir; *The Sheik Steps Out*, dir
1938   *Jezebel*; *There Goes My Heart*; *Topper Takes a Trip*
1939   *Exile Express*; *Gambling Ship*; *Juarez*; *Newsboys' Home*; *Rio*
1940   *Swamp Water*, prod

directed

    Earthbound; *Hudson's Bay*; *The Man I Married*
1941   *Dance Hall*; *The Great Commandment* (made in 1939, release delayed)
1942   *Life Begins at Eight-Thirty*; *The Pied Piper*; *Secret Agent of Japan*
1943   *Happy Land*; *The Moon Is Down*, and acted
1944   *And Now Tomorrow*
1945   *A Medal for Benny*
1946   *The Bride Wore Boots*; *Colonel Effingham's Raid*; *OSS*; *Temptation*; *Tomorrow Is Forever*
1947   *Something in the Wind*; *They Won't Believe Me*
1948   *The Miracle of the Bells*; *Mr. Peabody and the Mermaid*
1949   *Without Honor*
1950   *Destination Moon*; *The Great Rupert*; *Quicksand*
1951   *Santa Fe*, dir

After 1951 Pichel was not employed by major studios and worked with "rehabilitator" Roy Brewer, who, when he felt that Pichel's break with his former thinking was complete, went out of his way to find him work in the industry.

1953   *Martin Luther*, and acted
1954   *Day of Triumph*

Abraham Polonsky (b. 1910)

1947   *Body and Soul*, story, scr (AAn); *Golden Earrings*, co-scr
1948   *Force of Evil*, co-scr, dir
1951   *I Can Get It for You Wholesale*, scr

Polonsky was fired by 20th Century–Fox even before he testified in April 1951, when he took the Fifth Amendment. Blacklisted, he wrote scripts under pseudonyms for "You Are There" and other TV programs, fixed movie scripts on the black market, and published articles. In 1956 his *A Season of Fear* was published. Though Polonsky did not suffer financially, he received no screen credits until 1968.

1968 *Madigan*, co-scr
1969 *Tell Them Willie Boy Is Here*, scr, dir
1971 *Romance of a Horse Thief*, dir
1979 *Avalanche Express*, scr

Maurice Rapf (b. 1914)

1932 *Divorce in the Family*, co-story
1936 *We Went to College*, co-scr
1937 *They Gave Him a Gun*, co-scr
1938 *The Bad Man of Brimstone*, co-story; *Sharpshooters*, co-story
1939 *North of Shanghai*, co-story, co-scr; *Winter Carnival*, co-scr
1940 *Dancing on a Dime*, co-scr
1941 *Jennie*, co-scr
1942 *Call of the Canyon*, co-story
1946 *Song of the South*, co-scr
1949 *So Dear to My Heart*, co-adapt

Since Rapf was blacklisted in 1951, he has written and produced more than sixty educational and industrial films, and during the 1970s his critical writings appeared in *Life* and *Family Circle*. He taught drama at Dartmouth, where he was named adjunct professor and director of film studies in 1973.

Robert Riskin (1897–1955)

1931 *Illicit*, from his play, with Edith Fitzgerald; *Many a Slip*, from his play, with Edith Fitzgerald; *The Men in Her Life*, co-scr, dial; *Miracle Woman*, from his play *Bless You Sister*; *Platinum Blonde*, dial
1932 *American Madness*, story, scr, dial; *Big Timer*, dial; *Night Club Lady*, scr, dial; *Shopworn*, co-dial; *Three Wise Girls*, dial; *Virtue*, scr
1933 *Ann Carver's Profession*, from his story "Rules for Wives"; *Ex-Lady*, co-story; *Lady for a Day* (remade as *Pocketful of Miracles*, 1961), adapt, AAn
1934 *Broadway Bill* (remade as *Riding High*, 1950), scr; *It Happened One Night* (remade as *Eve Knew Her Apples*, 1945, and *You Can't Run Away from It*, 1956), adapt, AA
1935 *Carnival*, scr; *The Whole Town's Talking*, co-scr
1936 *Mr. Deeds Goes to Town*, scr, AAn
1937 *Lost Horizon*, scr; *When You're in Love*, scr, dir
1938 *You Can't Take It with You*, scr, AAn
1939 *The Real Glory*, assoc prod; *They Shall Have Music*, assoc prod
1941 *Meet John Doe*, scr
1944 *The Thin Man Goes Home*, co-story, co-scr, prod
1947 *Magic Town*, co-story, scr, prod

1950   *Mister 880,* scr
1951   *Half Angel,* scr; *Here Comes the Groom,* co-story, AAn, WGAAn

WGA Laurel Award, 1955

Robert Rossen (1908–1966)*

1934   *The Unknown Soldier Speaks* (documentary), dial
1937   *Marked Woman,* co-scr; *They Won't Forget,* co-scr
1938   *Racket Busters,* co-story, co-scr
1939   *Dust Be My Destiny,* scr; *The Roaring Twenties,* co-scr
1940   *A Child Is Born,* scr
1941   *Blues in the Night,* scr; *Out of the Fog,* co-scr; *The Sea Wolf,* scr
1943   *Edge of Darkness,* scr
1945   *A Walk in the Sun,* scr
1946   *The Strange Love of Martha Ivers,* scr
1947   *Body and Soul,* dir; *Desert Fury,* scr; *Johnny O'Clock,* scr, dir
1949   *All the King's Men,* scr (AAn, WGAA), dir (AAn), prod (AA, NYFCA, Best Film); *The Undercover Man,* prod
1950   *No Sad Songs for Me,* prod
1951   *The Brave Bulls,* dir, prod

In 1951 Rossen refused to name names before the committee. Blacklisted, he emigrated to Mexico, where he received a HUAC subpoena in 1953. In his second appearance, citing a change in political circumstances, he named names and detailed Party practices. Although he continued to work in film, he did not return to Hollywood.

1955   *Mambo* (It), co-scr, dir
1956   *Alexander the Great,* story, scr, prod, dir
1957   *Island in the Sun,* dir
1959   *They Came to Cordura,* co-scr, dir
1961   *The Hustler,* co-scr (AAn, WGAA), dir (AAn, NYFCA), prod (AAn, Best Film)
1962   *Billy Budd,* co-scr, uncredited
1964   *The Cool World,* from his play, with Warren Miller; *Lilith,* co-scr, dir, prod

Waldo Salt (b. 1914)*

1937   *Double Wedding,* contribution to dial, uncredited
1938   *The Shopworn Angel,* scr
1941   *The Wild Man of Borneo,* co-scr
1943   *Tonight We Raid Calais,* scr
1944   *Mr. Winkle Goes to War,* co-scr
1947   *A Likely Story,* addtl dial
1948   *Rachel and the Stranger,* scr, WGAAn
1950   *The Flame and the Arrow,* story, scr
1951   *M,* addtl dial

Salt was blacklisted after his testimony before the committee in 1950 and worked on films anonymously. On leaving Hollywood he wrote a folk opera and worked in New York pseudonymously as a TV writer and story editor.

1962 *Taras Bulba*, co-scr
1964 *Flight from Ashiya*, co-scr; *Wild and Wonderful*, co-scr
1969 *Midnight Cowboy*, scr, AA, WGAA
1971 *The Gang That Couldn't Shoot Straight*, scr
1973 *Serpico*, co-scr, AAn, WGAA
1975 *The Day of the Locust*, scr
1978 *Coming Home*, co-scr, AA, WGAA

(Robert) Adrian Scott (1912–1973)**

1941 *Keeping Company*, co-scr; *The Parson of Panamint*, co-scr; *We Go Fast*, co-scr
1943 *Mr. Lucky* (remade as *Gambling House*, 1950), co-scr
1944 *My Pal Wolf*, prod
1945 *Cornered*, prod; *Murder My Sweet*, prod
1946 *Deadline at Dawn*, prod; *Miss Susie Slagle's*, co-adapt
1947 *Crossfire*, prod; *So Well Remembered* (Br), prod

On November 24, 1947, Scott was cited for contempt of Congress and sentenced to one year in prison. Fired by RKO after the Waldorf meeting, he survived financially in Hollywood by writing TV scripts offered through a "front." In 1960 he co-wrote with Dalton Trumbo *Conspiracy of Hearts*, also sold through a front, and the following year emigrated to England, where he was hired as executive assistant to the head of MGM. In 1968 Scott returned to the United States, free-lancing in TV.

Budd Schulberg (b. 1914)

1937 *A Star Is Born*, co-scr, uncredited
1938 *Little Orphan Annie*, co-scr
1939 *Winter Carnival*, co-scr
1941 *Weekend for Three*, story
1943 *City Without Men*, co-story; *Government Girl*, adapt
1954 *On the Waterfront*, story and scr, AA, WGAA
1956 *The Harder They Fall*, from his novel
1957 *A Face in the Crowd*, story, scr, co-songs
1958 *Wind Across the Everglades*, scr, from his story "Across the Everglades"

Dalton Trumbo (1905–1976)**

1936 *Love Begins at Twenty*, co-scr; *Road Gang*, scr; *Tugboat Princess*, co-story
1937 *Devil's Playground*, co-scr; *That Man's Here Again*, contribution
1938 *Fugitives for a Night*, scr; *A Man to Remember*, scr
1939 *Career*, scr; *Everything Happens to Ann*, story; *Five Came Back*, co-scr; *The Flying Irishman*, co-story, co-scr; *Heaven with a Barbed Wire Fence*, story, co-scr; *The Kid from Kokomo*, story; *Sorority House*, scr
1940 *A Bill of Divorcement/Never to Love/Not for Each Other*, scr; *Curtain Call*, scr; *Half a Sinner*, story; *Kitty Foyle*, scr, AAn; *The Lone Wolf Strikes*, story; *We Who Are Young*, story, scr

1941 *Accent on Love*, story; *You Belong to Me* (remade as *Emergency Wedding*, 1951), story

1942 *The Remarkable Andrew*, scr from his novel

1943 *A Guy Named Joe*, scr

1944 *Tender Comrade*, story, scr; *Thirty Seconds over Tokyo*, scr

1945 *Jealousy*, original idea; *Our Vines Have Tender Grapes*, scr

On November 24, 1947, Trumbo was cited for contempt of Congress and sentenced to one year in prison. Hollywood's highest-paid screenwriter ($75,000 a script, according to his MGM contract), he was suspended without pay after the Waldorf meeting. Blacklisted, he smuggled out scripts from prison and sold them pseudonymously, and after his release, in 1951, co-scripted Joseph Losey's *The Prowler*. That year he emigrated to Mexico, where, anonymously and under such pseudonyms as "Marcel Klauber," "Sally Stubblefield," and "Les Crutchfield," he wrote the stories or worked on screenplays for *The Beautiful Blonde from Bashful Bend* (1949), *He Ran All the Way* (1951), *Roman Holiday* (1953), *The Carnival Story* (1954), *The Boss* (1956), *The Green-Eyed Blonde* (1957), *Wild Is the Wind* (1957), *Cowboy* (1958), *From the Earth to the Moon* (1958), *The Young Philadelphians* (1959), *Conspiracy of Hearts* (1960, with Adrian Scott), *Town Without Pity* (1961), and other films. In 1956, as "Robert Rich," Trumbo won an Academy Award (Best Motion Picture Story) for *The Brave One*, though he did not receive his Oscar until 1975. He was the first to emerge from the blacklist when in 1960 Otto Preminger announced that Trumbo had written his upcoming film, *Exodus*.

1960 *Exodus*, scr; *Spartacus*, scr, WGAAn

1961 *The Last Sunset*, scr

1962 *Lonely Are the Brave*, scr

1965 *The Sandpiper*, co-scr

1966 *Hawaii*, co-scr

1968 *The Fixer*, scr

1971 *The Horsemen*, scr; *Johnny Got His Gun*, scr from his novel, dir

1972 *FTA*, co-scr

1973 *Executive Action*, scr; *Papillon*, co-scr

WGA Laurel Award, 1970

Appendix II
The Screen Writers Guild Board,
1931–1953

1931

(Writers Club) *President* Howard Green *Members* Ralph Block, Alfred A. Cohn, W. Scott Darling, Tom Geraghty, Grover Jones, Gerrit J. Lloyd, Jane Murfin, Vernon Smith, Waldemar Young.

1932

(Writers Club) *President* Howard Green *Vice-President* Jane Murfin *Secretary* Vernon Smith *Treasurer* Frank E. Woods *Members* Ralph Block, Alfred A. Cohn, Oliver H. P. Garrett, Tom Geraghty, Grover Jones, Gerrit J. Lloyd, Waldemar Young.

1933

President John Howard Lawson *Vice-President* Frances Marion *Secretary* Joseph Mankiewicz *Treasurer* Ralph Block *Members* James A. Creelman, Oliver H. P. Garrett, Howard Green, Grover Jones, Dudley Nichols, Lawrence Stallings, Louis Weitzenkorn.

1934

President Ralph Block *Vice-President* Wells Root *Secretary* Tristram Tupper *Treasurer* Ernest Pascal *Members* Oliver H. P. Garrett, Rupert Hughes, John Howard Lawson, Wilfred MacDonald, Brian Marlow, Frances Marion, Seton I. Miller, Dudley Nichols, Arthur Ripley, Raymond Schrock, Courtenay Terrett.

1935

President Ernest Pascal *Vice-President* Seton I. Miller *Secretary* E. E. Paramore, Jr. *Treasurer* John Grey *Members* Ralph Block, Sidney Buchman, Lester Cole, Oliver H. P.

Garrett, Mary McCall, Jr., Edwin Justus Mayer, Dorothy Parker, Samson Raphaelson, Robert Riskin, Wells Root, Donald Ogden Stewart.

1936

President Ernest Pascal *Vice-President* Nunnally Johnson *Secretary* Robert N. Lee *Treasurer* John Grey *Members* William M. Conselman, Francis Faragoh, Frances Goodrich, Doris Malloy, Benjamin Markson, Seton I. Miller, E. E. Paramore, Jr., Allen Rivkin, Wells Root, Joel Sayre, Harlan Thompson, Charles Brackett.

1937

President Dudley Nichols *Vice-President* Charles Brackett *Secretary* Frances Goodrich *Treasurer* John Grey *Members* Sheridan Gibney, Albert Hackett, Dashiell Hammett, Lillian Hellman, Brian Marlow, Edwin Justus Mayer, Jane Murfin, Dorothy Parker, Samson Raphaelson, Morrie Ryskind, Donald Ogden Stewart.

1937–38

President Dudley Nichols *Vice-President* Charles Brackett *Secretary* Frances Goodrich *Treasurer* John Grey *Members* Sheridan Gibney, Albert Hackett, Dashiell Hammett, Lillian Hellman, Brian Marlow, Edwin Justus Mayer, Jane Murfin, Dorothy Parker, Samson Raphaelson, Morris Ryskind, Donald Ogden Stewart. *Alternates* Philip Dunne, Boris Ingster, Ring Lardner, Jr., Frank Partos, Tristram Tupper, Anthony Veiller.

1938–39

President Charles Brackett *Vice-President* Philip Dunne *Secretary* Maurice Rapf *Treasurer* Ring Lardner, Jr. *Members* Gilbert Gabriel, Sheridan Gibney, Dashiell Hammett, Lillian Hellman, Boris Ingster, Mary McCall, Jr., Dudley Nichols, Laura Perelman, Budd Schulberg, Donald Ogden Stewart, Anthony Veiller.

1939–40

President Sheridan Gibney *Vice-President* Sidney Buchman *Secretary* Dwight Taylor *Treasurer* Boris Ingster *Members* Ralph Block, Charles Brackett, Lester Cole, Philip Dunne, Mary McCall, Jr., E. E. Paramore, Jr., Gertrude Purcell, Wells Root, Dore Schary, Jo Swerling, Dalton Trumbo.

1940–41

President Sheridan Gibney *Vice-President* Sidney Buchman *Secretary* Dore Schary *Treasurer* Lester Cole *Members* Ralph Block, Jerome Chodorov, Lester Cole, Joseph Fields, Harry Kurnitz, Ring Lardner, Jr., John Howard Lawson, William Ludwig, George Oppenheimer, Maurice Rapf, Donald Ogden Stewart, Dwight Taylor.

1941–42

President Sidney Buchman *Vice-President* Ralph Block *Secretary* Robert Rossen *Treasurer* Lester Cole *Members* Claude Binyon, Charles Brackett, Marc Connelly, Joseph Fields, Sheridan Gibney, Mary McCall, Jr., Richard Maibaum, Stanley Rubin, Allan Scott, Dwight Taylor, Harry Tugend.

1942–43

President Mary McCall, Jr. *Vice-President* Lester Cole *Secretary* Frank Partos *Treasurer* Francis Faragoh *Members* Harold Buchman, Hugo Butler, Marc Connelly, Paul Jarrico, Talbot Jennings, Harry Kurnitz, Gladys Lehman, Jane Murfin, Waldo Salt, Allan Scott, Harry Tugend.

1943–44

President Mary McCall, Jr. *Vice-Presidents* Lester Cole, Sheridan Gibney, James Hilton *Secretary* Talbot Jennings *Treasurer* Hugo Butler *Members* Marc Connelly, Sheridan Gibney, James Hilton, Michael Kanin, Ring Lardner, Jr., Gladys Lehman, Jane Murfin, Maurice Rapf, Betty Reinhardt, Allan Scott, John Wexley.

1944–45

President Emmet Lavery *Vice-Presidents* James Hilton, Hugo Butler, Ring Lardner, Jr. *Secretary* Howard Estabrook *Treasurer* Michael Kanin *Members* Richard Collins, Oliver H. P. Garrett, Sheridan Gibney, Talbot Jennings, Gordon Kahn, John Howard Lawson, Elmer Rice, Dalton Trumbo.

1945–46

President Emmet Lavery *Vice-Presidents* Lester Cole, Howard Estabrook, Oliver H. P. Garrett *Secretary* Maurice Rapf *Treasurer* Harold Buchman *Members* Adele Buffington, Richard Collins, Philip Dunne, Sheridan Gibney, Gordon Kahn, Howard Koch, Mary McCall, Jr., Frank Partos, Marguerite Roberts, Robert Rossen.

1946–47

President Emmet Lavery *Vice-Presidents* Mary McCall, Jr., Howard Estabrook, Hugo Butler *Secretary* F. Hugh Herbert *Treasurer* Harold Buchman *Members* Melville Baker, James M. Cain, Lester Cole, Philip Dunne, Talbot Jennings, Ring Lardner, Jr., Ranald MacDougall, George Seaton, Leo Townsend.

1947–48

President Sheridan Gibney *Vice-Presidents* George Seaton, F. Hugh Herbert, Dwight Taylor *Secretary* Arthur Sheekman *Treasurer* Harry Tugend *Members* Robert Ardrey,

Art Arthur, Stephen Morehouse Avery, Claude Binyon, Charles Brackett, Frank Cavett, Oliver Cooper, Valentine Davies, Richard English, Everett Freeman, Paul Gangelin, Albert Hackett, Milton Krims, Ernest Pascal, Leonard Spigelgass.

1948–49

President George Seaton *Vice-Presidents* Oliver H. P. Garrett, Don Hartman, Wells Root *Secretary* Karl Tunberg *Treasurer* Valentine Davies *Members* Edmund Beloin, Warren Duff, Richard English, Erwin Gelsey, Edmund L. Hartmann, Karl Kamb, Arthur Kober, Gladys Lehman, Winston Miller, Richard Murphy, Sloan Nibley, Leonard Spigelgass, Dwight Taylor, Wanda Tuchock, M. Coates Webster.

1949–50

President Valentine Davies *Vice-Presidents* Ernest Pascal, Leonard Spigelgass *Secretary* Edmund L. Hartmann *Treasurer* Karl Tunberg *Members* DeWitt Bodeen, Richard Breen, Oscar Brodney, Harold Buchman, Morgan Cox, Warren Duff, Carl Foreman, Howard Green, F. Hugh Herbert, Jonathan Latimer, Winston Miller, Richard Murphy, Sloan Nibley, Frank Nugent, George Seaton, M. Coates Webster.

1950–51

President Karl Tunberg *Vice-Presidents* Edmund L. Hartmann, Leonard Spigelgass *Secretary* George Oppenheimer (resigned), Richard Murphy *Treasurer* Valentine Davies *Members* Marvin Borowsky, Richard Breen, Morgan Cox, Warren Duff, Carl Foreman, Ivan Goff (replacement for Murphy), Howard Green, F. Hugh Herbert, Virginia Kellogg, Jonathan Latimer (resigned), Mary McCall, Jr., Richard Murphy (prior to appointment as Secretary), Sloan Nibley, Frank Nugent, Walter Reisch, Allen Rivkin, George Seaton, Barry Shipman.

1951–52

President Mary McCall, Jr. *Vice-Presidents* Richard Murphy, Richard Breen *Secretary* Howard Green *Treasurer* Wells Root *Members* Marvin Borowsky (resigned), Robert Carson, Morgan Cox, Carl Foreman, Everett Freeman, Ivan Goff, Harold Greene, Dorothy Hughes, Virginia Kellogg, Ranald MacDougall, D. M. Marshman, Jr., John Monks, Jr., Sloan Nibley (resigned), Frank Nugent, Robert Pirosh, Walter Reisch, Allen Rivkin (resigned), Barry Shipman.

1952–53

President Richard Breen *Vice-Presidents* Valentine Davies, Ranald MacDougall *Secretary* David Dortort *Treasurers* D. M. Marshman, Jr., Leonard Spigelgass *Members* Adele Buffington, Robert Carson (resigned), Morgan Cox, Warren Duff, Everett Freeman, Ivan Goff (resigned), Harold Greene, Charles Hoffman, Dorothy Hughes, Curtis Kingston, Beirne Lay, Jr., Erna Lazarus, John Monks, Jr., Robert Pirosh, Walter Reisch, Barry Shipman, Leonard Spigelgass (resigned), Richard Tregaskis, Harry Tugend (resigned).

Index

Index

Index

A NOTE ON THE TYPE

The text of this book was set on the Linotype in a face called Times Roman, designed by Stanley Morison for The Times (London) and first introduced by that newspaper in 1932.

Among typographers and designers of the twentieth century, Stanley Morison has been a strong forming influence, as a typographical adviser to the English Monotype Corporation, as a director of two distinguished English publishing houses and as a writer of sensibility, erudition, and keen practical sense.

Composed by The Maryland Linotype Composition Corporation, Baltimore, Maryland.
Printed and bound by The Haddon Craftsmen, Inc., Scranton, Pennsylvania.

Design by Janice Willcocks Stern